MANY
NATIONS

LIBRARY
OF CONGRESS
RESOURCE
GUIDE

Contributors

Elizabeth B. Bazan, American Law Division, Congressional Research Service

Thomas J. Blumer, Law Library of Congress

Jennifer Brathovde, Prints and Photographs Division

James A. Flatness, Geography and Map Division

Patrick Frazier, Humanities and Social Sciences Division

James W. Gilreath, Rare Book and Special Collections Division

Judith Gray, American Folklife Center

John R. Hébert, Hispanic Division

Jerry Kearns

Karen Lund, Motion Picture, Broadcasting and Recorded Sound Division

John J. McDonough, Jr., Manuscript Division

Lee K. Miller

Roger Walke, Government Division, Congressional Research Service

MANY NATIONS

A LIBRARY OF CONGRESS

RESOURCE GUIDE FOR THE

STUDY OF INDIAN AND

ALASKA NATIVE PEOPLES

OF THE UNITED STATES

edited by PATRICK FRAZIER

and the PUBLISHING OFFICE

LIBRARY OF CONGRESS   Washington   1996

∞ The paper in this publication meets the requirements for permanence established by the American National Standard ANSI/NISO z39.48-1992. Permanence of Paper for Publications and Documents in Libraries and Archives.

Library of Congress Cataloging-in-Publication Data

Library of Congress.

Many nations : a Library of Congress resource guide for the study of Indian and Alaska Native Peoples of the United States / edited by Patrick Frazier and the Publishing Office.

p.   cm. — (Library of Congress resource guide)

Includes bibliographical references and index.

ISBN 0-8444-0904-9 (alk. paper)

——   —— Copy 3 z663 .M25   1996

1. Indians of North America — Library resources — Washington (D.C.)
2. Eskimos — Alaska — Library resources — Washington (D.C.)   3. Library of Congress.   I. Frazier, Patrick.   II. Library of Congress. Publishing Office.   III. Title.   IV. Series.

Z1209.2.U5L53   1996   96-42503
016.97304'97 — dc20   CIP

Designed by Adrianne Onderdonk Dudden

For sale by the
Superintendent of Documents
U.S. Government Printing Office
Washington, D.C. 20402

ON THE TITLE PAGE:
Tawa (Sun) Kachina, drawing by the author for the Zuni story "The Foster Child of the Deer" from *The Kachinas are Coming* by Gene Meany Hodge (Flagstaff, Arizona: Northland Press, 1967); E99.P9H66 1967 (LC-USZC4-4801). General Collections.

In Pueblo sacred rites, kachinas (or sacred personages) are represented by masked men. Pueblo children are instructed in the tribal religion through kachina effigies, or dolls, made by the men in the kivas, or ceremonial chambers, during breaks between ceremonies. This kachina represents the Zuni Sun Priest. The illustrations for this book of Pueblo mythology were based on the kachina dolls in the collections of the Southwest Museum of Los Angeles

CONTENTS

THE LAW LIBRARY OF CONGRESS   118

◆▼◆▼◆   GATEWAYS   ▲◆▼◆▲◆▼◆▲◆▼◆▲◆▼◆▲◆▼◆▲◆▼◆▼◆▲◆▼◆

♦▼♦▲♦▼♦▲♦   G A T E W A Y S   ▲♦▼♦▲♦▼♦▲♦▼♦▲♦▼♦▲♦▼♦▲♦▼♦▲

MOTION PICTURE, BROADCASTING AND RECORDED SOUND DIVISION   224

FOREWORD

When I became Librarian of Congress in 1987, I suggested that special guides be created to describe the Library's resources in major subject categories. The purpose was to connect related materials across different administrative divisions and formats and thus encourage broader public use of these invaluable collections.

Many Nations is the fourth such "resource guide" to Library of Congress holdings. Responding to increasing public interest in various aspects of America's heritage, the Library began a project to identify and describe the Library's vast collections related to American Indians and Alaska Natives some years ago. *Many Nations* was preceded by a guide to the Library's materials relating to black history and culture, *The African-*

American Mosaic. Like its predecessor, this publication was compiled by a team of Library staff members, the people who work with the collections on a daily basis, including librarians, reference and curatorial specialists, historians, analysts, and editors.

We hope that this attempt to describe our collections related to the rich and diverse Native American experience, from earliest accounts to the present day, will help make our resources more accessible for researchers and the general public—and may provide new perspectives in a rapidly growing area of study.

James H. Billington
Librarian of Congress

Raven, woodcut by John Frazer Mills, illustrating "The Wild Woman of the Woods" in *Once Upon A Totem* by Christie Harris (New York: Atheneum, 1963); E98.629 (LC-USZ62-115664). General Collections.

This story, from a book featuring the mythology of Northwest Coast peoples, stars raven, one of the emblems or totems of their legendary history. Raven leads a spirit boy to rescue children who had been captured and taken to her lair in the forest by Tezlemogk, an ugly ogress. Tricking the ogress with appeals to her vanity, the boy plucks the children from a salmon rack, where they have been hung to smoke, and sets them on the backs of friendly bears for the ride back to their village.

INTRODUCTION TO AMERICAN INDIAN RESEARCH AT THE LIBRARY OF CONGRESS

The serious researcher who is in the beginning stages of lengthy research on American Indian topics, and who has ample time to devote to such a project, would do well to make the Library of Congress a base from which to explore. For some projects, the Library's prodigious collections in a wide variety of formats may obviate the need to leave the base. Thousands of books contain information on North American Indians. The Library also holds what is probably the largest collection of manuscripts relating to American history—of which America's Indian people were an integral part—as well as extensive holdings of prints, photographs, broadsides, posters, government documents, laws and legal materials, films, videos, television programs, and sound recordings. If the Library does not have the material one needs, it likely has the resources to reveal where that material is. Further, the Library is only a short distance from three other major repositories of information regarding American Indian people, the Bureau of Indian Affairs, the Smithsonian's National Anthropological Archives, and the National Archives and Records Administration.

The size and complexity of the Library, however, dictate that a researcher's time will be most efficiently used, especially where travel is involved, by exhausting all of one's local and regional institutional resources to identify research guides, bibliographies, and catalogs that include Library of Congress holdings.

Library of Congress resources are formidable, and many have remained hitherto undiscovered, but its collections are not comprehensive (contrary to a long-held misconception, the Library of Congress does not have everything ever published). For example, the Library's collections are not significantly strong in linguistics, locally and tribally produced materials, or textbooks below college level. Other institutions, such as the Smithsonian Institution, the Newberry Library, the Library of the American Philosophical

Society, and the Huntington Library may have more concentrated and readily identifiable manuscript collections associated with Indian language, art, archaeology, or regional history. Nor is the Library the largest holder of Indian images, a distinction that the Smithsonian Institution's National Anthropological Archives probably holds. And the National Archives and Records Administration holds the official documents of the United States government relating to American Indian affairs.

Despite its own prodigious research collections and wealth of information on North American Indian people, the Library does not have a separate collection or section devoted to them. The nature of its broad subject divisions, the variety of formats, and the methods of acquisition have dispersed relevant material among a number of divisions. Those of the staff who deal with North American Indian topics within their general public service duties have frequently had to rely on one another to determine what may exist for research in various areas. The public, therefore, has not had an overall guide to the resources available for American Indian research in the Library. The purpose of this guide, then, is to facilitate the researcher's ability to encounter Indian people through the Library's collections and to enhance the Library staff's own ability to assist with that encounter.

Of several possible approaches to organizing the material for the guide, it was decided by the contributors and the editorial staff that an arrangement by the sections, divisions, and departments within the Library was the most feasible. It was further decided, given the Library's concentration on collections relating to United States history, that the guide would focus on North American Indians, excluding Mexico and Canada. The user should understand, however, that neither Indian groups nor collections of Library materials relating to them were necessar-

ily confined by borders. Thus one may find mention of both Canadian and Mexican tribes within these pages.

The Library patron, nevertheless, may still be perplexed by the overlap and redundancy of resources throughout the Library. The circumstances by which the Library acquires materials—copyright, gift, or purchase—and the departmentalization of the acquisitions unavoidably help create the confusion. A natural supposition, for example, is that individual prints and photographs will be found in the Prints and Photographs Division. Yet the American Folklife Center may hold a collection of photographs accompanying a group of American Indian recordings, or the Center's staff themselves may take photographs in conjunction with their own fieldwork. A collection of an individual's papers, also accompanied by photographs, may be acquired by the Manuscript Division, or a bound portfolio of prints may be retained by the Rare Book and Special Collections Division. Prints or photographs accompanying commercial music recordings will stay in the Music Division, a microfiche reproduction of photographs can be found in the Microform Reading Room, and electronically reproduced images may be located in various locations in the Library. And, of course, general books containing collections of prints and photographs will be located in the general book stacks. To give a sense of the diversity of subjects and formats to be found within each special collection division, and of their chronological spread, these chapters are each followed by a portfolio of images. Negative numbers are given in most cases. Page numbers for portfolio and other illustrations can be found in bold in the index under collection or item titles and appropriate subjects.

The nature of the relationship between American Indian people, the government, and the rest of America throughout its history has added to the complexity. The United States has dealt with Indian tribes as separate nations, as wards of the government, and as special citizens. Indian people have been studied in anthropology, archaeology, art, ethnology, law, literature, medicine, religion, and war. They are U.S. citizens, and yet they are members of tribal political units that have separate legal identities. It has not always been easy to classify information on these varied topics for a people whose status with the government and with the rest of society has so often been in flux. To help the researcher work though this maze of possibilities, the compilers have attempted insofar as possible to identify specific tribes or at least geographic ranges within collections. The user, therefore, should freely consult the index as a guide through the maze.

To further aid researchers, thematic summaries (which we have called Gateways) discuss some of the principal subject areas featured in the Library's collections, and can be used as thematic entry points to the Library divisions that hold relevant material. Page numbers for these gateways are listed in the Table of Contents. Space constraints have required that these summaries be kept brief; their length does not indicate an insensitivity to the great complexity of these subjects, each of which justifies a multivolume work of reference in its own right. They are intended as aide-mémoires and guideposts to researchers embarking on journeys of discovery across the Library's collections divisions.

Patrick Frazier

All-night dancing at Crow Fair, Crow Agency, Montana, August 1979. Photograph by Michael Crummett, Montana Project: MT9-MC24-10. American Folklife Center.

During a week of parades, giveaways, powwow dancing, feasting, and rodeo, the Crow renew social and kinship ties each August at the Crow Fair on their reservation near the Little Big Horn River in south central Montana.

ACKNOWLEDGMENTS

Creation of this resource guide was a complex undertaking, eventually spanning six years and involving a number of people beyond the primary contributors who, together, are the authors of this book. The assistance, advice, and ideas provided by these individuals enriched the guide, increasing its value to researchers and its appeal to general readers. Those of us on the List of Contributors who researched and wrote text for this publication thus wish to acknowledge and express our thanks to the following people for their assistance.

In the Publishing Office, Margaret E. Wagner started the process, assembled and organized the original contributors (Thomas Blumer, James Flatness, Patrick Frazier, Judith Gray, Jerry Kearns, and Lee Miller), and established a basic format with the editorial team. Sara Day, who took over coordination of the project as the Publishing Office editor, enhanced the guide's scope and presentation and encouraged more participants who helped unearth and describe additional material and write the Gateway summaries. Dr. Frederick E. Hoxie, former director of the D'Arcy McNickle Center for the History of the American Indian at the Newberry Library in Chicago, and now the Newberry's Vice President of Research and Education, reviewed the content and structure of the guide at the request of the Publishing Office, providing written suggestions which further helped the editors and contributors to strengthen its value to researchers.

Stephen James, chief of the Humanities and Social Sciences Division, deserves thanks for his patience and cooperation in allowing the editor generous time away from his regular duties to work on the guide. Thanks go to reference specialist Margaret N. Coughlan in the Children's Literature Center, and her chief, Sybille A. Jagusch, for their input to the children's literature portion of the guide. And thanks are due as well to Lyle Minter, head of the Government Publica-tions and Periodicals Section in the Serial and Government Publications Division, and to the head of the Newspaper Section, Frank Carroll, who reviewed the periodical text for accuracy.

In Rare Book and Special Collections Division, curator Rosemary Fry Plakas patiently accompa-nied researchers in the Rare Book stacks and made helpful suggestions. Clark W. Evans, refer-ence specialist, frequently answered the call for books that were needed for reproducing images.

James H. Hutson, chief of the Manuscript Di-vision, allowed participation by his staff, includ-ing assistant chief David Wigdor; early Ameri-can history specialist Gerard W. Gawalt; Civil War and Reconstruction specialist John R. Sell-ers; and twentieth-century political history spe-cialist John E. Haynes. Especially helpful were Michael Klein, Manuscript reference librarian, who did considerable work on an early version of the Manuscript portion, and Mary Wolfskill, head of the Reference and Reader Section, who guided us innumerable times. Jennifer Manning of the Congressional Reference Division of the Congressional Research Service, who is of Ar-kansas Cherokee heritage, also deserves credit for constructively reviewing drafts of this and other sections.

In the Law Library, legal research specialists Jim Martin and David Rabasca aided in track-ing down elusive bibliographic information. Re-search here was further aided by Susan E. Wat-kins, senior legal reference specialist, and Thomas Dan Burney, former rare book librarian. Outside of the Library, thanks go to attorney Don B. Miller of the Native American Rights Fund; at-torney Judy A. Leaming; and Fred E. Sanders, assistant chief of the Catawba Nation in South Carolina.

In the Prints and Photographs Division, Bernard F. Reilly, Jr., head, Curatorial Section, critiqued various drafts of the division's text, suggested illustrations, and reviewed captions.

Harry L. Katz, curator, Popular and Applied Graphic Arts, wrote captions for several illustrations. The division's chief, Stephen Ostrow, and the head of its Reference Section, Mary Ison, also cooperated in furthering progress. Catalogers Arden Alexander, Sarah D. Rouse, and Woody Woodis assigned negative numbers and checked catalogue data for most of the guide's illustrations.

Ralph Ehrenberg, chief of the Geography and Map Division, and Gary Fitzpatrick, geographic information systems specialist, read and commented on various stages of that section's drafts. In the Motion Picture, Broadcasting and Recorded Sound Division, reference librarian Rosemary Hanes and former head of the Documentation and Reference Center Patrick Sheehan suggested film titles, located various illustrations, and proofread various drafts of the MBRS chapter. Thanks also go to Samuel Brylawski and

Edwin M. Matthias, reference specialists in the Recorded Sound Reference Center, for suggesting record titles and illustrations, and for reading drafts.

In the Music Division, gratitude goes to acting chief Jon Newsom; donor relations officer Elizabeth Auman; and curator of the Miller Flute Collection Robert Sheldon. Wayne Shirley, music specialist, read the Music section's text and made additional suggestions. Vicky Wulff, dance specialist in the Performing Arts Library Section, also read and made suggestions on all texts referring to dance.

In the American Folklife Center, Joseph C. Hickerson, head of acquisitions, and the late Gerald E. Parsons, head of reference, gave valuable assistance. Thanks go also to Ives Goddard of the Smithsonian Institution's *Handbook of North American Indians Project*.

CONTRIBUTORS

ELIZABETH B. BAZAN earned a B.A. with high honors in anthropology from College of William and Mary (1974) and a J.D. from University of Maryland School of Law (1977). She was Law Clerk to Judge R. Dorsey Watkins, U.S. District Court for the District of Maryland (1977–79). A legislative attorney with the American Law Division of the Congressional Research Service since 1980, American Indian law is one of her many areas of expertise. She was a panelist on fractionated heirship lands, Annual Indian Law Conference, Fort Worth, Texas, held by the Indian Law Section of the Federal Bar Association; she has been a member of the FBA National Council since 1993.

THOMAS J. BLUMER, senior editor, Law Library of Congress, earned his doctorate in English from the University of South Carolina and is a recognized expert and consultant on Southeastern American Indian history and culture, with a particular emphasis on the Catawba Indians of South Carolina. He is the author of more than one hundred articles, the *Bibliography of the Catawba* (Scarecrow Press, 1987), and is working on a book-length study of the Catawba pottery tradition. He works directly for the Catawba Indian Tribal Council and is a frequent lecturer for museums and historical societies.

JENNIFER BRATHOVDE, reference specialist for Native American and western history materials in the Prints and Photographs Division, earned her masters degree in library science from the University of Washington, Seattle. Before coming to the Library in 1991, she received fellowships from the Newberry Library's D'Arcy McNickle Center for the History of the American Indian in Chicago and the Smithsonian Institution's National Anthropological Archives to develop guides for resource material related to American Indians at those institutions. An enrolled member of the Devil's Lake Sioux

Tribe in North Dakota, Brathovde is of Sisseton-Wahpeton ancestry.

JAMES A. FLATNESS has worked in the Library's Geography and Map Division for twenty-two years, initially as a reference librarian and more recently as the head of the division's Acquisitions Unit.

PATRICK FRAZIER, editor of this guide, is reference specialist in North American Indians in the Humanities and Social Sciences Division. He is the author of *The Mohicans of Stockbridge* (University of Nebraska Press, 1992) and *Portrait Index of North American Indians in Published Collections* (Library of Congress, 1992).

JAMES GILREATH is American history specialist in the Rare Book and Special Collections Division. His publications include *Thomas Jefferson's Library* (1989), and the introductions to the rare facsimile edition of *Catlin's North American Indian Portfolio* (Abbeville and the Library of Congress, c1989) and the Tiny Folios book *The North American Indian Portfolios from the Library of Congress* (Abbeville, c1993).

JUDITH GRAY, head of reference services for the American Folklife Center, is an ethnomusicologist who came to the Center in 1983 to work on the Federal Cylinder Project. She has cataloged and helped disseminate copies of the wax cylinder recordings made between 1890 and 1942 that document Native American songs and narratives. She regularly consults with individuals and tribal communities on aspects of cultural preservation.

JOHN R. HEBERT, senior specialist in Hispanic bibliography (Hispanic Division), assistant chief, Hispanic Division (1976–93), and the coordinator (1989–93) of the Library of Congress's five-year program *1492–1992: An Ongoing Voyage*

established to commemorate the Columbian Quincentenary, earned his doctorate in Latin American history at Georgetown University (1972). He has written extensively on eighteenth-century Spanish presence in the U.S. (the Spanish borderlands), historical cartography, and Latin American bibliography. Dr. Hébert curated the 1992–93 exhibition *An Ongoing Voyage: 1492–1992* and the traveling exhibition *In Their Own Voices*, which focussed on the use of American Indian language documents.

JERRY KEARNS is the former reference specialist for Native American and western history materials in the Prints and Photographs Division.

KAREN C. LUND of the Motion Picture, Broadcasting and Recorded Sound Division, has an M.A. in Cinema Studies and a certificate in Museum Studies from New York University. She compiled the guides *American Indians in Silent Film: Motion Pictures in the Library of Congress* (1992) and *A Selected Guide to Sound Feature Films and Television Programs with American Indian Content at the Library of Congress* (1995)

JOHN J. McDONOUGH of the Library's Manuscript Division specializes in the history of the nineteenth century's antebellum period. He is the compiler of *Members of Congress: A Checklist of Their Papers in the Manuscript Division, Library of Congress* (1980) and co-editor of *Witness to the Young Republic: the Journal of Benjamin Brown French, 1828–1870* (University Press of New England, 1989).

LEE MILLER, an ethnohistorian and screenwriter, is of Eastern Cherokee and Kaw heritage. She has an M.A. in anthropology from Johns Hopkins University. From 1989 to 1991 she served as a consultant for the Library of Congress's Columbus Quincentenary Program, *An Ongoing Voyage*, while also working on this guide. Ms. Miller was writer and head of research for *500 Nations*, the CBS television series, and is founder and CEO of the Native Learning Foundation, which seeks to establish culture and language immersion schools on Indian reservations.

ROGER WALKE is Analyst in American Indian Policy in the Congressional Research Service, Library of Congress. He is the compiler of the 1991 edition of *Federal Programs of Assistance to Native Americans* and holds an M.A. in anthropology from the University of Oregon (1975).

GENERAL COLLECTIONS

Cherokee Phoenix, New Echota, Georgia, April 10, 1828 (LC-USZ62-115659). Serial and Government Publications Division

Elias Boudinot, a Cherokee schoolteacher and missionary, began putting out the first Indian newspaper, the Cherokee Phoenix, *in 1828 in New Echota, Georgia. Printed in English and Cherokee, the four-page newspaper published Cherokee laws and described persistent alcoholism and other problems. In his first issue, Boudinot called for a time when "all the Indian tribes of America shall rise, Phoenix-like, from their ashes, and when terms like 'Indian depredations,' 'war whoops,' 'scalping knife,' and the like shall become obsolete and forever buried 'under deep ground.'" The paper closed after Boudinot refused to keep reports of divisions within the tribe over moving west to Indian Territory out of the paper.*

GENERAL COLLECTIONS

INTRODUCTION

For those who are initiating their research on American Indians in the Library of Congress, the general collections provide the best introduction. Their vastness, range, and accessibility can often completely answer a researcher's needs. Reprint publishing and the publishing of many manuscript and archival collections may obviate the need to consult special materials in other Library divisions or in other institutions where location and hours of access may make study difficult. Even if an answer to a research question lay outside the Library of Congress, part of these collections will reveal what is available elsewhere. Scholarly secondary works and bibliographies may also save time for a researcher either by adequately covering the subject being explored or by pointing to other resources.

Since the late nineteenth century the Library of Congress has been the depository for materials copyrighted in the United States. This process has been the major contributor to the Library's reputation as the largest holder of reference materials in the world. Additional acquisitions through purchase, gift, and exchange have brought the current total of volumes in the general collections to 16 million. In the classification span E51–E99, which contains the heaviest concentration of general works on North American Indian topics, there are approximately twenty thousand volumes. In addition, relevant bibliographies and Indian-related material in other general works and microforms swell these numbers considerably. And, of course, the numbers continue to grow.

Further, as the nation's library, the Library of Congress is naturally a main repository of information regarding the history and development of America. Since our indigenous peoples were an integral part of this country's history and development, and even predate it, the general collections have many resources to tell the American Indian story. In contemplating whether or not the Library of Congress has a particular book, therefore, it is probably safer to assume that it has, than that it has not.

The size and the physical layout of the Library's general collections, however, demand that, for serious study, researchers either be prepared to request specific materials or be able to spend considerable time discovering them. Whatever one's approach, the first contact a researcher should make is with a reference specialist in the Humanities and Social Sciences Division. These specialists are best equipped to help researchers navigate the sometimes-labyrinthine complexity of the collections through the numerous print and electronic passages.

USING THE COLLECTIONS

MAIN READING ROOM

LOCATION: Jefferson Building, 1st floor, Room LJ 100; telephone (202) 707-5522

HOURS: Monday, Wednesday and Thursday 8:30 A.M. to 9:30 P.M.; Tuesday, Friday and Saturday, 8:30 A.M. to 5:00 P.M.

ACCESS AND USE: No appointments necessary. The Library's bookstacks are closed to the public. Books and bound periodicals must be brought to the reading room (allow enough time for this procedure). Readers must also show a Library of Congress I.D. To obtain this user I.D. with photograph—valid for two years and now required in all public reading rooms—first time readers should apply to the reader registration station, Room G22, Jefferson Building.

INFORMATIONAL PUBLICATIONS: *Information for Researchers Using the Library of Congress*; *Doing Research at the Library of Congress: A Guide to Subject Searching in a Closed Stacks Library* by Thomas Mann, free booklets available by writing to: Library of Congress, National Reference Service, Washington, D.C. 20540.

The gateway to the general collections is the Main Reading Room. With approximately 70,000 reference volumes around its perimeter, on-line and CD-ROM reference sources, card and computer catalogs, and a staff of professional reference specialists, this reading room is the major entry point to Indian-related research.

The Catalogs

The key to the book collections is familiarity with the Library's subject headings and their various subdivisions used to narrow a given topic. That familiarity is gained through studying the compilation *Library of Congress Subject Headings*, currently a four-volume work that is usually available in large libraries. For study of Indians in general the heading "Indians of North America" exists for nearly all books dealing with Indians north of Mexico. Subdivisions cover particular aspects topically or geographically— "Art," "Biography," "Canada," "Great Plains," "Treaties," etc. One may also search directly under a tribal name, and similar subdivisions will apply, e.g. "Apache Indians—Basket making" or "Mohave Indians—Medicine." Anthropological, archaeological, and ethnological groupings also appear, such as "Clovis culture," "Moundbuilders," and "Woodland Indians." Further, a major branch of a given group may have its own heading, so that it is possible to search, for example, under Jicarilla Indians or Santee Indians. In short, if one has a specific subject in mind, it is best to search for it directly.

The transition from the card catalog to the computer catalog has created new advantages, and in some cases, new problems for American Indian-related topics. At present, the computer catalog is best used for publications cataloged since 1968, though older materials may be searched in a file that is undergoing bibliographic improvement. This file currently contains outdated subject terms, however, and may give a false impression of the amount of works available on a given topic. For assured coverage

GATEWAYS

At the time of European contact, "the Americas were inhabited by a complex mosaic of human societies, with an incredible diversity of languages, customs, and life-styles," according to anthropologists John Verano and Douglas Ubelaker. Native American cultures, evolving and interacting throughout their long existence on the continent, were ancient. Exactly how ancient no one knows for sure: Indian nations' origin stories often say they have always existed here, while most archaeologists agree that humans have been in North America for at least 12,000 years and probably longer, but disagree over how much longer they may have been here.

Native Americans were numerous and populated every part of North America. Most estimates of Native American population north of the Rio Grande, at the time of contact, fall in the range of 2–5 million people (the high estimate is 18 million and the low is 0.9 million).

Native American cultures covered a large range of political organization, from bands and tribes to chiefdoms and perhaps states. The degree of social stratification varied from egalitarian to genuine social classes. Some Native American groups, like the Inuit, were egalitarian, while others, like the Pacific Northwest Coast tribes, the Chumash of California, or the mound-builders of the Mississippi, had chiefs, commoners, and in some cases slaves.

In addition, there were hundreds of religions in North America. They varied from the individualistic vision-quest-oriented religions of the Great Plains, to the complex masked-dance rituals of the Pueblos, to the apparently temple-based religions of the mound-building Mississippian cultures.

In the area of kinship and marriage, Native American cultures exhibited as wide a variety of marriage customs, post-marriage residence, relations with in-laws, and family structures as can be found in the rest of the world. Their kinship structures (lineages, clans, etc.), forms of descent (patrilineal, matrilineal, or bilateral), kinship terminology systems, and life-cycle rituals (at birth, puberty, and death) were more various than those of contact-era Europe.

Students of culture have often made use of the concept of the "culture area," defined as a geographical area within which cultures are significantly similar to each other and dissimilar to the cultures of other such areas. In North America, the culture areas frequently distinguished include the Arctic, Sub-Arctic, Northwest Coast, Plateau, Great Basin, California, Southwest, the Plains, and the Eastern Woodlands (often divided into two culture areas, the Northeast and the Southeast).

Native American prehistoric culture evolved through numerous general and specific cultural stages. The two earliest general stages were the Paleo-Indian (up to about 8,000 years ago) and the later Archaic. As Archaic cultures differentiated, broad cultural traditions became more geographically localized, usually coming to characterize particular culture areas or smaller regions within them. For instance, the Woodland archaeological tradition (which included the famous Adena and Hopewell traditions) characterized most of the Eastern Woodland culture area following the Archaic, and was succeeded, in the Southeast, by the Mississippian tradition after about A.D. 800. Other culture areas also went through unique archaeological stages.

WHERE TO LOOK: Studies and evidence of pre-contact North American Indian life can be found in the General Collections, and in the Manuscript, Rare Book and Special Collections, Prints and Photographs, and Geography and Map Divisions.

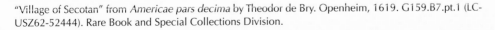

"Village of Secotan" from *Americae pars decima* by Theodor de Bry. Openheim, 1619. G159.B7.pt.1 (LC-USZ62-52444). Rare Book and Special Collections Division.

The engraving by Theodor de Bry of an Algonquian town on the Pamlico River estuary of North Carolina is a composite from drawings by John White, who visited the North Carolina and southern Virginia coast in 1585–86 and again in 1587. Shown in this engraving are typical aspects of Carolina Algonquians' economy, architecture, and religion. White depicted three crops of corn (ripe corn, sown in May, labeled 'F'; green corn, sown in June, 'G'; new corn, sown in early July, 'H'), as well as pumpkins ('I'), tobacco ('E'), and sunflowers (just above the tobacco).

of older works one should also check the card catalog, which will contain cross references that the computer catalog as yet does not. The cards also have more complete bibliographic information than do the pre-1968 computer entries. In browsing the card catalog for comprehensive subjects, one may visually be able to move from category to category within a subject area more easily than with a computer.

For works that the Library has cataloged since 1980, however, the computer catalog is the *only* access point. Two basic approaches to the computer files are known by the acronyms MUMS and SCORPIO. MUMS enables a keyword search in the author, title, subject, and series fields of a bibliographic record—an especially useful approach in locating material when one has only fragmentary citations. SCORPIO uses a more structured approach to searching but offers the ability to refine searches, for example, to specific

Internet Access to LOCIS

Through the Library of Congress Information System (LOCIS), Internet users have access to more than 27 million records in the following databases: **Library of Congress Online Catalog**, **Federal Legislation**, **Copyright Registrations**, **Braille and Audio Bibliographic Information**, **Library of Congress Guides and Organization Listings**, and **Foreign Law Abstracts and Citations**.

LOCIS may be reached using **telnet** or **tn3270**:

- **telnet** (or **tn3270**) to **locis.loc.gov** (or use the i.p. address 140.147.254.3)
- make database selections from the opening help screens
- 90 simultaneous Internet users are supported
- Hours of access (U.S.A. Eastern time): Monday–Friday, 6:30 A.M.–midnight
  Saturday, 8:00 A.M.–5:00 P.M.
  Sunday, 1:00 P.M.–5:00 P.M.

LOCIS may also be reached through the Library of Congress Gopher (**LC MARVEL**) and through the Library of Congress WWW site (**LC WEB**). Use Gopher client software or first connect to another Gopher in order to use LC MARVEL (The LC MARVEL address is **marvel.loc.gov**). To connect to LC's WWW site, use the Internet hypertext transfer protocol (**http**) to connect to the address **lcweb.loc.gov**. You may use LC MARVEL and LC WEB to connect to LOCIS, but in order to do so your Gopher client software and WWW browser or your Internet provider software must support the Internet **telnet** or **tn3270** function.

Assistance for searching LOCIS may be found on both LC MARVEL and LC WEB. The guides available through these services are also available on the LC anonymous **FTP** site. FTP to **ftp.loc.gov** and look in the **/pub/lc.online** directory. When using FTP, log in on anonymous and use your e-mail address or the word **guest** as a password.

languages or time periods. One can use either approach through the umbrella system, LOCIS. Navigating the computer catalog for basic searches has been made easier through the availability of ACCESS, a menu-driven, touch-screen system that is available in several of the Library's general and specialized reading rooms.

The Library's computer catalog is now available on-line through the Internet. In order to maximize efficient use of one's time in the Library, it is advisable to use the Internet beforehand, if available, in order to have the necessary classification number and bibliographic information needed for requesting books.

Besides the Library's on-line catalog for books, the computer system has files for public policy literature, federal legislation, and general magazine articles, all of which may yield information on Indian topics. In addition, the Library has CD-ROM versions of *Public Affairs Information Service*, *Social Science Index*, *Dissertation Abstracts* and Congressional Information Service's *Congressional Masterfile*, all of which are potential resources for Indian-related study.

❏ SELECTED BOOKS

In describing the Library's general holdings on Indian-related topics, their extent necessarily limits the discussion of specific titles to a selective sampling. Titles are selected following categories of American Indian study and related materials, illustrating the diversity of materials available; and are arranged alphabetically by title:

- Bibliographies and Guides
- American Archaeology, Ethnology, History
- Political Affairs
- Language and Literature
- Children's Literature
- Local History and Genealogy

Bibliographies and Guides

In the initial stage of any research, bibliographies provide an efficient first step to determine what has already been written on a given topic. In the Library of Congress, bibliographies are separately cataloged within the classification Z. As of this writing the Library holds more than five hundred fifty bibliographies related directly to North American Indians, including for example, nineteen from the *Native American Bibliography Series* by The Scarecrow Press. Hundreds of other bibliographies exist, however, of a local, regional, or topical nature that may contain significant Indian-related citations.

Several works that have proved useful are on the reference shelves in the Main Reading Room. Among them are such wellknown bibliographies as *A Bibliographical Guide to the History of Indian White Relations in the United States* by Francis Paul Prucha (Chicago: University of Chicago Press, 1977) and its 1982 supplement; *Native Americans: An Annotated Bibliography* by Frederick E. Hoxie and Harvey Markowitz (Pasadena, Calif.: Salem Press, 1991); and *Ethnographic Bibliography of North America* by George Peter Murdock (4th ed. New Haven: Human Relations Area Files Press, 1975) and its 1990 supplement.

To retrieve a relevant bibliography that may be in the stacks, one simply searches the computer or card catalog under the appropriate subject heading, with "Bibliography" as the subheading—"Hopewell Culture—Bibliography," for example. Then, as with all book stack requests, one submits a request slip in the appropriate reading room.

Guides at the Library of Congress to Holdings in Other Institutions

Within the Z and CD classifications are catalogs and guides to other institutions' holdings, sources that may expand research possibilities. A representation of titles in the Library's collections appear below. Although some of them are dated, they may be uncommon in other libraries and they offer excellent starting points to locate works or collections that may be hard to find or are unique to the institution.

Biographical and Historical Index of American Indians and Persons Involved in Indian Affairs. 8 vols. Boston: G. K. Hall, 1966; Z1209.H85

A copy of a file kept until 1965 by the Department of the Interior library that contains citations to tribes, Indian individuals, and persons in Indian affairs who are mentioned in books, journals, treaties, and other publications.

Catalog of the Manuscripts of the Massachusetts Historical Society. 7 vols. Boston: G. K. Hall, 1969; Z1295.M39 1969
—First Supplement. 2 vols. Boston: G. K. Hall, 1980; Z1295.M39 1969 suppl.

Since Massachusetts was the New England province most interactive with Indian groups during the colonial era, the papers of some of its populace are often valuable for research. More than 1,100 entries appear under the subjects "Indian affairs" and "Indians," but one may also need to search under individual names, Indian or non-Indian.

Catalog to Manuscripts at the National Anthropological Archives. 4 vols. Boston: G. K. Hall, 1975; Z1209.2.N67 N37 1975 (fol.)

This catalog reproduces card entries for manuscripts generated mostly by the Smithsonian Institution's Bureau of American Ethnology between 1879 and 1965. The collections reflect holdings mostly on North American Indians and are especially rich in vocabularies, grammar notes, and linguistic texts. Tribes, individual names, geographical areas, and broad topics are inter-filed alphabetically. Approximately eighty drawings mainly by Indian artists are also listed.

Dictionary Catalog of the American Indian Collection: Huntington Free Library and Reading Room, New York. 4 vols. Boston: G. K. Hall, 1977; Z1209. H85 1977

Based on an inventory and shelflist through 1976, this set reproduces card entries for more than 35,000 volumes of books and periodicals regarding indigenous peoples of the Western Hemisphere. There are broad topical headings as well as subject arrangements by tribe or location.

Dictionary Catalog of the Edward E. Ayer Collection of Americana and American Indians in the Newberry Library. 16 vols. Boston: G. K. Hall, 1961; Z1201.N45
—First Supplement. 3 vols. Boston: G. K. Hall, 1971

A catalog of about 100,000 pieces as of 1971, it contains citations for books, maps, atlases, and periodicals. A significant portion of the listings includes materials on Canadian, Caribbean, Central American, Hawaiian, Mexican, Philippine, and South American indigenous peoples.

The Dictionary Catalog of the Pacific Northwest Collection of the University of Washington Libraries. 6 vols. Boston: G. K. Hall, 1972; Z1251.N7 W33 1972 (fol.)

This catalog lists mostly monographs, but includes some manuscripts and theses. Among American Indian holdings, the concentration is on tribal groups of the Northwest. The arrangement follows the Library of Congress cataloging scheme (see discussion on p. 3).

A Guide to Cherokee Documents in Foreign Archives. William L. Anderson and James A. Lewis. Metuchen, N.J.: Scarecrow Press, 1983; Z1210. C46A53 1983

A Guide to Cherokee Documents in the Northeastern United States. Paul Kutsche. Metuchen, N.J.: Scarecrow Press, 1986; Z1210.C46K87 1986

Two titles from the Native American Bibliography Series. The first identifies official documents in Canada, France, Great Britain, Mexico, and Spain, the bulk of which are in Great Britain. The second chronologically lists and annotates 6,257 entries from manuscript collections in 20 public and private libraries in the Northeast. Nearly 4,600 of these are from Harvard University's Houghton Library. Contrary to its title, it also lists entries from the William L. Clements Library at the University of Michigan, the Newberry Library in Chicago, and the State Historical Society of Wisconsin.

A Guide to Manuscripts Relating to the American Indian in the Library of the American Philosophical Society. Compiled by John F. Freeman. Philadelphia: American Philosophical Society, 1966; Z1209.F7 (Q11.P612, v. 65)
—Supplement. Compiled by Dathal Kendal. Philadelphia: American Philosophical Society, 1982; Z1209.F7 Suppl.; (Q11.P612, v. 65 s)

Very strong in Indian language collections, the society's guide and its supplement contain more than 5,100 entries from about 300 collections. Other historical and ethnological data, including recordings, also appear. The entries are arranged alphabetically by tribes, language families, and geographic areas. Generous indexes facilitate locating material.

Guide to the National Anthropological Archives, Smithsonian Institution. By James R. Glenn. Washington, D.C.: National Anthropological Archives, 1992; Z1209.2.U5 N38 1992

This guide describes 600 collections that contain more than 6,000 linear feet of archives. The collections consist of documents from the Smithsonian's own anthropological and archaeological

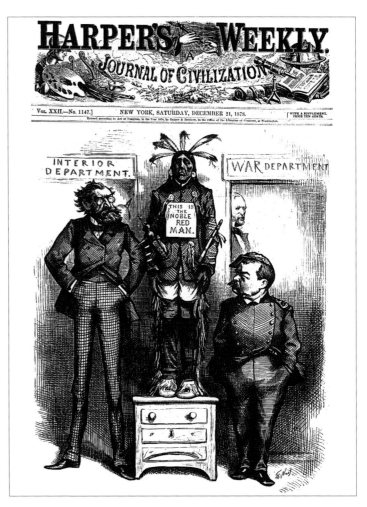

"The New Indian War. Now, no sarcastic innuendoes, but let us have a square fight," wood engraving from *Harper's Weekly*, December 21, 1878. AP2.H32 (LC-USZ62-55403). General Collections (Microform) and Prints and Photographs Division.

In December 1878, with the latest bill before Congress to transfer the Bureau of Indian Affairs back to the War Department (it had been switched to Interior in 1849), Secretary of the Interior Carl Schurz appeared before a joint committee and presented the case against transfer so effectively that the bill was killed in the House. The political cartoon shows the disputed "noble red man" standing on a bureau, holding a peace pipe in the direction of Schurz and a tomahawk in the direction of General Philip Sheridan, head of the army's Division of the Missouri—with the retiring figure of General William Tecumseh Sherman, commanding general of the army, in the doorway.

work and that of others since the late nineteenth century, as well as materials donated by other institutions and by persons such as missionaries, frontier army officers, settlers, and explorers. Materials include manuscripts, field notes, correspondence, photographic lots and other items. Many entries list correspondents and Indian tribes.

Guide to Records in the National Archives of the United States Relating to American Indians. Compiled by Edward E. Hill. Washington, D.C.: National Archives and Records Service, 1982; Z1209.2.U5H54 1982

The records cited in this work document the United States' relations with Indian tribes, predominantly through the Bureau of Indian Affairs. Although pre-federal and early federal period records exist here, the majority cover the period from the mid-nineteenth to the mid-twentieth centuries.

Historical Records Survey

Compiled under the auspices of the Work Projects Administration, these are inventories of early county and state archives that may also include manuscript collections. They occasionally contain entries specifically mentioning Indians, but more frequently one must infer from the types of records represented that Indians may be included. Search in the catalog under the heading "Historical Records Survey. Ohio," for example. Each entry has its own bibliographical information and classification number.

The Spanish Archives of New Mexico. Compiled by Ralph Emerson Twitchell. 2 vols. Cedar Rapids, Mich.: The Torch Press, 1914; CD3394 1914

An English-language inventory giving brief descriptions and excerpts from about 20,000 documents relevant to the Southwest from 1621 to 1821. Some are translated and printed in entirety in this guide. The interactions between Indians and the Spanish colonials suffuse these documents, which relate to land transactions, civil and military affairs, and mission efforts. Although the original records are in Santa Fe, the Manuscript Division has a microfilm edition, as well as a microfilm edition of *Mexican Archives of New Mexico,* covering 1821–46.

American Archaeology, Ethnology, and History

The vast majority of the Library's published North American Indian material is found in the classification span E51–E99, encompassing at this writing approximately 20,000 volumes. Here are found archaeological and ethnological publications from government and private institutions, tribal histories, captivity narratives, and most of the Indian-related topics from pre-Columbian times to the present. Besides the thousands of scholarly secondary works in class E, published primary sources exist, just a few notable examples of which are:

Papers of the Peabody Museum of Archaeology and Ethnology, Harvard University. Cambridge, Mass.: Harvard University Press, 1888?–; E51.H337

Although worldwide in scope, the majority of this series concentrates on North, Central, and South American archaeology and ethnology, and of these most deal with archaeology. Many of the studies are extensive and illustrations of sites and artifacts are plentiful. While the series' volume numbers are sequential, the dates of publication are not. One needs the volume number, therefore, when requesting these publications. Both the series and individual authors and titles within it can be located through the computer catalog.

Bureau of American Ethnology *Annual Report.* Washington, D.C.: GPO, 1879–80–1930–31; E51.U55, and the BAE *Bulletin.* Washington,

D.C.: GPO, 1887–1971; E51.U6. (Note: another set of the *Annual Report* is under the class number GN2.U5. See also the microform title *Periodicals by and about the North American Indian* in the Microform Reading Room section of the guide).

These publications represent the work of American anthropologists, ethnologists, and archaeologists working under the aegis of the Smithsonian Institution from the late nineteenth century forward. Nearly all of the work involved North American Indian topics and produced pioneering studies of continuing value. The Reports ceased in 1930 with the publication of volume 48, which is a subject index to the previous volumes. The Bulletin ceased publication with number 200, which is a list of all of the Bureau's previous publications, with an index to authors and titles. Many of the titles that appeared in these series were also cataloged separately by the Library of Congress and may be found under other classification numbers.

The American Indian and the United States: a documentary history. Compiled by Wilcomb E. Washburn. 4 vols. New York: Random House, 1973; E93.W27

A selection of documents that have figured significantly in the development of Indian-U.S. relations. The principal sources are reports of the commissioners of Indian affairs, congressional debates, judicial decisions, treaties, and acts of Congress.

The New American State Papers: Indian Affairs. 13 vols. Wilmington, Del.: Scholarly Resources, c1972; E93.U938

Materials drawn from the original *American State Papers* published between 1832 and 1861 (also in the Library's collections), as well as Congressional documents after 1817, and the Legislative Records Section of the National Archives. Bringing together these scattered and sometimes rare documents into one set gives the researcher a concentrated source with which to study U.S. relations with Indian people from the federal period up to the Civil War. Further, in the early years these documents contained presidential messages and the reports of the Commissioner of Indian Affairs, as well as letters, petitions, and other documents submitted to Congress by persons involved with Indian groups and by Indian groups themselves. The volumes are divided into categories for general affairs, the Southeast, and the old Northwest.

The E class also represents American history in general and contains valuable resource material in the form of both secondary works and published primary source materials relevant to Indian history. All of the published papers of the Presidents, for example, particularly the early ones, contain much information. Similarly, published official documents and papers of other historical figures involved in Indian events exist in the general collections. Examples include:

New American World: a documentary history of North America to 1612. Edited by David B. Quinn. 5 vols. New York: Arno Press, 1979–; E101.N47

A large sample of mostly sixteenth and seventeenth century English and translated French, Spanish, and Portuguese documents relating to the earliest explorations and settlements in America. The first volume also contains classical, medieval, and Muslim writings on the concept of the world and the possibility of undiscovered lands, as well as Norse accounts of Vinland, and those of yet-to-be-confirmed pre-Columbian visitors to this continent. Where narratives of contact with indigenous peoples appear, and where the accounts are not overly embellished for European consumption, the documents offer interesting glimpses at how each group's observations and experiences with the other may have shaped the course of subsequent relations.

The Papers of Chief John Ross. Edited by Gary E. Moulton. 2 vols. Norman: University of Oklahoma Press, c1985; E99.C5R82

Landowner, farmer, trader, merchant, slaveholder, and preeminent political figure among the Cherokee, John Ross was deeply involved in the significant and tumultuous affairs of the Cherokee in the first half of the nineteenth century. The papers span the era from the War of 1812 (briefly) to the onset of the Civil War and reflect Ross's personal life as well as his prolific efforts on behalf of the Cherokee, especially during the removal period.

The Papers of Sir William Johnson. 13 vols. Albany: The University of the State of New York, 1921–62; E195.J62

As England's principal agent for Indian affairs in northern colonial America, as wealthy landowner in the New York's Mohawk Valley, and as husband to a prominent Mohawk woman, Johnson was an influential and knowledgeable figure in Indian affairs from the 1740s until his death in 1774. His papers span 1738 to 1788, with the bulk covering the period from the French and Indian War until 1770.

Territorial Papers of the United States. 28 vols. Washington, D.C.: GPO, 1934–1975; E173.C3

Official papers and correspondence involving

"Witchitaw village on Rush Creek," lithograph by James Ackerman from *Exploration of the Red river of Louisiana, in the year 1852* by Randolph B. Marcy; assisted by George B. McLellan. Sen. Exec. Doc., 33rd Cong., 1st Sess. (Washington, D.C.: U.S. War Department, 1854). F377.R3U51 (LC-USZ62-11478). General Collections.

Capt. Randolph B. Marcy was sent by the federal government to find the headwaters of the Red River, with Bvt. Capt. George B. McClellan (later Union commander in chief during the first part of the Civil War) as second in command. He failed to find the river's source but, trained at West Point in figure, topographical, and landscape drawing, he produced a number of informative illustrations for his report. He drew one of the many large Wichita farming villages encountered in 1852, some of which contained as many as a thousand grass and pole lodges.

what were the territories east of the Mississippi River in the late eighteenth and early nineteenth centuries. Many of the issues discussed in these documents affected Indian people directly or indirectly. The volumes are grouped into areas north and south of the Ohio River (the old Northwest and old Southwest), Alabama, Arkansas, Florida, Illinois, Indiana, Louisiana-Missouri, Michigan, Mississippi, Orleans, and Wisconsin.

Texas Indian Papers. Edited by Dorman H. Winfrey and James M. Day. 4 vols. Austin: Texas State Library, 1959–61; E78.T4T42

Printed transcripts of the Indian Papers from the Archives Division of Texas State Library. Although coverage is from 1825 to 1916, only one document from each of these years appears. The majority date from the 1830s through 1879. The papers were generated by several departments within Texas government, including its own Bureau of Indian Affairs of the Republic in 1844 and 1845. Sources include letters, minutes of council meetings with tribes, treaties, and accounts and supply lists by traders, agents, and others involved with Indian people. Numerous tribes are dealt with, particularly the Alabama, Caddo, Cherokee, Choctaw, Comanche, Delaware, Keechai, Kickapoo, Kiowa, Lipan, Shawnee, Tawakoni, Tonkawa, Waco, and Wichita.

Closely following the E class in importance is the classification F below the number 1000, devoted to local United States history. Located here are valuable sources of information such as the publications of historical societies, many of which print primary source documents from their collections. Several compilations of colonial records and archives such as those of New York, Pennsylvania, and South Carolina, are also very fruit-

ful, as are the accounts of travelers, explorers, missionaries, and administrative officials. Below is a sampling of titles:

Anza's California Expeditions. Herbert Eugene Bolton. 5 vols. Berkeley: University of California Press, 1930; F864.B68

Expeditionary and colonizer Juan Bautista Anza's diaries and other sources relative to his excursions and encounters with Indians in Arizona and California.

Early Western Travels 1748–1846. Edited by Reuben Gold Thwaites. 32 vols., with index. Cleveland: A. H. Clark Co., 1904–7; F592.T54

An extensive compilation of annotated reprints of early travel accounts and diaries, most of which described encounters with Indians.

The Expeditions of John Charles Frémont. Edited by Donald Jackson and Mary Lee Spence. 4 vols. in 3, plus map portfolio. Urbana: University of Illinois Press, 1970–80; F592.F852

These volumes contain journals, correspondence, and other papers relating to Frémont's several explorations and travels throughout the West to Oregon and California in the 1840s and 1850s. Frémont made numerous observations of the land and its original occupants, and his first journal had enthusiastic reading in the East.

The Jesuit Relations and Allied Documents. Edited by Reuben Gold Thwaites. 73 vols. Cleveland: Burrows Bros. Co., 1896–1901; F1030.7. C96

Extensive published primary sources relevant to the Jesuit missions in eastern North America during the seventeenth and eighteenth centuries. Volumes 72 and 73 comprise an index.

Life, Letters and Travels of Father Pierre-Jean DeSmet, S.J. 1801–1873. Edited by Hiram Martin Chittenden and Alfred Talbot Richardson. 4 vols. New York: F. P. Harper, 1905; F591.S63

FUR TRADE

Perhaps the most important early Indian-colonial trade was the fur trade, beginning in the early sixteenth century and continuing well into the nineteenth. Beaver became the major item but other furs (otter, ermine, marten, fox, raccoon, and lynx) as well as hides (moose, caribou, deer, and elk) were also significant. The fur trade was important not only in eastern-central North America but also in the Spanish colonies, in Alaska, and later in western North America. Indians also supplied the buffalo robe trade in the nineteenth century.

Prominent European trade goods included guns, ammunition, knives, beads, axes, hatchets, hoes, cloth, blankets, mirrors, and body paint. Many of these items were technologically more efficient or more durable versions of items Indian people already used, but other items, most notably liquor, were new to the people and wrought havoc on the native population, as did the diseases carried by the Europeans.

Participation in the fur trade represented a major change from subsistence hunting, since the latter focused primarily on mammals that could supply food for a community. The search for small fur-bearers caused hunters and their families to disperse in winter (when the pelts were thickest) so as not to compete for—and totally deplete—the limited number of animals in a given territory. While Indian participants helped shape the fur trade (going many miles out of their way, if need be, to visit the trader with the best quality goods),

in some cases they were also, in effect, trading self-sufficiency for acquired needs.

Depending in part on pre-existing trade routes between Indian groups, European trade-good suppliers sometimes relied on coastal groups to carry materials inland and to return with furs. The Russians in Alaska, however, did the fur seal and sea otter hunting themselves initially, before becoming dependent on Aleuts for these animals. While some companies established a network of trading posts, the French "coureurs de bois" travelled the inland waterways to rendezvouz with Indian clients.

The fur trade was characterized by international rivalry in both hemispheres: the French competed with the British, and the British with the Americans, and both of the latter with the Russians. Principal rival firms included the Hudson's Bay Company, the North West Company, the American Fur Company, and the Russian-American Company. Trade partnerships became military alliances in more than one war; thus, for example, the Dutch West India Company sold guns to their Iroquoian trade partners, but not to any Algonquians.

WHERE TO LOOK: The General Collections, Rare Book and Special Collections, Manuscript, Prints and Photographs, and Geography and Map Divisions, and the Law Library.

"Praevalebit Aequior" (Grease takes precedence), cover woodcut from *The American Magazine and Monthly Chronicle*, Vol. I, No. 6 for March 1758. AP2.A2A5 (LC-USZ62-115627). Rare Book and Special Collections.

This magazine was founded during the French and Indian War for distribution both in England and in the colonies. The woodcut, by an unidentified artist, shows an Indian whose loyalty is being sought by French and English competitors bearing different trade items. On the left, an Englishman carries a Bible and a bolt of cloth while the Frenchman on the right offers a tomahawk and a money purse. Though doubtlessly laden with contemporaneous value judgments about the items being offered and about the Indian and French figures, this illustration documents a British realization that Indian people had options regarding alliances based on their own preferences.

THE AMERICAN MAGAZINE,

PRÆVALEBIT ÆQUIOR.

AND

Monthly CHRONICLE for the BRITISH Colonies.

Vol. I. Nᵒ. VI. For MARCH 1758.

CONTAINING.

I. DEBATES in MARYLAND.
II. PHILOSOPHICAL MISCELLANY.
III. MONTHLY ESSAYS.
IV. POETICAL ESSAYS.

V. HISTORY of the WAR in NORTH AMERICA.
VI. MONTHLY CHRONICLE

To be continued (Price *One* Shilling *Pennsylvania* Currency each Month)

By a SOCIETY of Gentlemen.

Veritatis cultores, Fraudis inimici.

PHILADELPHIA.

Printed and Sold by WILLIAM BRADFORD, at the Corner-House in *Front* and *Market-Streets*.

Journals and letters from the 1840s through the 1860s of the Jesuit missionary who travelled widely from St. Louis to the Straits of Juan de Fuca, establishing missions and relations with numerous tribes of the Northwest. He also served as an intermediary between the government and the Indians during peace and war. Tribes such as the Arapaho, Blackfeet, Coeur d'Alene, Crow, and others appear in his narrations.

The Mountain Men and the Fur Trade of the Far West. Edited by Le Roy Reuben Hafen. 10 vols., with bibliography and index. Glendale, Calif.: A. H. Clark Co., 1965–72; F592.M74

A scholarly and well-footnoted secondary biographical source on the trappers and fur traders in the Upper Missouri region, the Southwest, and the Oregon country. The subjects covered are the actions of the men for whom relations with Indian people were an integral part of their personal and business life.

Papers Concerning Robertson's Colony in Texas. Compiled and edited by Malcolm McLean. Fort Worth: Texas Christian University Press, 1974–; F389.M17

Documents relative to a colonization effort in the 1820s and 1830s to place several hundred families along the Brazos River between Austin and Fort Worth in an area that now encompasses thirty-one counties. The settlement was near several Indian groups, and entries appear on the Caddo, Cherokee, Comanche, Shawnee, Tawakoni, Waco, and others. The Library currently has eighteen volumes in this continuing series, including the unnumbered introductory volume. Volume 6, covering March 6 through December 5, 1831, is titled "The Campaigns against the Tawakoni, Waco, Towash, and Comanche Indians."

The Papers of William Penn. Edited by Mary Maples Dunn. 5 vols. Philadelphia: University of Pennsylvania Press, 1981–1987; F152.2.P3956 1981

Volumes 2 and 4 of this series are the most relevant for studying the dealings of this prominent Quaker governor of Pennsylvania, whose legacy of fair play with Indians was respected by tribes in that colony for generations.

The Susquehannah Company Papers. Edited by Julian Parks Boyd and Robert Joseph Taylor. 11 vols. Ithaca, N.Y.: Cornell University Press, 1930–71; F157.W9S97

Correspondence and other papers of the company involved in eighteenth-century land speculation in the Wyoming Valley of Pennsylvania and subsequent conflicts with the Delaware and Six Nations.

Political Affairs

See the discussion of this area in the Law Library section under "*State Documents*" (p. 132). Materials under this classification (J) must be requested in either of the general reading rooms in the Adams Building or the Jefferson Building.

Language and Literature

Recent years have seen an explosion of interest in Native American linguistics. Language-related books for North American Indians (classification PM), including grammars, dictionaries, and glossaries, are cataloged under either the tribal name or the language group—"Ojibwa language," "Dakota language," "Siksika language," etc. The majority of studies and examples of Indian legends, literature, poetry, religious texts, and song lyrics, however, may be found variously cataloged in ethnology (E), anthropology (GN), and American literature (PS). One would search in the card or computer catalog, for example, under "Navajo Indians—Legends," or "Navajo Indians—Poetry," but "American literature—Indian authors," for collective studies of Indian-

Walter Richard West (Wah-Pah-Nah-Yah), a Cheyenne and director of art at Bacone College, the only Indian college in the United States in the 1950s, checked the stories retold by Grace Jackson Penney in this exhaustively researched book of Cheyenne folklore against his own childhood memories. According to the story of "How the Raven Got to be Black" a great white raven caused the near starvation of the Cheyenne camp by scaring away the buffalo in the area everytime the hunters tried to surprise them. A guardian spirit allowed the hunters to approach and kill buffalo by deafening them to the white raven's warning cries. He then tricked and captured the treacherous bird, and carried it back to the camp. Piling green wood on a tipi fire, he let the raven hang in the hole above it, squawking and flapping until it turned black.

generated prose. Works of individual American Indian authors appear under the individuals' names.

While the Library generally does not assign subject headings to fictional works, exceptions include ethnic groups and places. Thus, researchers wishing to study the treatment of American Indians in fiction may search under the various Indian-related headings such as those described earlier, with "Fiction" as the subheading. In addition, one may find Indian characters and topics in fiction where locale is the dominant theme. The heading "West (U.S.)—Fiction," is an example.

Lesser-Known Languages Collection

This small collection contains a smattering of miscellaneous uncataloged pamphlets, school texts, and religious tracts in boxes labeled according to language or ethnic group. Each box may contain one or more publications. Tribes represented are: Aleut, Cherokee, Chipewyan, Chippewa, Cree, Creek, Dakota, Eskimo, Fox (Mesquakie), Hopi, Kalispel (a catechism, which actually indicates Flathead), Koyukon, Micmac, Mohawk, Navajo, Pima, Tlingit, and Zuni.

Children's Literature

The Library of Congress holds perhaps the country's largest concentration of children's books. These books are integrated into the General Collections by subject area and are maintained for the scholarly study of children's literature itself, not as a collection for use by children. Because nearly all of the books come to the Library through copyright deposit, they represent a broad spectrum of publishing without the filtering process of selection.

These works may be of interest to researchers wishing to trace the historical depiction of American Indians in children's texts and their illustrations.

CHILDREN'S LITERATURE CENTER

LOCATION: Jefferson Building, Main Reading Room Gallery (temporary); telephone (202) 707-5535

HOURS: Monday–Friday 8:30 A.M. to 5:00 P.M.

ACCESS AND USE: Appointments preferred, but not necessary. Although two reference specialists are available during the above hours, children's books are available from the General Collections through the Main Reading Room and are subject to its hours and criteria.

For nonfiction, the Library assigns the subheading "Juvenile literature" to those works on a given topic aimed at an audience below college level. The assignment of, and changes within, subject headings for Indian-related fiction is somewhat complicated, but the following strategy should facilitate searching for children's books:

1. Search the desired subjects in the card or computer catalog under the subject heading established in *Library of Congress Subject Headings*, discussed earlier.

2. Under this heading, refine the search to the subheadings "Fiction" and "Juvenile fiction."

3. For children's fiction, select only those titles with a classification designation PZ5 or higher.

In the prefatory pages of volume 1 of *Library of Congress Subject Headings* a listing of headings used for children's literature appears. These headings sometimes go beyond the normal Library of Congress subject headings and should be reviewed for American Indian topics. For example, Indian language readers for helping children learn English or an Indian language may be found under a heading such as "Hopi lan-

guage—Readers," while bilingual texts of folklore appear under "Hopi language materials."

Reference aids and bibliographies can often help fill research gaps that cataloging does not address, and it is therefore advisable to consult with the Children's Literature Center staff.

Local History and Genealogy

LOCAL HISTORY AND GENEALOGY READING ROOM

LOCATION: Jefferson Building, Ground floor, Room LJ G20 (temporary); telephone (202) 707-5537

HOURS: Same as Main Reading Room

ACCESS AND USE: No appointments necessary. All reference books relating to local U.S. history, family histories, and genealogical research should be requested from this room.

The Local History and Genealogy Reading Room contains reference collections that specifically relate to local U.S. history, family histories, and genealogical research. All books on these subjects must be requested from this room. Virtually all of the genealogical resources are secondary, however, and researchers looking for primary genealogical materials will need to consult other archives and repositories that hold relevant documents. For published genealogies on individual tribes, one should search the computer or main card catalog under the name of a tribe, with "Genealogy" as the subheading. Reference specialists in the reading room will also help researchers.

The surge of interest in genealogy has spawned numerous publications on genealogical research, some of which are relevant to Indians. But as complex and time consuming as genealogical research can be for non-Indian ancestry, it is much more so for Indian ancestry, which is frequently recorded only in the oral traditions of families themselves or exists in diverse archival records at the federal, state, or local level. Among the few publications that exist, the vast majority deal with the Cherokee and the other Indians belonging to the so-called Five Civilized Tribes (Choctaw, Chickasaw, Creek, and Seminole), and these may only be valuable for identifying individual names rather than tracing genealogy.

❏ SELECTED BOOKS

Following are a few useful reference titles, which are located within the reading room:

Campbell's Abstract of Creek Indian Census Cards and Index. Compiled by John Bert Campbell. Muskogee, Okla.: Phoenix Job Printing Co., 1915; E99.C9C18

A compilation of Creek tribal families based on census records, with some references to Freedmen census citations. Information includes individuals' names, age, sex, Indian blood ratio, names of mother and father when known, and whether living or dead at the time of the census.

Cherokee Emigration Rolls 1817–1835. Transcribed by Jack D. Baker. Oklahoma City: Baker Publishing Co., c1977; E99.C5B27

Lists of those Cherokee scheduled to emigrate from Alabama, Georgia, North Carolina, and Tennessee to Indian Territory. Information varies among the different rolls, which may include the head of a family, the number in the family, genders, and slaves.

The Final Rolls of Citizens and Freedmen of the Five Civilized Tribes in Indian Territory. Compiled by U.S. Commission to the Five Civilized Tribes. Washington, D.C.: GPO, 1907; E78.I5U27

This and its companion volume, *Index to the Final Rolls . . . ,* provide the name, sex, age, Indian "blood degree," and tribal roll number for individuals as of 1907. With the exception of blood degree, the same information appears for the Freedmen among the tribes.

The Osage Annuity Rolls of 1878. Louis F. Burns. 3 vols. Fallbrook, Calif.: Burns, c1980–81; E99. O8B87

More than 2,200 names appear here grouped within tribal bands by family, listing the age, sex, and family relationship. Most of the names are the original Osage language names. The compiler provides an alphabetical index to the names, as well as an index of the Indian names as they would appear in English.

Our Native Americans and Their Records of Genealogical Value. Kay E. Kirkham. 2 vols. Logan, Utah: Everton Publishers, c1980–84; Z1209.2. N67K57

A useful guide to the primary sources—governmental, tribal, and private—available for potential genealogical research. This source should probably be the researcher's first stop on a genealogical journey.

PERIODICALS

Bound issues of periodicals with Indian-related topics are scattered throughout the Library's collections in appropriate subject classifications. The Library has substantial holdings of titles such as *American Anthropologist, Ethnohistory,* and *Plains Anthropologist.* It also holds most of the publications of significant institutions and museums, such as those of the American Museum of Natural History, the American Philosophical Society, Chicago's Field Museum of Natural History, the University of Michigan's Museum of Anthropology, and Yale University.

Holdings of periodicals generated by Indian groups themselves are spotty, due to the ephemeral nature of many of them. The Library does have, however, privately produced microform collections of American Indian periodicals, described in the section on the Microform Reading Room. If one does not know a specific periodical title desired, it is best to consult a bibliography

"The Nation's Ward," chromolithograph by Grant Hamilton from *Judge*, June 20, 1885. AP101.J8 (LC-USZC4-4802). General Collections (Microform) and Prints and Photographs Division.

"The Reason of the Indian Outbreak. General Miles declares that the Indians are starved into rebellion," unattributed chromolithograph from *Judge*, December 20, 1890. AP101.J8. (LC-USZC4-4101, color; LC-USZ62-56003, black and white). General Collections (Microform) and Prints and Photographs Division.

Native Americans were targets of ridicule in the illustrated satirical weeklies that flourished in America after the Civil War. Cartoonists usually portrayed them as murderous warriors or shiftless beggars taking advantage of the nation's largesse. Occasionally, however, they were depicted with more sympathy, as victims of corrupt federal agents.

such as James P. Danky's *Native American Periodicals and Newspapers, 1828–1982* (Z1209.2.U5D36 1984). Librarians can assist in checking holdings of individual titles.

Current, unbound issues of periodicals are held in the Newspaper and Current Periodicals Reading Room, Madison Building, 1st floor, Room LM 133 *(same hours as the Main Reading Room)*. In some cases, depending on acquisitions decisions, only a few months of current issues may be kept. In other cases, titles may be retained for a longer period to determine the feasibility of adding them to the permanent collections. Many Indian-generated periodicals may fall into either of these categories, and a researcher should check with reading room staff for particular titles.

This reading room also holds all of the Library's newspaper collections, both in paper copy and microform. The Library has several eighteenth-century domestic and foreign newspapers, as well as numerous nineteenth-century papers. Most of the eighteenth-century issues date from the last two decades of the period, although a few titles, such as the *New York Gazette*, Philadelphia's *The American Weekly Mercury*, and Williamsburg's *The Virginia Gazette*, date from the first half of the century. And for a British slant on American news, the collections include London's *Daily Advertiser* from 1731 to 1795. Other British and European papers may also be of interest.

While newspaper accounts for these eras may not be as highly regarded as other historical sources, they are in some instances the only accounts extant. Colonial American newspapers, for example, frequently relayed official government announcements verbatim or copied reports from foreign papers or from each other. But occasionally they also relayed correspondence on events from individuals—correspondence that may not have subsequently survived. In addition, occasional editorial opinion and advertisements of the period may offer insights into the popular perception of American Indians.

For eighteenth-century papers, researchers should check a four-volume, loose-leaf compilation prepared by the staff and held in the reading room. It lists the papers by state, and by city within each state, with a detailed chronological list of the holdings of each title. Another reference work, *A Check List of American Eighteenth Century Newspapers in the Library of Congress* (Washington, D.C.: Library of Congress, 1936; reprinted by Greenwood Press, 1968), originally compiled by John Van Ness Ingram, and revised and updated by Henry S. Parsons, may be available in other large libraries. For the nineteenth and twentieth centuries, staff member Paul E. Swigart compiled an eleven-volume work, *Chronological Index of Newspapers for the Period 1801–1967 in the Collections of the Library of Congress*.

The Library's holdings of nineteenth-century general periodicals also afford sources for Indian images and articles. *Harper's Weekly* and *Frank Leslie's Illustrated* series, for example, carried images illustrating Indian-related stories, while *Puck* and *Judge* carried many caricatures on Indian themes. These periodicals are on microfilm in the Microform Reading Room, but separate illustrations culled from paper copies also exist in the Prints and Photographs Division.

MICROFORM

The distribution of research materials through microforms has significantly enhanced scholarly study since the second world war. Reproductions from numerous institutions and the policy of interlibrary loan have made manuscripts, archives, newspapers, illustrative materials, rare books, and pamphlets from all over the globe much more available to researchers than was previously possible. Further, microforms prolong the life of original documents by reducing the need for handling them directly. Through both acquisitions and preservation filming of its own collections the Library of Congress has

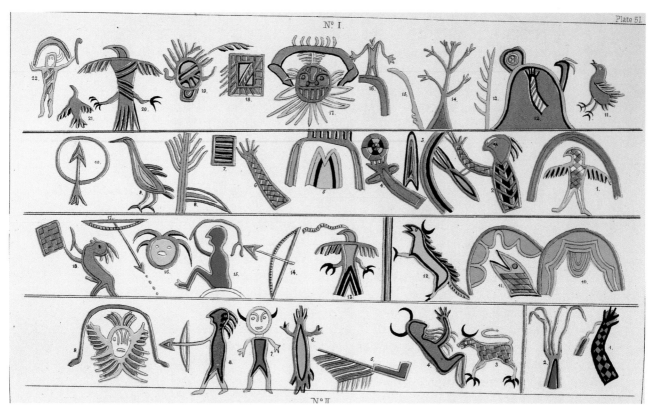

"Meda Songs," chromolithograph by James Ackerman after Seth Eastman from volume 1 of *Historical and Statistical Information Respecting the History, Condition and Prospects of the Indian Tribes of the United States* by Henry R. Schoolcraft (Philadelphia: Lippincott, Grambo & Co., 1851). E77.S381 (LC-USZC4-4803). General Collections.

Schoolcraft, a former Indian agent (whose papers are held by the Library's Manuscript Division), began work on his massive six-volume encyclopedic work on American Indians while he was employed by the Indian Office in 1847. He recruited Capt. Seth Eastman of the U.S. Army to make hundreds of drawings and watercolors of tribal ceremonies, landscapes, artifacts, pictographs, tools, costumes, weapons, musical instruments and maps. According to Schoolcraft, this is an exact facsimile of an Ojibwa music board— "one of those tablets of pictorial notation" used as prompters for songs of the tribe's Meda Society.

thousands of microform titles available. General and specialized reading rooms usually have microform collections appropriate to their subject or format responsibilities.

MICROFORM READING ROOM

LOCATION: Jefferson Building, 1st floor, Room LJ 107 (temporary); telephone (202) 707-5471

HOURS: Same as those for Main Reading Room

The Microform Reading Room is virtually a library unto itself. In addition to books that have been microfilmed for preservation purposes, several special collections relevant to the study of American Indians are available here. Reference specialists can assist with research guidance to the collections, and published guides to many of the collections are available.

❐ SELECTED COLLECTIONS

Microform titles relevant to American Indian study as of this writing are grouped thematically, and then arranged alphabetically, as follows:

- Ethnology
- Government Relations
- Historical Research Collections
- Periodicals
- Reform Organizations

Ethnology

HRAF. New Haven, Conn.: Human Relations Area Files, 1958–; Microfiche 1013

This collection of reproduced pages of articles, books, and manuscripts includes ethnological and anthropological studies of tribes or cultural groups. Holdings through 1987 contain studies on about fifty tribes, arranged by topic such as religious beliefs, methods of warfare, etc.

North American Indians: Photographs from the National Anthropological Archives, Smithsonian Institution. Compiled by Herman Viola. Chicago: University of Chicago Press, 1974; Microfiche 5020

This microfiche collection of nearly 4,700 photographs consists mainly of individual or group portraits, but also includes representations of artifacts, architecture, ceremonies, and crafts. Arranged alphabetically by tribe, it also supplies negative numbers that may be used to request prints from the National Anthropological Archives.

The Northwest Coast Collection of American Indian Art. Boston: G. K. Hall & Co, 1987; Microfiche 91/7000

A color reproduction of Northwest Coast artifacts held by the Museum of Mankind, London. Although the sharpness of the images in this 35-fiche set is not perfect, it is still an absorbing, useful representation of nearly 1,500 objects of stone, ivory, bone, wood, leather, and fiber-woven utensils, implements, clothing, effigies, and furnishings collected mainly between 1800 and 1875. Many of the objects display the unique design and intricate carving that pay tribute to indigenous artistry.

The Peabody Museum : a Visual Record of Artifacts. The Peabody Museum of Archaeology and Ethnography, Harvard University. Photography by Hillel Burger. Catalog by Barbara Isaac. Boston: G. K. Hall, c1990; Microfiche 91/7018 (G); Guide 273

Five of eight color fiche contain approximately 380 images of North American Indian art, artifacts, and clothing, as well as early European-American paintings and drawings of Indian subjects selected from the museum's collections. Some items are attributed to collections from the Lewis and Clark expedition. Among the Indian groups represented are Aleut, Eskimo, Haida, Tlingit, and others of the Alaska and the Northwest; California people such as the Karok and Hupa (Hoopa); Hopi, Navajo, and Zuni of the Southwest; Crow, Mandan, Sioux, Chippewa, Huron, Choctaw, Cherokee, and Seminole; a few Northeastern tribes; and prehistoric cultures of the Anasazi, Hopewell, Mississippian, and Mimbres. Two of the three remaining fiche cover Mesoamerica and South America. A guide accompanies the collection and describes the items.

University of South Dakota American Indian Oral History Collection. Sanford, N.C.: Microfilming Corp. of America, 1979; Microfiche 85/200; Guide AI3.O7, no. 2

The Library has Part II of this collection, which largely includes personal experiences and

"Washington, D.C.—Photographing an Indian delegation, in C. M. Bell's studio, for the government," wood engraving from *Frank Leslie's Illustrated Newspaper*, September 10, 1881. AP2.L52. LOT 4391-F (P&P). (LC-USZ62-77077). General Collections (Microform) and Prints and Photographs Division.

Charles Milton Bell (1848–93) was one of Washington's leading portrait photographers during the last quarter of the nineteenth century. He may be best known today for his photographs of Native Americans, which he began to produce in 1873. He was assigned by Ferdinand V. Hayden of the U.S. Geological Survey of the Territories to photograph as many of the Indian visitors to the capital as possible during this period of intense treaty negotiations. Cooperative chiefs were apparently rewarded with a trip to the photographer's studio. From the end of the Hayden Survey in 1879 until the 1890s, Bell also made photographs of Indians for the Department of the Interior and the Bureau of American Ethnology. The C. M. Bell Studio Collection is among the holdings of the Library's Prints and Photographs Division.

reminiscences of more than two hundred Indians and non-Indians associated with them. Recorded in the late 1960s, most of the interviews cover a variety of topics, reflecting the ethnic reawakening of the period. In some instances, an interviewee's age, religious affiliation, and degree of Indian blood is given. The majority of tribes represented are Chippewa and various branches of the Sioux. Others included are: Apache (1 interviewee), Cheyenne (1), Coeur d'Alene (3), Colville (1), Cree (1), Crow (17), Flathead (1), Hidatsa (1), Kalispel (1), Navajo (1), Ponca (1), Pueblo (1), Spokane (8), and Winnebago (10). In an unusual instance of cataloging, each individual's name has been entered in the Library's computer catalog.

Government Relations

Annual Report, 1838–1943, of the Office (Bureau) of Indian Affairs. Washington, D.C.: Library of Congress Photoduplication Service, 1974; Microfilm 04093.

These reports include each Indian agent's summary of the previous year's activity among the people under his jurisdiction. A published set of reprinted reports from 1824 to 1847 is available from the book collections under the call number E93.U715a.

British Manuscripts Project. Washington, D.C.: Library of Congress Photoduplication Service, 1941–45; Microfilm 041; Guide: Z6620.G7U5

Among the millions of manuscript pages filmed, the most germane to Indian matters are those of the Jeffery Amherst Papers in the War Office, and these are relevant mainly for the French and Indian War from late 1758 through 1763, with some material touching on Pontiac's rebellion. The collection is prodigious, nonetheless, comprising more than fifty reels for this period, and includes frequent correspondence with Amherst's officers and with William Johnson on Indian participation.

Also useful are the Colonial Office papers for Georgia, Maryland, Massachusetts, New Hampshire, New Jersey, New York, North Carolina, Pennsylvania, and South Carolina, consisting mainly of papers of the governors and correspondence between them and the Board of Trade in London. Indian-related material is scattered, and it is best for a researcher to have a particular date or correspondent in mind. Much of this same material, however, may be published or appear in the *State Records Microfilm* described below. A checklist exists for this collection, giving principally the correspondents' names and dates of coverage.

The FBI files on the American Indian Movement and Wounded Knee. Edited by Rolland Dewing. Frederick, Md.: University Publications of America, 1986; Microfilm 88/359; Guide 105–150

This collection of twenty-six reels consists of memoranda from agents, office reports, letters, protest literature, and some periodical clippings that deal not only with AIM (the American Indian Movement) but also with numerous protests, demonstrations, and government property occupations by Indians throughout the country. Most of the material is dated 1973, and nearly half of it represents coverage of the Wounded Knee incident of that year.

Some sections of reports are blacked out, and some papers are deleted entirely by an invocation of cited exemptions under the Freedom of Information Act.

Indian Claims Commission. New York: Clearwater Publishing Co., 1973–82; Microfiche 90/7052 (negative image); Guide 238a–b

This collection represents more than half a million pages from the commission's files in the National Archives. Set up to hear and determine tribal claims against the United States, the commission operated mainly from 1947 to 1978. Its files contain not only important background information on specific claims (nearly all of which were based on inadequate compensation for land purchases), but also historical documents from public and private sources, cartographic and illustrative material, retrospective mineral and land appraisals, and expert testimony by ethnologists, historians, and anthropologists. The collection is, therefore, not only valuable as a reference source itself, but as a guide to other sources that may produce further information. The collection is divided into five segments, and researchers should determine which section they wish to view:

1. *The decisions*. The commission's findings of fact, opinions, orders, and final awards.

GATEWAYS

Six European countries—Spain, Great Britain, France, the Netherlands, Sweden, and Russia—at one time or another, between 1500 and 1867, established a colonial presence within what is now the continental United States.

Spain was the first of these European powers to establish a permanent settlement in the present-day continental United States, in 1565 in Florida. Further Spanish settlement followed in the American Southwest after 1598, Texas after 1700, California from the mid-eighteenth century on, and the Mississippi Valley from the eighteenth century. Spanish administration generally lasted until Mexican independence, in 1821, but this varied for Florida and the Mississippi Valley.

The first permanent English settlement was in 1607 in Virginia, and lasted along the Atlantic Coast until American independence in 1783, and lasted elsewhere (the Great Lakes region, the Pacific Northwest) as long as the mid-nineteenth century. France, while initially based in Canada, was active in the present United States from 1608 until 1763, and then again from 1800 to 1803 in the Mississippi Valley. The Dutch colonial efforts were shortlived, beginning in 1609 in the central Atlantic Coast region and ending in 1664 with the English conquest of New Netherland. Swedish settlement, chiefly for trading purposes, lasted from 1638 until their ouster by the Dutch in 1655. Russian traders and others were active in

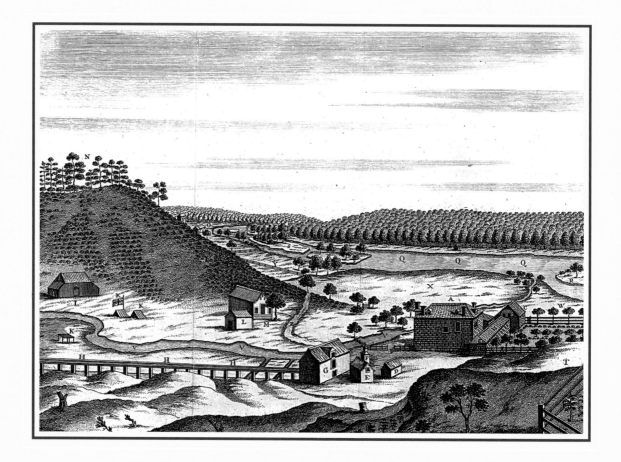

present-day Alaska from 1741 to 1867 (when the U.S. purchased the territory) and for a while in California (1812–44).

Each of the European colonial nations had to develop a means of handling Indian relations. Their solutions varied markedly from country to country and all changed, to some degree, over time. These differing solutions had differing effects on the many Indian peoples.

For all the European colonial powers except Spain, the national government in Europe at first eschewed direct administration of colonies, whether the colonial purpose was trade or settlement. Instead, administration of both the colony and Indian relations, in the Western Hemisphere, was left to private entities—chartered trading companies, individual traders, or proprietors and grantees of landed estates. These private entities were subject to varying methods and amounts of national government oversight, but it was oversight exercised from Europe.

The Dutch, Swedish, and Russian governments, during the period of each country's colonial presence, did not establish administrative structures in the Western Hemisphere to govern colonies and handle Indian relations. The English and French governments eventually did. New France was transferred to royal control in 1663 and became a crown colony, with royal administrators, in 1674. (The Louisiana province was a separate crown colony.) The French king appointed a governor and an *intendant* for each of the two provinces; the latter official was in charge of Indian tribal relations. The English experience varied with each of its numerous colonies along the Atlantic coast, since, while the English king did appoint colonial governors, each colony handled its own Indian relations. It was not until 1755 that the British government set up a system of Indian superintendencies (one northern, one southern) and only in 1763 that the royal government assumed exclusive jurisdiction over Indian affairs.

Spain's holdings in the present United States began as royal colonies, but its systems for dealing with Native Americans changed several times during its long colonial tenure. Usually a military *presidio* and a mission shared the immediate supervision of an Indian population in each area, under the control of a governor and the viceroy. After 1763, however, in most (but not all) regions, Indian administration was secularized, and *presidios* assumed complete jurisdiction. In the Mississippi Valley, however, the Spanish government used traders, much like the other colonial powers.

WHERE TO LOOK: Library collections bearing on European colonial administration of Indian affairs include the Law Library, the General Collections (including the Microform Reading Room), and the Manuscript, Geography and Map, and Rare Book and Special Collections Divisions. Note especially the photocopies, transcriptions, and microfilm of British, French, and Spanish archival documents.

"A North View of Fort Johnson drawn on the spot by Mr. Guy Johnson[,] Sir W. Johnson's Son," from *The Royal Magazine, or Gentleman's Monthly Companion*, October 1759. APR.R7 (LC-USZ62-9288). Rare Book and Special Collections Division.

William Johnson (1715–74), a 1738 Irish immigrant to an uncle's upstate New York estate, became a major British colonial diplomat in Indian affairs, especially with the Iroquois, as well as a military leader and a very wealthy land speculator and fur trader. In 1755 he was appointed the first northern superintendent of Indian affairs. In 1739 he had acquired Fort Johnson on the Mohawk River in New York and had made it a leading site for Indian councils and trade. The Indian council house is labeled "I," the Indian camping ground is "K," the Mohawk River is "Q," and Johnson's residence is "A."

Arrangement is by volume and page numbers listed in the guides mentioned below.

2. *Expert testimony*. Written, professional ethnological and historical reports, as well as retrospective appraisals of land and minerals. Arrangement is by docket number. Many of the expert testimonies have also been published by Garland Publishing, Inc., and are in the general book collections.

3. *Transcripts of oral expert testimony*. Oral testimony was allowed in the early years of the commission's operation, and this segment contains less material than the written testimony. Arrangement is by document number.

4. *The briefs*. These provide both the Indian and the government positions, backed up by all the references and citations used to support their cases. It is here that one will find excerpts from primary sources and the references to them that make the section a valuable resource guide and bibliography. Arrangement is by docket number.

5. *GAO and GSA reports*. These are accounts by the General Accounting Office and the General Services Administration of the actual disbursements made to a tribe under a treaty that was the basis of a claim. As such it may contain a historical record of related disbursements for the tribe. Arrangement is by date of the original treaty in question.

A two-volume guide divides the series by the written expert testimony and decisions, and further by a table of cases, tribe, state, author, and docket number. These guides can be somewhat confusing because of the collection's different sections and access points, and one should check both volumes under all headings to insure adequate coverage.

Reports of the Commissioner to the Five Civilized Tribes. Arlington, Va.: University Publications of America, c1975; Microfilm 88/240; Guide 105–121

This collection brings together the annual reports from 1894 to 1920 and special documents relating to the division of tribal lands among individuals of the Cherokee, Chickasaw, Choctaw, Creek, and Seminole tribes. Known as the Dawes Commission, it generated numerous documents, including legal decisions, samples of census rolls, genealogical charts, allotment maps, and discussions of the conditions among the tribes.

State Records Microfilm. Washington, D.C.: Library of Congress in association with the University of North Carolina, 1941–50; Microfilm 1550; Guide, *A Guide to the Microfilm Collection of Early State Records*. Edited by Lillian A. Hamrick. Washington, D.C.: Library of Congress Photoduplication Service, 1950; Z663.96.G8 or Z1223.5. A1 U47

Also known as Records of the States or Early State Records, this collection contains approximately 1,700 reels of film with nearly 3 million pages of colonial and state legislative, executive, judicial, and Indian records from the eighteenth and nineteenth centuries, many of which are in manuscript form. The guide (cited above) outlines the various record groups under each state and provides the reel numbers. The guide itself was compiled in segments and amended, so a careful perusal is necessary to glean as many records as possible.

A Guide to the Microfilm Collection of Early State Records: Supplement. Washington, D.C.: Library of Congress Photoduplication Service, 1951. Lists "Records of American Indian Nations," which are part of the *State Records Microfilm*; Microfilm 1551.

The records include mostly manuscript sources filmed in eight state archives and historical societies. A major portion of the material is from the Indian Archives of the Oklahoma Historical Society, where nearly all of the Cherokee records were filmed. The guide supplement provides cursory descriptions of the contents and reel numbers. The sections on newspapers and miscellany should also be checked for material from early newspapers, broadsides, proclamations, and some manuscripts that may also contain relevant information, though the *Guide* may not cite it. Following are descriptions of notable collections from the "Records of American Indian Nations," and a few items from the "Miscellany," arranged by state.

Connecticut

Connecticut Archives: Indians 1647–1820. A manuscript work useful for study of Connecticut's relations with Indians. Indexes to topics and tribes appear at the beginning of each of the two volumes. A majority of entries concern land issues, and among the tribes represented are Massachusett, Mohegan, Pequot, Pocumtuc, Scaticook, and Tunxi, as well as Mohawk.

In the "Miscellany" section for Connecticut is a 1770 text called "The Moheagon Indians against the Governor and Company of Connecticut," which includes an introductory history of the Mohegan, followed by tracts that deal with Uncas and his progenitors' claims to certain Connecticut lands.

Kansas

Letterbook of John Beach, Indian agent for the Sac and Fox of Iowa and Kansas (478 pages). Dating from June 1840 to August of 1847, this collection consists of Beach's letters to the U.S. commissioner of Indian affairs, the governor of Iowa, other Indian agents and sub-agents. No letters from his correspondents appear.

Constitution and Laws of the Sac and Fox Nations, 1888 (30 pages), including tribal laws adopted between 1885 and 1887. An eight-page supplement includes laws adopted in 1889.

Massachusetts

The topics are not Massachusetts Indians, but the contents are from volumes 60 and 61 of the Massachusetts Historical Society's Timothy Pickering Papers. These volumes deal with Indian relations and treaties in 1790 and 1791 with the tribes then occupying the old Northwest Territory, comprising the present states of Illinois, Indiana, Michigan, Ohio, and Wisconsin. Among tribes involved either directly or diplomatically are the Delaware, Miami, Mohawk, Oneida, Seneca, Shawnee, Stockbridge, Tuscarora, and Wyandot. A full microfilm set of the Pickering Papers is in the Manuscript Division.

Michigan

In the "Local Records" section appears a manuscript journal in French on Pontiac's Conspiracy, from the Burton Historical Collection in Detroit. It is rather faded and some of the pages are torn.

New Mexico

In the Miscellany section, as part of the official record book of Don Manuel Alvarez, American consul at Santa Fe, is a printed version in Spanish of the diaries of several New Mexican militia officers from an 1839 campaign against the Navajo (8 pages)

New York

Four reels of microfilm contain reproductions from the Henry O'Reilly Papers, called "O'Reilly's Western Mementos." Relating to the Iroquois from 1784 to 1820, the papers are important for study of post-Revolutionary New York's involvement in Indian affairs and land acquisition prior to the federal government's assumption of that role. The primary tribes involved were the Six Nations—Cayuga, Mohawk, Oneida, Onondaga, Seneca, and Tuscarora.

The miscellany section for this state contains an eclectic assembly of eighteenth-century documents and treaties, many of which were printed and have been subsequently issued elsewhere. A 1718 map of the country of the Five Nations and the tribes of the Great Lakes appears, as do a few 1840s issues of the journal, "The Mental Elevator," a Seneca language publication from the tribe's Buffalo Creek reservation.

Oklahoma

Fourteen reels contain Cherokee documents dating from the 1820s to 1906, the bulk of material covering the latter half of the nineteenth century. These are documents generated by the Cherokee themselves as they began adopting Anglo-American social and political culture in the early nineteenth century. They contain records of the national council, legislative journals, several editions of the laws and constitution, records of the supreme court, and annual reports of administrative officers such as the treasurer, the board of education, medical superintendent, high sheriff, commission on citizenship, insane asylum supervisors, and the editor of the *Cherokee Advocate*.

The legislative journals are good sources for identifying names of influential and politically active Cherokee. The laws and constitution, in both Cherokee and English, provide a look at the transition from tribal and clan law to Anglo-American oriented procedure from 1808 forward. They also reflect the social condition of women, blacks, and mulattoes, as well as the attempts to regulate potential or actual intrusions from non-Indian groups. With this material (on reel 1 of M.2a-B:C) is a 48-page compilation, in-

Cherokee Phoenix, New Echota, Georgia, April 10, 1828 (LC-US262-115660). Serial and Government Publications Division (detail)

cluding letters, titled "Communication of the Delegation of the Cherokee Nation to the President of the United States . . . ," which discusses the Cherokee role in the Civil War. Further discussion of the Civil War appears in the letterbook of Stand Watie, July 1863 to July 1864, and proceedings and laws of the executive council (M.2a-E.1). Note: much of this material is also kept in the Law Library, which provided some of the documents filmed.

Annual reports of officers. 1880–1906. Combined with "Messages of the principal chief" (M.2a-D.2) and the minutes of some of the administrative officers' meetings (M.2a-D.24), these reports provide insights to some of the social and economic issues facing the tribe at the turn of the century.

M.2X contains miscellaneous Cherokee documents, as well as some for the Creek, Osage, and Seminole. It also includes an 1850 compilation of an Ottawa alphabet and portions of the New Testament in Ottawa.

The records of the remaining four of the so-called "Five Civilized Tribes" are not as comprehensive as those of the Cherokee, since most of their records were not available at the time of microfilming. The bulk of material for the Chickasaw, Choctaw, Creek, and Seminole consists of tribal laws and editions of constitutions, many of which are in the native languages as well as English. The laws, nonetheless, reflect interesting social issues, such as the Indians' relations with the blacks and whites living among them. A few other items of interest are listed below.

Reel 2 of M.2b-B:C contains a "Compact between the several tribes of the Indian Territory," a legal agreement to resolve intertribal issues among the Five Civilized Tribes and the Caddo, Comanche, Delaware, and Wichita tribes.

Journal of the General Council of the Indian Territory, 1870–85. A council of all the tribes in Indian Territory, which by this time included Ottawa, Shawnee, Quapaw, Seneca, Wyandot,

Peoria, Sac and Fox, and Osage. The sixth annual conference of 1875 was a pan-Indian congress of numerous tribes, many of whom described their respective conditions, and who sought advice from the more acculturated tribes about following their style of living.

Journal of the Union Mission to the Osages in Arkansas, 1820–26 (Mss. 314 pages).

Pennsylvania

The Penn Manuscripts, 1687–1801. Most of the material dates from the 1750s, especially the French and Indian War, and some of it has been published. Journals of Conrad Weiser appear, as do reports by George Croghan, Daniel Claus, and Moravian missionaries. Among the tribes included are the Cherokee, Delaware, Miami, Nanticoke, Shawnee, Six Nations, Susquehanna, and Wyandot.

Rhode Island

One hundred and thirty-four manuscript items on the Narragansett cover the period from 1735 to 1859 and deal with land problems, tribal dissensions, and oversight issues, primarily involving the Ninigret family.

South Carolina

Two reels contain the original manuscript volumes on Indian affairs from the *Colonial Records of South Carolina*, including the *Journals of the Commissioners of Indian Trade* from September of 1710 to August of 1718; *Documents Relating to Indian Affairs*, from 1750 to 1760; and the *Journal of the Directors of the Cherokee Trade* from 1762 to 1765. These documents have also been published by the University of South Carolina Press, however, and are, therefore, more easily read in printed form. The journals of the commissioners are available by Library of Congress class number E78.S6S65, and the *Documents . . . and Journal of the Directors . . .* are available by E78.S6S6. Predominant among the tribes included are Catawba, Cherokee, Chickasaw, and Creek, but entries also appear for Tuscarora and smaller tribes such as Congaree, Pee Dee, Waccamaw, and Yuchi.

Historical Research Collections

American Culture Series 1493–1875. Ann Arbor, Mich.: University Microfilms, 1956–76; Microfilm 01291; Guide: Z1215.A583

This is a series of early books and pamphlets filmed from the collections of numerous institutions, including the Library of Congress. The Library did not acquire reels one through twenty-six, which contain about forty titles on Indians out of more than two hundred titles.

The guide for this series has an author, title, and subject index with general headings and subheadings under "Indians of North America" and under specific tribes.

Doctoral Dissertation Series. Ann Arbor, Mich.: University Microfilms International, 1938–.

The Library of Congress has those dissertations that are part of the University Microfilms Project, and for which an abstract identification number appears after an entry in *Dissertation Abstracts.* A special guide, *North American Indians: a Dissertation Index* (Ann Arbor, Mich.: University Microfilms International, 1977; Z1209.2.N67U54 1977, and supplement 1979), identifies by author and by key word those works on Indians between 1904 and 1976. Other dissertations date from 1861, and comprehensive indexes for the series exist in the Main Reading Room reference collection. In addition, *Dissertation Abstracts Ondisc*, a CD-ROM database also available in the Main Reading Room, provides comprehensive coverage from 1861 forward, with the added convenience of quick, current indexing and display of the abstracts in one source.

Library of American Civilization. Chicago: Library Resources, 1971–72; Microfiche 1008; Guide: Z1236.L45

A collection of books, pamphlets, periodicals, public and private documents relating to all aspects of American life and literature from the fifteenth century to World War I. Most of the coverage, however, is the nineteenth and early twentieth centuries. A four-volume guide provides an author, title, and subject index that follows Library of Congress subject headings as of 1972, and a "biblioguide," which arranges the material under broad disciplinary headings.

Pamphlets in American History. Glen Rock, N.J.: Microfilming Corp. of America, 1978; Microfiche 1014; Guide: Z1236.M54

Group I of this series contains more than 1,500 rare Indian-related pamphlets from the late eighteenth to the early twentieth centuries. Topics of these tracts are diverse: Indian biographies, missionary and government activities, wars, sermons, speeches, and essays on Indian affairs, education, tribal charters, constitutions and laws, ethnological observations, and linguistic tracts.

The guide provides author, title, and subject indexes.

Western Americana, 1550–1900. 2 vols. New Haven, Conn.: Research Publications, 1975; Microfilm 51566; Guide: Z1251.W5W48

This collection of over 7,000 titles, assembled with the cooperation of Yale University and the Newberry Library, represents basic published sources—many of them rare or not easily available—for study of the exploration, settlement, and development of the Trans-Mississippi West. They consist mainly of personal narratives by participants in the frontier experience, but also include other relevant works.

A two-volume guide provides catalog entries arranged by author and subject. Topics on Indians are entered either under the general heading "Indians of North America" and its subdivisions, or under specific tribes.

Periodicals

American Indian Periodicals from the State Historical Society of Wisconsin. New York: Clearwater Publishing; Bethesda, Md.: University Publications of America, 1981–; Microfilm 94/2119; Guide 359

Thirteen reels contain forty-one titles of American Indian-produced periodicals.

American Indian Periodicals in the Princeton University Library. New York: Clearwater Publishing, 1981–; Microfiche (o) 92/6012

More than 2,000 microfiche represent about 130 titles produced by American Indian groups and Indian interest organizations. There is some overlap with the titles that follow.

Periodicals by and about the North American Indian. Glen Rock, N.J.: Microfilming Corp. of America, 1974; Microfilm 90/8032; Guide 260. *Periodicals by and about North American Indians, 1923–1981.* Bethesda, Md.: Congressional Information Service, 1982; Microfilm 94/2118; Guide 341

Because of changes in the microfilm publishers, the Library received the two parts of this series at different times; hence, the different titles and microfilm and guide numbers. The series by Microfilming Corporation contains forty-two reels of the Smithsonian Institution's Bureau of American Ethnology bulletins from 1887 to 1971,

and its annual reports from 1879 to 1931. The series by Congressional Information Service contains eighty-two reels of publications produced by Indian groups themselves. There is partial overlap with the previous title.

Reform Organizations

Annual Report of the Executive Committee of the Indian Rights Association, 1883–1934. Philadelphia: The Association, n.d.; Microfilm 38754; and the Association's *Publications* (1st series, 1882–92, Microfilm 8124E; 2nd series, numbers 1–99, [#19 and #35 missing] 1893–1915, Microfilm 04190); Guide 17

This organization has concerned itself with the protection of the legal rights and welfare of American Indians. Included among the various publications are its constitution and by-laws, statements by Indian individuals, pamphlets on Indian related issues, accounts of conditions among tribes, and public addresses. Some of its pamphlets may also appear in the General Collections or among other microform series described below. See also the association's listing under the Manuscript Division.

Archive of the Fourth Russell Tribunal on the Rights of the Indians of the Americas. Zug, Switzerland: IDC, 1985; Microfiche (w) 87/203 (E); Guide 124 (in English and Spanish)

Organized by a private Dutch group called the Workgroup Indian Project, in cooperation with the Bertrand Russell Peace Foundation, the tribunal had an eleven-member jury that met in Rotterdam in 1980 to consider alleged violations of the rights of the Indians in the Americas. The collection contains seventy groups of documents, forty-seven of which relate to the cases presented to the tribunal. Twelve of these involve Indians within the United States and five involve those in Canada. Each case may include historical documents, statements and testimony by Indian representatives, articles, legal briefs, and correspondence. The guide contains a checklist of materials in each document group, as well as an index of topics and tribes.

The Library of World Peace Studies. Edited by Warren F. Kuehl. New York: Clearwater Publishing Co., 1978–82; Microfiche 90/10 (H) (negative image); Guide 244

This microfiche collection contains the proceedings of the *Annual Meeting of the Lake Mohonk Conference in Behalf of the Civilization and Legal Protection of the Indians of the U.S.* from 1883 to 1929. This gathering at various times included benevolent association representatives, ministers, journalists, active or retired government and military officials, and others interested in the welfare of American Indians. Theodore Roosevelt and Rutherford B. Hayes, for example, were among the attendees who met to discuss and to offer solutions for problems in Indian affairs. The diversity of professions represented among the participants gives an interesting glimpse at the attitudes toward Indian people and experiences with them. Each proceeding has a subject index. A separate, printed compilation exists of these indexes, *The Lake Mohonk Conference of Friends of the Indian: Guide to the Annual Reports*, with an introduction that discusses the Mohonk conferences.

Tribal Records

(NOTE: See also the section on Oklahoma under the *State Records Microfilm* in the Government Relations section, pp. 30–31)

Major Council Meetings of American Indian Tribes. Frederick, Md.: University Publications of America, c1982; Microfilm 88/253; Guides 134a, 134b

Divided into two sections covering 1911–56 and 1957–70, this collection was selected from documents in the National Archives' Record Group 75, Bureau of Indian Affairs central classified files. Tribes included are the Arapaho, Cherokee, Cheyenne, Chippewa, the Mississippi Band of Choctaw, intertribal meetings of the Five Civilized Tribes of Oklahoma, Klamath, Seminole, Sioux, and Ute.

MULTIMEDIA FORMATS

American Indian studies are becoming part of the rapidly developing electronic media. A few titles specifically dealing with Indian topics have begun to appear in CD-ROM format, including multimedia publications containing text, visuals, and sound recordings. These formats enable a user to experience in one sitting a broad range of Indian research that might otherwise require visits to different locations. This is an evolving area of technology, as well as reference and research, and the Library's policies and services are developing accordingly.

Titles and subjects in electronic formats are generally searchable in the Library's computer catalog. A researcher interested in electronic formats for American Indian subjects may first wish to check locally in guides such as *CD-ROMS in Print* to identify particular titles and the equipment needed to handle them, and then call ahead to see if the Library has them and if they can be read here. As of this writing, however, machines are not available in the main or related reading rooms to read CD-ROMs.

SPECIAL COLLECTIONS

While the general collections can satisfy many research needs, other materials in the Library's special collections offer an additional wealth of potential for Indian-related pursuits. Rare and illustrated books, broadsides, manuscripts, government documents, laws and legal materials, visual materials—from photographs to posters, maps, music and recorded sound, motion pictures, television shows, and documentaries are all available to help researchers gain a more extensive view of Indian affairs. In the sections that follow, each of these special areas are discussed. Keep in mind that in an institution the size of the Library of Congress, with its ongoing acquisitions and its continuing analysis of materials already held, none of the sections below represents a complete listing of the Library's holdings. It is wise always to consult reference librarians and specialists, whose assistance can be as valuable, or more so, than a printed guide.

"Pehriska-Ruhpa," by Karl Bodmer in *Reise in das innere Nord-America in den Jahren 1832 bis 1834* by Prince Maximilian Alexander Philipp von Wied-Neuwied (Koblenz, 1839–41). E165.W64, atlas (LC-USZC4-4804, color; LC-USZ62-9183, black and white). Rare Book and Special Collections Division.

This Minnetarre (Hidatsa) warrior, and principal leader of the Dog Society in his village, is shown in a magnificent ceremonial costume. Members of the Real Dog Society were expected to be daring and brave in battle. Eighty-one hand-colored copperplate engravings after Swiss artist Karl Bodmer's magnificent and accurate watercolors of Plains Indians can be found in the picture atlas accompanying Prince Maximilian's two-volume account of their travels up the Missouri River.

RARE BOOK AND SPECIAL COLLECTIONS DIVISION

INTRODUCTION

The Rare Book and Special Collections Division holds the books that are the foundation stones for the Library of Congress. Thomas Jefferson's personal library, purchased by Congress in 1815, resides here. Jefferson maintained an active interest in American Indians and their languages and the division that preserves his library is appropriately rich in accounts by European and American explorers, settlers, missionaries, and historians of encounters with Indian peoples.

The Library did not create a separate Rare Book and Special Collections Division until 1934 when it moved into its present reading room and stack area, but the institution had been actively seeking out collections of rare materials since the visionary Ainsworth Rand Spofford was Librarian of Congress (1864–97). The purchase of the large private library of Peter Force, the Russian collection of Gennadii Yudin, and 3,000 fifteenth-century books from Otto H. Vollbehr, as well as gifts from many donors, including the large library of Joseph Meredith Toner and the collection of John Boyd Thacher, a leading nineteenth century authority on the history of discovery, necessitated a separate, secure quarters and staff. Between 1943 and 1979, Lessing J. Rosenwald presented to the Library 2,600 rare illustrated books—its finest single collection of rare books—including some of the earliest images made by Europeans of North American Indian peoples, collected and published by Theodor de Bry.

Today the division's collections—including well over one hundred separate collections with their own indexes—amount to approximately 650,000 books, broadsides, pamphlets, theater playbills, title pages, prints, posters, photographs, and medieval and Renaissance manuscripts.

These abundant materials include many key works for the study of the early contact between

Europeans and various American Indian groups, beginning with two copies—one illustrated—of Columbus's printed letter announcing his discovery of the Americas and calling the people there "los Indios." Accounts of early encounters with Indian peoples in North America include those of Hernando de Soto in the Southeast and Southwest, with significant references to Indian political alliances, and distinctive cultures from Florida to eastern Texas; Alvar Nuñez Cabeza de Vaca's autobiographical work on his 1520s to 1530s trek across Texas and the near southwest; René de Laudonnière's personal remembrances of the ill-fated French colonization in Florida in the 1560s and his impressions of the Timucua and other Atlantic coastal groups; Samuel de Champlain's various early seventeenth-century descriptions of the peoples and places of Canada and Maine; as well as many first hand accounts of European explorers, expedition leaders, colonizers, and missionaries as they for the first time met and tried to describe Indian cultures in what is now the United States.

The division also has rich collections on British colonial administration, the American Revolution, the early American republic, and the westward movement of explorers and settlers in the nineteenth century. Period documentation of contacts with Indian tribes includes copies of the famous pre-Civil War portfolios of color lithographs depicting Indian individuals and tribes. These valuable visual records of Indian life before the invention of photography were enhanced recently by the addition of a copy of Prince Maximilian Alexander Philipp von Wied-Neuwied's *Reise in das innere Nord-America in den Jahren 1832 bis 1834* (Coblenz, 1839–41), including the supplemental picture atlas of eighty-one hand-colored copperplate engravings after paintings by Karl Bodmer of Plains Indians. The division also holds a complete set of the most extensive photographic record of Indian tribes of the early twentieth century: Edward S. Cur-

tis's twenty-volume *The North American Indian*, with twenty portfolios of photogravures (Seattle and Cambridge, Mass., 1907–30). The Prints and Photographs Division holds contact prints made from Curtis's large-format negatives, many of which were not published by him.

Many of these works have appeared also in reprint form, which can be found normally in the Library's General Collections. While in most cases little distinction exists between the intellectual content of the original imprint and the reprinted, e.g., facsimile, editions, opportunities for comparison of editions and to physically use the original edition exist. More recent, non-rare editions may include translations into English, indexes, supplementary documents, and scholarly assessments that intervening researchers have provided. Yet, it is important to review the original source to ascertain the original contents and to obtain the "feel" of the historic document. In addition, researchers and curators looking for high quality illustrations for publication or exhibitions will find a wealth of material in original editions.

Although much of the materials held by the Rare Book and Special Collections Division describe Indian peoples from a European and Euro-American point of view, colored by classical or religious influences and cultural and personal biases, they should not be dismissed as mere examples of cultural imperialism. In the absence of written and pictorial records by Indian peoples themselves, these documents often provide the only documentation we have. By looking at them with keen awareness of the probable bias of their authors, a researcher can at the very least understand the motivations of those who recorded the encounters.

Not all European depictions of Indian life need be treated with a high degree of suspicion. For example, it has been broadly accepted that John White's drawings between 1584 and 1587 of Carolina Algonquians are living, vigorous expressions of a non-European culture. His drawings, transferred into prints under the direction of Theodor de Bry, serve as invaluable documents in the study of pre-European Carolina Tidewater history.

An educated writer, such as Giovanni da Verrazzano, produced a many-sided account of a voyage of exploration, but his knowledge of classical tales about the barbarians known to Mediterranean cultures often distorted his account of what he saw, or thought he saw. Often the simple seaman or soldier, a Bernal Diaz del Castillo, Hans Staden, or Miles Philips, brought the new scene and the newly envisaged cultural landscape most sharply and objectively to light. Although necessarily hardened toward potential adversaries, soldiers and sailors often had a considerable capacity for identifying with the enemy. Many of the most useful narratives are by such individuals.

On the other hand, the cleric, and more especially the missionary, was often likely to distort by condemnation and exaggeration the non-compatible culture. These individuals observed the new cultures primarily with the thought of transforming their ideology, and this kept the great majority of them from seeing clearly what it was that they proposed to alter. There were exceptions. Bartolomé de las Casas tried hard, if not too clearly, to see the conquest from the American Indian point of view; Gonzalo Fernández de Oviedo y Valdés expressed his disgust at their practices yet gave some of the best descriptions of the way the American Indian peoples got things done; Richard Hakluyt swayed between his strong Protestant reaction against paganism and his objective curiosity about the non-European world and its inhabitants.

The Jesuits, who sought to apply a detached and critical intelligence to the problems of conversion, pushed aside the more elementary missionary misconceptions of non-European and non-Christian society. In the Jesuit letters, the external descriptions provided by lay travellers were paralleled by attempts to reveal the inner character of the non-European societies.

The researcher will find two works especially useful in sorting through the various accounts that have provided some of the first and perhaps most compelling images of American Indian peoples and society. They are *The Discovery of North America* by W. P. Cumming, R. A. Skelton and D. B. Quinn (London: Elek, 1971; E101 .C96) and *The Exploration of North America 1630–1776* by W. P. Cumming, D. B. Quinn, et al. (London: Elek, 1974; E121 .E9 1974c).

USING THE COLLECTIONS

RARE BOOK AND SPECIAL COLLECTIONS READING ROOM

LOCATION: Jefferson Building, 2nd Floor, Room LJ 206; telephone (202) 707-5434

HOURS: Monday through Friday, 8:30 A.M. to 5:00 P.M.

ACCESS AND USE: Researchers are required to present a Library of Congress photo ID card when they register and to use pencil when taking notes. Any requests for photocopying materials, including microfilming and the preparation of photoprints or color transparencies, must be directed to the Library's Photoduplication Service.

Catalogs

Because nearly four-fifths of the division's material consists of a group of collections built around specific subjects, chronological periods, geographical areas, formats, and authors, only a portion of the total holdings—the general, or classified, collection of books—is represented in the main catalog of the Library of Congress. The division's own dictionary catalog contains 650,000 cards that provide access to almost the whole of the division's collections by author or other form of main entry and, in some instances, by subject and title also. In addition to this central card catalog, the division has created over one hundred special card files describing individual collections or special aspects of books from many collections.

Special Collections

Indian-related material can be found in many special collections in addition to the general book collection:

American Almanac Collection: 3,896 titles; seventeenth through nineteenth centuries

American and Foreign Magazines Collection: 3,872 titles; seventeenth to early twentieth centuries

American Imprints, 1640–1800: 16,990 titles

Bible Collection: 1,471 titles; early editions and rare issues in many languages, including Indian languages

Broadside Collection: 30,500 items; mostly American single-sheet publications; sixteenth to twentieth centuries. See *Catalog of Broadsides in the Rare Book Division, Library of Congress* (Boston: G. K. Hall & Co., 1972; Z1231.B7 A5)

Dime Novel Collection: 35,000 titles; popular paperback fiction, nineteenth and early twentieth centuries

Documents of the First Fourteen Congresses: 12,922 titles

Benjamin Franklin Collection: 850 titles; publications written, printed, edited, or published by Franklin

Henry Harrisse Collection: 414 items; publications pertaining to early exploration of America

Lessing J. Rosenwald Collection: 2,653 titles; illustrated books, fifteenth through twentieth centuries. See *A Catalog of the Gifts of Lessing J. Rosenwald to the Library of Congress* (Wash-

ington, D.C.: Library of Congress, 1977; Z881.U5 1977)

Spanish American Imprint Collection: 368 titles; books from various Latin American countries, sixteenth to nineteenth centuries

John Boyd Thacher Collection: 5,193 items, including incunabula and early Americana. See *The Collection of John Boyd Thacher . . .* (Washington, D.C., 1931; Z881.U5 1931)

Wagner-Camp Collection: 451 titles; Western Americana selected from Henry R. Wagner's and Charles L. Camp's bibliography *The Plains and the Rockies* (San Francisco, 1921; Z1251.W5 W2)

❑ SELECTED BOOKS AND COLLECTIONS

This brief description of some of the rich variety of materials in the Library of Congress's Rare Book and Special Collections Division is intended to suggest in general terms to researchers the broad parameter of materials that one can find on American Indian topics from the late fifteenth to the twentieth century. Individual researchers, with different intents and interests, should be able to uncover equally specific, rare, and exquisite records. Selections are arranged thematically and then chronologically, as follows:

- Early Contact: Discoverers and Explorers
  Early Spanish Contact
  French and English in the East and South
    of North America
  Spanish Penetration of the Southwest
  Spanish American Imprint Collection
  French Contacts in the Upper Midwest
  Jesuit Relations
  Contacts on Northwest Coast and California
- Captivity Narratives
- Government Documents: Franklin treaties
- Bible Collection

- Indian Portfolios: Prints and Photographs
- Nineteenth Century Exploration and Travel in the American West: Documentary, Popular, and Fictional Accounts
    Wagner-Camp Collection
    The Dime Novel Collection
- Twentieth Century Decorative Arts

Early Contact: Discoverers and Explorers

The following examples of the rich varieties of materials available for the study of the initial contact of European and American Indian cultures in the Rare Book collections serve merely as the extreme tip of a large iceberg. The thousands of records reporting on multiple Indian cultures by European rivals vying for control in what is now the United States, such as those pitting the Spanish against the French or French against the English, and so on, or by proponents of conflicting religious views seeking souls in the Americas, provide researchers with ample descriptions, from different perpectives and with different intentions, of Indian cultural, political, and economic activities during the initial contact with Europeans.

Early Spanish Contact

Although the scope of this guide is generally limited to America north of Mexico, the division holds copies of some of the classic works describing Columbus's discovery of Caribbean islands and the subsequent Spanish colonization of the hemisphere. These works provided the first representation for Europeans of American Indian peoples and their influence endured for generations:

Historia Baetica. Carol Verardi. [Basel]: I[ohann] B[ergmann, de Olpe], 1494; Incun.1494.47 Voll H15942

This edition of Columbus's 1493 letter announcing the discovery of what became known as America has several woodcuts, including a depiction of the Spanish ship landing on Hispaniola with native people gathered on shore watching the arrival (see Rare Book portfolio). Since Columbus thought that he had arrived in the East Indies, the letter incorrectly uses the name Indian to describe the indigenous peoples of the Americas, the generic identification that endured. Columbus wrote that both the men and women wore no clothes and were timid, guileless, and generous. His letter spread quickly throughout Europe, with numerous editions in various languages published within a year, an astonishing number for a fifteenth-century book; these included versions in Rome, Florence, Paris, Basel, and Antwerp.

In addition to this edition, which was published bound with an epic poem celebrating Christian Spain's triumph over the Moors at Granada, the Library possesses an even earlier edition of Columbus's 1493 letter, the second Roman edition in Latin entitled *Epistola de insulis nuper inventis* (Thacher Collection No. 731; Incun.1493.C6). It was printed after April 30, 1493, only two months following Columbus's return to Europe from his first voyage.

De orbe nous decades. Pietro Martire d'Anghiera. Alcala: A. Guillelmi, 1516; Thacher Collection No. 635; E141.A58 1516

Commonly known as Peter Martyr's *Decades,* this is a collection of his letters sent from Spain to prominent individuals in Italy attesting to the news of the early Spanish voyages to America, including those of Columbus and Vespucci. Martyr continued Columbus's characterization of the American Indian peoples as noble savages living in a paradise without books, laws, and, as he put it, "lying judges." This description, which followed his *P. Martyris Angli mediolanensis opera, legatio babylonica, oceani decas . . .* (Sevilla, 1511;

E141.A5 1511a Thacher Collection), which contains a map showing the southern tip of Florida, echoed through many of the other early exploration and discovery accounts. These included *La historia general delas Indias* by Gonzalo Fernández de Oviedo y Valdes (n.p., 1535; E141.O92) and also his *Libro XX. De la segunda parte de la general historia de las Indias* (Valladolid, 1535; E141.O942), José de Acosta's *Historia natural y moral de las Indias* (Seville, 1590; E141.A283), and André Thevet's *Historia dell'India America* (Venice, 1561; E141.T43).

Brevissima relacion de la destruycion de las Indies. Bartolomé de las Casas. Seville: S. Trugillo, 1552; F1411.C25

If Peter Martyr described the Indian peoples of the Indies as living in paradise, Dominican priest Bartolomé de las Casas described their rough treatment under Spanish rule as virtually living in hell. Las Casas recounted for the Spanish court the mutilations inflicted by Spaniards on the American Indians and the fact that dogs were kept to hunt them down. He personally expressed his horror to Spain's King Charles V in pressing for the passage of the New Laws related to the treatment of Indian peoples in the Americas. His impassioned pleas are landmarks in the description of European and American Indian contact, and were heavily used by those opposed to Spanish successes in the Americas to create the Black Legend regarding Spain's legacy there. Also important is his *Aqui se cotiene treynta proposiciónes muy jurídicas*, published in Seville in 1552 (F1411.C24).

La Florida del ynca. Garcilaso de la Vega, el Inca. Lisbon: P. Crasbeeck, 1605; E125.S7G1

Garcilaso de la Vega, the mestizo son of an Incan princess and a Spanish conquistador in Peru, wrote an extraordinarily rich book on Hernando de Soto's 1539–42 expedition through Spanish Florida to East Texas, based on eye-witness accounts. In this work, he praised both Spaniards and Indian leaders, providing oral record from both sides; especially noteworthy is the speech of Florida cacique Acuera to Soto. *La Florida del ynca*, completed in 1599, contained one of the earliest descriptions of multiple Indian cultures in the southeastern and trans-Mississippi portions of the United States in confrontation with a sizeable Spanish expeditionary force. Instances of cooperation with, and opposition to, that force filled Garcilaso's writings. This remarkable account is filled with valuable information on Indian land use, inheritance, size of communities, agricultural production and variety, trading activities, intra- and inter-tribal relationships, military prowess, and numerous religious and social practices. In addition to a full record of the Soto expedition, the author described subsequent Spanish efforts in Florida, which then included most of southeastern United States, through the ill-fated Jesuit mission to Ajacan in the Chesapeake Bay area in 1570–71. A French translation, *Histoire de la Floride* (Paris: G. Clovzier, 1670; E125.S7 G31), and a twentieth-century English translation, *The Florida of the Inca; a history of the adelantado, Hernando de Soto, Governor and Captain General of the kingdom of Florida, and of other heroic Spanish and Indian cavaliers* (Austin: University of Texas Press, 1951; E125.S7 G26), are also in the Library of Congress.

French and English Contact with East and South Coasts of North America

L'Histoire Notable de la Floride Sitvée en Indes Occidentales. René Goulaine de Laudonnière. Paris: G. Auvray, 1586; F314.L37

An original non-illustrated edition of Laudonnière's account of his voyages in the early 1560s to Florida and his experiences among the Timucua during his attempt to establish a Huguenot colony there, this edition also includes

GATEWAYS

At the time of contact, the region that became the United States was filled with hundreds of tribes speaking a multiplicity of languages and dialects and occupying a range of habitats. One result of this diversity and fragmentation was the emergence of complicated alliances and antagonisms among Indians and with Europeans; another was the dependence of Europeans on the local people for their very survival. At first, groups usually welcomed Europeans and only later resisted them.

While parallel settlements occurred, conflicts developed as European peoples attempted to force their cultural practices on existing structures, disrupting long-established living patterns and often leaving a legacy of fear and hostility. Devastating diseases, warfare, and occasionally enslavement reduced American populations drastically. Yet, in vast stretches of America, no European contact occurred until long after the initial voyages of exploration were completed. Ultimately, Indian societies endured significant disruption to customs, practices, and spiritual beliefs. But these societies did survive and adapt to the presence of Europeans in their midst.

Europeans—French, Spanish, Portuguese, and English—arrived in the sixteenth century sporadically, in small numbers, and in pursuit of various objectives. With the exception of fishermen, whalers, and fur traders, none of the Europeans found what they sought. There was no passage to Asia, nor were there great accumulated riches of gold and silver. Nor did Europeans confront an untamed wilderness but, in many areas, encountered densely settled populations who carefully managed and utilized the land and its plant and animal life. The Hurons of the Great Lakes region, among others, lived in semipermanent villages of 800 to 1,600 people. Some of the largest and militarily strongest groups, such as the Five Nations of the Iroquois and the Creek, were able to dictate the terms of their relationship with Europeans.

Spanish forays into the region began early in the sixteenth century. These expeditions included those of Hernando de Soto in the Southeast and Vázquez de Coronado in the Southwest. At that time, attempts to settle and exploit the Southwest all but ceased until the end of the century with the expedition of Juan de Oñate and the arrival of the Franciscan missionaries. Spanish activity in Florida resulted in the founding of St. Augustine in 1565. In the late sixteenth century, the English under Walter Raleigh attempted unsuccessfully to found a settlement in the mid-Atlantic region.

With permanent European settlements in the seventeenth century, relations with the Indian tribes became uneasy and frequently hostile. The two worlds—European and Indian—remained for the most part sharply separated and fundamentally at odds, notwithstanding alliances made for purposes of trade or war.

WHERE TO LOOK: Material for the era of European exploration can be found in the General Collections, Rare Book and Special Collections, Manuscript, Prints and Photographs, and Geography and Map Divisions, and the Law Library.

"Outina defeats Potanou with the aid of the French," from *Brevis narratio* by Theodor de Bry (Frankfurt, 1591). F314.L33 (LC-USZ62-370). Rare Book and Special Collections Division.

Chief Outina used the French in his battle against the enemy Potanou in 1564 in Florida. Outina placed the French soldiers at the front of the attack and in a short time routed Potanou. The French were used in similar fashion by a number of the Indian leaders in Florida as the French desire to reach gold and silver sources required the support of various warring factions of Florida Indians.

an account of Dominique de Gourgues' 1568 reprisal raid on the Spanish in Florida.

La Floride Française, Scènes de la Vie Indienne, Peintes en 1564. Charles Germain Marie Bourel de la Roncière. Paris: Les Editions nationales, 1928; F314.L33

This work reproduces in color Jacques Le Moyne de Morgues' original sixteenth-century drawings and watercolors of American Indian life in Florida and South Carolina, when Le Moyne accompanied René de Laudonnière's expedition to establish a Huguenot colony.

A briefe and true report of the new found land of Virginia. Thomas Hariot. Francoforti ad Moenum: Typis I. Wecheli, sumtibus vero T. de Bry, 1590; Rosenwald Collection no. 723; F229.H27 1590

In 1585 Hariot sailed on an exploration with Sir Walter Raleigh, to what is now known as North Carolina. Raleigh's expedition made contact with American Indian peoples throughout the voyage, and his party explored inland, giving Europe some of the most detailed accounts of Indian culture. The artist John White accompanied the explorers and made detailed watercolors of Indian villages and customs. Though first published in 1588 without illustrations, this 1590 edition contained uncolored engravings based on White's observations. Hariot's account was included in a larger effort by Theodor De Bry to compile sixteenth-century exploration narratives for the Americas, which he published in Frankfurt between 1590 and 1634.

A census of the Library's holdings of De Bry's works appears on pages 236–39 in *A Catalog of the Gifts of Lessing J. Rosenwald . . .* (Washington, D.C.: Library of Congress, 1977; Z881.U5 1977). The catalog describes Rosenwald's magnificent collection of illustrated books and manuscripts, produced between the fifteenth and twentieth centuries, that was given to the Library for the most part between 1943 and 1975. Few items

pertain to Native Americans; his rich group of De Bry's works is an exception.

New English Canaan or Newe Canaan. Thomas Morton. Amsterdam: J. F. Stam, 1637; F67.M88

Morton provides a descriptive account of the Indian peoples of New England, especially in Massachusetts, at the point of early contact with the English. He describes the language, religious beliefs, architecture, and clothing styles of the people, as well as the geographical setting.

A Briefe Narration of the Originall Undertakings of the Advancement of Plantations into the Parts of America. Ferdinando Gorges. London: Printed by E. Brudenell, for N. Brook, 1658; F7.G66 pt. 2

Gorges, a prominent seventeenth-century English military figure who never went to America, sponsored a few unsuccessful attempts to colonize New England. This title, one of a series of pamphlets called "America Painted to Life," is the only substantive account of his colonial endeavors. His description of New England and its Indian peoples are secondhand, although he received information from three Indians who were brought to England in 1605.

Histoire de la Louisiane, contenant la découverte de ce vaste pays; sa description géographique; un voyage dans les terres; l'histoire naturelle, les moeurs, coûtumes & religion des naturels, avec leurs origines; deux voyages dans le nord du nouveau Mexique, dont un jusqu'à la Mer du Sud. . . . Antoine Simon Le Page du Pratz. Paris: De Bure, 1758; F372.L54

Le Page du Pratz's three-volume work contains an extensive account, with illustrations, of the Natchez people of the Mississippi Valley. The work is based on his long involvement with the Natchez, which included day-to-day life, hunting trips, and occasional war parties against neighboring communities. The work provides especially rich detail regarding the religion and the political structure of the Natchez society.

The memoirs of Lieut. Henry Timberlake, (who accompanied the three Cherokee Indians to England in the year 1762) containing whatever he observed remarkable, or worthy of public notice, during his travels to and from that nation. Henry Timberlake. London, 1765; E99.C5 T6

Timberlake's work provides a description of the Cherokee nation and culture at the time the British were seeking alliance with them against the French in the middle of the eighteenth century. This work includes a map of the Cherokee communities along the Tennessee River in the vicinity of Fort Loudoun.

A concise natural history of East and West Florida. Bernard Romans. New York, 1775; F314.R75

Romans serves as an important source of information on the Indian peoples of the Gulf Coast area of the United States, with special references to, and descriptions of, the Chickasaw, Creek, and Choctaw. His account, prepared following the British expansion into Spanish East and West Florida after the British capture of Havana during the French and Indian War, was intended for both military and economic purposes. It speaks frankly about British relations with various Indian peoples of the southern area.

Spanish Penetration of the Southwest

"Relatione del Reverendo Fra Marco da Nizza" in *Terzo volume delle navigationi nel quale si contengono al mondo nuovo.* Giovanni Battista Ramusio. Venetia: Giunti, 1556; G159.R2 vol. 3 1556

While the French and English were primarily absorbed in exploring the Atlantic coastal area of North America, the Spanish, in addition to settlements in Florida, and after conquering Mexico, undertook a penetration into what is now the southwestern United States, especially New Mexico. Fray Marcos, as he is popularly known, was inspired to make his incursion in 1539 after hearing tales of fabulous cities of gold to the north of Mexico. Fray Marcos's mission underscores one of the motives of the early European contacts with American Indians, which was the search for wealth. Fray Marcos found the Pueblo Indians friendly but lacking the gold he sought.

Giovanni Battista Ramusio, who compiled *Navigatione et viaggi,* issued in three volumes in Venice between 1550 and 1556, was one of the most important publishers of accounts of voyages and explorations to America (along with the Englishman Richard Hakluyt). In addition to Fray Marcos's account in this volume, the accounts—some with illustrations—of the expeditions of Alvar Núñez Cabeza de Vaca, Francisco Vásquez de Coronado, Giovanni da Verrazzano, and Jacques Cartier appear.

Noticias de la Nueva California. Francisco Palou. 4 vols. San Francisco: E. Bosqui, 1874; F864.P2

A native of Spain, Father Francisco Palou arrived in Mexico in 1749 with fellow Franciscan Junipero Serra. Two decades later, Palou was president of the missions in what was then called Old California, now Baja California, and Serra was missions president of New California, with his base in Monterey. Later, Palou directed the missions in New California and recorded his observations of mission life and individual missions, around which were gathered many American Indian communities. In general, Palou writes of a peaceful coexistence between the Spanish missionaries and those California Indians who converted to Catholicism.

SPANISH-AMERICAN IMPRINT COLLECTION

Palou's *Noticias* is part of the Division's general collection, but the researcher should also consult the Spanish-American Imprint Collection in the Division, which contains many works relating to New Spain, including Miguel Venegas's *El apostol Mariano representado en la vida del V.P. Juan Maria de Salvatierra, de Compania de Jesus,*

GATEWAYS

Religious conversion of Indian people was an adjunct to the expansion of empire and trade of several of the colonizing European nations. Usually, a desire to convert native peoples to Christianity was accompanied by attempts to convert them to European ways of life and ally them politically against other competing European nations. Indian groups that chose to accept missions did so with varying degrees of enthusiasm, but seem to have viewed them as both a means to extend their spirituality and to accommodate cultural differences between them and the new Americans. Often, however, missions and the competing Christian sects presented confusing and divisive choices for tribes and opened a wedge for further inroads by non-Indians.

Spain relied on missions in California, the Southeast and the Southwest, along with civilian and military settlements, to expand territory and to curb the advances of other nations. Similarly, New France sought to convert Indian tribes to Catholicism and French civilization through the Capuchins and Jesuits, who were particularly ac-

tive in the areas along the present U.S./Canadian border. The Jesuits, especially, compiled extensive records of their efforts.

One of the Puritans' stated purposes in settling New England was conversion of its native people to Christianity, but the practice was somewhat limited. Massachusetts and Rhode Island established a few missions in the seventeenth and eighteenth centuries, but Indian-colonial wars and waves of European immigrants with more secular interests lessened missionary fervor.

Missionary efforts continued, however, by Catholics and various Protestant sects, throughout the country into the nineteenth and twentieth centuries. And mission records comprise rich sources for study relating to North American Indian culture.

WHERE TO LOOK: The General Collections and almost every specialized division of the Library, particularly the Manuscript and Prints and Photographs Divisions.

Feast day at San Estevan del Rey Mission, Acoma Pueblo, New Mexico. Photographed by Charles F. Lummis, c.1890. LOT 2840 (LC-USZ62-29347). Prints and Photographs Division.

The church in the background of Lummis's photograph was built under Franciscan direction in the mid-seventeenth century. After Franciscans gave up residence a century later, tribal clan and religious leaders assumed its management. The mission had become sacred to the Acoma, as had their pre-Christian religious kivas, and the church was similarly protected from public view on occasions. In this scene, a statue of a saint is carried in a procession from the church to the site of feast day dances.

fervoroso missionero en la provincia de Nueva-Espana, y conquistado apostolico de las Californias (Mexico: Maria de Ribera, 1754; F864.S18) and *Relación histórica de la vida y apostólicas tareas del venerable padre fray Junípero Serra, y de las misiones que fundó en la California Septentrional, y nuevos establecimientos de Monterey* (Mexico: Felipe de Zuniga y Ontiveros, 1787; F864.S48). There is a card index in the Rare Book Reading Room to the Spanish-American Imprint Collection. The entries are arranged by date, printer, and place of publication.

French Contacts in the Upper Midwest

Nouvelle découverte d'un très grand pays situé dans l'Amérique, entre le Nouveau Mexique, et la Mer Glaciale, avec les cartes, & les figures nécessaires, & de plus l'histoire naturelle & morale, & les avantages qu'on en peut tirer par l'establissem.des.colon . . . Louis Hennepin. Amsterdam: Chez A. van Someren, 1698; F352.H61

Hennepin travelled extensively in the Illinois and Mississippi River sections of the upper midwestern part of the United States. He describes through words, images, and maps the variety of Indian societies in the region, reflecting on the multiplicity of languages in use.

Nouveaux voyages de Mr. le baron de Lahontan, dans l'Amérique Septentrionale, qui contiennent une relation des différents peuples qui y habitent; la nature de leur gouvernement; leur commerce, leurs coûtumes, leur religion, & leur manière de faire la guerre. Louis Armand de Lom d'Arce, baron de Lahontan. La Haye: Chez les frères l'Honore, 1703–04; F1030.L152

Lahontan's famous account about the Indian peoples of the St. Lawrence and the eastern Great Lakes region is filled with a rich variety of materials on various Indian groups, their practices, languages, and arts of war. This work contains some of the earliest illustrations of the articles used by Algonquian, Huron, and Iroquois peoples to hunt, to fight, and to travel. A special section of the work, "Petit dictionaire de la langue des sauvages Iroquois," is complemented by additional glossaries of French-Algonquian and French-Huron words. A graphic description of a battle, in the same form as the midwestern winter counts, is found herein. The book contains numerous maps of the area covered by his account.

Two additional works related to the French in Canada and the northern part of the United States include Gabriel Sagard's *Dictionaire de la langue huronne nécessaire à ceux que n'ont l'intelligence d'icelle* (Paris: Chez Denys Moreau, 1632; F1030.S13) and Joseph François Lafitau's *Moeurs des sauvages amériquains, comparées aux moeurs des premiers temps* (Paris: Saugrain l'ainé, 1724; E58.L16). Lafitau's work is especially useful for the study of American Indians, containing rich illustrations of customs and practices.

Histoire de l'Amérique Septentrionale . . . Claude Charles Le Roy Bacqueville de la Potherie. 4 vols. Paris: J.-L. Nion et F. Didot, 1722; F1030.B11

Bacqueville, comptroller-general of the marines and fortifications in Canada for a brief period in the late 1690s, recounts his experiences and those of his contemporaries and predecessors, including Nicolas Perrot and Louis Frontenac. There is considerable discussion of groups such as the Iroquois, Abenaki, Huron, Ottawa, Illinois, Potawatomi, and Sac and Fox. Several interesting illustrations appear. An English translation and condensed version of both Perrot's and Bacqueville's accounts appear in *The Indian Tribes of the Upper Mississippi Valley and Region of the Great Lakes . . .* , edited by Emma Helen Blair (Cleveland: Arthur H. Clark, 1911; E78.N8 B63)

JESUIT RELATIONS

The division possesses a comprehensive collection of original editions and reprints of what is known as the Jesuit Relations. These include works of Paul Le Jeune, Jacques Gravier, Jérôme Lallemant, Jean de Quen, and Paul Ragueneau. These accounts were the equivalent of annual reports to superiors in France about Jesuit efforts to convert the Indian people in Canada, the upper Midwest, and the lower Mississippi Valley during the seventeenth and eighteenth centuries. The most convenient way to identify these items in the Rare Book Reading Room is under the subject heading "Jesuits. Letters from Missions (North America)."

Two distinctive series of publications are found within this large body of materials. One numbered series includes primarily original seventeenth- and eighteenth-century Paris imprints appearing in the Rare Book collection under the classification F1030.7.Z632 (a total of forty-one works). Another numbered series appears as nineteenth-century reprints of original works prepared under the direction of John Dawson Gilmary Shea, who was a major compiler of information on the Catholic Church in the United States and Canada. Some twenty-six facsimiles of original works appeared between 1850 and the 1880s in Shea's Cramoisy Press Series (F1030.7.C57). The Cramoisy Press (Paris) had been a seventeenth- and eighteenth-century publisher of Jesuit Relations.

Separate from these series but of major importance for the documentation of Jesuit descriptions of American Indian peoples are the works of Father Pierre Jean de Smet, including his *Voyages aux montagnes Rocheuses, et une année de séjour chez les tribus indiennes du vaste territoire de l'Oregon . . .* (Malines: P. J. Hanicq, 1844; F592.S633), *New Indian sketches* (New York: D. & J. Sadlier, 1863; E77.S64 1863), and *Missien van dem Oregon en reizen naer de Rotsbergen en de bronnen der Colombia* (Gent: Schelden, 1849; F880.S635). In these books he provides early descriptions of the Salish and Siksika (Blackfeet),

including a Salish catechism and a Kootenai glossary.

Contacts on Northwest Coast and California

Geschichte der reisen, die seit Cook an der Nordwest . . . Edited and compiled by Georg Forster. Berlin: Voss, 1791; F851.5.F73 1791

This three-volume illustrated work contains late eighteenth-century descriptions of the Northwest Coast and its people by explorer-adventurers George Dixon, John Meares, Nathaniel Portlock, and fur trader John Long. English language accounts of these encounters are available in other editions in the Rare Book collection and in the General Collections.

Noticias de la provincia de Californias en tres cartas de un sacerdote religioso, hijo del Real convento de predicadores de Valencia a un amigo suyo. Luis Sales. Valencia: Los hermanos de Orga, 1794; F864.S16

Father Sales provided a description of the character and the religion of the Indian peoples of both Baja and Upper California, including references to the peoples of San Diego, Monterey, and the Northwest Coast near Nutka.

Voyage pittoresque autour du monde, avec des portraits de sauvages d'Amérique, d'Asie, d'Afrique, et des îles du Gran ocean. Louis Choris. Paris: Firmin Didot, 1822; G420.K84 C5

This work, dedicated to the Emperor of Russia, provides a description of the tribes and places encountered during the Russians' second voyage around the world. Of particular significance are the descriptions of the Indian groups of California (in the San Francisco Bay area), the Aleutians, and the peoples of the Bering Strait region. This illustrated compilation contains numerous images of the people, dances, arms and utensils, boats, artifacts, and transcribed music of each of the three groups.

Captivity Narratives

If earlier descriptions of American Indians portrayed them as peaceful and living in an idyllic state, another picture emerged as the British began to occupy Indian lands and met resistance. Indian peoples were described as vicious savages, especially in the genre known as captivity narratives.

The Sovereignty and Goodness of God, Together with the Faithfulness of His Promises Displayed: Being a Narrative of the Captivity and Restauration of Mrs. Mary Rowlandson. Mary Rowlandson. Boston: T. Fleet, 1720; E87.R862

Mary Rowlandson's is one of the best known examples of this genre. She describes her capture by a band of Indian peoples after a frontier skirmish and what she terms her enslavement. She pictures the Indian peoples in her book as warlike and nomadic, mocking the European settlers. The captivity narrative was an influential force in the creation of American Indian images, and there are many examples from the seventeenth- through the late nineteenth-century, as primarily English settlers pushed westward from the Atlantic Coast. Many accounts, such as Rowlandson's book first printed in 1685, had enduring readership; an edition issued as late as 1930 is in the Rare Book collection.

Those captivity narratives printed before 1800 in what is now the United States are generally housed in the division's pre-1800 Collection, one of the largest collections of this sort of material in the country. After 1800, they are generally found in the division's general book collection and can be located by searching under the subject heading "Indians of North America—Captivity Narratives." One particularly descriptive title published in Providence, Rhode Island in 1815 gives

an excellent sense of the captivities themes: *An Affecting Narrative of the Captivity and Sufferings of Mrs. Mary Smith, Who, with Her Husband and Three Daughters Were Taken Prisoners by the Indians, in August Last and after Enduring the Most Cruel Hardships and Torture of Mind by the Indians for Sixty Days (in which time She Witnessed the Tragical Death of her Husband and Helpless Children) Was Fortunately Rescued from the Merciless Hands of the Savages by a Detached Party from the Army of the Brave General Jackson Now Commanding at New Orleans* (Providence, 1815; E87.S663 1815a).

Government Documents: Franklin treaties

Some of the most important sources for understanding American Indian culture and history are government documents of all types, since the United States government has been the principal institution to deal formally with Native Americans. Government documents, however, are not collected in one place in the Library of Congress. For example, the Benjamin Franklin Collection, purchased by the U.S. government in 1882, consists of the books and manuscripts carried to England by William Temple Franklin, Benjamin's grandson, in order to write a biography of his grandfather. The books became part of the Rare Book and Special Collections Division's holdings and the manuscripts are located in the Library's Manuscript Division.

An Account of the Treaty Held at the City of Albany. Philadelphia: Printed by Benjamin Franklin, 1746; E99.17.P4

This example of one of the many treaties between the government and various Indian tribes is from the division's outstanding Franklin collection. In it, representatives from Massachusetts, Connecticut, Pennsylvania, and New York inform the Iroquois of the hostilities between the

English and the French at the start of King George's War. The Iroquois promised the English that they would not allow any of the Indians allied with the French to cross their land, and the British colonists promised protection from the French. Often in these treaties, American Indian peoples are reported to speak in a stilted and romanticized way that many historians believe to be more the product of the English reporter on the scene than a true depiction of Indian manners and pattern of speech.

The Franklin treaties are gathered together and reprinted with an introduction by Carl Van Doren and notes by Julian P. Boyd in *Indian Treaties Printed by Benjamin Franklin, 1736–1762* (Philadelphia: The Pennsylvania Historical Society, 1938; E95.I64). References to other treaties, regardless of printer, can be found in the division's card catalog under the heading "Indians of North America—Treaties." The same heading can be used to search the computer catalog for any treaties added to the division after its card catalog was closed in 1990.

Bible Collection

Within this collection are American Indian language prayer books, hymnals, and bibles, including an original edition of the first Indian Bible, colonial missionary John Eliot's translation into the Massachuset language.

The . . . Holy Bible . . . Containing the . . . Old Testament . . . and the New Translated into the . . . Indian Language. Cambridge: Samuel Green and Marmaduke Johnson, 1663; BS345.A2E4 1663

This bible, commonly referred to as the Eliot Indian Bible, was the first complete bible published in what is now the United States. It was a remarkable feat. Only primitive conditions for printing English language texts existed in seventeenth-century Massachusetts. Not only did the Puritans have to develop a written language for the Massachuset Indians but they also had to create the individual type fonts to print it. The Eliot Indian Bible is housed in the division's large Bible Collection in which are found many other later Indian bibles, including those in Iroquois and Cherokee. A later edition, *Mamusse . . . Wunneetupanatamwe . . . Up-Biblum God ; ; ; Naneeswe . . . Nukkone Testament* (Cambridge: Printeeuoop Nashpe Samuel Green, 1685; BS345.A2E4 1685), is also in the collection.

Cherokee Gospel Tidings. Goingsnake, Indian Territory: Presbyterian Mission Press, 1898–1902; E99.C5 C404

A Cherokee language religious periodical, with some sections in English, for which the division has issues covering 1898 to 1902. The Cherokee were the first Native Americans to have their own alphabet and writing system, invented by Sequoyah in the nineteenth century. This rare periodical, printed in the Cherokee syllabary, was meant to be used during Sunday services.

Indian Portfolios: Prints and Photographs

The lithographic revolution of the 1830s and 1840s allowed the widespread dissemination of pictures to all classes of society. Public interest in the West was answered by entrepreneurs involved in Indian administration, such as Thomas L. McKenney, and by expeditionary artists who recorded and interpreted what they saw in precise illustrations to accompany factual descriptions. Between 1843 and 1863 the federal government alone published almost thirty different illustrated survey reports of the trans-Mississippi West (see the Law Library and Prints and Photographs sections also). Most of these pictures are suffused with the lessons and attitudes of European Romanticism and to a greater or lesser degree reveal the changing

Anglo-European attitudes toward American Indians: from exotic specimens to "savages" to "uncivilized" enemies, to remnants of a doomed and disappearing race. These monumental documents of United States Indian life, treasures in most cases, were part of a general treatment of Indian societies in the Americas, produced by such individuals as Alexander Freiherr von Humboldt in South America and Mesoamerica, Jean Baptiste Debret in Brazil, and John Lloyd Stephens and Frederick Catherwood in the Yucatan.

History of the Indian Tribes of North America. Thomas L. McKenney and James Hall. Philadelphia: E. C. Biddle, 1836–44; E77.M13

An original edition of McKenney and Hall's compilation of biographies and hand-colored engravings of portraits of Indian individuals by early painters, such as Charles Bird King and James Otto Lewis, this work is one of the few sources for color likenesses of prominent Indian leaders from east of the Mississippi River. Thomas L. McKenney amassed many Indian artifacts and portraits as superintendent of Indian affairs, particularly the more than one hundred portraits in his Indian Gallery, which he began in 1821. McKenney was dismissed from his government position by Andrew Jackson's administration in 1830.

Reise in das innere Nord-America in den Jahren 1832 bis 1834. Prince Maximillian Alexander Philipp von Wied-Neuwied. 2 vols., and atlas. Coblenz, 1839–41; E165.W64

Prince von Wied-Neuwied's book, which was translated into English as *Travels in the Interior of North America* (London, 1843; E165.W65), is one of the most magnificent works produced about the U.S. Midwest and its Indian inhabitants before the Civil War. Von Wied-Neuwied brought with him on his travels up the Missouri River a

Swiss artist named Karl Bodmer. The eighty-one hand-colored copperplate engravings in this book are based on Bodmer's delicate watercolors of the Midwestern and Western landscape and Indian life, the first truly accurate depictions of American Indians to reach the general public. Bodmer was the most accomplished artist to paint Plains Indians and his contemporaries attested to his strict attention to detail.

The French edition of the work, *Voyage dans l'intérieur de l'Amérique du Nord, exécuté pendant les années 1832, 1833 et 1834...* (Paris: A. Bertrand, 1840–43; E165.W66 Copy 3 Atlas), is one of the few completely colored aquatint reproductions of eighty-one of artist Karl Bodmer's lustrous paintings of the West, including scenes and portraits of the Arikara, Assiniboine, Blackfeet, Hidatsa, Mandan, and Sioux.

North American Indian Portfolio. George Catlin. London, 1844; NE2527.C4 1844

An original edition of hand-colored lithographs of Catlin's paintings of Plains Indians and their culture in the 1830s. Catlin's work, and that of his contemporary Karl Bodmer (see above), provided the first portfolios of images of western American Indians in their own setting.

If the authors of some works, represented by Mary Rowlandson's captivity narrative described above, saw American Indians as savages, others, such as George Catlin, went to another extreme. Catlin was a moderately successful portrait painter on the East Coast of the United States who, according to his own story, when he saw a group of American Indians who had travelled from the West, was taken with the idea of becoming their pictorial biographer and spent most of his life journeying from the upper to the lower Plains painting scenes of Indian life. He later took his paintings and the artifacts that he had collected to London where he exhibited them and had this book made, copying some of the paintings.

The *North American Indian Portfolio*, though highly romanticized and not artistically distinguished, nevertheless depicts many scenes, otherwise unknown pictorially from contemporary sources, of such activities as "Indian Ball Play," which resembled modern-day lacrosse, the Buffalo Dance, and hunting activities. Catlin believed the American Indian way of life was being destroyed by encroaching European settlements and that the closer the Indian peoples were to East Coast civilization the more they were corrupted. Indeed, historians and anthropologists have long considered his prints to be useful sources.

The division has a fine group of material relating to Catlin, including the page proofs for his *The Manners, Customs, and Condition of the North American Indians* (London, 1841; E77 .C377), his *Nord-Amerikas Indianer och de, under ett attaaright vistande bland de vildaste af deras stammar* (Stockholm, 1848; E77.C3818 1848)), which is a Swedish edition of his *The Manners* but illustrated with miniature reproductions of the hand-colored images in the large *Portfolio of the North American Indian* rather than with the simple line sketches found in the American and English editions; a salesman's sample for a quarto edition of the large oversized folio *Portfolio of the North American Indian*, and ephemera in the Broadside Collection relating to the sale of his books and his exhibits of Indian artifacts in London.

The North American Indian. Edward S. Curtis. 20 vols. and 20 portfolios of photogravures. Seattle and Cambridge, Mass.: E. S. Curtis, 1907–30; E77.C97

Edward Curtis's photographs provide a romantic and sometimes staged view of American Indians. He found many parallels between himself and George Catlin and wanted to create a description in photographs of what he considered to be a vanishing people and its way of life. The division has one of the 500 original twenty-volume published sets, with twenty large portfolios, of Curtis's photogravure prints produced during his nearly three-decade effort to record native life, particularly in the Plains, Southwest, California, and Northwest, a venture that was financed by J. Pierpont Morgan.

Originally a society photographer, as Catlin was initially a painter of East Coast society, Curtis produced photographs in a soft-focused sepia tone that self-consciously sought a spiritual look, bordering on mysticism.

Nineteenth-Century Exploration and Travel in the American West: Documentary, Popular, and Fictional Accounts

Wagner-Camp Collection

The Wagner-Camp Collection is named for Henry R. Wagner and Charles L. Camp's bibliography *The Plains and the Rockies* (San Francisco, 1921; Z1251.W5 W2 1921), which was revised in 1982 for a fourth edition by Robert H. Becker, a copy of which is in the division's reading room (1251.W5 W2 1982). *The Plains and the Rockies* is, by its own description, an annotated "bibliography of exploration, adventure and travel in the American West" consisting of 429 titles. The earliest entry was printed in 1801 and the latest was first issued in 1865, though later editions of some of these books were produced after this date. It is impossible to characterize these books in a general way except to say that they are the classic works describing the westward movement by those who participated. They tell the story of the first fledgling moves toward the Mississippi, to the spread of U.S. settlers across the Plains, to the treks up the Oregon Trail and down the Santa Fe Trail.

Such classic Western books as Josiah Gregg's *Commerce of the Prairies* (New York, 1844; F800.G8),

Zenas Leonard's *Narrative of the Adventures of Zenas Leonard . . . Who Spent Five Years in Trapping for Furs, Trading with the Indians* (Clearfield, Pa., 1839; F592.L36 1839), Alonzo Delano's *Life on the Plains and Among the Diggings, Being Scenes and Adventures of an Overland Journey to California: With . . . Mistakes and Sufferings of the Emigrants, the Indian Tribes, the Present and Future of the Great West* (Auburn, Buffalo, 1854; F593. D33) and Francis Parkman's *The California and Oregon Trail* (New York, 1849; F592.P24) are included. As might be expected, many of the depictions of Indian peoples are negative because they resisted the occupation of their lands. However, accounts compiled by the exploring expeditions sponsored by the government to study the West or to plan a railroad route across the continent contain rich materials.

Ethnologists and artists often accompanied such expeditions and their observations provided much of what is known about contemporary Indian societies. Such reports as Amiel Whipple's and Joseph Ives' in *Reports of Explorations and Surveys . . . for a Railroad Route from the Mississippi River to the Pacific Ocean* (Washington, D.C., 1855–60; F593.U58) are rich in information and extremely important in influencing legislators in Congress, who were destined to play a crucial role in the history of American Indian people.

The Dime Novel Collection

Approximately 35,000 items comprise this collection of the popular pulp fiction of the nineteenth and early twentieth centuries. Dime novels rose to prominence in the publishing industry after the U.S. Civil War (1861–65) and are so named because of their price, although many were sold for a little more as the century wore on. They were widely distributed, sold in railway stations and cars, newsstands, and other popular gathering places. Always highlighting sensationalism,

an action-packed plot, simple characterization, and an uncomplicated narrative, dime novels quickly became very important for helping to shape the country's perception of itself. Many titles are also useful for a study of the literary portrayal of American Indians, portrayals that undoubtedly helped form popular impressions.

The cover art on some of these novels is in itself revealing. It often depicts frontiersmen and American Indians locked in mortal combat, with the pages of the text always revealing that the Indian lost the fight. The titles of some of the books give a fair indication of the typical contents: *Hunters and Redskins*, *The Shawnee Witch*, *Panther Jack*, and *Malaeska, the Indian Wife*. While there is no subject guide to this fiction, bibliographies and series guides can help to identify genres that may be fruitful. Reference staff can also offer informed guidance.

Twentieth-Century Decorative Arts

With the turn of the twentieth century, a small group of Californians became fascinated with Pueblo Indian arts and actively collected the beautiful blankets, pots, and baskets of the New Mexican pueblos. The group's interest sparked a worldwide movement that valued the grace and originality of Indian design of all kinds. During the early years, especially, a number of books about the artifacts and designs were published in limited editions, many of which had original photographs tipped into their pages in order to more accurately portray the elegant objects. Because of their rarity and fragility many of these books are housed in the division.

American Indian Designs. Philadelphia: H. C. Perleberg, 1925–30; E98.A7W5

This two-volume work, called separately "Series one" and "Series two," contains seventy-two plates with over four hundred New Mexican Indian designs from prehistoric to modern times. Indian peoples included are the Laguna, Zuni, Cochiti, Mimbres, Casas Grandes, San Ildefonso, Acoma, Santo Domingo, Jemez, and Tewa. Explanatory texts accompany the designs.

Kiowa Indian Art: Watercolor Paintings in Color by the Indians of Oklahoma. Compiled by Oscar Brousee Jacobson. Nice: C. Szwedicki, c1929; E98.A7J17

This compilation contains thirty mounted watercolors of Indian portraits and ceremonial representations by Monroe Tsa-to-ke, Steve Mopope, Jack Hokeah, Spencer Asah, and Bouge-tah-smokey.

Pueblo Indian Painting: 50 Reproductions of Watercolor Paintings by Indian Artists of the New Mexican Pueblos of San Ildefonso and Sia. Nice: C. Szwedicki, c1932; E98.A7P88

A treasury of ceremonial and religious art by Velino Herrera, Julian Martínez, Miguel Martínez, Richard Martínez, Encarnación Peña, Alfonso Roybal, Louis Roybal, Abel Sanchez, Awa Tsireh, and Romando Vigil is found in this work.

Decorative Art of the Southwestern Indians. Compiled by Dorothy Smith Sides. Santa Ana, Calif.: Fine Arts Press, 1936; E98.A7S53

This work contains fifty color plates of pottery, basket, and textile designs. Tribes and pueblos represented are the Acoma, Apache, Chemehuevi, Cochiti, Hopi, Laguna, Maricopa, Mimbres, Mohave, Navajo, Papago, Pima, San Ildefonso, Sia, and Zuni.

Pueblo Indians of New Mexico as They Are Today: Twenty Photographs in Color by David Hare. New York, 1941; E99.P9H25

This is a collection of twenty 8" x 10" portraits in color taken at fifteen pueblos.

A Book of Plains Indians. By Leonard Baskin and Fritz Scholder. Northampton, Mass.: Gehenna Press, 1994; E77.5.S36 1994

A book containing fourteen monotype illustrations with accompanying text of the Sioux, Cheyenne, and Crow Indian peoples by the combined creative talents of Leonard Baskin and Fritz Scholder. Scholder is considered to be a leading American Indian painter. This publication is limited to twenty-six copies.

"Their manner of fishing in Virginia" from *A briefe and true report of the new found land of Virginia* by Thomas Hariot (Frankfort, 1590). F229.H27 1590 Rosenwald (RBSC neg. 454 and LC-USZC4-4805, color, LC-USZ62-576, black and white). Rare Book and Special Collections Division.

Thomas Hariot and artist John White, members of the English Roanoke Island settlement in 1585-86, made detailed and admiring reports on American Indian methods of agriculture and food preparation and use. According to Hariot, the Indian peoples "have likewise a notable way to catche fishe in their Rivers. For whear as they lacke both yron and steele, they faste unto their Reedes or longe Rodds, the hollowe tayle of a certain fishe like to a sea crabbe in steede of a poynte, wehr with by nighte or day they stricke fishes, and take them opp into their boates."

"Insula hyspana" from *De insulis in mari Indico nuper inventis* by Christopher Columbus in *Historia Baetica* by Carlo Verardi (Basel, 1494). Incun 1494 .V47 Voll H15942 (LC-USZC4-4806). Rare Book and Special Collections Division.

In his pursuit of recognition and fame, Christopher Columbus had published, in Latin, a letter to the world at large concerning his "recently found islands." This earliest printed record of America contained the first use of the term Indian to name the peoples of America. This edition included curious illustrations depicting the peoples and the places he had encountered on his first voyage. All of the illustrations evolved from the imagination of the publisher.

"Timucua Dugouts and typical houses," color facsimile of engraving from *La Floride Française: Scènes de la vie Indienne peintes en 1564* by Theodor de Bry and Charles de la Roncière (Paris, 1928). F314.L33 (LC-USZC4-4807, color; LC-USZ62-31870, black and white). Rare Book and Special Collections Division.

The image of a Timucua dugout canoe and a dwelling, drawn in 1564 by Jacques Le Moyne de Morgues from observation, shows a party of Indians bringing in a harvest for storage. Le Moyne said that "there are in that region a great many islands, producing abundance of various kinds of fruits, which they gather twice a year, and carry home in canoes, and store up in roomy low granaries built of stones and earth, and roofed thickly with palm-branches and a kind of soft earth fit for the purpose."

"Virginia" from *The generall Historie of Virginia, New-England, and the Summer Isles; with the names of the adventurers, planters, and governours from their first beginning, ano: 1584 to this present 1624* by John Smith (London, 1624). F229.S61 (LC-USZ62-116706). Rare Book and Special Collections Division.

John Smith's map of Virginia provides information on substantial areas that were not visited by the English. The data were provided by the skilled cartographers of Powhatan who described streams, communities, and natural features to the English expedition. The scene at top left shows the leader Powhatan in council.

"The defeat of the Pequot Indians in Connecticut in 1637. The figure of the Indians' fort or Palizado in New England And the maner of the destroying It by Captayne Underhill And Captayne Mason" from *Newes from America* by John Underhill (London, 1638). E83.63.U55 (LC-USZ62-32055). Rare Book and Special Collections Division.

The Pequots were a dominant Indian tribe in seventeenth-century New England. For several years after English settlers landed in the Connecticut River Valley, the two groups lived in peace. But, as colonists moved farther into Pequot lands, war broke out. In 1637, colonists and their Mohegan and Narragansett allies, under John Mason, attacked the main Pequot village at night. Several hundred defenders, including women and children, were burned alive. By the end of the Pequot War, the tribe was virtually wiped out.

"Raquetes" (Snow Shoes) from *Nouveaux voyages . . .* by Baron de Lahontan (LaHaye, 1703). F1030.L152 (LC-USZ62-115626). Rare Book and Special Collections Division.

Comparing Indian snowshoes to European tennis rackets, Lahontan observed, "By the help of this Contrivance they walk faster upon the Snow, than one can do with Shoes upon a beaten path . . . [without them it would be] impossible not only to hunt and range the Woods, but even to go to Church."

"Le transport du Grand Soleil" from *Histoire de la Louisiane* by Antoine S. Le Page du Pratz (Paris, 1758). F372.L54 (LC-USZ62-115625). Rare Book and Special Collections Division.

According to Le Page du Pratz, the Natchez lived under a theocracy where the state, the people, and their resources were devoted to the religious establishment. The head of the state was the Sun. By worshipping the human Sun, they also worshipped the true Sun. They built high mounds on which they erected temples so that the earthly Sun could converse with his elder brother, the heavenly Sun.

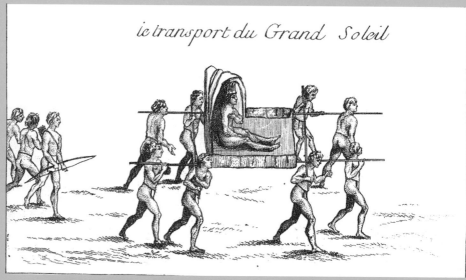

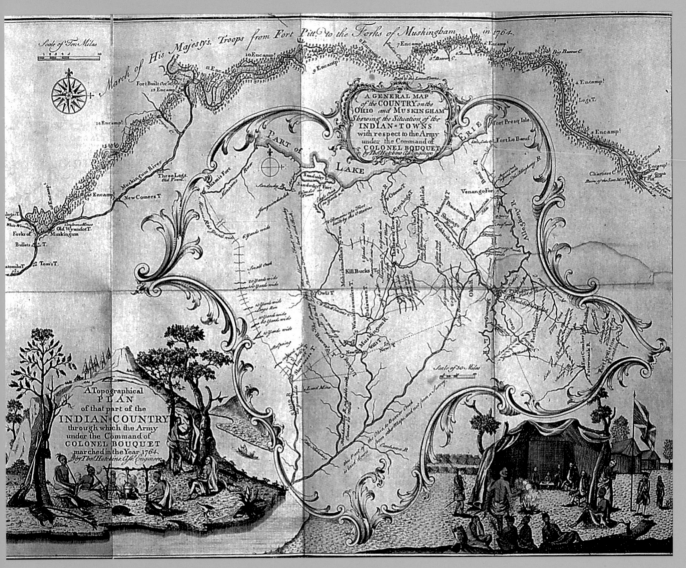

"Topographical plan of Indian country from Smith's account of the Expedition Against the Ohio Indians" by Thomas Hutchins from *An historical account of the expedition against the Ohio Indians, in the year 1764* by William Smith (Philadelphia, 1765). E83.76.S65 (LC-USZC4-4809). Rare Book and Special Collections Division.

Cartographer Thomas Hutchins accompanied British Colonel Henry Bouquet on an expedition to relieve Fort Pitt from a siege by tribes involved in Ottawa Chief Pontiac's rebellion against incursions into the Ohio area. Tactical graphics such as this usually accompanied narratives of British campaigns.

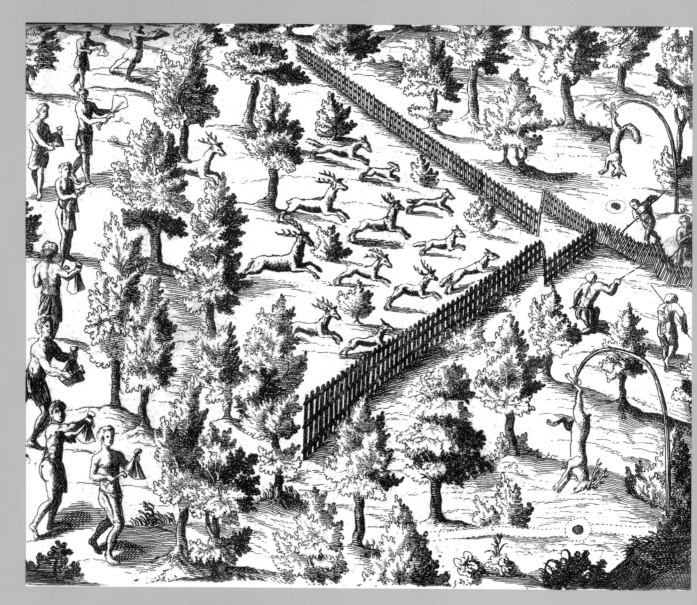

[Deer hunting], engraving from *Les Voyages du Sieur de Champlain* by Samuel de Champlain (Paris, 1613). F1030.1.C446
.R3 (LC-USZ62-116707), Rare Book and Special Collections Division.

*It was not always individual stealth that provided food for Indian stomachs. This illustration from Champlain's travels in the
Northeast renders a method of capturing large amounts of game for the kill. Similar practices were observed in other parts
of the country, where fire may have been part of the driving force. In the West, bison were sometimes herded over cliffs.*

[Indian sugar camp, showing sap collection from maple trees] from *The American aboriginal portfolio* by Mary Henderson Eastman (Philadelphia: Lippincott, Grambo & Co., 1853). E77.E125 (RBSC neg. 2672, also LC-USZ62-115628). Rare Book and Special Collections Division.

In her book, Dahcotah; or, life and legends of the Sioux around Fort Snelling *(New York, 1849), Mary Henderson Eastman, wife of artist and army officer Seth Eastman, observed the sugar extraction processes. "After the scalp-dance had been performed long enough, the Dahcotahs turned their attention to making sugar. Many groves of sugar trees were in sight of their village, and on this occasion the generous sap rewarded their labors . . . when the medicine men announced that they must keep the sugar-feast, all left their occupation, anxious to celebrate it . . . they were all occupied with the construction of their summer wigwams, which are made of the bark of trees, which must be peeled off in the spring."*

"Ball-play," color lithograph from *North American Indian Portfolio* by George Catlin (London, 1844). NE2527.C4 1844 (LC-USZC4-4810). Rare Book and Special Collections Division.

Catlin attempted to chronicle the Indian people of America and their lifeways in his North American Indian Portfolio. *This view depicts Choctaws near Fort Gibson, Oklahoma, to which they had been forced from their lands in Alabama and Mississippi. The ability of the people to preserve in their new home such customs as their ball-play is the underlying message of Catlin. In the game—the forerunner of lacrosse—players attempted to throw or carry a ball between goal posts, cradling the ball in webbed rackets while running or passing it to teammates.*

"Dog sledges of the Mandan Indians," aquatint by Karl Bodmer from *Reise in das innere Nord-America in den Jahren 1832 bis 1834* by Prince Maximilien Alexander Philipp von Wied-Neuwied (Coblenz, 1839-41). E165.W64 (RBSC neg. 1494A and LC-USZC4-4811). Rare Book and Special Collections Division.

Dogs were used by various Indian peoples in America for numerous functions. For the Dakota, the dog was used for hunting, dragging the travois, or as a packer. Among the village tribes, the dog was used for pulling the sled, for hunting, and for food during famine and for special ceremonies, and as a pack animal and guard dog. Bodmer's illustration, made in 1834, shows two dogs dragging a toboggan of the Mandan Indians along the frozen Missouri River.

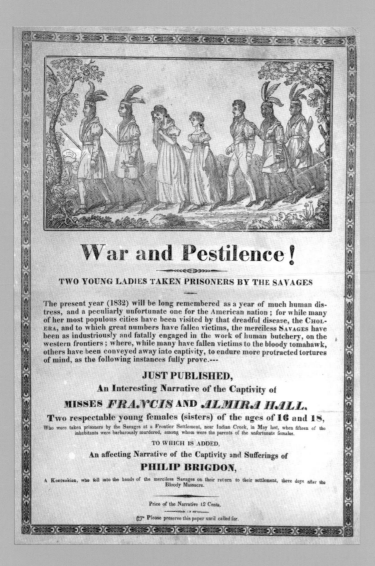

War and Pestilence!

TWO YOUNG LADIES TAKEN PRISONERS BY THE SAVAGES

The present year (1832) will be long remembered as a year of much human distress, and a peculiarly unfortunate one for the American nation ; for while many of her most populous cities have been visited by that dreadful disease, the CHOLERA, and to which great numbers have fallen victims, the merciless SAVAGES have been as industriously and fatally engaged in the work of human butchery, on the western frontiers ; where, while many have fallen victims to the bloody tomahawk, others have been conveyed away into captivity, to endure more protracted tortures of mind, as the following instances fully prove.---

JUST PUBLISHED,
An Interesting Narrative of the Captivity of
MISSES *FRANCIS* AND *ALMIRA HALL,*

Two respectable young females (sisters) of the ages of **16** and **18**,

Who were taken prisoners by the Savages at a Frontier Settlement, near Indian Creek, in May last, when fifteen of the inhabitants were barbarously murdered, among whom were the parents of the unfortunate females.

TO WHICH IS ADDED,
An affecting Narrative of the Captivity and Sufferings of
PHILIP BRIGDON,

A Kentuckian, who fell into the hands of the merciless Savages on their return to their settlement, three days after the Bloody Massacre.

Price of the Narrative 12 Cents.

☞ Please preserve this paper until called for.

Published MONTHLY.   Novel Series, NUMBER 71.

BEADLE'S DIME NOVELS

THE CHOICEST WORKS OF THE MOST POPULAR AUTHORS

ONE DIME

THE LOST TRAIL.

NEW YORK:
BEADLE AND COMPANY, 118 WILLIAM ST.
General Dime Book Publishers.

FAR LEFT: *War and Pestilence! Two young ladies taken prisoners by the savages . . . to which is added, an affecting narrative of the captivity and sufferings of Philip Bridgon,* [1832]. Broadside collection, portfolio 230, No. 9. Also in *Narrative of the capture* (New York, 1833). E83.83 .N24 (LC-USZ62-43902). Rare Book and Special Collections Division.

From the beginnings of European exploration and settlement in the sixteenth century through the end of the nineteenth century, Indian captivity was very much a historical reality for countless explorers and settlers living on the edge of the American frontier, and in one form or other it touched the fears of those for whom it was a possibility. While the authenticity of such narratives varied, they were appealing to early American audiences since they combined dramatic form, thrilling adventure, exotic context, and seemingly personal relevance. The account above is based on the reported captivity of Sylvia and Rachel Hall by Sac and Fox Indians in Illinois.

LEFT: Front cover of *The Lost Trail, Beadle's Dime Novels, Number 71* (New York: Beadle and Company, 18). Dime Novel Coll. (LC-USZ62-75779). Rare Book and Special Collections Division.

Covers like this for the popular melodramatic fiction of the late nineteenth century served as thrillers for readers who likely never had contact with Indian peoples. They also reinforced one of the Indian stereotypes that persisted for generations.

LEFT: "Massacre of the Whites by the Indians and Blacks in Florida. The above is intended to represent the horrid Massacre of the Whites in Florida, in December 1835, and January, February, March and April 1836, when near Four Hundred (including women and children) fell victims to the barbarity of the Negroes and Indians," woodcut from *Authentic narrative of the Seminole War* (Providence, 1836). E83.835 .A94 (LC-USZ62-366). Rare Book and Special Collections Division.

This depiction of anti-Indian sentiments published during the Second Seminole War illustrates in part the attack of Maj. Francis I. Dade and his contingent of approximately one hundred men by Seminoles and Blacks. Such accounts heightened concerns over racially motivated warfare.

INDIAN LAND FOR SALE

GET A HOME OF YOUR OWN ❋ EASY PAYMENTS

PERFECT TITLE ❋ POSSESSION WITHIN THIRTY DAYS

FINE LANDS IN THE WEST

IRRIGATED IRRIGABLE   GRAZING   AGRICULTURAL DRY FARMING

IN 1910 THE DEPARTMENT OF THE INTERIOR SOLD UNDER SEALED BIDS ALLOTTED INDIAN LAND AS FOLLOWS:

Location.	Acres.	Average Price per Acre.	Location.	Acres.	Average Price per Acre.
Colorado	5,211.21	$7.27	Oklahoma	34,664.00	$19.14
Idaho	17,013.00	24.85	Oregon	1,020.00	15.43
Kansas	1,684.50	33.45	South Dakota	120,445.00	16.53
Montana	11,034.00	9.86	Washington	4,879.00	41.37
Nebraska	5,641.00	36.65	Wisconsin	1,069.00	17.00
North Dakota	22,610.70	9.93	Wyoming	865.00	20.64

FOR THE YEAR 1911 IT IS ESTIMATED THAT **350,000** ACRES WILL BE OFFERED FOR SALE

For information as to the character of the land write for booklet, "INDIAN LANDS FOR SALE," to the Superintendent U. S. Indian School at any one of the following places:

CALIFORNIA: Hoopa. COLORADO: Ignacio. IDAHO: Lapwai. KANSAS: Horton. Nadeau.

MINNESOTA: Onigum. MONTANA: Crow Agency. NEBRASKA: Macy. Santee. Winnebago.

NORTH DAKOTA: Fort Totten. Fort Yates. OKLAHOMA: Anadarko. Cantonment. Colony. Darlington. Muskogee, Pawnee.

OKLAHOMA—Con. Sac and Fox Agency. Shawnee. Wyandotte. OREGON: Klamath Agency. Pendleton. Roseburg. Siletz.

SOUTH DAKOTA: Cheyenne Agency. Crow Creek. Greenwood. Lower Brule. Pine Ridge. Rosebud. Sisseton.

WASHINGTON: Fort Simcoe. Fort Spokane. Tekoa. Tulalip. WISCONSIN: Oneida.

WALTER L. FISHER,
Secretary of the Interior.

ROBERT G. VALENTINE,
Commissioner of Indian Affairs.

Indian Land For Sale. U.S. Dept. of Interior [Washington, 1911] Broadside Portfolio 240, no. 24, (RBSC neg). Rare Book and Special Collections Division.

A Department of the Interior advertisement of about 1911—with a photograph of Not Afraid of Pawnee, a Yankton Sioux—offers surplus Indian land for sale. A total of 150,000 acres of Indian land was sold in 1911 for $2,500,000, an average of $16 per acre.

ABOVE: "Danse des habitants de Californie à la mission San Francisco" from *Voyage pittoresque autour du monde, avec des portraits de sauvages d'Amérique, d'Asie, d'Afrique, et des iles du Grand ocean . . .* by Louis Choris (Paris: Firmín Didot, 1822); G420.K84 C5 (RBSC neg. 2945). Rare Book and Special Collections Division.

As part of the 1816 Russian von Kotzebue expedition, Choris visited the pueblo of San Francisco, where he found fifteen hundred Indians in the Spanish mission community. Although attending mass on Sunday, the Indian participants followed it with a ritual dance in the cemetery in front of the mission house, wearing traditional regalia.

RIGHT TOP: "A Chinook Lodge [Oregon Territory, 183-]," engraving by R. W. Dodson, from a sketch by Alfred Agate in volume 4 of *Narrative of the United States Exploring Expedition* by Charles Wilkes (Philadelphia, 1844). Q115.W6 v.1-5. (LC-USZ62-31244). Rare Book and Special Collections Division.

The United States Exploring Expedition of 1838-42 was led by Lt. Charles Wilkes and included a large scientific corps and three artists. After extensive exploration of the Pacific and Antarctic, their final effort was to make a survey of North America's Northwest coastline north of the Columbia River. One result was many drawings representing native lifestyles. The Chinook, who were the great traders of the region, built large semisubterranean cedar plank houses with gabled roofs. Sleeping platforms were arranged along the side walls.

RIGHT BOTTOM: "Intérieur d'une cabane de Caloches, Ile de Sitkha," from *Voyage autour du monde* by Fedor Petrovich Lütke (Paris, 1835–36). G420.L93, Rare Book and Special Collections Division for text volumes. Illustration in atlas volume; G2860.L8 1835 copy 2 Vault (LC-USZ62-115629). Geography and Map Division.

The Russian expedition under Captain Fedor P. Lütke explored the coasts of Kamchatka, Anadyr Gulf, Bering Strait and other places in the Pacific Ocean and the Sea of Okhotsk. Lütke circumnavigated the globe from 1826 to 1829; his publication brings to us some of the earliest images of the people of the far Northwest Coast of America.

LEFT: "Wedding Ceremony" by Steve Mopope in *Kiowa Indian Art: Watercolor Paintings in Color by the Indians of Oklahoma* by Oscar Brousse Jacobson (Nice, France: C. Szwedicki, 1929). E98.A7 J17 (LC-USZC4-4812). Rare Book and Special Collections Division.

Steve Mopope's brilliantly illuminated, stylized work is part of a larger, limited edition portfolio on Oklahoma Indian peoples. Mopope was one of the Kiowa Six, a group of artists who launched the renaissance of southern Plains painting after World War I with an emphasis on dance and elaborate and decorative costumes. Their work was among several efforts during the first half of the twentieth century to document and idealize Indian cultures at a time when much concern existed over their assumed loss.

LEFT BELOW: ". . . then upon one knee, uprising, Hiawatha aimed an arrow, . . . ," photogravure after Frederic Remington from *The song of Hiawatha* by Henry Wadsworth Longfellow (Boston and New York: Houghton, Mifflin and Company, 1891). PS2267.A1 1891 (LC-USZC4-4813). Rare Book and Special Collections Division.

Noted United States artists, such as Frederic Remington, repeatedly used the Indian peoples as a rich source for their work. Here, in contrast to his well-known scenes of Indian/white conflict, Remington illustrates Longfellow's famous work memorializing past glories of a declining culture.

RIGHT: "Tah-Col-O-Quoit," hand-colored engraving from *History of the Indian Tribes of North America* by Thomas Loraine McKenney and James Hall (Philadelphia: E.C. Biddle, 1836-44). E77.M13 (LC-USZC4-4814) Rare Book and Special Collections Division.

McKenney and Hall's work provides an interesting description of the migrations of the Sauk (or Sac), to which the warrior Tah-Col-O-Quoit belonged. The Sac settled originally along the St. Lawrence River, near the Atlantic but they were driven progressively toward the Great Lakes by the French and other Indian peoples. They waged war with the Iroquois, collided with the Wyandot on the southern shore of Lake Erie, allied with the Fox on Lake Michigan, and ultimately, in the time of McKenney and Hall, had reached the Rock River area, in Illinois. Tah-Col-O-Quoit (Rising Cloud) was a member of the 1824 Sac and Fox delegation to Washington. His portrait was painted by Charles Bird King.

MANUSCRIPT DIVISION

INTRODUCTION

The Manuscript Division's holdings of more than fifty million items in eleven thousand collections document all aspects of American history and culture and include some of the nation's greatest manuscript treasures. Represented are the papers of twenty-three of the presidents of the United States, their cabinet members, many of their colleagues and adversaries in the Senate and House of Representatives, members of the Supreme Court and federal judiciary, military officers and diplomats, artists and writers, scientists and inventors, and other prominent Americans, as well as records of organizations whose existence reflects aspects of our country's evolution. Many of these collections reveal individuals' private lives in addition to professional or political careers, suggesting how their origins, family relationships, personal experiences, motivations, prejudices, and humor affected their public behavior and activities.

Although several hundred divisional collections focus on Native Americans and document their role in the creation and development of the United States, only rarely does one find in the extant record a manuscript or a document originating in the hand of an American Indian. The predominant viewpoint expressed is that of non-Indians, including colonialists, military officers, missionaries, administrators, politicians, or public officials, many of whom actively established and supported the long-term policies that have defined relations between America's governments and North American Indians. The significance of the manuscripts lies in their evidentiary value, that is they are the primary sources upon which the study of the past is based. Without them we would be largely unable to understand the actions of individuals and evaluate their accomplishments within the larger context of the history of the United States. Types of manuscripts included are letters, diaries, journals, notebooks, logs, scrapbooks, subject files, photographs, legal and financial papers, and other materials in a variety of formats.

The division's holdings document the course of American Indian history before and following the appearance of European settlers in the Americas down to the present. Narratives and letters of early missionaries speak of their attempts to evangelize the Indian nations of North and South America, and constitute some of the earliest materials informing us of the cultural and political interaction of complex and highly ordered societies. For example, the substantial records of the Russian Orthodox Greek Catholic Church in Alaska chart its earliest efforts to convert and Russify the native populations of that region: its records (in Russian) of vital statistics, kept by clergy who adopted the dual roles of ecclesiastic and civil servant, have long been appreciated by descendants who wish to discover the date of birth, death, or marriage of an indigenous Alaskan ancestor.

In their desire to communicate with Indian tribes, many missionaries studied Indian languages and at times produced prayer books and bibles in these languages. For example, a Micmac prayer book devised by a French missionary, Father Chrestien LeClerq, who lived among the Micmac in the 1670s, is composed of hieroglyphic characters. However, the Division's richest collection of vocabularies of North American Indian languages—largely those of the Indian peoples of California—was formed by naturalist, ethnologist, and linguist Clinton Hart Merriam.

In addition to missionary accounts, the papers of explorers, fur traders, pioneers, and other frontiersmen, as well as military officers and colonial leaders, document areas of Indian life in pre-Revolutionary America. Printer and pub-

lisher Peter Force amassed a monumental collection of original manuscripts and transcriptions for publication in his *American Archives*, originally planned as a history of America to 1789. The collection, which was purchased for the Library of Congress in 1867, includes a wide range of materials relating to interaction with Indian peoples. Examples include documents on Anglo-Indian treaty negotiations; a formal appeal of the Mohegan Indians against the colony of Connecticut in 1746; and a letter to the Archbishop of Canterbury requesting missionaries, drafted for four sachems and dually inscribed in cursive and glyphic signatures, at Boston, Massachusetts, July 21, 1710. The Spanish-American experience with the Indian is also reflected in the Force collection.

Following the Revolutionary War, the history of American Indians is almost inextricably involved with the federal government's evolving Indian policy. The gradual termination of tribal land ownership over the years and the forced removal of entire tribes from their established lands in the east to settlements west of the Mississippi, and then on to reservations, is documented in the papers of presidents, congressmen, secretaries of the interior, Indian commissioners and agents, and military officers. Papers of such presidents as George Washington, Andrew Jackson, and William Henry Harrison; of military commanders Duncan McArthur, John McAllister Schofield, Philip Henry Sheridan, William Tecumseh Sherman, Hugh Lenox Scott, and many others; and of such Indian agents as George Croghan and Return Jonathan Meigs, reveal attitudes and policies of the country's leadership toward American Indians, and trace the course of military and diplomatic interaction as the rim of the frontier moved further westward.

Fortunately, there were some during the periods of expansion who recognized the value of recording the traditions, customs, and relations of societies whose members were forced to accept an approximation of their original cultures. Henry Rowe Schoolcraft, explorer, author, and ethnologist, was preeminent among these. His voluminous papers include correspondence; various Indian vocabularies; his *Algic Researches*; his "Muz-ze-ni-e-gun" and other manuscript magazines; and notes on Indian history, mythology, and language.

Many manuscripts of the late nineteenth and early twentieth centuries document attempts by the federal government to reform the administration of Indian affairs. The papers of secretaries of the interior Carl Schurz and Harold L. Ickes are especially useful as are those of members of congress, such as Clinton Presba Anderson, Henry Laurens Dawes, Robert M. La Follette, Sr., and Thomas J. Walsh, who attempted to change the legal and physical lot of American Indians. Among the congressional papers are those of Robert Latham Owen, one of the first two U.S. senators from Oklahoma and an enrolled Cherokee, a fiscal expert who co-authored the Federal Reserve Act of 1913.

Finally, the division's voluminous judicial papers offer another rich area for research. The papers of Associate Supreme Court Justice Smith Thompson, for example, include the manuscript of his memorable Supreme Court dissent in *Cherokee Nation* v. *Georgia* (1831). At issue was whether or not the Cherokee were to be considered a foreign nation, subject to repressive state laws. Chief Justice John Marshall denied that they were a foreign nation, whereas Thompson in his dissent argued that the Cherokee Indians had long been treated as a nation by the U.S. government. Thompson could not turn the mood of President Andrew Jackson, a long-time advocate of removing the Indians to land west of the Mississippi, nor of Congress, which had the year before enacted the Indian Removal Act.

USING THE COLLECTIONS

MANUSCRIPT READING ROOM

LOCATION: Madison Building, 1st floor, Room LM 101; telephone (202) 707-5387

HOURS: Monday through Saturday, 8:30 A.M. to 5:00 P.M.

ACCESS AND USE: No appointments necessary, except with staff historians. Because the Manuscript Division's holdings are rare, valuable, and irreplaceable, their use is limited primarily to patrons conducting serious research. Student access is generally limited to those engaged in graduate study. First-time researchers are required to read and sign a form agreeing that they will abide by the formal rules and regulations for using the reading room. All researchers must complete a registration card every two years and must present a Library of Congress photo I.D. card at the time of registration. Pencils, note cards, and note paper are provided. Only materials essential to research are allowed in the reading room. As a rule researchers are permitted to make copies of original manuscript material on the photocopiers in the reading room, with the exceptions of bound documents, fragile items, or collections that have restrictions on photoduplication.

The division's reference staff is available to provide information about the division's holdings and on related topics important to successful research, such as the nature of the copyright law (Title 17, United States Code) as it applies to unpublished manuscripts, restrictions on the use of certain materials, procedures for obtaining duplicates of documents through the Library's Photoduplication Service, and reference books and finding aids pertaining to manuscript sources.

The division also has several staff historians who specialize in particular eras or fields of American history. They are available for personal consultation with researchers, and their areas of expertise are: Colonial era and early American history to 1825; National period to

1861; Civil War and Reconstruction to 1900; Twentieth-century political history; African-American history; American literary history and culture; and the history of science and technology.

Access to the collections is through the on-line master record of manuscript collections. Researchers are also referred to one or more of the following general finding aids:

Master Record of Manuscript Collections

The basic guide to the division's holdings is the *Master Record of Manuscript Collections*, which consists of two parts. The first, *Master Record I*, lists collections alphabetically by the name of the individual or organization whose documents are collected and includes brief descriptions of the entries. *Master Record II* generally contains more detailed catalog descriptions of the collections including the types of material, the major topics represented, and the names of principal correspondents. It indexes the names and key terms found in the collection descriptions. Although there are printed volumes for *Master Record II* in the Manuscript Reading Room, they were last printed in mid-1986. Since this file is on-line as part of the MUMS (Multiple Use Marc System) database, researchers should consult it by computer for the most up-to-date information. Commands for information from the manuscript file should be qualified with "f=mss" preceded by a semicolon. For example, to search for information on the subject of Indians, the command should be "find s indians;f=mss."

Registers

Detailed finding guides or registers exist for virtually all of the division's larger collections. Approximately 1,800 are available for reader use in the reading room. Most include information about the provenance and administration of the collection, a scope and content note, an organizational or biographical history or chronology, a description of the various series, and a container list (or reel list if the collection, or portions of it, have been microfilmed).

Presidential Papers Indexes
(*see "Selected Collections" section*)

National Union Catalog of Manuscript Collections

The standard and most comprehensive guide to the holdings of manuscript repositories in the United States is the multi-volume National Union Catalog of Manuscript Collections (Washington, D.C.: Library of Congress, 1959–93), commonly known as *NUCMC*. Approximately 1,880 of the division's collections have been reported to *NUCMC* since it began publication. Beginning in 1988, the catalog information has been made available in a machine-readable format on RLIN (Research Libraries Information Network). The 1993 volume is the last printed catalog to be published; all future catalog information will be available only through RLIN or OCLC (Online Computer Library Center).

Numerous other helpful guides, indexes, and checklists to various collections have been compiled by the division and by others. Researchers should consult with the reference staff to determine the most efficient approach for their topics.

❑ SELECTED COLLECTIONS

This presentation of the Manuscript Division's rich resources is arranged initially by the division's principal representative collections containing Indian material, and then thematically:

- Force Collection
- Schoolcraft Papers
- Presidential Papers
- Congress and Indian policy
- Federal Judiciary
- Secretaries of the Interior
- Indian Commissioners, Agents, and Traders
- Indian Wars
- Explorers and Adventurers
- European Colonial Administrations
- Missions and Missionaries
- Indian Languages
- Historians, Anthropologists, Ethnologists, and Other Students

To be sure, such categories are somewhat arbitrary and overlapping. Andrew Jackson was not only the seventh President of the United States but also had a lengthy military career that affected many Indian lives during the War of 1812 and the Seminole Wars in Florida; Peter Force, a historian, gathered papers of military men; the administrative papers of colonial powers contain material related to missions, Indian wars, and other themes. But such categories can help a potential researcher better understand the sometimes overwhelming complexity of American Indian history as it is represented in the Manuscript Division.

This selection of the Manuscript Division's holdings of material relating to American Indians can only suggest their richness. While original items are stressed, there is also extensive photocopied material available for researchers. The researcher should be aware that the Manuscript Division has maintained a widespread acquisitions program with respect to manuscript collections in other American repositories and in foreign repositories and that these microfilmed collections are a very valuable resource for students of American Indian peoples. For instance, the Foreign Copying Program, begun in 1905, has brought to the Library several million pages of manuscripts copied from several hundred libraries in twenty-four foreign countries. Much of this material, especially from the colonial period, contains information about American Indians.

NOTE: Accompanying the official names of the collections listed below are the span dates—the dates of the first and last manuscripts in the collection—as well as the availability of a finding aid. Collections that have also been recorded on microfilm are cited accordingly.

Force Papers

The Peter Force Papers and Collection (span 1170–1961; finding aid)

The Library of Congress manuscript, rare book, and map Americana collections owe much to Peter Force, a printer who moved to Washington during the early nineteenth century. A student of American history, he amassed an enormous collection of printed and manuscript sources—dating chiefly from 1750 to 1868—for his multi-volume *American Archives — A Documentary History. . . .*

Those few collections within the Force Papers that are substantially about American Indian peoples will be noted in the relevant thematic sections of this chapter. Other Force material relating to them is scattered through the various collections he gathered together and may be divided into two parts—originals and transcripts. These collections are cataloged within the confines of an overall, comprehensive guide to the Force Collection, and many of them can be viewed on microfilm.

ORIGINALS

Andrews, Joseph Gardner. Papers (1795; microfilm)

The diary (Jan. 1–Dec. 31, 1795) kept by Andrews (b. 1768?) as an army surgeon at Fort Defiance, Ohio (Northwest Territory) includes numerous accounts of meetings with Indian groups.

Atkinson, Theodore. Papers (1724–54) and *Journal* (1727; transcript; both on microfilm)

An Indian commissioner, Atkinson (1697–1779) kept a journal of a journey (Jan. 15–May 14, 1724) through New York to Canada on a diplomatic mission to Governor Vaudreuil relating to problems with Indians and violations of the Treaty of Utrecht. Another diary, of Atkinson's journey (June 3–July 19, 1754) from New Hampshire to Albany, N.Y., to negotiate a treaty with the Six Nations, was annotated and published in 1907 by the Society of Colonial Wars (E186.3.N58). The Force Collection also contains a transcript of Atkinson's 1727 journal of a conference between Massachusetts and New Hampshire commissioners and the Norridgewock, Penobscot, and Wawenoc Indians.

Chalmers, George. Collection (1640–1825; microfilm)

The journals, papers, reports, and records collected by this historian (1742–1825) relate to his broad interest in British colonial administration and include a Mohegan appeal to the Assembly of Connecticut (1746) which can also be seen in *State Records Microfilm* for Connecticut in the Microform Reading Room section.

Force, Manning Ferguson. Papers (1678–1846; microfilm)

Letters, patents, commissions, pamphlets, maps, and other papers relating to French exploration of the Mississippi River collected by Manning Force (1824–99), a lawyer, army officer, and historian.

Jesuit Relations Collection (1632–1847; microfilm)

French original documents, English translations, and one 1847 pamphlet, E. B. O'Callaghan's "Jesuit Relations of Discoveries and Other Occurrences in Canada and the Northern and Western States of the Union, 1632–72," and narratives relating to Mississippi missions, missions at Detroit, drunkenness among Indians, war against the Iroquois, request from St. Louis for "gifts" for Indian nations, and Father Pierre Millet's captivity and treatment among the Iroquois.

Lincoln, William. Papers (ca. 1830; microfilm)

The notes, extracts, and other papers of lawyer and antiquarian Lincoln (1801–43) relate to the history, languages, and customs of the Indians of New England, as well as the Mohawk and Osage.

Penhallow, Samuel. Manuscript (1726; microfilm)

"History of the wars of New England with the Eastern Indians continued" is the account by Penhallow (1665–1726), a New Hampshire official, of a voyage to the Penobscot in Maine carrying supplies from Lieutenant Governor William Partridge. It mentions Penobscot and Pigwacket Indian Wars and the involvement of France and England, Pemaquid Fort, and a missionary to the Norridgewock.

Strange, Robert. Manuscript (no date)

Strange (1796–1854), lawyer and U.S. senator from North Carolina (1836–40), sent the two-volume manuscript of his novel entitled "Eoneguski, or the Cherokee Chief," to Peter Force who published it for private circulation in 1839. The novel describes Indian traditions in the region of Fayetteville, North Carolina, where Strange resided.

TRANSCRIPTS

Fleete, Henry. Journal (July 4, 1631–February 22, 1632; microfilm)

Account of a voyage to America by Fleete (fl. 1621–54), including "customs of those Indians

GATEWAYS

Federal Indian policy has passed through various identifiable phases or periods, as circumstances have changed and policymakers have responded by emphasizing different options. While the long-time goal was acquisition of Indian lands, the policy question was what to do about the Indians occupying the lands. In the nineteenth and early twentieth centuries, policymakers debated among three broad options: removal of Indians to other areas, segregation in enclaves, and assimilation. Of course, these options were not mutually exclusive. Later in the twentieth century the policy debate expanded to include the option of Indian tribal autonomy and self-development.

Among the periods generally identified by historians (although with some disagreements on dates) are the following eras:

- *early treatymaking and trade*, from ratification of the Constitution (1789) to about 1830;
- mass *removal* of tribes across the Mississippi River, from about 1830 to about 1850;
- concentration of tribes on *reservations*, from about 1850 to 1887;
- *allotment* of reservation lands and assimilation of individual Indians, from 1887 to about 1925 (or to 1933);
- *reform* and reorganization, the "Indian New Deal," from about 1925 (or 1933) to the late 1940s (or 1953);
- *termination* of federal-tribal relations, from the late 1940s (or 1953) to the early 1960s (or 1975); and
- tribal *self-determination*, from the mid-1960s (or 1975) to the present.

See other topical summaries for discussions of particular periods in federal Indian policy.

Since 1824 the Bureau of Indian Affairs (BIA)—called at various times, formally or informally, the Office, or Department, of Indian Affairs or the Indian Service—has been the key federal agency to carry out federal Indian policies and programs. Initially created by the Secretary of War, the BIA was statutorily authorized by Congress in 1834, two years after it authorized a commissioner of Indian affairs. In 1849 Congress moved the BIA from the Department of War to the new Department of the Interior. Congress finally assigned a major federal Indian program to an agency other than the BIA in 1954, when it moved health care programs from the BIA to a new Indian Health Service in the then Department of Health, Education and Welfare. In the 1969s and 1970s a number of other federal departments also added important new federal Indian programs. The BIA remains, however, the most comprehensive federal Indian agency. Indian affairs achieved greater salience within the Interior Department in 1977, when President Jimmy Carter created the position of assistant secretary of the interior—Indian affairs, with authority over the BIA and the commissioner.

WHERE TO LOOK: Library collections with materials relevant to federal Indian policy and the BIA include the Law Library, the Manuscript Division, the Microform Reading Room, the Local History and Genealogy Reading Room, the Rare Book and Special Collections Division, the Geography and Map Division, the Prints and Photographs Division, and the General Collections.

"Move On." Has the Native American no rights that the naturalized American is bound to expect?, wood engraving by Thomas Nast from *Harper's Weekly*, April 22, 1871. AP2.H32. LOT 4391-H (LC-USZ62-53856). Prints and Photographs Division and General Collections (Microform).

Nast's political cartoon advocating enfranchisement of Indians includes figures representing Irish, German, English, Scots, French, and Asian immigrants. They are shown voting, along with an African-American, while an Irish policeman indicates to an Indian that he is not wanted at the polls. While some Indian bands had been granted citizenship by Congress, debate continued over citizenship for all Indians, and over whether the Fourteenth Amendment (adopted in 1868) made Indians U.S. citizens. The cartoon's title, intentionally or not, captures one of the cardinal aims of nineteenth-century Indian policy.

living along the rivers and harbors of Maryland and Virginia."

Gates, Horatio. Papers (1777; microfilm)

Correspondence, orderly book, and reports on the Philadelphia and Saratoga campaigns by Gates (1728–1806), a Continental Army general, include information on Indian alliances. (The division also has a 20-reel microfilm collection of Gates's papers from the New-York Historical Society, 1726–1828).

Georgia Committee of Correspondence. Records (1762–71; microfilm)

Consists chiefly of letters from the Provincial Committee of Safety to colonial agent William Knox concerning frontier defense during the French and Indian War and negotiation with Creeks over land.

St. Clair, Arthur. Papers (1772–93; microfilm)

Post-Revolutionary War correspondence of this army officer (1736–1818), as governor of the Northwest Territory, concerns Indian affairs, fortifications, and trade on the Western frontier; also a letter (November 10, 1791) from Michael McDonough describing Saint Clair's November 4 defeat by an Indian alliance.

Scottow, Joshua. Journal (1677; microfilm)

Titled "Narrative of ye voyage to Pemaquid," the journal describes the participation by Scottow (1618–93) in negotiations and an abstract of a treaty with the Pemaquid.

South Carolina, Provincial Congress. Records (1770–76; microfilm)

Letters and reports concerning the Indian situation on South Carolina's western frontier.

Sprague, William Buell. Collection (1702–83; microfilm)

The collection of Sprague (1795–1876), a clergyman and author, includes correspondence (1755–74) to and from Sir William Johnson, superintendent of Indian affairs in the northern colonies.

Stevens, Phineas. Journals (1749 and 1752; microfilm)

Journals kept during two journeys to Canada by Stevens (1706–56) to negotiate the release of Massachusetts soldiers and civilians held prisoner by the French and their Indian allies.

Schoolcraft Papers

The Schoolcraft Papers are the division's leading collection on Indian matters. A published guide, *Henry Rowe Schoolcraft: A Register of His Papers In the Library of Congress*, goes into great detail on the contents.

Schoolcraft, Henry Rowe. Papers (1788–1906; finding aid; microfilm)

Schoolcraft (1793–1864) was the Indian agent at Sault Ste. Marie and Mackinac Island, superintendent for Indian affairs for Michigan (1836–41), leader of expeditions throughout the Great Lakes region, member of Michigan's legislative council, ethnologist studying and reporting on the Iroquois of New York State, and compiler and editor of the six-volume *Historical and Statistical Information Respecting the History, Condition, and Prospects of the Indian Tribes of the United States* (Philadelphia, 1851–57) for the Office of Indian Affairs. The general correspondence and the journals in the collection are rich sources of information about the working of an Indian agency at the time. Schoolcraft also interviewed American Indians on Mackinac Island between May and September 1837 about their personal and tribal histories and constructed vocabularies for the Ojibwa, Mandan, Costanoan, and

Cushna, a branch of the California Maidu. A separate section of the collection contains manuscripts of the many articles and speeches he wrote about American Indian peoples. There is also a brief manuscript of Indian maxims. Many of Schoolcraft's accounts of his visits to and observations among Indian tribes have been published, but his papers include considerable unpublished correspondence and other materials. Poems by Schoolcraft's first wife Jane Johnston Schoolcraft, who was part Chippewa, are included in the Poetry File.

Presidential Papers

The establishment of the Presidential Papers Program by Congress at the Library of Congress in 1957 has been, and continues to be, of permanent importance for the study of national culture. The program's purpose was to preserve and to make widely accessible presidential papers in the Library's collections. The presidents listed below are represented in the Manuscript Division by major groups of personal papers, whose span dates are noted in parentheses, and are recorded in finding aids which contain full writer-recipient indexes. All are on microfilm:

George Washington (1592–1937)
Thomas Jefferson (1606–1902)
James Madison (1751–1836)
James Monroe (1758–1839)
Andrew Jackson (1775–1860)
Martin Van Buren (1787–1910)
William Henry Harrison (1734–1939)
John Tyler (1691–1918)
James K. Polk (1775–1891)
Zachary Taylor (1814–1931)
Franklin Pierce (1820–69)
Abraham Lincoln (1774–1931)
Andrew Johnson (1814–1947)
Ulysses S. Grant (1843–1969)

James A. Garfield (1831–81)
Chester A. Arthur (1843–1960)
Grover Cleveland (1859–1945)
Benjamin Harrison (1787–1938)
William McKinley (1847–1901)
Theodore Roosevelt (1759–1920)
William Howard Taft (1784–1930)
Woodrow Wilson (1786–1957)
Calvin Coolidge (1915–32)

The papers of former presidents beginning with Herbert C. Hoover are in the custody of presidential libraries, administered by the National Archives and Records Administration. There is also a Rutherford B. Hayes Library in Fremont, Ohio; the John and John Quincy Adams papers are in the Massachusetts Historical Society; the Millard Fillmore Papers are in the Buffalo and Erie County Historical Society; the James Buchanan papers are in the Historical Society of Pennsylvania; and the Warren G. Harding papers are in the Ohio Historical Society. The Manuscript Division has microfilm copies of all of them.

Among those listed above, a few have particular relevance for this guide and are described in chronological order:

The *George Washington Papers* are important for his years as a military leader during the French and Indian War (1754–63) and the Revolution, as a Virginia commissioner to the Ohio Indians, as well as for his tenure as president during the post-Revolutionary frontier conflicts. One of the formative statutes in federal Indian policy, the 1790 Trade and Intercourse Act, was enacted during his first term.

The *Thomas Jefferson Papers* provide evidence of the third president's insatiable curiosity about almost everything, and the lives and customs of American Indian peoples were no exception. He, more than any other president, was interested in the culture of American Indians. He studied their languages and compiled vocabularies of them (they were stolen in 1809), excavated a burial mound, and collected native artifacts. American Indians visited his homes in his youth and adulthood, and his papers include an early drawing of burial mounds in Ohio Territory. Though he did not as president engage in any military activity against American Indian tribes, he nonetheless thought that they must be assimilated into white culture to survive or be inevitably forced to move west.

The *James Monroe Papers* show the fifth president's impact on American Indian policy from the Confederation Congress of the 1780s through the War of 1812 and the First Seminole Indian War. They also document the expansion of government economic and educational support of the Indians.

The *Andrew Jackson Papers* illustrate the seventh president's long public career and its unprecedented effects on American Indians' lives. Though his military career is best known by his repulse of the British at New Orleans during the War of 1812, Jackson (1767–1845) received that command through his decisive campaign against the Creeks culminating in the Battle of Horseshoe Bend (1814). Later, during the Seminole War, exceeding his order to intervene in the area, he precipitously invaded Florida, capturing the Spanish town of Pensacola (1818). After election as president in 1828, he made his long-held view that all Indian tribes should be moved west of the Mississippi River a centerpiece policy of his administration, a decision that profoundly affected the course of American Indian history.

The *William Henry Harrison Papers* consist of his correspondence and military papers, largely from the period 1796–1841, with special emphasis on Indian campaigns and treaties. A letter-book of 1812–13 relates to incidents of the War of 1812 on the western borders. Also of interest are reports of the February 3, 1813, Indian conference at Fort Feree, Ohio, the 1838 Tippecanoe Almanac, and speeches about Indians (1813, 1836).

The *Zachary Taylor Papers* cover his military career against Indians during the War of 1812 in Indiana and Illinois Territory. Later, he served during the Black Hawk War and followed that service with a stint during the Second Seminole War that led to a key U.S. military victory in the Battle of Okeechobee in 1837.

The *Theodore Roosevelt Papers* show that he was interested in Indian affairs and on at least one occasion attended the Lake Mohonk Conference concerned with the acculturation and legal protection of Indian groups. As president, he once sought the advice of photographer and journalist Charles F. Lummis, a harsh critic of federal Indian policy, in developing his own administration's Indian programs.

Congress and Indian Policy

Members of Congress and their staffs have significantly affected American Indians and American Indian history in four ways: as elected representatives from states with substantial Indian populations, through dealings with the Bureau of Indian Affairs and its predecessors, by service on either the Senate or House committees handling Indian affairs, and as persons passing legislation affecting American Indians. Following is a selection from more than 900 collections representing a range of these activities.

Anderson, Clinton Presba. Papers (1938–72; finding aid)
    Anderson (1895–1975) was a representative (1941–45) and senator (1949–73) from New Mexico. His administrative and legislative files

contain correspondence with constituents and the Department of the Interior regarding New Mexican Indian claims and affairs. Other files relate to the Pueblos, Klamath, Ute, and Fort Berthold Indians; the New Mexico Association of Indian Affairs; the Santa Fe Indian School; Blue Lake; the Santa Fe Bureau; Indian irrigation problems; and Mescalero Apache lumber and ranching operations.

Borah, William E. Papers (1905–40; finding aid)

The papers contain files marked Indian Affairs for each Congress from 1907 through 1940, and respectively for the tribes within the Idaho constituency of Senator Borah (1865–1940).

Cutting, Bronson Murray. Papers (1899–1950; finding aid)

Cutting (1888–1935), a United States senator from New Mexico from 1927 to 1935, kept a general correspondence file dealing with matters relating to constituents, many of whom were Native American. He had a special interest in the Mescalero Apache.

Dawes, Henry Laurens. Papers (1833–1933; finding aid)

Dawes (1816–1903) had a major impact on Indian affairs. The highlight of his long service as U.S. representative (1857–75) and senator (1875–93) from Massachusetts was the passage of one of the most significant pieces of legislation affecting American Indian people, the 1887 Dawes Severalty Act (or General Allotment Act—see Reservations, Agents, and Allotments gateway, pp. 156–157). Dawes also was chair of the Commission to Administer the Tribal Affairs of the Five Civilized Tribes (1893–1903) and his records for this period are valuable for understanding internal political factions, especially among the Choctaw, and the problems of freed blacks once owned by American Indians, who had settled on Indian land.

La Follette, Robert M., Sr. (1844–1925) section in the *La Follette Family Papers* (1844–1973; finding aid)

Congressman (1885–91), governor of Wisconsin (1901–5), and senator (1906–25), La Follette (1855–1925) was one of the strongest legislative supporters of Indian rights during the Progressive era and advocated allowing Indians greater control of their resources. His unusually rich files are arranged by tribe, including most prominently the Chippewa, the Crow, the Five Civilized Tribes, the Menominee, the Oneida, the Osage, and additionally the Tomah Indian School. The division also has microfilm of the Robert La Follette Sr. papers in the State Historical Society of Wisconsin.

Morgan, John Tyler. Papers (1840–1907; finding aid)

The wide ranging interest in Indian affairs of this Alabama senator (1824–1907) included his desire to see Oklahoma, New Mexico, and Washington territories, all areas with dense Native American population, achieve statehood.

Owen, Robert Latham. Papers (1920–41)

Owen (1856–1947), lawyer, banker, Indian agent to the Five Civilized Tribes, U.S. senator from Oklahoma (1907–25), and Cherokee Tribal Council member, was one of a small number of U.S. congressmen of Indian descent. A co-author of the Federal Reserve Act of 1913, his papers relate primarily to fiscal causes of depressions and arguments for government control of currency and credit.

Pittman, Key. Papers (1898–1951; finding aid)

In addition to his substantial office files relating to his work on the Senate Committee on Indian Affairs and correspondence with the Bureau of Indian Affairs, Key Pittman (1872–1940), senator from Nevada from 1913 to 1940, had a

GATEWAYS

Congress, under current law, is considered to have plenary power over federal Indian policy. In other words, statutes passed by Congress, and treaties ratified by the Senate, control what relationship, if any, the federal government will have with American Indian and Alaska Native tribes and villages. The major debates over Indian policy have eventually ended up in Congress. Most major shifts in Indian policy have been marked by congressional legislation, including the Indian Trade and Intercourse Act of 1790, the Indian Removal Act of 1830, the General Allotment Act of 1887, the Indian Reorganization Act of 1934, the termination resolution of 1953, and the Indian Self-Determination and Education Assistance Act of 1975. The major federal agencies dealing with Indians—currently the Bureau of Indian Affairs and the Indian Health Service—have been authorized by Congress.

Congress has exercised its control by passing statutes, ratifying some 370 treaties, approving agreements, appropriating funds, and exercising its oversight function. Treaties ratified by the Senate were the chief vehicle for relationships with individual tribes until 1871, when, at the House of Representatives' insistence, a proviso in the annual Indian appropriations bill forbade further negotiation of treaties with tribes. After that act, agreements between the federal government and tribes had to be approved by both houses.

To carry out its Indian policy functions, Congress has worked through a variety of committees (standing, select, special, joint) and subcommittees, although each house had a permanent committee on Indian affairs from the 1820s to 1947 (and, in the Senate, since 1984).

Indians have at times been members of Congress. The earliest members publicly identified as Indian were Kansas Representative and later Senator Charles Curtis (1893–1907 in the House,

1907–13 and 1915–29 in the Senate) and Oklahoma Senator Robert Latham Owen (1907–25). They have been followed by six more representatives and one additional senator.

WHERE TO LOOK: Congress's ongoing discussion of Indian policy can be found not only in floor debates (in the *Congressional Record* and its predecessors) but also in hearings, documents, prints, and reports, as well as in the personal papers of members of Congress. Library collections in which to follow this debate, or to determine the legislative history of a particular act, are the Law Library, the Manuscript Division, the Microform Reading Room, the Geography and Map Division, and the General Collections

ABOVE: *U.S. commissioners and delegations of Sioux chiefs visiting Washington, October 15, 1888.* LOT 12566 (LC-USZ62-92959). Prints and Photographs Division.

The commissioners shown here, standing with the Sioux chiefs on the steps of the Senate wing of the Capitol, were led by Richard H. Pratt (first row, fourth from right) of Carlisle Indian School. They had failed to gain Sioux acceptance of an earlier 1888 statute authorizing the break-up and diminution of the Great Sioux Reservation in Dakota Territory. The Sioux leaders had come to Washington to try to negotiate better terms from Congress and the secretary of the interior. Subsequently, a new and more generous offer enacted in 1889 gained grudging approval by the requisite three-quarters of eligible (i.e., adult male) Sioux voters.

OPPOSITE PAGE: Robert Latham Owen. Unknown photographer, c.1908. BIOG FILE. (LC-USZ62-115124). Prints and Photographs Division.

Owen (1856–1947), an enrolled Cherokee, was the second Indian elected to the U.S. Senate and one of the first two senators elected from Oklahoma. He served from 1907 to 1925. Lawyer, educator, publisher, Indian agent, and banker, Owen championed progressive causes in Congress, especially national monetary reform. See the description of his papers in the Manuscript Division chapter.

special interest in the Indian school at Elko and the Temoak bands of Western Shoshone.

Walsh, Thomas James. Papers (1910–34; finding aid)

Like Robert La Follette, Sr., and Key Pittman, Thomas Walsh (1859–1933), senator from Montana (1913–33), was a member of the Senate Committee on Indian Affairs. The papers contain information on American Indian affairs from 1901 until 1934, including correspondence, memoranda, and legislation about the openings of the Fort Peck Indian Reservation, the Crow Indian Reservation, the Blackfeet Reservation, as well as issues concerning the Fort Assiniboine Military Reservation, the sale of the lands of the Flathead Reservation, and the relief of the Crow Indians. Walsh's papers also contain those of John Edward Erickson, who finished out Walsh's term after his death in office.

Federal Judiciary

The division's collections include the nation's largest corpus of the papers of chief justices and associate justices of the U.S. Supreme Court, as well as of the many judges of the lower federal courts who played leading roles in American life and of lawyers who practiced in federal courts. Many of these justices and judges presided over major cases involving Indian claims and rights and their papers are likely to contribute significantly to research on these subjects. The Supreme Court, for example, has decided cases concerning almost every aspect of Indian life, including the determination of a tribe's existence and an individual's membership in a tribe.

CHIEF JUSTICES OF THE SUPREME COURT

Oliver Ellsworth (term of office: 1796–99)
John Marshall (1801–35)
Roger B. Taney (1836–64)
Salmon P. Chase (1864–73)

Morrison R. Waite (1874–88)
Melville Weston Fuller (1888–1910)
William Howard Taft (1921–30)
Charles Evans Hughes (1930–41)
Harlan Fiske Stone (1941–46)
Earl Warren (1953–69)

Associate justices are also well represented. For the Warren Court alone, the division holds the papers of Hugo L. Black, William O. Douglas, Felix Frankfurter, Harold H. Burton, Robert H. Jackson, William J. Brennan, Jr., Byron R. White, Thurgood Marshall, and Arthur J. Goldberg.

Of these, the very large collection of William O. Douglas may be singled out for evidence of support of the rights of North American Indians:

Douglas, William O. Papers (1801–1980; finding aid)

Douglas (1898–1980), who lived near Washington's Yakima Reservation as a boy, and who retained an association with it and with some of its residents, has been cited for the consistency of his record in Indian decisions. Over the period 1939–74 he was on the side of the Indian in thirty-nine of forty-seven decisions. In his Supreme Court files are a variety of materials bearing on such cases as *United States* v. *Santa Fe Railroad* (1941); *Northwestern Bands of Shoshone Indians* v. *United States* (1944); *Menominee Tribe of Indians* v. *United States* (1967); and *Mescalero Apache Tribe* v. *Jones, et al* (1972).

Secretaries of the Interior

The role of the secretary of the interior in Indian affairs has varied over time and has historically been, especially in the nineteenth century, more directly engaged than it is today. Though the federal-Indian relationship is complex and multifaceted, in general the Department of the Interior has been the major agency managing federal concerns with American Indians. Among these are the administration of public land held in trust for American Indians and other trust assets, and handling or sharing in government services, such as social welfare, education, health, local law enforcement, and the courts.

Fisher, Walter Lowrie. Papers (1879–1936; finding aid)

A rich source of information for his years as secretary of the interior between 1911 and 1913, the papers of Walter Fisher (1862–1935) relate particularly to the Oklahoma Indians.

Garfield, James Rudolph. Papers (1879–1950; finding aid)

Garfield (1865–1950), son of President James A. Garfield, was Theodore Roosevelt's appointee as secretary of the interior (1907–9). The papers include carefully kept diaries, correspondence, office files, and files of legal cases.

Ickes, Harold LeClair. Papers (1815–1969; finding aid; part on microfilm)

Ickes (1874–1952), who had a lifelong concern for the American Indian, was one of the most prominent secretaries of the interior and an outspoken conservationist who became involved in efforts to improve the economic and cultural status of tribes and protect them from aggressive exploitation. The papers cover his years as secretary of the interior (1933–46), during which time his support of John Collier, commissioner of Indian affairs, led to what some have termed "the Indian New Deal." Together they brought about the termination of the fifty-year-old allotment policy and pushed through Congress the Indian Reorganization Act of 1934.

Schurz, Carl. Papers (1842–1932; finding aid; microfilm)

The papers provide perhaps the earliest record of a secretary of the interior's attempt to root out corruption in the Bureau of Indian Affairs. In doing so, Schurz (1829–1906) dismissed the commissioner of Indian affairs and reorganized the agents, discharging many of them during his tenure between 1877 and 1881. He also resisted concerted attempts to transfer oversight of American Indians back to the War Department, where it had resided until 1849.

Indian Commissioners, Agents, and Traders

The subject of Indian agents frequently overlaps with topics falling under the division's Reference Index headings for Congress, the War Department, Department of the Interior, and Indian Wars. The following are representative of Manuscript Division holdings on this subject:

Bonaparte, Charles. Papers (1760–1921; finding aid)

A lawyer, civil service reformer, and U.S. attorney general (1906–9), Bonaparte (1851–1921) was a Theodore Roosevelt appointee to the U.S. Board of Indian Commissioners (1902–4), during which time he was charged with an investigation into abuses against Indians in Indian Territory. A box of documents is related to this investigation, as well as to later matters involving Indians between 1912–17.

Crittenden, John J. Papers (1782–1888; finding aid; microfilm)

A commissioner of Indian affairs as well as a U.S. attorney general and Kentucky senator and governor, Crittenden (1787–1863) left papers which include information on Cherokee treaties (1847), Seminole removal, Seneca reservation lands, Georgia's desire for Creek lands (1825), appointment of agents to treat with Sioux for lands (1850), and Kiowa and Comanche wars (1861).

Croghan, George. Papers (1768; finding aid; microfilm)

Part of the *Peter Force Collection*, the papers of Croghan (d. 1782), the principal deputy to the British government's superintendent for Indian affairs in the Northern district for fifteen years, contain the minutes of a 1768 conference between Croghan and the chiefs of the Ohio and western Indian tribes, including treaty negotiations with the Six Nations, Delaware, Shawnee, and Wyandot.

Ewing, George Washington. Papers (1829–1910)

This merchant, banker, and land speculator's family and business correspondence, account book, documents, and assembled printed material reveal his perception of Indian affairs and land speculation in the wide sweep of what is now Kansas, Indiana, Missouri, Illinois, and Wisconsin. Ewing (1804–66) and his brother acquired Indian lands as debt settlements by Shawnee and other northern tribes.

Franklin, Benjamin. Papers (1726–1907; finding aid; microfilm)

An index to *List of the Benjamin Franklin Papers in the Library of Congress*, compiled by Worthington C. Ford (1905) shows several entries for "Indians," including observations on treaty-making power of inhabitants of Pennsylvania, remarks on a plan for regulating Indian trade, remarks concerning the "savages" of North America, and 1787 letters to a Cherokee Indian "noblewoman" and a Cherokee chief.

Johnston, George. Papers (1824–27)

The collection consists of his 120-page "Journal of George Johnston in the North West" (August 29, 1824–May 16, 1827), written in the form of letters from posts on the Red River, from Sault Ste. Marie, Fond du Lac, Flameau, and La Pointe, while trading with Indian groups for the American Fur Company.

Kendall, Amos. Papers (1835–1909; part photocopies; microfilm)

Correspondence and other papers, chiefly 1835–80, relate primarily to the work of Kendall (1789–1869), attorney for the Cherokee Nation, on behalf of Cherokee claims and treaties.

McKee, John. Papers (ca. 1792–1825)

An Indian agent and congressman from Alabama, McKee (1771–1832) was appointed commissioner to the Cherokee in 1792 and two years later made temporary agent. In 1802 he became an agent to the Choctaw. During the Creek War he was active in persuading other tribes to remain at peace with the U.S. He helped negotiate the peace treaty with the Choctaw in 1816 and the Treaty of Dancing Rabbit Creek (1830). Although the McKee Papers were badly burned in a fire before they were donated to the Library, four containers of letters are legible.

Medill, William. Papers (1834–64)

Medill (ca. 1805–65) was commissioner of Indian affairs from 1845 to 1849. Some of his correspondence relates to Indian schools, removal of Indians from Wisconsin, Cherokee treaties, and other aspects of Indian relations.

Meigs, Return Jonathan I, II, and III in *Meigs Family Papers* (1772–1862; microfilm)

An agent to the Cherokee (1801–23), Return Jonathan Meigs I (1740–1823) was active in persuading other tribes to remain at peace during the Creek War. He was genuinely sympathetic to the Indians and worked hard to improve their lives through instruction and direction. The collection also includes papers of his son, Return Jonathan Meigs II (1764–1825), governor of Ohio, and correspondence of his grandson, Return Jonathan Meigs III (1801–91), a lawyer and attorney general of Tennessee, concerning primarily the removal of Creek from Alabama and Choctaw from Mississippi Territory (1831–34).

Morgan, George. Papers (1775–1822; part transcripts and photocopies; microfilm)

Morgan (1743–1810) was an agent to the Delaware tribe in what was called the Middle Department of the Colonies. As Indian agent during the Revolution, he dealt with the Delaware, Shawnee, Mingo, and Wyandot tribes in Virginia and Pennsylvania. Papers include a report (1789) on the settled territory of the Ohio and Mississippi Rivers, and letters from Hancock, Lafayette, and others concerning Indian affairs.

MICROFILM

Panton Leslie & Co. Papers (1780–1815; finding aid; 26 reels)

Operating in Florida from the late eighteenth through the mid-nineteenth centuries, this firm generated tens of thousands of documents relevant to its trade with the Cherokee, Chickasaw, Choctaw, Creek, Seminole, and other southeastern tribes. More than 8,000 documents in English and Spanish were selected from various collections for this microfilm edition.

Indian Rights Association Papers (1864–1973; finding aid; 136 reels)

Microfilms of originals in the Historical Society of Pennsylvania, Philadelphia. For forty years from its founding in 1882 in Philadelphia, the Indian Rights Association was the major non-governmental group to which Indians could turn for protection and support and was the primary source for non-Indians of information about Indian affairs. In addition to its purpose of protecting the interests and general welfare of the Indians, the IRA also initiated, supported, or opposed government legislation and policies designed to "civilize" the American Indian.

Indian Wars

Collections relating to military history are among the most important and numerous held by the Manuscript Division. The division's holdings contain material for the broad spectrum of wars that erupted between Indian peoples and whites, and perhaps those most often represented are the first two Seminole wars in Florida and the battles that flared across the Great Plains after the Civil War. The Seminole wars are especially well represented in the *James Monroe Papers* and *Andrew Jackson Papers (see the Presidential Papers section).*

The following collections are among those containing war-related materials:

Anderson, Robert. Papers (1819–1919; part photocopies; finding aid)

Anderson (1805–71) served in the U.S. Army during the Black Hawk War, Seminole wars, and the Cherokee removal.

Brown, Jacob Jennings. Papers (1812–28; microfilm)

As a major general in command in the North during the War of 1812, Brown (1775–1828) became interested in the Indians beyond matters of military strategy. His papers include "Memorandum of the Tribes of Indians in the North-West. . . . ," with various statistics on the tribes and their ways of life.

Burt, Elizabeth. Papers (1797–1917; microfilm)

Burt (1839–1936), the wife of an army officer, wrote letters to her daughter describing relations with Indian people, including Shoshone Chief Washakie, and military life at Forts Bidwell, Bridger, Laramie, D. A. Russell, Sanders, Washakie, Missoula, Smith, Omaha, and Robinson. The papers also contain her typescript autobiography, "An Army Wife's Forty Years in the Service, 1862–1902."

Carlton, Caleb Henry. Papers (1831–1954; finding aid)

Military papers, letters, and diaries from the army service of Carlton (1836–1923) in the 3rd, 7th, 8th, and 10th cavalries during the Plains Wars mention the Comanche, Wichita, Kiowa, Caddo, Cheyenne, Chemehuevi, Sioux, Snake, and Nez Perce; Schofield's attack on a Comanche camp; and the Indian leaders Quannah Parker, Satanta, and Dull Knife.

Carson, Christopher "Kit." Collection (1842–69)

The collection of papers of Carson (1809–68), famous trapper, guide, Indian agent, and colonel of the 1st New Mexico Volunteers, includes the headquarters letterbook for Carson's Navajo expedition in New Mexico, July 11, 1863–May 17, 1864. The expedition ended Navajo armed resistance to the United States.

Clinch, Duncan Lamont. Papers (1834–59)

Clinch (1787–1849) was commander of Fort King and other Florida fortifications at the start of the Second Seminole War (1835–42). An order book and a letterbook include his observations about alleged depredations committed by Seminoles and escaped slaves aligned with them.

Clinton, George and James. Collection (1776–91; microfilm)

James Clinton (1733–1812) was a Continental Army officer and public official. His 1779 orderly book mentions a treaty with the Six Nations, the relations of different tribes to the English and Americans, and orders given during the expedition against the Iroquois in New York.

Drennan, Daniel. Papers (1861–1904; part transcripts; finding aid)

Military secretary to General Philip Sheridan (1865–88), Drennan (1840–1905) left papers relating to Sheridan and other Civil War officers,

including two drafts of annual reports (1877 and 1883) submitted to the secretary of war by William T. Sherman as General of the Army, and giving much detail on the Nez Perce uprising and other Indian campaigns. Papers include news clippings of Sitting Bull, Geronimo, Custer, Lt. John G. Bourke, the 1870 massacre of Piegans in Montana, and many other Indian-related matters.

Flournoy, Thomas. Papers (1812–46; microfilm)

Correspondence, including copies of Flournoy's letters, is largely concerned with his command of the 7th Military District from headquarters at New Orleans during the War of 1812. In the South, the war principally involved combat with the Creek Indians. In 1820, Flournoy (1775–1857) was appointed U.S. commissioner to bring about a treaty with the Creek Indians of Georgia.

Godfrey, Edward Settle. Papers (1863–1933; finding aid)

Material relates to various Indian engagements in the West in which Godfrey (1843–1932) was involved, especially the battles of the Washita, Little Big Horn, and Bear Paw Mountains.

Hatch, John Porter. Papers (1843–68)

The papers consist primarily of letters written home by Hatch (1822–1901), an army officer, describing his service in campaigns against the Navajo and the Gila Apache in New Mexico and Texas between 1851 and 1861.

Heintzelman, Samuel Peter. Papers (1822–1904; finding aid; microfilm)

Correspondence, diaries, journals (1825–72), military papers, maps, and clippings cover this army officer's participation in the Seminole and Creek Wars in Florida and Georgia (1835–42) and his command of a fort among the Yuma Indians in the 1850s. Heintzelman (1805–80) developed a deep interest in Indian culture and his journals contain information especially about the Colorado River tribes.

Hitchcock, Ethan Allen. Papers (1810–73; finding aid)

The long military career of soldier and author Hitchcock (1798–1870), a grandson of Revolutionary patriot Ethan Allen, included Indian duty in the Northwest from 1837 to 1840. In 1841, he investigated the frauds against the Cherokee, resulting in a highly controversial report that the War Department tried to suppress. Correspondence and a journal are particularly relevant to his service in Florida, which involved campaigns against the Seminole and their removal west of the Mississippi. He also saw duty on the Louisiana frontier in 1845, in the Mexican War, and as commander of the Military Division of the Pacific.

Hughes, Robert Patterson. Papers (1865–1909)

Among the small collection of papers of Maj. Gen. Hughes (1839–1909) is an eight-page letter he wrote to his wife when he was a captain in the 18th Infantry and an aide-de-camp to Gen. Alfred H. Terry. Written on June 30, 1876, five days after the Battle of the Little Big Horn, it describes the massacre of Custer's command (Hughes was one of the first officers to reach the scene) and includes a hand-drawn map keyed to his remarks.

Jesup, Thomas Sidney. Papers (1789–1907; finding aid)

The official papers of this army quartermaster general relate to his service in the War of 1812, the Second Seminole War, and the Mexican War. As U.S. commanding general (1836–38) against the Seminole, Jesup (1788–1860) engineered the capture of Osceola. The correspondence in the

collection is largely between Jesup and his fellow army officers.

Kautz, August Valentine. Papers (1846–1945; finding aid)

Descriptive material accumulated by Kautz (1828–95), an army officer, about Oregon and Washington territories and the Indian nations there, includes information on the trial and execution of Nisqually Chief Leschi; diaries (1857–95); news clippings on Apache, Mohave, Hualapai, Warm Springs, Rogue River, Nisqually, Yakima, Puyallup, the Puget Sound War, Wounded Knee, and views on anglicizing Indian people.

McAdoo, William Gibbs. Papers (1786–1941; finding aid)

The collection of this secretary of the treasury (1913–18) and senator from California (1933–39), William Gibbs McAdoo (1863–1941), contains early family papers, among which are the letterbooks (1806–15) of Gen. John Floyd (1769–1855), who led Tennessee state troops in campaigns against the Creek, and the diaries, letterbooks, order books, and scrapbooks of Charles R. Floyd (1797–1845), a Marine officer who led Georgia state troops against the Cherokee. This portion of the collection is available only on microfilm.

McArthur, Duncan. Papers (1783–1848)

McArthur (1772–1839) was active in military and Indian affairs in the Northwest, beginning with campaigns against the Shawnee in 1790. The papers include military documents during his command of the Army of the Northwest (1814–15), when his task was to wrest influence with tribes of the old Northwest from the British. In 1816, he served as Indian treaty commissioner, resulting in cession of Indian lands in

WARFARE

Indian groups engaged in their own rivalries, battles, and ritualized contests before and after the arrival of Europeans. But it is the warfare between Indians and the new Americans that dominates the printed record. Many of the earliest contacts between North American Indians and European explorers were hostile, from an eleventh-century Norse attack on Northeast coast natives to Spanish battles in the Southeast and Southwest in the sixteenth century. Indeed, friction between Indians and North American colonists developed into war only fifteen years after the settlement of Jamestown, and continued intermittently until the late nineteenth century. Although the onset of conflicts may have been triggered by various events, the principal condition producing antagonism was the relentless American territorial expansion that threatened the Indian way of life.

The location of Indian-white wars in North America moved gradually, and unevenly, inward from the Atlantic Coast and northward from Mexico. In the seventeenth century, wars occurred mostly in eastern and northeastern North America near the coast, in areas of British and Dutch colonization, as well as in the Southwest, an area into which the Spanish empire had expanded. In the eighteenth century, before the American Revolution, the northeastern Indian-white wars generally occurred farther inland, reaching into the Great Lakes area, while new wars started in the Southeast. These eastern wars involved British and French colonists and traders. Indian-Spanish warfare, meanwhile, continued in the Southwest, and began in California. Indian-Russian warfare also started in Alaska in the eighteenth century. From the beginning of the American Revolution to 1850, the new nation's battles with Indians took place chiefly in the Northeast, Old Northwest, and Southeast, and also moved west of the Mississippi River. In the rest of the nineteenth century, the final Indian-U.S. wars mainly took place in the Pacific Northwest, the Southwest, and the Plains.

Indian resistance was never taken lightly and could be costly if done so. Indian tribes had intimate knowledge of their own lands and resources and often frustrated and prolonged government counter efforts. Geronimo, Osceola, and Chief Joseph and his co-leaders, for example, demonstrated leadership strategies that put their adversaries to considerable trouble and expense. And the outcome of the Battle of the Little Big Horn is just the most publicized example of Indian military successes that shocked the non-Indian public. The war conducted by Wampanoag leader King Philip (Metacomet) and his allies in 1675 and 1676 is considered to be proportionally the most costly American war in terms of human life and material losses. Colonial losses were estimated at 600 men, 1,200 houses burned, and 8,000 head of cattle lost. The Indian side of the ledger, however, bespeaks the ultimate outcome of continued conflicts with whites where battles might be won but the war lost—3,000 Indian men, women, and children were killed, and the Wampanoag nation was nearly obliterated.

WHERE TO LOOK: The General Collections through the Main Reading Room, and virtually every special collection.

Attack of the Seminoles on the Block House. Lithograph, 1837. PGA—Gray & James (A size). (LC-USZ62-11463, also LC-USZC4-2397, color). Prints and Photographs Division.

For seven years, from 1835 to 1842, the Seminole Indians of Florida fiercely resisted attempts to remove them from their homeland. The battle depicted in this lithograph took place at Lake Okeechobee on December 25, 1837. Zachary Taylor won promotion to brigadier general for his leadership in the fight. The Seminole wars are richly documented in collections in the Manuscript Division.

Ohio to the U.S., and later represented Ohio in congress (1823–25).

McCarthy, Michael. Papers (1865–1905; microfilm)

McCarthy (b. 1845) served continuously as a sergeant in Co. H of the 1st U.S. Cavalry from 1869 to 1879. His journal, memoir, and scrapbook cover his part in the Modoc War in California (including the capture of Captain Jack) and southern Oregon (1872–73), while stationed at Fort Harney, Oregon, and in the Nez Perce campaign, Idaho Territory. He was awarded the Congressional Medal of Honor for his actions at the Battle of White Bird Canyon, June 17, 1877.

Nash, Edwin R. Diary (August 3–September 26, 1865)

Nash's diary describes a two-month period when, as a member of the Powder River Expedition, he led Omaha Indians against Dakotas.

Pershing, John Joseph. Papers (1882–1971; finding aid; microfilm in part)

The papers of Pershing (1860–1948) contain materials relating to his early career with the 6th Cavalry during the 1886–90 Apache campaigns in Arizona and New Mexico; his participation in the Sioux campaigns in South Dakota (1890–91); and his role in the round-up of Cree Indians for deportation to Canada.

Pratt, Richard Henry. Papers (1862–1964; part transcript)

Pratt (1840–1924) was an army officer in wars against the Kiowa, Comanche, Cheyenne, and Arapaho, and commanded Tonkawa scouts in Texas and Indian scouts in Oklahoma. He was ordered to accompany Kiowa prisoners to Fort Marion, Florida, and became interested in educating them. Pratt's interest led to a seminal role in the development of Indian education. He was an organizer of the Indian education department at Hampton Institute, Va., and founder and su-perintendent of Carlisle Indian School. The collection includes his manuscript autobiography and typewritten copies of his military record and Civil War diary (the originals of which are at Yale University, together with his Carlisle Indian School papers).

Reid, John. Papers (1802–42)

Reid (1784–1816) served as Andrew Jackson's aide-de-camp in the War of 1812, involving campaigns against the Creek and at New Orleans. Letters written to family members almost weekly relate in full the events of that time (1813–16). Reid was co-author of *Life of Andrew Jackson, Major General in the Service of the United States*, 1817.

Rhodes, Charles Dudley. Papers (1885–1940)

A typescript copy of his journal, "Diary Notes of a Soldier" (1885–1919), relate particularly to the service of Rhodes (1865–1948) as a 6th Cavalry officer during the 1890 Brulé Sioux (or Pine Ridge) War, involving the Ghost Dance.

Root, Elihu. Papers (1863–1937; finding aid)

Root (1845–1937) was Theodore Roosevelt's secretary of war (1899–1904). Army reports and correspondence (1890–95) deal with the 1890 U.S. attack on the Sioux at Wounded Knee.

Schofield, John McAllister. Papers (1837–1906; finding aid)
Sheridan, Philip Henry. Papers (1853–88; part transcripts; finding aid)
Sherman, William Tecumseh. Papers (1759–1897; part photocopies; finding aid; microfilm)

These three large collections chronicle the actions of successive commanders-in-chief of the "Army of the Frontier" following the Civil War when they oversaw the relocation of American Indians from their tribal lands on the Plains and in the Black Hills onto reservations. Both Sheridan (1831–88) and Schofield (1831–1906) also had substantial experience fighting Indians before the Civil War. Schofield was dispatched to Florida during the Second Seminole War; Sherman (1820–91) saw duty against the same tribe in that state during the 1840s; and Sheridan faced the Yakima in the Pacific Northwest.

Scott, Hugh Lenox. Papers (1845–1981; part photocopies; finding aid; partial microfilm)

The papers include details of this army officer's campaigns against the Sioux, Nez Perce, and Cheyenne between 1876 and 1883, including observations about Custer, Chief Joseph, and the Apache. Scott (1853–1934) also studied Plains Indian languages for the Army and the Smithsonian Institution (there are materials on Plains sign language and a grammar book of Dakota). He was a member of the Board of Indian Commissioners from 1919 to 1933.

White, John Chester. Memoir (1861–1921)

An officer in the 17th, 19th, and 21st Pennsylvania Volunteers and the 11th U.S. Infantry, White's memoir includes comments on the conduct of Indian soldiers during the Civil War and on the western frontier.

Explorers and Adventurers

The division holds several collections that describe the experiences of Euro-American explorers through country occupied by Indian tribes before and after they were confined to reservations.

Beale, Edward Fitzgerald section in *Beale Family Papers* (1801–1957; finding aid)

E. F. Beale (1822–93) was appointed general superintendent of Indian affairs for California and Nevada by President Fillmore in 1852. His 1858 journal relates to a survey through Indian country for a wagon road from Arkansas to the Colorado River.

Chittenden, Newton H. Papers (1873–1920)

More of an adventurer than an explorer, Chittenden's scrapbooks record his travels across the continent in 1884, 1888, and 1889. He traveled 3,400 miles on burro and foot through the Southwest, Northwest Coast, and Central Plains. The collection includes descriptions and hand-drawn copies of Indian rock paintings; a photo album of Indian tribes from the Southwest and California (Yuma, Cahuilla, and Hopi); photographs of Northwest Coast artifacts Chittenden collected; and general Plains pictures.

Freeman, Thomas. Collection (1806–73; finding aid; microfilm)

This small segment of the *Peter Force Collection* contains a 141-page manuscript entitled "An Account of the Red River, in Louisiana, drawn up from the returns of Messrs. Freeman and Custis to the War Office of the U.S. who explored the same, in the year 1806." The report was published very early in the nineteenth century (there is a copy in the Rare Book and Special Collections Division). In 1804, Jefferson commissioned Freeman (d. 1821) and Peter Custis to explore what would soon be part of the Louisiana Purchase. During their voyage, they classified and described the flora and fauna, and visited the largest settlement of the Caddo Indians and the Coushatta Village.

Ingraham, Joseph. Journal (1790–92; microfilm)

Ingraham (1762–1800) was a navigator, trader, and explorer whose 208-page journal describes a voyage of the brigantine *Hope* from Boston to the Sandwich Islands (Hawaii), stopping on the Northwest Coast. It includes descriptions and color illustrations of Indians.

Lander, Frederick West. Papers (1836–94; finding aid; microfilm)

Printed and manuscript material represents the efforts of Lander (1821–62), chief civil engineer for the Northern Pacific Railroad, to find an alternate route to the Oregon Trail and his consequent negotiations with the Paiute led by Chief Winnemucca, especially when he acted as special agent for Indians along the Honey Lake Wagon Road in 1858 and 1859.

McClellan, George B. Papers (1823–98; finding aid; microfilm)

The voluminous papers of army officer McClellan (1826–85) include diaries, correspondence, reports, military papers, and field and engineering notebooks relating to his participation in two expeditions in which he encountered Indians: the 1851 Red River Expedition and the 1853–54 Pacific Railway Survey in Washington Territory. Of particular interest is McClellan's manuscript report "The Indian Inhabitants of Washington Territory," which contains appendices and a Comanche alphabet.

Nicollet, Joseph Nicholas. Papers (1832–43; microfilm)

Nicollet (1786–1843) was a scientist and geographer who visited the upper Mississippi during the 1830s and compiled a variety of notes about the tribes of the region, including dictionaries and grammars of the Dakota and the Ojibwa. He also made observations about the Choctaw and the Osage. The papers include journals of Francis A. Chardon concerning his experiences at and around Fort Clark in the upper Missouri country among the Mandan and Gros Ventre.

Peale, Titian Ramsay. Journals (1819–42; microfilm)

Peale (1799–1885) was artist and assistant naturalist with the Stephen Long Expedition by steamboat down the Ohio and Mississippi Rivers and up the Missouri, during which he kept a journal (May 3–August 1, 1819). The collection also includes his 1838–42 journals when he was naturalist with the U.S. Exploring Expedition.

Volume 7 relates to Oregon and California, and includes references to encounters with Indians. The latter was published as *Overland Journey from Oregon to California*, G. Dawson, ed., 1957 (E856.E174 vol. 36); also Microform 84/128E; also as part of *Titian Ramsay Peale and His Journals of the Wilkes Expedition*, Jessie Poesch, ed., 1961 (Q11.P612 vol. 52, pp. 190–8.)

Talbot, Theodore. Papers (1837–67; microfilm)

Talbot's diary, "Notes of a Journey" (1843–44), kept on Frémont's second expedition, describes the route across Kansas and along the Oregon Trail. He encounters numerous Indian tribes and characterizes the Shawnee and Delaware as "remarkably brave and intelligent," and the Pawnee as ferocious. Talbot also touches briefly on the Sioux and the Shoshone.

Weber, Charles Henry. Journal (1859; part transcript)

Observations as he traveled between St. Louis, Missouri, and Fort Benton, Montana, via the Missouri and Yellowstone Rivers, May 28–August 16, 1859. Weber visited, and gave a literate and entertaining account of, a number of Pawnee, Omaha, Sioux, and other tribal settlements.

European Colonial Administrations

The Manuscript Division's coverage of the administration of Indian affairs during the Colonial period is particularly full. The Force Collection, which contains considerable material on the thirteen original colonies, is described earlier in this section. Collections describing Spanish colonial administration are strongly represented in original and copied material. Most likely to answer researchers' needs in this subject area, however, are the massive records copied from European archives and libraries through the Foreign Copying Program.

Connor, Jeanette M. Thurber. Papers (1565–1927; transcripts and photocopies)

Historian Connor (d. 1927) assembled one of the finest collections relating to the early Spanish history of Florida, including materials on Florida and Georgia Franciscan missions to Indians, the Timucua Indians, and the French in Florida. It includes photocopies and transcripts of documents from Spanish, French, and English repositories.

East Florida Papers (1737–1858; finding aid; microfilm)

When Spain ceded all of Florida to the United States in 1821, the treaty brought these Spanish colonial papers into American hands. These Spanish-language diplomatic, military, economic, judicial, legal, and administrative archives of the colonial government of East Florida are primarily for the period of its second occupation, 1783–1821, and include orders and decrees, censuses, and other vital records. Relations with the Indians loom large in these records.

Lowery, Woodbury. Collection (1522–1803; transcripts)

Lowery (1853–1906) copied material from the Spanish Archives relating to Spanish settlements, primarily in Florida, but also in California, Louisiana, New Mexico, and Texas, the subject of his *The Spanish Settlements Within the Present Limits of the United States* (New York: G. P. Putnam's Sons, 1905); F314.L91

Russian Orthodox Greek Catholic Church in Alaska. Records
(*see Missions and Missionaries*)

Woodbury, Levi. Papers (1668–1897)

Woodbury (1789–1851) was a governor of New Hampshire, U.S. senator, and Supreme Court justice, whose Miscellaneous Papers Series include an autograph album containing two treaties (1714 and 1717) made in New Hampshire with New England nations, including the Amassacontoag (Amaseconti), Kennebec, Narakamigock (Rocameca), Norridgewock, Penacook, Penobscot, Pigwacket, and Saco. This series also contains the 1668 will of Pomantaquash, the "Black Sachem," as well as a 1687 Nipmuc land deed.

MICROFILM

Spanish Archives of New Mexico (1621–1821; 22 reels)

These are the official records of Spanish central and local government, including census and court records. The originals are at the New Mexico Records Center and Archives, Santa Fe.

FOREIGN COPYING PROGRAM

Except for brief interruptions during the two World Wars, the Library's Foreign Copying Program has been carried on continuously since 1905. The result is a collection of reproductions—handwritten, photostatic, and microfilm—of several million manuscripts from archives and other collections throughout the world. These reproductions are especially rich for the Colonial period for manuscripts copied in Great Britain, Spain, and France, whose military and governmental activities in America often involved Native Americans. In general, most copying has been carried on in each country's principal national repositories: the British Library and the Public Records Office in Great Britain; the Bibliothèque Nationale and the Archives Nationales in France; and the Archivo Historico Nacional and the Archivo General de Indias in Spain.

Missions and Missionaries

Narratives and letters of early missionaries speak of their attempts to evangelize the Indian nations of North and South America and constitute some of the earliest materials informing us of the cultural and political interaction of two disparate societies. Missionaries were generally the first to attempt to write down and compile vocabularies for the languages of the tribes with whom they were interacting. While the Manuscript Division does not hold many collections of original material pertaining to missionary work, it does hold microfilm or transcripts for several major missionary collections in other institutions (see Microfilm).

Copway, George. Collection (1858)

A Chippewa chief, Methodist missionary, and author, Copway (1818–63) discusses 'civilization' of Indian nations, and the role of Congress in appropriating funds toward that end for education and similar programs in his letters. One letter is signed by eighteen Midwestern chiefs.

Post, Christian Frederick. Papers (1758–59; finding aid; microfilm)

Post (1710?–85), whose papers are in the *Peter Force Collection*, served as a Moravian lay missionary and an emissary of the Pennsylvania government to the Ohio Indians. The papers include contemporary copies of journals he kept while working among the Indians of the Ohio (July 15, 1758–October 25, 1759), as well as minutes of a conference in Philadelphia with the Cayuga Indians (February 8–9, 1759) and of an Indian conference at Fort Duquesne, Pittsburgh (October 24–25, 1759).

Russian Orthodox Greek Catholic Church in Alaska. Records (1733–1938; finding aid; microfilm)

These Russian-language records are the division's most important collection of original materials about missionary work with American Indians. Although primarily ecclesiastical, they encompass the broader life of the various Aleut, Eskimo, and Tlingit Indian communities in the vast area of Alaska under the Church's jurisdiction. The priests who compiled the records not only served their church but also acted as agents of the Russian Imperial government and assisted the Russian-American Company, which had a monopoly on trade in the area. In order to convert the natives and establish bilingual schools the priests worked diligently to learn the native dialects. The records contain translations of Christian texts, dictionaries, grammars, primers, and prayer books in native languages, as well as numerous statistical records of conversions and invaluable genealogical information, such as dates of births, deaths, and marriages, Native and Christian names, places of origin, and the like. Approximately two hundred photographs are also present in the records.

Smith, George Nelson. Papers (1835–79; microfilm)

Smith (b. 1807) was a Presbyterian minister, educator, and farmer who kept thirty-seven journals (1840–79) while performing missionary work among the Indians of southwestern Michigan.

Zuni Indian Mission. Records (1732–34; microfilm)

Three volumes in Spanish of events at Zuni pueblo in New Mexico contain lists of births, deaths, and marriages.

MICROFILM

American Board of Commissioners for Foreign Missions. Papers (Unit 6: Missions on the American Continents, 1811–1919; finding aid; 134 reels)

Reels 736 through 793 of Unit 6 cover missions to such tribes as the Cherokee, Pawnee, Choctaw, Sioux, Ojibwa, Stockbridge, Osage, Chickasaw, and Indians in Oregon.

American Home Missionary Society. Papers (1816–94; 385 reels)

Composed of Congregational, Presbyterian, Dutch Reformed, and Association Reformed churches, the society's papers contain some Indian material on missions to the Indian Territory, George Henry Atkinson's notes on the Indian nations of Oregon and Washington states, and the Oregon Indian wars.

American Indian Correspondence Collection (1833– 93; 35 reels)

Microfilms of originals in the Library of the Presbyterian Historical Society, Philadelphia, containing almost 14,000 letters from Presbyterian missions. The material discusses Indian religion, culture, relations with the U.S. government, and tribal factionalism. Tribes included are: Apache, Assiniboine, Blackfeet, Cherokee, Chickasaw, Chippewa, Choctaw, Creek, Crow, Dakota, Fox, Iowa, Kickapoo, Missouri, Mohawk, Navajo, Nez Perce, Omaha, Oto, Ottawa, Pawnee, Potawatomi, Pueblo, Sac, Santee, Seminole, Seneca, Shawnee, Shoshone, Sioux, Spokane, Teton Sioux (Lakota), Wea, Winnebago, Uinta Ute, Umatilla, Ute, and Zuni.

Missionary Society of Connecticut. Papers (1759– 1948; 20 reels)

Congregational Church of Connecticut's original records at Congregational House, Hartford, Conn., including those concerning an Indian mission project (1800–4) and later correspondence relating to tribes in Oklahoma Territory and the Southwest.

The Moravian Mission Among the Indians of North America (1739–1800; 40 reels)

The originals (mostly in German) in the Moravian Church Archives, Bethlehem, Pennsylvania, include missionaries' journals and diaries; word lists, dictionaries, and grammars (in Creek, Mohawk, Onondaga); sermons to children in Delaware; and the works of missionaries David Zeisberger and John Heckewelder. Contains material on the Cherokee, Chippewa, Creek, Delaware, Mohican, Nanticoke, Onondaga, and Shawnee from missions in Connecticut, Georgia, Indiana, New York, Ohio, Oklahoma, Ontario, and Pennsylvania.

The Manuscript Division also has an extensive collection of photostats of the Church archives in Germany regarding the Church in the U.S. (mostly in German script).

Santa Barbara Mission Collection (1768–1844)

Photocopies of originals in the Santa Barbara Mission Archives, California. Documents are in Spanish and relate primarily to Junipéro Serra, Indian missions, the "pacification" of the Apache, reductions, conversions, and the missions at San Xavier, San Ildefonso, San Juan, and Candelaria.

Company for the Propagacion of the Gospell in New England and the Parts Adjacent. Letterbook . . . (1688–1761; 1 reel) (formerly Society for . . .)

Original at University of Virginia includes letters to the Company commissioners in America concerning, among other things, the education of Indian children and the settlement of Indian people on their own lands.

FOREIGN COPYING PROGRAM

Among the records relating to missionary work copied in foreign repositories are the following:

Bolognetti, Cardinal Mario. Collection (1555– 1709)

Bressani, Francisco Giuseppe. Jesuit Relation (1659)

Church of England, Diocese of London. Archives of the Bishop of London at Fulham Palace (1629– 1829)

Church of England, Province of Canterbury. Manuscripts of the Archbishop of Canterbury at Lambeth Palace Library (1595–1864)

Münchner Jesuiten Kollegium. Correspondence (selections of letters from Jesuit missions in America)

Society for the Propagation of the Gospel in Foreign Parts Records (1701–1901)

GATEWAYS

More than two hundred different languages were spoken among tribes north of Mexico at the time of European contact. These languages, like those of Indo-European origin, can be grouped into larger families according to their linguistic similarities. Among these families are Algonquian, Athabaskan, Caddoan, Eskimo-Aleut, Iroquoian, Kiowa-Tanoan, Muskogean, Penutian, Salish, Siouan, and Uto-Aztecan. An Algonquian language like Shawnee is as different from the Athabaskan Navajo language as French is from Chinese. The need to communicate over such linguistic boundaries led to the development of sign language on the Plains and to the use of "trade languages," such as Chinook jargon along the Columbia River valley in the Northwest and the use of Comanche in the Southwest.

Within a linguistic family, some languages were so similar as to be essentially dialects. The language cluster (though not the "political" entity) Europeans called "Sioux" consists of Lakota (Teton), Dakota (Santee-Sisseton), and Nakota (Assiniboine and Stoney)—indicating the use of "L," "D," or "N," respectively, at a given position in a word that means the same thing in all three language groups. A further complication arises with Yankton and Yanktonai, both of which have some Dakota and some Nakota characteristics.

Tribal names in Euro-American documents reflect, in part, the east-to-west sequence in which many contacts were made. For example, the Algonquian-speaking people of the Great Lakes region referred to their traditional enemies to the west by the name of "nadessioux" (an Ottawa word for "those people" joined to the French plural suffix), from which we derive the collective name "Sioux." In recent years, communities have been asserting their own names for themselves—Tohono O'odham for Papago, Mesquakie for Fox, Quechan for Yuma, and so on.

Adding to the proliferation of names was the fact that Indian linguistic features were heard differently by various European groups. The same tribal name that was heard as "Chippewa" (voiceless, aspirated "ch" and "p") by English speakers, for example, was heard as "Ojibwa" (voiced, unaspirated "j" and "b") by the French.

In general, Indian languages north of Mexico were not written down nor did the people use the elaborate pictographs of the Mesoamerican region. Contemporary written forms derive basically from Euro-American phonetic transcriptions. Native people did, however, develop a variety of mnemonic devices and some syllabaries, the most famous of which is the Cherokee syllabary created around 1821 by Sequoyah.

Numerous tribes today are involved in language preservation and revival programs.

WHERE TO LOOK: The American Folklife Center, General Collections, the Rare Book and Special Collections, Manuscript, and Geography and Map Divisions, the Recorded Sound Reference Center of Motion Picture, Broadcasting and Recorded Sound Division, and the Law Library.

"Se-quo-yah," from *History of the Indian Tribes of North America* by Thomas L. McKenney (Philadelphia: E. C. Biddle, 1836–44). E77.M13 (LC-USZC4-4815; LC-USZ62-1292, black and white). Rare Book and Special Collections Division.

This is the only likeness of Sequoyah, inventor of the Cherokee syllabary to which he is pointing. Not literate in English or other European languages, Sequoyah devised his writing system using symbols that in some cases look like Roman letters. Each symbol, however, consists of a consonant, or consonant cluster, together with a vowel: that which looks like "A" for example, stands for the syllable "go," while "K" stands for "tso."

Indian Languages

Two collections lend support to the interest in Native American languages that has been referred to in other collections mentioned in this chapter (for example, see Henry Rowe Schoolcraft section and *Hugh Scott* in Indian Wars section).

Merriam, Clinton Hart. Papers (1873–1938; finding aid; partial microfilm)

The papers of this naturalist, zoologist, linguist, and ethnologist (1855–1942) contain 125 volumes of his journals (1873–1938), with indexes, and numerous sets of Indian vocabularies with accompanying large-scale manuscript maps showing the distribution of all known Indian tribes in California and Nevada. Among the languages included—not all from that region—are: Achumawi, Algonquian, Bannock, Cahuilla, Chemehuevi, Chimariko, Chinook, Choctaw, Chowchilla, Chumash, Cocopa, Crow, Ennesen (Salinan), Hualpi (Hualapai), Havasupai, Hupa, Kahto (Cahto), Kammei (Kamia), Karok, Klamath, Lolahnkok (northern Sinkyone), Luiseno, Maidu, Mattol (Mattole), Miwok, Mohave, Monache, Mono, Nekanni, Nisenan, Panamint, Papago, Pima, Pomo, Sahaptin, Salish, Seminole, Serrano, Shasta, Shoshone, Soolahtelukan (Wiyot), Tlohomtol (New River Shasta), Tolowa, Tsennahkennes (Wailaki), Tubatulabal, Washo, Wintu, Yokuts, Yuki, Yuma, and Yurok.

Townsend, John Kirk. Vocabularies (1835)

An ornithologist, Townsend (1809–51) collected vocabularies of languages that white traders and Indians used to communicate with each other in the Pacific Northwest, especially along the Columbia River to the Puget Sound, including the Carrier (Takelhé), Cayuse, Chinook, Kootenai, Nisqually, Nez Perce, Puyallup, Skaywamich (Skokomish), Suquamish, and Walla Walla. These vocabularies were not entirely from indigenous languages but rather combined local languages, English, and French.

MICROFILM

Gallatin, Albert. Papers (1783–1847; 46 reels)

Gallatin (1761–1849), secretary of the treasury under presidents Jefferson and Madison, and an ambassador and banker, published the first reasonably comprehensive classification of the American Indian languages of North America (1836) and a work on Indian vocabularies (1848) and founded the American Ethnological Society. The division also holds a small original collection of Gallatin's correspondence while secretary of the treasury (1801–14), including an 1826 letter to Thomas L. McKenney, commissioner of Indian affairs.

Historians, Anthropologists, Ethnologists, and Other Students

In addition to the Force, Schoolcraft, Merriam, and other papers, the Manuscript Division has acquired several collections of research papers and records amassed by historians, anthropologists, ethnologists, and others interested in aspects of American history related to Indian peoples.

Borglum, [John] Gutzon. Papers (1895–1960; finding aid)

Borglum (1867–1941), the sculptor who designed and sculpted the presidents' heads on Mount Rushmore, became an advocate for the struggling Oglala Sioux at the nearby Pine Ridge Reservation, South Dakota. He solicited aid, argued against further depletion of the buffalo, and worked to change the image of Indians. The papers of his brother, Solon Hannibal Borglum, also reveal an interest in Indian peoples.

Cline, Howard Francis. Papers (1608–1972; finding aid)

Among the papers of Cline (1915–72), a noted ethnohistorian who specialized in Mesoamerica, are materials on California Indian, Creek, Seminole, Apalachee, Yamassee, and Jicarilla Apache land claims and Spanish Indian policy.

Ghent, William James. Papers (1876–1942; finding aid)

Ghent (1866–1942) was an author and journalist whose papers contain the original diaries of Edward S. Godfrey and Holmes O. Paulding, participants in the Battle of the Little Big Horn, and files of clippings, notes, and printed material on many subjects, including Buffalo Bill, Custer, various forts, battles, and chiefs. Tribes mentioned are the Apache, Cherokee, Crow, Kaw, Nez Perce, Osage, and Sioux. Ghent also corresponded with Mrs. George Custer and twentieth century historian of the West Frederick S. Dellenbaugh.

McGee, William John. Papers (1822–1916; finding aid)

Voluminous letters and writings by W J (sic) McGee (1853–1912), a self-taught ethnologist and geologist, cover the period when he was ethnologist in charge of the Smithsonian's Bureau of American Ethnology (1893–1903) and in charge of the anthropological and historical exhibit of the Louisiana Purchase Exposition in St. Louis (1903–5), which is extensively documented.

Mead, Margaret. Papers and South Pacific Ethnographic Archives (1838–1987; finding aid)

Columbia University sponsored Margaret Mead (1901–78) in her studies of the Omaha Indians in Nebraska. A small section of this vast collection documents her investigations that eventually led to the writing of *The Changing Culture of an Indian Tribe*, 1969.

Price, Vincent. Papers (1883–1992; finding aid)

The papers include materials that document the abiding interest of actor Price (1911–93) in American Indian art as collector and member of the Indian Arts and Crafts Board of the Department of the Interior (1957–71) and the Institute of American Indian and Alaska Native Culture and Arts Development. In 1958, he also was a member of the Indian Art of America Committee.

Quinn, David B. Papers (1000–1988)

This contemporary historian's notes, compiled for more than twenty books on discovery and exploration of the Americas, forms an archive of the meeting of American Indian and European cultures.

Squier, Ephraim George. Papers (1841–88; finding aid; microfilm)

Part of the papers of this diplomat, archaeologist, anthropologist, and ethnologist (1821–88) reflect his interest in American Indian history. His correspondence, drawings, and diagrams relating to the Indians of the Mississippi Valley shed light on his research for *Ancient Monuments of the Mississippi Valley*, 1847, first publication of the new Smithsonian Institution.

MICROFILM

Boas, Franz. Papers (ca. 1858–1942; 44 reels)

Microfilm of the personal and professional correspondence, diaries, and family papers of the great anthropologist Boas (1858–1942) in the American Philosophical Society Library, Philadelphia. Materials cover anthropology and linguistics in the United States and the development of their study.

Draper, Lyman Copeland. Papers (1735–1890; 134 reels; finding aid)

Originals at the State Historical Society of Wisconsin of this monumental collection assembled by historian Draper (1815–91) on the trans-Allegheny frontier, encroachment on Indian lands, and on friendly and hostile Indian-white relations. Significant Indian-related components of Draper's collection include his Daniel Boone collection, "Border Forays" and "Frontier Wars" collections, the papers of scouts and Indian fighters Samuel Brady and Lewis Wetzel, and papers of Joseph Brant, George Rogers Clark, Thomas Forsyth, and Simon Kenton. Among nations prominently represented are the Catawba, Cherokee, Chickasaw, Chippewa, Choctaw, Creek, Delaware, Fox, Miami, Mohawk, Ottawa, Potawatomi, Seneca, and Shawnee.

Griffith, D. W. (David Wark). Papers (1897–1954; 36 reels)

Griffith (1875–1948) directed many films about Indians (a selection is listed in the Motion Picture, Broadcasting section). His original papers are at the Museum of Modern Art, New York.

Iroquois Indians: A Documentary History of the Diplomacy of the Six Nations and Their League (1665–1921; 50 reels)

A comprehensive collection of manuscript, archival, and published primary sources from widely scattered repositories dating from the mid-seventeenth century through the early nineteenth century, this microfilm is also a valuable aid for the study of many other tribes who interrelated with the Iroquois throughout this period.

Kroeber, Alfred Louis. Papers (1948, 1957)

Kroeber (1876–1960), famous for his study of Ishi, sole survivor of a small band of Yahi Indians, gave the manuscript drafts and corrected typescripts for two of his books to the Library: *Anthropology* (1948) and *Style and Civilizations* (1957). The remainder of his papers are at Berkeley.

U.S. Work Projects Administration Collection. Records (1627–1940)

These extensive transcriptions of records covering Utah history, including Mormon diaries, journals, autobiographies, life sketches, interviews, and local histories, as well as transcriptions of interviews with pioneer Utahans, are replete with references to Indians. Also, the records of the WPA's Folklore Project contain files on "Indian lore," state by state.

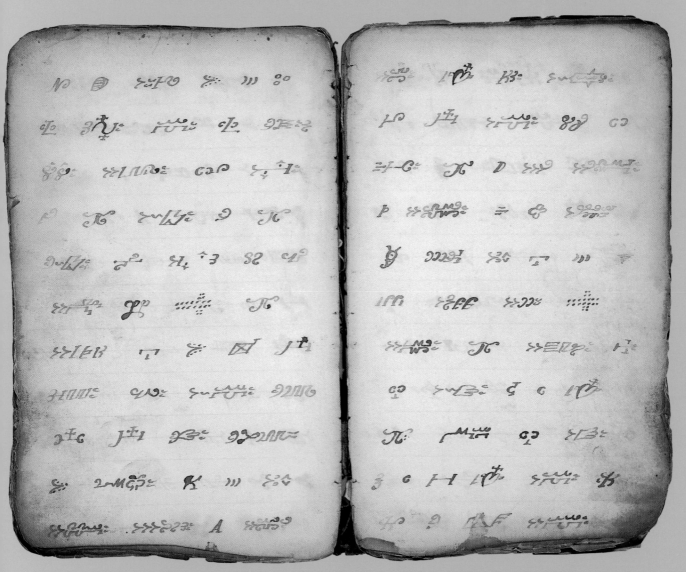

Pages from a Micmac prayer book, 17th century [?]. Miscellaneous Manuscripts Collection (LCMS-35956-156). Manuscript Division.

Although of uncertain provenance, this volume appears to be written in a system of symbols or hieroglyphic characters employed by Father Chrestien LeClercq. The Micmacs, associated primarily with the maritime provinces of Canada, were also found in adjacent areas of Maine. Conversion of the peoples of the Americas was considered to be central to the goal of bringing them into "civilized" society.

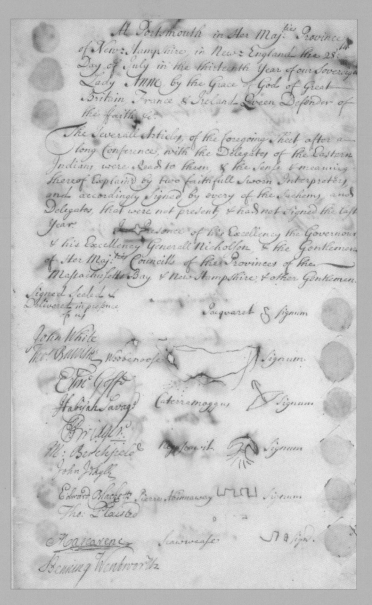

The opening paragraphs of a paper by Benjamin Franklin—"Remarks concerning the Savages of North America." It is not known when Franklin wrote this paper, but it was first published as a pamphlet in England in 1784. Benjamin Franklin Papers (LCMS-21451-21). Manuscript Division.

"Savages we call them, because their Manners differ from ours, which we think the Perfection of Civility. They think the same of theirs." Franklin, in contrasting the two civilizations, is very respectful of that of the Indian.

Indian treaty signed at Portsmouth, New Hampshire, July 28, 1714. Levi Woodbury Papers (LCMS-12930-S116 and C17). Manuscript Division.

The "Eastern Tribes," which had been allied with the French, submitted on July 13, 1713, following the end of Queen Anne's War. The delegates and sachems of the tribes met at Portsmouth a year later with representatives of the provinces of Massachusetts Bay and New Hampshire to sign this treaty. Pictographs and English and French names were used by the Indian signatories. The treaty brought temporary peace to the northern frontier, following several years of violent warfare.

John Reid to Betsy [Reid], Fort Williams, Alabama, written on April 1, 1814, during the course of Andrew Jackson's campaign against the Creek Indians in the War of 1812. John Reid Papers (LCMS-37507-1). Manuscript Division.

Reid, who was Jackson's aide-de-camp, tells his wife that on March 27, 1814, Jackson's forces had "gained the most signal victory that has ever been obtained over Indians," having destroyed the power of the Creek at the Battle of Horseshoe Bend on Alabama's Tallapoosa River. The Creek had occupied a well-fortified position and Jackson was forced to storm its walls. Reid remarked that the "enemy fought with the bravery of desperation; but at length were cut to pieces."

Draft in Jefferson's hand of his second Inaugural address, March 4, 1805. Thomas Jefferson Papers (LCMS-27748-276). Manuscript Division.

Jefferson, who had a deep interest in American Indians, and frequently commented upon them, devoted two long paragraphs to them in his second inaugural address. Although regarding Indians "with the commiseration their history inspires," he recognized that they had been "overwhelmed" and were being "driven before" the "stream of overflowing population from other regions . . . ." In notes for this address he spoke of promoting the "work of humanizing our citizens towards these people . . . ."

Letter from Andrew Jackson to his wife Rachel, April 8, 1818, describing warfare against the Indians in Florida. Andrew Jackson Papers (LCMS-27532-3). Manuscript Division.

Early in Andrew Jackson's 1818 invasion of Spanish Florida, during which he conducted a swift and decisive campaign against the Seminole Indians, he wrote to his wife Rachel describing the grisly side of such warfare. Thirty Indians had been killed, and the "miskasooky" towns of the Seminoles near Tallahassee destroyed. To Jackson these towns were "the modern Sodom and Gomorrow," in which "upwards of fifty fresh scalps from the infant to the aged matron" had been found.

Charles Henry Weber's journal entry of July 18, 1859. Charles Henry Weber Papers (LCMS-35956-147). Manuscript Division.

Weber's journal describes a trip to Fort Benton, Montana, via the Missouri and Yellowstone Rivers, on board the steamboat Spread Eagle, *May 28–August 16, 1859. The journey was undertaken to determine the limit of steamboat navigation on these rivers. Weber comments frequently on the Indians encountered along the way, and his touch is generally light and his reportage enthusiastic and interesting. In this entry he describes a horse-drawn travois used for "children and small packages."*

Photograph of Henry Rowe Schoolcraft. (LC-USZ62-34719). Prints and Photographs Division.

Draft of Henry Rowe Schoolcraft's letter of December 19, 1855, to Henry Wadsworth Longfellow. Henry Rowe Schoolcraft Papers (LCMS-39115-12), Manuscript Division.

Henry Wadsworth Longfellow, in a letter of December 14, 1855, to Henry Rowe Schoolcraft, had expressed his appreciation and gratitude for the work Schoolcraft had done to call attention to Indian legends and mythology, thereby contributing to the poet's The Song of Hiawatha. *Schoolcraft's letter in response mentions having "perused the poem with equal avidity & high gratification."*

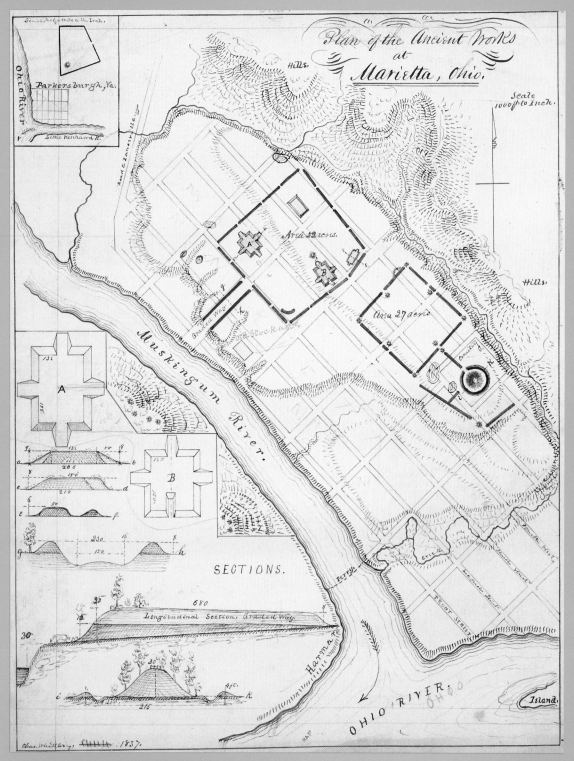

"Plan of the Ancient Works at Marietta, Ohio" by Charles Whittlesey, 1837. Ephraim George Squier Papers (LCMS-41087-3). Manuscript Division.

Ephraim George Squier (1821-88), journalist, diplomat, and archeologist, is renowned for his Ancient Monuments of the Mississippi Valley *(1847), the first volume to be published by the newly founded Smithsonian Institution. Included in his papers is this 1837 plan made by Charles Whittlesey (1808-86), geologist, topographical engineer, and student of ancient Indian culture.*

Portion of Battiste Good's "Winter Count." Pictograph water color roll backed with linen and mounted on panels, 1907. Miscellaneous Manuscripts Collection (LCMS-35956-159). Manuscript Division.

Battiste Good (1821–1908?) was a Brulé Dakota living at the Rosebud Agency, South Dakota, when he made this copy of a winter count in 1907. Winter counts were used to mark significant events. A circle of lodges represents a cycle of years, and individual years also depicted buffalo hunts, fights with neighboring tribes, famines, and other particular occurrences.

Page four of a letter of high Indian policy from Gen. William T. Sherman to Gen. Philip H. Sheridan, Headquarters, Army of the United States, Washington, D.C., August 12, 1876. Philip H. Sheridan Papers (LCMS-39768-1). Manuscript Division.

Less than two months after the Battle of The Little Big Horn two of the great commanders of the Civil War discuss the status of the Sioux Indians. Sherman was commanding general of the army at the time, and Sheridan headed the Division of the Missouri. The situation remained volatile, and Sherman, who had been in touch with President Grant, thought it advisable that "all the Sioux nation be kept under close military surveillance till they can again be trusted to civil agents."

Photograph of orchestra on St. Paul Island, c. 1890s. Records of the Russian Church in Alaska (LCMS-38695-27). Manuscript Division.

This small orchestra, made up of native (Aleut) and non-native members, is gathered on remote St. Paul Island, part of the Pribilof or Fur Seal Islands in the Bering Sea some three hundred miles from the Alaskan mainland. The island is only thirty-five square miles in area and has a population of well under one thousand.

Photograph of a "Japanese Drill" at Immaculate Conception Indian Boarding School, Stephan, South Dakota, 1899. Solon Borglum Papers (LCMS-35956-158). Manuscript Division.

The American sculptor, Solon Borglum, noted for his cowboy, horse, and Indian pieces, spent the summer of 1899 in South Dakota at the Crow-Creek Reservation (Fort Thompson) making studies for an Indian group he was planning. This unusual cross-cultural photograph appears in Borglum's papers without further explanation.

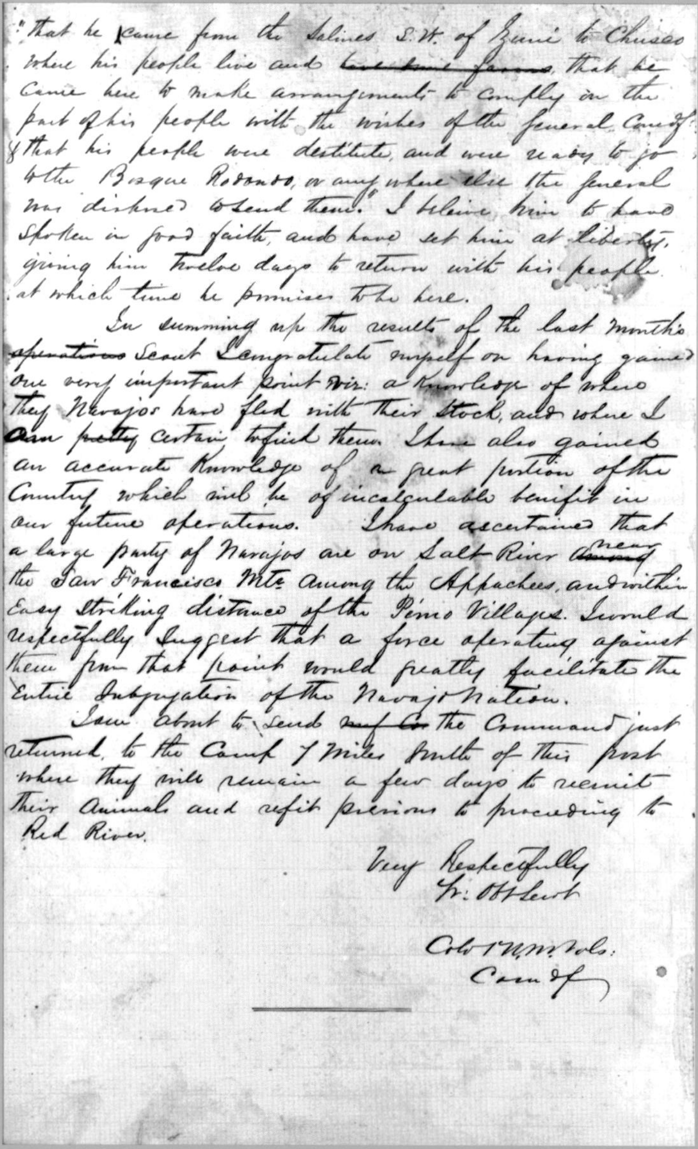

[Handwritten letter, left column — Col. Christopher "Kit" Carson's headquarters letterbook:]

". . . that he came from the Salines S.W. of Zuni to Chusca where his people live and . . . that he came here to make arrangements to comply on the part of his people with the wishes of the General Comdg. & that his people were destitute, and were ready to go to the Bosque Redondo, or any where else the General was disposed to send them." I believe him to have spoken in good faith, and have set him at liberty, giving him twelve days to return with his people, at which time he promises to be here.

In summing up the results of the last month's operations I congratulate myself on having gained one very important point viz: a knowledge of where they Navajos have fled with their Stock, and where I am pretty certain to find them. I have also gained an accurate Knowledge of a great portion of the Country which will be of incalculable benefit in our future operations. I have ascertained that a large party of Navajos are on Salt River near the San Francisco Mts. among the Apaches, and within Easy Striking distance of the Pimo Villages. I would respectfully Suggest that a force operating against them from that point would greatly facilitate the Entire Subjugation of the Navajo Nation.

I am about to Send the Command just returned, to the Camp 9 miles South of this post where they will remain a few days to recruit their Animals and refit previous to proceeding to Red River.

Very Respectfully
C. Carson
Col. 1 N.M. Vols.
Comdg

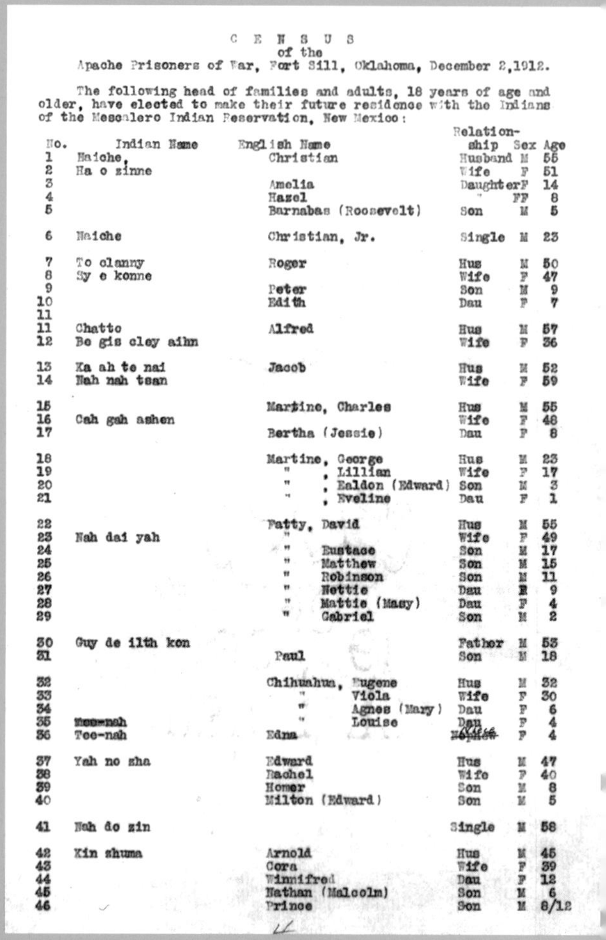

CENSUS
of the
Apache Prisoners of War, Fort Sill, Oklahoma, December 2, 1912.

The following head of families and adults, 18 years of age and older, have elected to make their future residence with the Indians of the Mescalero Indian Reservation, New Mexico:

No.	Indian Name	English Name	Relationship	Sex	Age
1	Naiche	Christian	Husband	M	55
2	Ha o zinne		Wife	F	51
3		Amelia	Daughter	F	14
4		Hazel		F	8
5		Barnabas (Roosevelt)	Son	M	5
6	Naiche	Christian, Jr.	Single	M	23
7	To olanny	Roger	Hus	M	50
8	Sy e konne		Wife	F	47
9		Peter	Son	M	9
10		Edith	Dau	F	7
11					
11	Chatto	Alfred	Hus	M	57
12	Be gis cley aihn		Wife	F	36
13	Ka ah te nai	Jacob	Hus	M	52
14	Nah nah tsan		Wife	F	59
15	Cah gah ashen	Martine, Charles	Hus	M	55
16			Wife	F	48
17		Bertha (Jessie)	Dau	F	8
18		Martine, George	Hus	M	23
19		", Lillian	Wife	F	17
20		", Baldon (Edward)	Son	M	3
21		", Eveline	Dau	F	1
22	Nah dai yah	Fatty, David	Hus	M	55
23			Wife	F	49
24		", Eustace	Son	M	17
25		", Matthew	Son	M	15
26		", Robinson	Son	M	11
27		", Nettie	Dau	F	9
28		", Mattie (Mary)	Dau	F	4
29		", Gabriel	Son	M	2
30	Guy de ilth kon		Father	M	53
31		Paul	Son	M	18
32		Chihuahua, Eugene	Hus	M	32
33		", Viola	Wife	F	30
34		", Agnes (Mary)	Dau	F	6
35	Mumwnah	", Louise	Dau	F	4
36	Tee-nah	Edna			
37	Yah no sha	Edward	Hus	M	47
38		Rachel	Wife	F	40
39		Homer	Son	M	8
40		Milton (Edward)	Son	M	5
41	Nah do zin		Single	M	58
42	Kin shuma	Arnold	Hus	M	45
43		Cora	Wife	F	39
44		Winnifred	Dau	F	12
45		Nathan (Malcolm)	Son	M	6
46		Prince	Son	M	8/12

Census of Apache prisoners of war held at Fort Sill, Oklahoma, December 2, 1912. Hugh L. Scott Papers (LCMS-39297-3). Manuscript Division.

The Apaches at Fort Sill had been incarcerated since the surrender of Geronimo in 1886. Gen. Hugh L. Scott was overseeing their release in 1912, and this census, which lists 264 individuals, was taken in order to give the prisoners an opportunity to decide whether to settle in Oklahoma or on the Mescalero Reservation in New Mexico. One of the Apaches, speaking through an interpreter, said: "For twenty-eight years I have been a prisoner of war and I have got married a prisoner of war and got children as prisoners of war and I do not understand for what reason I am for twenty eight years a prisoner of war . . . ."

Final page of a report of August 31, 1863, recorded in Col. Christopher ("Kit") Carson's headquarters letterbook (1863-64). Christopher Carson Papers (LCMS-35956). Manuscript Division.

Kit Carson, guide, Indian agent, and soldier, was serving as a colonel in the 1st New Mexico Volunteer Infantry during the Civil War. In 1863 he was charged with campaigning against the Mescalero Apache and Navajo. In writing of his preparations he spoke of having gained "a knowledge of where the Navajos have fled . . . and where I am certain to find them," and looked ahead to "the entire subjugation of the Navajo Nation."

Scrapbooks compiled by Newton H. Chittenden. Newton H. Chittenden Papers (LCMS-91413-1). Manuscript Division.

Newton H. Chittenden, adventurer and author, wandered throughout the Pacific Northwest and California during the latter years of the nineteenth century recording his observations of the Indians he encountered and on the artifacts of their past.

Browning, Montana.
February 23rd, 1915.

Honorable Franklin K. Lane,
Secretary of the Interior,
Washington, D.C.

Dear Sir:

  We, the Blackfeet Indians are now looking to you to help us a little more. You helped us
once when you took Agent McFatridge away from here.
Now we ask you to help us again, when you send us
a new Agent.

  Two years ago Chief Curly Bear and many
of our other Chiefs and Councilmen and head men went
to Washington and told you about our troubles. While
in your City we met a good white man, his name is
Martin J. Bentley, and we had a long talk with him.
What he said to us and what we said to him we have
told our people. We are thinking about that yet. We
know that the Great Spirit does not want us to set
down and let trouble catch us. He wants us to work
and push until we get what is right. We know that
when we work right we sleep well. The earth is our
mother. She holds a plenty for us all. We must find
the way to get it. We can't get it now in the old
Indian way. The game is gone. We must dig it out of
the ground. We think Mr. Bentley can show us how.
We have made a lot of noise about our bad Agents.
Send us this man because we know a good man when we
see him. We know him in a different way from the
White man's way. We may be mistaken about Mr. Bentley but if we are xiiii we will kick ourselves and
not kick you.

    Respectfully submitted,

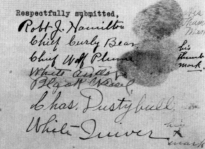

Robert J. Hamilton, et al., members of the Blackfeet tribe,
to Franklin K. Lane, Browning, Montana, February 23,
1915. Robert M. LaFollette Family Papers (LCMS-29165-3).
Manuscript Division.

*Senator Robert M. LaFollette had long service on the Sen-
ate's Indian Affairs Committee and his papers include a
very large "Indian Affairs File" that incorporates materials
from the Interior Department's Office of Indian Affairs. This
letter, from a "Blackfeet" folder, has an additional twelve
pages of signatures attached—278 signatures in all—many
with accompanying thumbprints.*

Mr. Chairman, the Gentlewoman from Arizona and members
Gentlemen of the Committee:

  It is gratifying to me to appear for the first time before the
House Committee on Indian Affairs in behalf of H.R. 6234, the Thomas-
Rogers Oklahoma Indian Welfare bill, the most important piece of Indian
legislation to come before Congress since the passage of the modified
Wheeler-Howard bill a year ago. My interest in Indian affairs has
extended over many years. It is based on personal acquaintance and
sympathy with many Indians and several Indian tribes. Few achievements
of the present Administration have given me more personal satisfaction
than the effort, successful so far but not completed, to bring about a
basic reorganization of federal Indian policy and the Indian Service.

  This reorganization, this effort to place the Indian on a sound
economic foundation, to make him self-supporting and to give him the
right of civic self-determination, is now under way everywhere, except
in Oklahoma, the state which contains almost one-third of the country's
total Indian population. The bill now before this committee proposes
to extend to the Oklahoma Indians the enlarged measure of federal protection, aid and guidance now available to all Indians outside of
Oklahoma.

  The members of this committee apparently are in full agreement on
the principal features of the bill. I have heard of no opposition to
the proposal to supply land to Oklahoma's landless Indians, to assist
in the organization of Indian cooperative groups for economic purposes,

(all carbons to Lear)

Retained copy of a letter from Harold L. Ickes to Robert F.
Jones, Washington, July 22, 1943. Harold L. Ickes Papers
(LCMS-27011-7). Manuscript Division.

*Harold L. Ickes, as secretary of the interior in the cabinet
of President Franklin D. Roosevelt, puts his well-known
spirit and temper on display in behalf of the American Indian. Deriding a speech made on the floor of the House of
Representatives by Congressman Robert F. Jones of Ohio,
as one of "labored facetiousness," Ickes went on to give a
succinct account of the Roosevelt administration's
beneficial treatment of the Indian.*

First page of Associate Justice William O. Douglas's draft of his dissenting opinion in *The Northwestern Bands of Shoshone Indians v. The United States.* October Term, 1944. William O. Douglas Papers (LCMS-18853-1). Manuscript Division.

The Northwestern Bands of Shoshone Indians were seeking to "recover from the United States damages estimated at fifteen million dollars for the taking of some fifteen million acres of the lands held by aboriginal or immemorial title." The opinion of the Court was that "no recovery may be had." In his dissent Justice Douglas alluded to an 1863 treaty and asserted that the negotiation of the treaty's provisions constituted "plain recognition by the United States that it was dealing with people who had the power to grant these rights . . . ." A note from Justice Felix Frankfurter to Douglas declared: "This is a spirited opinion reflecting the justice which the law here requires. I am glad to join it."

Indian schoolchildren visiting the Southern Plains Indian Museum in Anadarko, Oklahoma. Photograph, U.S. Department of the Interior, Indian Arts and Crafts Board. Copy in Vincent Price Papers (LCMS-36905-1). Manuscript Division.

Many of the items in the museum's exhibit were by members of the Comanche, Kiowa, Cheyenne, Arapahoe, Caddo, Wichita, and Delaware tribes. Vincent Price, who took an intense interest in Native American art, was a long-time member of the Interior Department's Indian Arts and Crafts Board.

THE LAW LIBRARY
OF CONGRESS

INTRODUCTION

Research in Indian law provides entree into a world of unique, complex, and fascinating legal issues. These issues may require knowledge of constitutional law, federal law, tribal law, state law, international treaties, or some combination of these. Constitutional, treaty, statutory, and regulatory language must be examined. Recourse to legislative history of various enactments may be a valuable asset in evaluating legislative intent.

In Indian law, areas of inquiry may range from taxes to criminal law, from Indian gaming to child custody, from environmental issues to tribal sovereignty, and beyond. Almost every area of legal specialization has its counterpart in Indian law. In addition, those working in American Indian legal studies must be conversant with the full range of historical, anthropological, and ethnological resources and possess skills which take them across disciplinary lines, often into waters that are difficult to chart. Broad scholarly perspectives are needed.

A few examples may be illustrative of the multi-faceted nature of the legal issues involved in the field of Indian law. A water rights dispute may necessitate an examination of Indian reserved water rights under *Winters* v. *United States*, 207 U.S. 564 (1908), which held that implicit in the creation of a reservation is the reservation of sufficient water to accomplish the purposes for which the reservation was created. To quantify Indian reserved water rights for a particular reservation, expert testimony may be necessary to determine the amount of water sufficient to irrigate all of the practicably irrigable acreage on the reservation. Resolution of such a dispute may necessitate federal litigation; or, under the McCarran Amendment, 43 U.S.C. § 666, Indian water rights may be among those addressed in a general state water adjudication. Alternatively, resolution of issues surrounding Indian reserved water rights may result in a negotiated settlement involving tribal, federal, state, and local parties. To become effective, such a settlement agreement may require ratification by federal legislation, or by both federal and state legislative action.

Similar complexity is reflected in questions regarding Indian hunting and fishing rights. Such disputes often arise in areas where tribal religious, subsistence, and commercial interests may be in competition for a limited resource with local commercial interests and a recreational hunting or fishing industry which may bring substantial income into state and local economies. Expert testimony with respect to the historical, religious, and economic factors involved may provide perspective and context. Such cases may require an examination of federal treaties with pertinent Indian tribes regarding on- and off-reservation hunting and fishing rights. Court interpretations of similar or identical treaty language may provide added illumination.

Federal litigation may be precipitated by a dispute over the applicability of federal, state, and tribal laws and regulations on fish and wildlife. A question may also arise as to whether the Endangered Species Act, 16 U.S.C. § 1531 *et seq.*, applies to a particular fact situation. If a tribal right to take fish or to hunt is established, historical, cultural, and ethnographic expertise may be required to determine what traditional methods of hunting or fishing may legally be used by tribal members today. Expert testimony as to fluctuations in the size of a fish or animal population may lead a federal court to take continuing jurisdiction over a matter for years, particularly where preservation of the species is at issue.

Even when treaty rights are established through litigation, questions may arise as to which tribes now extant are entitled to share the benefits of particular treaty rights as descen-

dants or successors in interest of the treaty signatory tribes. Generally treaty rights inure to the benefit of the tribe or tribes, and only derivatively to the individual members of that tribe. This issue becomes more complex if some of the modern descendants of the signatory tribes are not now federally recognized tribes. A question may then arise as to whether they may participate in those treaty rights.

Attorneys who specialize in American Indian legal issues today understand the complexity of this demanding branch of law and the depth of research that must be brought to it. Historians, anthropologists, archaeologists, and experts from other disciplines may be called upon to provide background in the litigation process. While historical documentation proceeds, a mass of pertinent federal laws must be located and assimilated. Consideration also must be given to state laws that affect the issues at hand as well as a growing panorama of tribal laws. Tribal laws are taking on more weight in U.S. courts today because of a change in philosophy regarding tribal autonomy and a shift in tribal relations with the federal government.

The collections of the Law Library of the Library of Congress afford researchers a wide array of resources with which to pursue Indian law issues. To begin to address such intricate issues, one may wish to start with an overview of the subject area. A number of hornbooks, treatises, and case books available in the Law Library Reading Room may provide an avenue into this area of the law. A law review article on the subject being explored can also provide illumination, and the Law Library's law reviews are legion.

Once a preliminary course is charted, the Law Library can offer a vast array of federal materials to further the legal inquiry. In addition to federal laws, both codified and uncodified, and treaties, comprehensive legislative history materials are available. These include the *Annals of Congress*, the *Register of Debates*, the *Congressional Globe*, the *Congressional Record*, committee reports and hearings, and House and Senate Journals. The earliest legislative materials may be accessed in the *American State Papers* which are included in the Law Library's microfilm collection. Some of the personal journals of the members of the early Congresses may also be found among the Law Library's resources.

A complete collection of federal trial and appellate court decisions is also part of the Law Library resources. In addition, the Law Library maintains a large collection of appellate and Supreme Court records and briefs. These can often stimulate ideas for persuasive approaches to particular issues and can act as springboards into fruitful lines of research to support those approaches.

If state materials are needed, current and historical state laws are available, as are reporters containing state case law. If early state treaties with Indian tribes are necessary, as in cases involving Eastern land claims, the arrival in the Law Library of *Early American Indian Documents: Treaties and Laws, 1607–1789* may prove to be a boon to research (see discussion under *Law Library General Collections—Colonial and Early American Materials*). If the Law Library's collections do not include state treaties or legislative history materials needed to pursue a particular area of inquiry, recourse to the general collections or to state legislative reference services may provide further information.

The Law Library's collection of tribal laws and constitutions is growing, although not yet exhaustive. Tribal laws and constitutions are playing an increasing role in today's complex Indian legal issues.

In some areas of Indian law study, international materials are also an integral part of the resources which must be examined. For example, a dispute over fishing or whaling in international waters may necessitate an examination of fishing or whaling treaties with Canada or other affected nations. A question regarding free passage rights or duty-free passage rights of tribes whose ancestral lands traverse the United States / Canada border may require an examination of Article III of the Jay Treaty of 1794 with the 1796 Explanatory Article, Article IX of the Treaty of Ghent of 1815, the Treaty of Spring Wells of 1815, 8 U.S.C. § 1359, and pertinent case law, as well as more recent American and Canadian laws and regulations, and tribal laws implementing those rights. In addition, the relationship of the federal government with the Pueblo Indian tribes originally stemmed, in part, from the Spanish and Mexican laws which defined the relationship that those governments had with the Pueblo Indian tribes prior to the acquisition of the lands they occupied by the United States under the Treaty of Guadalupe Hidalgo (1848).

The Law Library possesses a substantial collection of international treaties and bilateral agreements, as well as legal materials from many nations around the world. Its resources can provide the means to gain historical and legal perspectives upon such matters.

USING THE COLLECTIONS

LAW LIBRARY READING ROOM

LOCATION: Madison Building, 2nd floor, Room LM 201; telephone (202) 707-5079

HOURS: Monday, Wednesday and Thursday 8:30 A.M.–9:30 P.M.; Tuesday, Friday and Saturday 8:30 A.M.–5:00 P.M.

ACCESS AND USE: Closed Sunday except to Congress when in session. The Law Library book stacks are closed to the public. Requested materials must be brought to the reading room. Allow adequate time for this procedure. Bring photo identification with you. A staff of professional legal reference specialists will be available to assist you. Appointments are advised, and photo ID and pencils are required, for use of rare book material.

The resources of the Law Library of Congress, the largest law library in the world, are very rich in American Indian materials A reference staff assists readers in utilizing the collections, including federal, state, tribal, and international materials.

Catalogs

A researcher may use the author/title card catalog in the Law Library Reading Room (new card entries closed December 1980), or may utilize the Library's own on-line research tools. Both SCORPIO and MUMS services may be accessed through the Library of Congress Information System. These two services provide on-line searching capabilities within the Library of Congress Catalog. Computer terminals and instruction sheets are available in the Law Library Reading Room to enable researchers to determine what parts of the Law Library collections will be of greatest assistance to them.

Major Reference Works

When beginning research into an unfamiliar area of Indian law, an examination of major reference works may prove invaluable. The three most commonly used law texts are:

Felix S. Cohen's Handbook of Federal Indian Law. Charlottesville, Va.: Michie Bobbs-Merrill, 1982; KF8202.P75 1994

The first edition of this monumental work. printed in 1941, was written by Felix Cohen, Chairman of the Board of Appeals at the Department of the Interior. It represents the first comprehensive text addressing substantive laws, appropriation acts, and treaties affecting American Indians. The most recent edition of this text was published in 1982.

American Indian Law, Cases and Materials. R. N. Clinton, N. J. Newton, and M. E. Price. Charlottesville, Va.: Michie Co., 1991; KF8204.5.L38 1991

Cases and Materials on Federal Indian Law. David H. Getches, Charles F. Wilkinson, and Robert A. Williams. 3rd edition. St. Paul, Minn.: West Publishing Co., 1993; KF8204.5 G47 1993

These two books are teaching texts which use selected cases, accompanied by explanatory text and supplementary notes and questions, as a means of learning principles of Indian law.

Other useful texts available through the Law Library Reading Room include:

American Indian Law Deskbook. Conference of Western Attorneys General, N. J. Spaeth, Chair, Editing Committee; J. Wrend, and C. Smith, Chief Editors. Niwot, Colo.: University of Colorado Press, 1993; KF8205.A76 1993

American Indian Treaties, The History of a Political Anomaly. F. P. Prucha. Berkeley, Ca.: University of California Press, 1994; KF8205.P75 1994

Documents of United States Indian Policy. Edited by F. P. Prucha. Lincoln and London, Neb.: University of Nebraska Press, 1990; KF8205.D63 1990

Early American Indian Documents: Treaties and Laws, 1607–1789 (see discussion on page 127)

Indian Law Reporter, Volumes 20, 21, and 22. Oakland, Calif.: American Indian Lawyer Training Program, Inc., 1993–95; KF8201.A3I5

Each year, this loose-leaf binder series compiles decisions on Indian law topics from the United States Supreme Court, the United States Courts of Appeals, the United States District Courts, the United States Court of Federal

GATEWAYS

The British, French, Dutch, and Swedish all entered into treaties with North American Indian nations. Within the bounds of the 13 colonies, British colonial treaty-making started as early as 1607, when the Virginia colonists signed a treaty with the Powhatan Confederacy, and extended to 1775, by which time at least 175 treaties had been signed. Treaty-making by the new United States with the Indian tribes, both by the Continental Congress (1774–88) and under the Constitution (1789–1871), was modeled on the practices that the British and Indians had developed during their nearly 170 years of diplomacy preceding the Revolution. The United States government's first Indian treaty was concluded in 1778 with the Delaware Nation.

Treaties under the Constitution are agreements between the United States and independent nations that are ratified by the Senate and signed by the President. In fact the first two treaties ever submitted to the Senate under the Constitution, in 1789, were ones with the Six Nations (Iroquois) and with six Northwest Territory tribes. The last Indian treaty the United States ratified was in 1869, with the Nez Perce. In 1871 Congress prohibited any further treatymaking (as defined under the Constitution) with Indian nations. This prohibition resulted both from the House of Representatives' objections to its exclusion from treaty approval (while still having to appropriate funds for treaty obligations) and from growing objections by Indian policy-makers to treating Indian tribes as independent nations.

Between 1778 and 1871 the United States ratified about 370 treaties with Indian nations. A number of additional agreements with tribes were never ratified.

After 1871 the federal government continued to make agreements with Indian nations, but they had to be passed as regular laws by both houses of Congress. Between 1871 and 1913 Congress approved at least ninety-six such agreements with tribes. The United States still uses the statute process to make agreements with tribes, especially to settle claims.

From the U.S. government's point of view, the purposes of Indian treaties were various, from the securing of peace and friendship to the cession of land. As U.S. power waxed, tribal land cessions became the predominant purpose of treaties and agreements. From an Indian point of view, treaties reserved lands, other rights, and tribal self-governmental status and were meant to gain a cessation of military or other hostile activities. Furthermore, since treaties also varied in the fairness and equity of their terms, negotiation, and tribal ratification, they became the basis for many Indian claims.

Indian treaties remain important because they are—with the Constitution, statutes, executive orders, and Supreme Court decisions—the basis both of Indian tribes' unique status in the U.S. political system and of the federal government's trust relationship with Indian tribes and special programs for Indians.

WHERE TO LOOK: Library collections bearing on Indian treaties include the Law Library, the Manuscript Division, the Microform Reading Room, the Geography and Map Division, and the General Collections.

"View of the treaty ground at Prairie du Chien, Michigan Territory [now Wisconsin], in 1825" by Lehman and Duval after a painting by James Otto Lewis, from *The Aboriginal Port-Folio* by J. O. Lewis (Philadelphia, 1835). E89.L66 (LC-USZC4-4816, without caption, and LC-USZC4-510, with caption, both color; LC-USZ62-32586, with caption, black and white). Rare Book and Special Collections Division.

Not a land cession treaty, the agreement signed here on August 19, 1825, was a U.S. attempt to set boundaries and make peace among the Eastern Sioux, Lake Superior Ojibwa (Chippewa), Sac and Fox, Menominee, Iowa, and Winnebago, and parts of the Ottawa and Potawatomi.

Claims, state courts, and tribal courts. Also included are decisions from various miscellaneous proceedings by, for example, the Interior Board of Indian Appeals or the United States Tax Court.

Irredeemable America, The Indians' Estate and Land Claims. Edited by I. Sutton. Albuquerque, N.M.: University of New Mexico Press, 1985; KF8208.I77 1985

Native American Rights Fund National Indian Law Library Catalog: An Index to Indian Legal Materials and Resources. Boulder, Colo.: Native American Rights Fund, 1973–; KF8201.A1N38

The Rights of Indians and Tribes, The Basic ACLU Guide to Indian and Tribal Rights. Edited by S. L. Pevar. Carbondale and Edwardsville, Ill.: Southern Illinois University Press, 1992; KF8210.C5P48 1992

❑ SELECTED RESOURCES

A more detailed familiarity with some of the resources available for Indian legal studies at the Law Library may assist researchers in making maximum use of the collections. While the Law Library's own wide-ranging primary and secondary materials—in hard copy, microfiche, and microfilm—are divided between the division's rare book and general collections, recourse may also be taken to a vast array of materials in other parts of the Library of Congress. Some fundamental areas of research, with selected resources, are organized and described in the following discussion. References are made to useful materials located elsewhere in the Library where appropriate:

LAW LIBRARY RARE BOOK COLLECTION
- Colonial and Early American Materials
- Great Britain, Acts of Parliament
- Indian Territory

- Twentieth-Century Tribal Constitutions and Corporate Charters

LAW LIBRARY GENERAL COLLECTIONS
- Treaties
- Colonial and Early American Materials
- Federal Documents
    Legislative Branch Materials
    Executive Branch Materials
    Judicial Branch Materials
- State Documents
- Tribal Documents
- International Materials

LAW LIBRARY RARE BOOK COLLECTIONS

Colonial and Early American Materials

Although the emphasis in researching American Indian legal issues is federal law, legal research into many Indian legal questions (particularly those relating to Eastern tribes) must begin with the Colonial period. The Law Library Rare Book Collection is a good place to begin research for those tribes with the longest histories of contact with the non-Indian world. Indian-related materials will be found within various collections of statutes for the colony or state in question. Good examples are:

The Statutes at Large of South Carolina, 1632–1838. Edited under Authority of the Legislature by Thomas Cooper (vols. 1–5) and David J. McCord (vols. 6–10). Columbia, S.C.: A. S. Johnson, 1836–40; Law Office S.C.-1

The Statutes at Large: Being a collection of all the Laws of Virginia, From the First Session of the Legislature in the year 1619. Edited by William Waller Hening. Richmond (vols. 1–12), 1809–23, and Philadelphia (vol. 13), 1823; Law Office KFV2425.2 1619

Both of these sets of statutes are fully indexed. The materials for other colonies may not be so well organized. For instance, a researcher must examine each volume of the *Rhode Island Acts and Resolves* (Law Office R.I.-1) in order to locate all citations on a particular subject. *Hening's Statutes* are also available through the Law Library's stack collections. These will always be used in preference to the rare book collections, where they are available.

Because of a lack of indexes and reference guides for these rare materials, it is advisable to use all standard printed and automated catalogs available, including MUMS and SCORPIO, the card catalog located in the Law Library Reading Room (new card entries closed December 1980), and the National Union Catalog, pre-1956. Even this kind of cautious research may not be adequate. For instance, legislation from the Colony of Virginia is most thoroughly identified by examining the entire Virginia collection by index and/or table of contents for each volume.

Great Britain, Acts of Parliament

The Law Library Rare Book Collection also contains a large number of acts passed by the Parliament of Great Britain during the colonial period. These are arranged in volumes by reigning monarch and year (Law Office Gt Brit I 33 Geo 2 1763, for example). Again, ascertaining whether or not this collection contains American Indian material requires a volume-by-volume approach.

Indian Territory

The Rare Book materials also include a limited number of volumes devoted to Indian Territory. Perhaps the most important of this Indian Territory documentation is the seven-volume *Indian Territory Reports*, 1900–09 (Law Office Ind. Terr.),

compiled by James Frank Craig, which provides many insights into the management of Indian Territory. Other valuable resources include:

Rules of the United States Court of Appeals, Indian Territory. South McAlester, Okla.: News Print, 1903; Law Office Ind. Ter. 6 Rules Ct. App. 1903

Revised Leasing Regulations of June 11, 1907, Governing Leasing of Lands of Members of the Five Civilized Tribes. Washington, D.C.: GPO, 1907; Law Office Indian Tribes

Annotated Statutes of the Indian Territory Embracing All Laws of a General and Permanent Character. Compiled by Dorset Carter. St. Paul, Minn.: West Publishing Co., 1899; Law Office Indian Terr. 2 1899

A small but historically valuable collection housed among the Law Library's rare book materials comprises legal materials published by the "Five Civilized Tribes" in Oklahoma, part of Indian Territory at the time of publication. Some of these constitutions, codes, and acts are in the languages of the publishing nation: Cherokee, Chickasaw, Choctaw, and Creek, for instance. Some are bilingual editions, in both Indian languages and English.

Twentieth-Century Tribal Constitutions and Corporate Charters

A sizeable part of the Law Library's Rare Book Collection consists of twentieth-century tribal constitutions and tribal corporate charters for a little more than two hundred of the three hundred and thirty recognized tribal groups currently residing in the Lower Forty-eight. A number of Alaskan Indian villages and communities are also represented. These may be accessed by the call number "Law Office Indian Tribes" plus the name of the group.

LAW LIBRARY GENERAL COLLECTIONS

Treaties

The current relationship between the United States government and many Indian tribes may stem in part from the terms of one or more treaties negotiated prior to March 3, 1871. In some cases, earlier treaties between the same nation and Great Britain should be consulted as well. As a rule, these treaties delineate rights and territories ceded by the Indian nation to the United States. Other rights and territories are retained. In addition, the treaty language may include guarantees of hunting, fishing, or gathering rights; may define annual annuities to be paid by the United States to the tribe or tribes; may provide for peaceful relations between the parties; and may commit the United States to the provision of some educational benefits, among other terms. To understand the current impact of a given treaty, a researcher would benefit from an examination of the details of the treaty language, its historical context, and the way in which the tribe or tribes would have understood its terms, and any subsequent history, along with any relevant statutes and case law. To pursue this field of inquiry, a number of the resources available in the Law Library may be of help, including:

A Compilation of all the Treaties Between the United States and the Indian Tribes Now in Force as Laws. Washington, D.C.: GPO, 1873; E95.U6 1873

The needed citations are provided.

United States Statutes at Large. 1789 to present; KF50.U5

This multi-volume set contains the text of ratified treaties signed by the United States with Indian tribes during the treaty-making period, which ended in 1871. Volume 7 contains a compilation of all Indian-U.S. treaties signed between 1778 and 1842. The texts for treaties signed between 1846 and 1871 are found in the appropriate volume of the *U.S. Statutes at Large*. A full set of *Statutes at Large* is located in the reading room.

Indian Treaties, 1778–1883. Compiled by C. J. Kappler. New York, N.Y.: InterLand Pub., 1972; KF8203 1972b

A one-volume compendium of treaties with Indian tribes.

Indian Affairs, Laws and Treaties. Compiled by C. J. Kappler. Washington, D.C.: GPO, 1903; KF8203 1972

This multi-volume set contains general laws relating to Indian affairs, along with pertinent acts of the United States Congress, Executive Orders, proclamations, treaties, and agreements.

In addition, the Law Library's microfiche collection includes the *American State Papers, Documents, Legislative and Executive of the Congress of the United States*, 1st through 19th Congresses, 1789–1827 (Gales and Seaton, 1832). Class II of this collection includes a wide array of documents relating to Indian affairs, including documents accompanying Indian treaties. A related resource is *The New American State Papers: Indian Affairs*, drawn from the original *American State Papers*, published from 1832 to 1861 (E93.U938), included in the General Collections (see the discussion of these materials in the General Collections portion of this guide, p. 11).

Some commentaries to the treaties and additional copies of the texts are generally classified in E (General Collections) and many original imprints are located in the Library of Congress Rare Book and Special Collections Division.

Since understanding the most subtle points made in treaties remains crucial, a steady stream of commentary continues to be published in law reviews. These law reviews are accessed through the *Index to Legal Periodicals* (K9.N32) and the *Current Law Index* (K33.C87), both located in the Law Library Reading Room. Materials from 1980 to the present may also be accessed through "LegalTrac," a CD-ROM database.

Many texts of Indian treaties were published as monographs as part of their promulgation. These are not found in the Law Library collections but in the Rare Book and Special Collections Division and may be located through SCORPIO.

Colonial and Early American Materials

When researching the history of tribes in the eastern part of the United States, contemporaneous documents can provide valuable insights. Materials providing such illumination may be found in the following multi-volume source, and among the state materials discussed in a separate section of this chapter.

Early American Indian Documents: Treaties and Laws, 1607–1789. General Editor, A. T. Vaughan. Frederick and Bethesda, Md.: University Publications of America, 1979–; KF8202 1979

The Law Library has thus far received eight volumes of this on-going, ambitious compilation of colonial documents relating to North American Indians. These volumes cover Pennsylvania and Delaware treaties, 1629–1737 (Vol. I); Pennsylvania treaties, 1737–1756 (Vol. II); Virginia treaties, 1607–1722 (Vol. IV); Virginia treaties, 1723–1755 (Vol. V); Maryland treaties, 1632–1775 (Vol. VI); New York and New Jersey treaties, 1609–1682 (Vol. VII); Georgia Treaties, 1733–1789 (Vol. XI), and the Revolution and Confederation (Vol. XVIII). Included in this effort are reliable texts of important Indian-related documents ranging from treaties to minutes of meetings to correspondence about events of importance.

Federal Documents

The Law Library houses a large number of government publications concerning Indian nations dating from the foundation of the republic to the present. Although the colonies dealt individually with tribes within their boundaries, and the states also engaged in some direct contact and treaty-making with Indian tribes, a Proclamation under the Articles of Confederation, constitutional language, and a series of Trade and Intercourse or Non-Intercourse acts beginning in 1790 emphasized the plenary authority of the federal government over Indian affairs. While much of the early documentation was concerned with treaties, it quickly expanded to cover a wide range of topics such as health, education, law, and culture. Codified and uncodified federal statutes are part of the Law Library's collection, as is a complete set of the decisions of the federal trial and appellate courts. A review of some of the other significant federal resources in the Law Library's collection may also be of assistance.

Legislative Branch Materials

HOUSE AND SENATE COMMITTEE REPORTS

Several sources can be used to explore the House and Senate Committee Reports on bills which have been reported out of committee. Among these sources are:

GATEWAYS

American Indians and Alaska Natives today may be members of tribes that are recognized by the federal government, by their state government but not the federal government, or by neither government. At the end of 1994 there were about 565 federally recognized Indian entities, including 225 Alaska Native villages and 13 recognized sub-groups of larger entities. Most federally recognized tribes outside Alaska are located on federal reservations (Alaska Native villages are not considered reservations by the federal government, although there is one federal reservation in Alaska and one recognized council). Most federally recognized tribes, with or without reservations, and most Alaska Native villages have a tribal (or village) government. Many of the governments are based on written tribal constitutions adopted under the Indian Reorganization Act (IRA) and related acts, but many others are based either on non-IRA written constitutions or on traditional tribal governments without a written constitution. The federal government deals with all these types of tribal government. Most tribal governments have a legislative body, an executive branch, and a tribal judicial system. The relationships of the executive and judicial arms to the legislative branch vary from tribe to tribe.

Most members of federally recognized tribes do not live on a federal reservation or in an Alaska Native village. Many members live *near* their reservation. A large proportion, however, live away from their reservation, often in a city. These are often lumped together under the term "urban Indians." "Urban Indians" is a flexible term and may include enrolled tribal members, persons eligible for membership who have not enrolled as members, members of non-federally-recognized tribes, and persons who consider themselves Indians but are not members of any one tribe. Cities with large urban Indian populations include Chicago, Los Angeles, San Francisco, Minneapolis-St. Paul, Phoenix, New York, and other major U.S. cities. Urban Indians do not constitute tribes and do not have tribal governments in the cities where they live, but they have created urban Indian centers that provide cultural support, a social and political focus, and counselling services for employment, substance abuse problems, housing, and many other needs.

To be eligible for most (but not all) federal programs specifically established for Indians, an Indian must be a member of a federally recognized tribe. Most BIA programs are additionally restricted to tribal members living on or near the reservation. (A few BIA programs—mostly educational—are available to tribal members living off the reservation.) Indian Health Service programs are chiefly for members of federally recognized tribes but are available in some urban areas (at urban Indian health clinics) as well as on or near reservations. Other federal programs for recognized tribes may or may not be restricted to reservation areas, depending on the service offered.

WHERE TO LOOK: Library collections with materials relevant to tribal governments, federal recognition, federal programs, urban Indians, and similar topics include the General Collections, the Microform Reading Room, the Law Library, the Manuscript Division, and the Geography and Map Division.

Navajo Tribal Council committee listening to industry presentations, in the Council House in Window Rock, Arizona, the Navajo Nation's capital, in 1966. U.S. News & World Report Collection (LC-U9-15608, Frame 9/9A). Prints and Photographs Division.

United States Congressional Serial Set. Washington, D.C.: G.P.O., Serial Set.

A valuable resource in accessing these materials is Steven L. Johnson's *Guide to American Indian documents in the Congressional Serial Set, 1817–1899* (KF8201.A1J63). The Law Library has a complete set of these volumes, which contain many documents relevant to Indian affairs. Among these are House and Senate Reports on bills reported out after committee consideration. These also include House and Senate documents. The *U.S. Congressional Serial Set* may contain petitions from Indian groups, reports of explorations, letters, and reports to Congress on Indian matters, and many other materials. Volumes 1 to 7915 of the *Serial Set* are accessible only through microfiche, unless the fiche is unreadable. These materials may be accessed through the *U.S. Serial Set Index, 1789–1969* (Z1223.Z9C65 1975) located at the reference desk in the Law Library Reading Room. A CD-ROM version of the general *Serial Set* index, entitled *Congressional Masterfile 1789–1969*, and its supplement for 1970 to the present, *Congressional Masterfile II*, may be accessed on computer terminals in the Thomas Jefferson Building's Computer Catalog Center.

U.S. Senate Executive Documents & Reports, 1817–1969. Washington, D.C.: Congressional Information Service, 1987

This reference source is available at the reference desk of the Law Library Reading Room. It covers documents and reports not published in the U.S. Serial Set.

U.S. Code Congressional and Administrative News. St. Paul, Minn.: West Publishing Co., 1941–; KF48.W45

The texts of measures enacted into law are published in the *U.S. Code Congressional and Administrative News*, along with some of the perti-

nent committee reports on the legislation. This resource began in 1941.

CONGRESSIONAL HEARINGS

For congressional hearings held before 1970, the title of the hearing and committee information can be found in the *U.S. Congressional Committee Hearings Index (1833–1969)* (KF40.C56), located in the Law Library Reading Room. A second index, the *Congressional Information Service Index and Abstract* (KF49.C62) is used for hearings held after 1969. This publication, also located in the Law Library Reading Room, indexes and abstracts congressional hearings, documents, reports, and committee prints, but does not cover *The Congressional Record*. In addition, the CIS (Congressional Information Service) Masterfile in the Thomas Jefferson Building indexes congressional hearings. Most of the hearings themselves, however, are in the General Collections prior to 1970. From 1970 to the present, all hearings are included in the Law Library stack collection.

As a possible alternative source of current congressional hearings, researchers may wish to look at the federal depository library collection in Room LM 133 of the Madison Building. Some unpublished congressional hearings may be identified through two indexes, *Unpublished U.S. Senate Committee Hearings, 1823–1964* (KF40.C55 1986) and *Unpublished U.S. House of Representatives Committee Hearings, 1833–1936* (KF40.C54 1988). The Law Library Reading Room has both of these indexes. Original transcripts of unpublished congressional hearings may be found at the National Archives.

The Serials Division holds unpublished U.S. Senate executive documents and reports. The originals are kept in a secured area, but copies are available on microfiche. The Congressional Information Service (CIS) has compiled an index to many of the U.S. Senate executive documents and reports.

CONGRESSIONAL DEBATES

The floor debates on matters before the United States House of Representatives or the United States Senate are contained in a series of publications, all of which are available in the Law Library collections. These include:

Annals of Congress, 1789–1824
Register of Debates, 1824–37
Congressional Globe, 1833–73
The Congressional Record, 1873–present

These materials from 1789 to 1901 are available only in microform, unless the microform version is unreadable. The indexes for these titles from 1789 to the present are kept in the Law Library Reading Room. Another useful index kept in the Law Library Reading Room is A. W. Greely's three-volume *Documents of First Fourteen Congresses, 1789–1817* (Z1223.A 1973). Full text of *The Congressional Record* from 1951 to the present is available in hard copy in the Law Library Reading Room, and editions from earlier years are kept in the closed stacks. These materials are also available on microfilm in the Law Library Reading Room. The Law Library also has the *House Journal* and *Senate Journal* for each Congress, which can shed further light upon the activities of each house of Congress during a given session or Congress, and can provide a more comprehensive access approach to *The Annals of Congress*.

BILLS INTRODUCED IN THE HOUSE OR SENATE

The Law Library collection also contains a set of all of the versions of the bills introduced in the House or the Senate under classification KF16. The early bills are on microfilm, related *American State Papers* on microfiche, and more recent bills are available in hard copy. The bills from 1789 to 1921 (for the 1st to the 66th Congresses) are only available in microform. This collection of bills permits a researcher to observe the evolution of

bill language during the legislative process. If a researcher wishes to view hard copy of early legislative and executive materials, he or she may examine *The New American State Papers: Indian Affairs*, drawn from the original *American State Papers* published from 1832–61 (E93.U938), included in the General Collections. (See the discussion of these materials in the General Collections portion of this guide, p. 11.)

Executive Branch Materials

In addition to the extensive legislative and judicial resources in the Law Library, a wide range of Executive Branch materials are also available. Among them are:

Presidential Executive Orders and Proclamations, 1789–1983. Washington, D.C.: Congressional Information Services, 1987; KF70.A55 1987

This source, available at the Law Library Reading Room reference desk, contains a nearly complete set of executive orders that can provide useful insights into presidential involvement in Indian Affairs. Those proclamations and executive orders issued after 1936 are also found in Title 3 of the *Code of Federal Regulations* (KF70.A3 1949) in the Law Library Reading Room. Proclamations and executive orders also appear in:

Federal Register; KF70.A2

Weekly Compilation of Presidential Documents, 1965 to present; J80.A284

U.S. Code Congressional and Administrative News; KF48.W45

The texts of executive orders and proclamations are only available from this resource from 1944 to the present.

Proclamations are also found in the *Statutes at Large*. A complete set is available in the Law Library Reading Room.

The published *Public Papers of the Presidents* (J80.A283) are housed in the Serials Division and the Main Reading Room rather than in the Law Library.

FEDERAL REGULATIONS

Federal regulations promulgated by Executive Branch departments and agencies are published in the *Federal Register* (KF70.A2) and codified in the *Code of Federal Regulations* (KF70.A3 1979). Many of the regulations pertinent to Indian affairs are contained in Title 25 of the *Code of Federal Regulations*.

Opinions of the Solicitor of the Department of the Interior Relating to Indian Affairs, 1917–1974. Washington, D.C.: U.S. Dept. of the Interior, 1979; KF8204 1917.

These opinions deal with important matters concerning such topics as the management of the Bureau of Indian Affairs, the interpretation of laws of importance to Indians, land resource issues, and tribal government powers.

The Law Library Reading Room also has the CIS checklist of *U.S. Executive Branch Documents, 1789–1909.* This index may prove helpful in accessing materials which may be of use in Indian legal research.

Judicial Branch Materials

A complete collection of federal trial and appellate court decisions is also part of the Law Library resources. Further, the Law Library maintains a large collection of appellate and Supreme Court records and briefs.

State Documents

While federal law plays a preeminent role in Indian legal studies, there are a number of circumstances in which a knowledge of state law is crucial to a comprehensive understanding of legal issues affecting a tribe. For example, there are a few states which have some degree of civil or criminal jurisdiction over Indian tribes within their borders because of a federal delegation of such jurisdiction under P.L. 83-280, Act of August 15, 1953, as amended; 18 U.S.C. § 1162; 25 U.S.C. §§ 1321-1326; 28 U.S.C. §§ 1360 and 1360 note (often referred to simply as Public Law 280 or P.L. 280). In some parts of the country, state hunting and fishing cases involving Indians may be part of the backdrop to federal litigation in this field of law. Under the McCarran Amendment, 43 U.S.C. § 666, Indian reserved water rights may be adjudicated as part of general state water adjudications. Sometimes interstate compacts are pertinent to a particular area of inquiry. As these examples suggest, state laws and state court decisions may be a necessary part of research in a particular Indian law dispute. Codified versions of state laws (under classifications KFA-KFW) and state case law (under classifications KFA-KFW for individual state reporters, or under classification KF for those decisions printed in a regional reporter series such as *Atlantic Reporter* or *Southern Reporter*) are available in the Law Library Reading Room.

Other state documents are located in the General Collections under classification J. Materials in this classification must be requested in either of the general reading rooms in the John Adams Building or the Thomas Jefferson Building. Classification J contains the published proceedings of state executive and legislative bodies. State legislative materials are arranged alphabetically by state in the J87 (politics) classification of the General Collections. As a rule, these materials include the journals of the state's house and senate, and house and senate bills. Some states also print governors' reports, legislative journals, and various and sundry annual reports, some of which pertain to Indians. This is most apt to be the case with states with large Indian populations such as

Arizona, New Mexico, and Oklahoma. However, the situation is complicated by emerging splinter groups and urban Indian communities. Some of these groups have state recognition and some are actively seeking federal recognition. As a result, legislative materials may be found in the printed volumes of nearly every state.

A thorough check of indexes and other finding aids must be made when approaching the legislative papers of any particular state. A researcher should note that the indexes are not consistent as to how Indian materials may be categorized. For example, it may be assumed that the heading "Indian" or the name of the particular tribe should be checked. However, a recent Virginia legislative journal indexed Indian materials under "Virginia History." Normally, it might be safe to assume that such an index would include the names of the several tribes—Chickahominy, Pamunkey, and Mattaponi—which have called Virginia home for many centuries; but this index does not mention these ancient communities. Once again, the place to begin research on these "State Indians" is in the legislative materials published by the state in question. These are found under the J87 (politics) classification in the General Collections.

The General Collections also contains a large body of legal materials classified under JK. These materials, including special reports and manuals, are not in alphabetical order but are shelved according to region. Such materials should be accessed through automated finding aids such as MUMS and SCORPIO. A firm grasp of each state's history is needed to determine if any of these miscellaneous volumes might produce information relevant to the Indian group being researched.

A few notable examples of early period titles appear below:

General Index to the Documents of the State of New York. Albany, N.Y.: James B. Lyon, 1891; J87.N75d

A checklist of documents from 1777 to 1888 arranged under subject headings that include specific tribes.

Report of the Governor of Oklahoma to the Secretary of the Interior. 17 vols. in 5. Washington, D.C.: GPO, 1891–1907; J87.O51

Reports during Oklahoma's status as a territory.

The Journal of the Commons House of Assembly. Edited by J. H. Easterby. Columbia, S.C.: Historical Commission of South Carolina, 1951; KFS1818.2 1736 (now in Law Library)

South Carolina's colonial legislative records dating from 1736. The Law Library currently has volumes through 1752.

Messages of the Governors of Tennessee. Compiled by Robert H. White. 8 vols. Nashville: Tennessee Historical Commission, c1952–1972; J87.T216

Covers 1796–1907. Index.

Executive Journals of the Council of Colonial Virginia. Edited by H. R. McIlwaine. 6 vols. Richmond: Virginia State Library, 1925–1966; J87.V588

Journals of the House of Burgesses of Virginia. Edited by H. R. McIlwaine. Richmond: Virginia State Library, 1619–1776; J87.V6

An Index to Governors' Messages (Wisconsin). Madison, Wisc.: Wisconsin Historical Records Survey, 1941; J87.W66

The messages themselves have the call number J87.W62.

Tribal Documents

As the various Indian nations become increasingly involved in the management of their own affairs, their tribal governments are naturally beginning to generate official legal documents.

However, it is often difficult to locate such materials. Some are classified with the general American Indian collections under E and others may be found in any number of places, such as with the political collections under J. If these materials are obviously legal in nature, they become part of the Law Library collections.

While the Law Library's collection of tribal legal materials is not exhaustive, it does contain a number of useful resources. For example, the Navajo Nation was once governed by a constitution and a corporate charter. Today, as a result of the Indian Self-Determination and Education Act, Public Law 93-638 (88 Stat. 2203), the Navajo have endeavored to provide their nation with the full range of twentieth-century legal materials. The Law Library collections contain the *Navajo Tribal Code* (KF8228.N3A5), which covers such topics as tribal administration, domestic relations, education, elections, land, law and order, parks, wildlife, and Navajo/U.S. relations. The *Navajo Court Rules* (KF8228.N3A5) includes rules of court, civil, and criminal procedure, probate and appellate procedure, and the rules of evidence. The *Navajo Reporter* (KF8228.N3A5) discusses landmark decisions made within the Navajo Nation court system. Another example of the Law Library's collection of tribal laws is the *Cherokee Nation Code Annotated*, 2 vols. (St. Paul, Minn.: West Publishing Co. 1993; KF8228.C5A5 1993).

In addition to the hard copy materials relating to tribal laws, the Law Library's microfiche collection includes *Indian Tribal Codes: A Microfiche Collection of Indian Tribal Law Codes*, edited by Ralph W. Johnson (Marian Gould Gallagher Law Library, University of Washington School of Law, Research Studies Series, 1981). While neither comprehensive nor up-to-date in all respects, this source is one of the largest compilations of such codes available. Introductory materials for this collection are available in hard copy in the Law Library.

Smaller tribal groups may not have generated such extensive published materials. But the number of Indian tribes now in the publishing business, including the publication of legal materials, is growing. Researchers should work on the assumption that such sources exist rather than on the assumption that none are to be found.

International Materials

Under some circumstances, historical and contemporary international materials may also assist researchers engaged in Indian legal studies. For example, early Spanish laws and royal ordinances and early Mexican laws may shed light upon early American treatment of the Pueblo tribes or the California tribes. *See, e.g.,* among the pertinent Spanish laws relating to the Pueblo Indians, the Act of March 21, 1551; the Act of December 1, 1573; the Act of October 10, 1618; the royal cedula of July 12, 1695; the decree of February 23, 1781; the decree of January 5, 1811; and Decree 31 of February 9, 1811. For relevant early Mexican legal materials regarding the Pueblo Indians, see the Plan of Iguala of February 24, 1821; the Treaty of Cordova of August 24, 1821; the Declaration of Independence of October 6, 1821; and the Act of August 18, 1824. Early Russian materials may be illuminating in setting some of the issues relating to Alaskan natives in their historical context. Further, modern international treaties may impact upon such Indian law issues as the exercise of traditional hunting and fishing rights.

The Law Library has an extensive collection of international treaties and bilateral agreements. Contemporary and historical legal materials are also available from many foreign nations, either in English or in the original language. The Law Library rare book collections include some materials which may also be of interest, such as the Russian Imperial Collection.

In addition, the Law Library resources include numerous law reviews from foreign nations. The Law Library's professional staff includes an impressive array of specialists in the laws of many foreign nations. Finally, some early historical materials pertinent to Indian law issues may also be reprinted in secondary sources, such as general texts relating to Indian law, or may be referenced in the records, briefs, or decisions arising out of related litigation in United States courts.

"Buffalo Dance, Pueblo of Zuni, NM," lithograph by Ackerman after R. H. Kern in *Report of an Expedition down the Zuni and Colorado rivers* by Capt. L. Sitgreaves, Corps Topographical Engineers. Senate Exec. Doc. No. 59, 32nd Congress, 2nd Session, Washington, D.C., 1853. KF12.U5; "Cocopas" in *Report upon the Colorado River of the West*, Senate Exec. doc. No.__, 36th Congress, 1st Session, Washington, D.C., 1861. KF12.U5; and "Sketch of part of the March and Wagon Road of Lt. Col. Cooke from Santa Fe to the Pacific Ocean, 1846–7. . .," in House Exec. Doc. No. 41, 30th Congress, 1st Session, Washington, D.C., 1848 (Serial Set 517). The last of these three has been removed from the serial set volume and is now being kept in the Geography and Map Division. Lt. Col. Cooke's report appears in this volume at pp. 549–63. Law Library.

Three reports of government-funded expeditions which encountered Indian cultures provide examples of the kind of material one might unexpectedly find in a congressional document from the Law Library collection. These reports and other survey expeditions contain vibrant illustrations and accounts of the Indian tribes encountered; plants, animals and fossils found; ruins discovered; and maps of the routes taken and surrounding areas.

"Chemehuevis" in *Report upon the Colorado River of the West . . .* , Exec. doc No._, 36th Congress, 1st session, Washington, D.C., 1861. KF12.U5 (LC-USZC4-4817). Law Library.

Another illustration from Report upon the Colorado River *shows Chemehuevi Indians at a point in their history when contact with non-Indians was minimal. Such reports provide a vital historical link to early contacts with Indian tribes. The illustrations, maps, and written records of these expeditions provide a contemporaneous view of the lands, flora and fauna, weather conditions, and topography. They also reflect some of the perspectives and experiences of those early travelers and of the Indian peoples they encountered.*

[35]

and in every such case the Vestry of the respective Parish where such Gift or Grant hath been made, and the Quantity not ascertained, as aforesaid, may demand and take of such Lands, for the use of the Church, and thereto adjacent, Two Acres, and no more, which they shall cause to be Surveyed and staked out, and make Returns of two Certificates thereof, one of which must be Recorded in the County Court, and the other in the High Court of Chancery, there to be Registred *in Perpetuam rei Memoriam*, as aforesaid.

And be it further Enacted by the Authority aforesaid, by and with the Advice and Consent aforesaid, That where the Vestry of any Parish within this Province have or shall think convenient to place either Church or Chappel of Ease within their respective Parishes, for the better conveniency of their Parishioners, but the owner or owners of such Land chosen out and appointed by such Vestry, as aforesaid, for the use of their Parish aforesaid, either refuse to make Sale thereof, or are unreasonable in his or their demands for the same, or otherwise incapacitated by *Non-age, non sana Memorea*, or *beyond the Sea*, that then and in every such Case the respective Vestrys of the respective Parishes shall apply themselves to the Commissioners of the County Court whereto they belong, upon whose application the said Commissioners shall forth-with grant their Warrants to the Sheriff of their County, thereby requiring him, at a certain Day and Time, to be by them nominated and appointed, to impannel a Jury of substantial Free-holders next adjacent to the Land in quest aforesaid, which said Commissioners and Jury aforesaid shall proceed in all things as by an other Act of Assembly (entituled, *An Act impowering the Commissioners of the several and respective Counties to take up and purchase Land for their County Court Houses*) they are directed, not exceeding two Acres, as before in this Act mentioned and exprest, any thing in this Act or any other ordained to the contrary notwithstanding.

And purchase Land for building Churches &c. by Warrant in Nature of Ad quod Damnum.

An Act declaring that the Grantees of Land lying within the *Indians* Land may have Action of Trespass against such Persons as cut Timber off their Land on pretence of having bought the same of the *Indians*.

BE it hereby Enacted and Declared by the *Queens most Excellent Majesty*, by and with the Advice and Consent of her Majesty's Governour, Council and Assembly of this Province, and the Authority of the same, That the falling, mauling and carrying away of Timber, or purchasing or receiving any Timber by any Person or Persons upon pretence of having bought the same of the *Indians*, or upon any unlawful pretence whatsoever on or from off any Lands within the Bounds of the *Indians* Land, whereof any other person or persons have in him, her or them the Fee, be judged, deemed and accounted a Trespass; and whosoever shall purchase or receive, fall, maul or carry away Timber, as aforesaid, shall be deemed and adjudged Trespassers, and shall be lyable to Action or Actions of Trespass, and the Persons grieved shall and may recover their Damages accordingly, as if the Grantee or Patentee aforesaid did actually occupy and enjoy such Land, and had improved it, any Law, Act of Assembly or Usage to the contrary notwithstanding.

I 3   An

"An Act declaring that the Grantees of Land lying within the Indians Land . . . " in *The Laws of the Province of Maryland Collected into one Volumn* (Philadelphia, 1718). KFM1225.2 1692b (LC-USZ62-116678). Law Library.

This act gave land grantees within "Indians Land" a right to seek damages for trespass from persons cutting, purchasing or receiving timber from the grantees' land on the pretense that the timber was bought from the Indians or under any other unlawful pretense. It provides an insight into concerns related to the legality of eighteenth-century land acquisitions from Indian tribes. Such concerns eventually led the British Crown to assume responsibility for all Indian land transactions. This right passed to the United States.

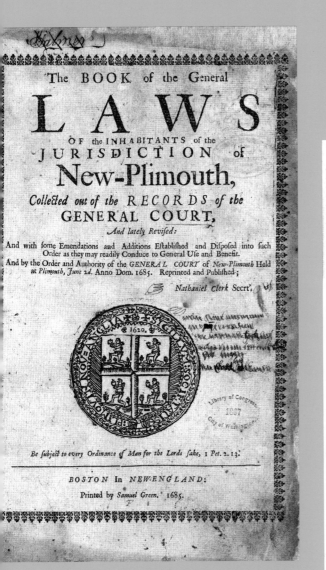

Title page and "Indians" in *The Book of the General Laws of the Inhabitants of the Jurisdiction of New-Plimouth* (Boston, 1685). Law Office Mass.1685 (LC-USZ62-116708, above, LC-USZ62-116709, right). Law Library.

Volumes such as this one found in the Law Rare Book Collection provide insights into some of the fears the early settlers experienced and their legal approaches to Indian-white contacts. Section 4 reflects an effort to give equal protection to property owned by the Indians.

"An Act for the Government and Protection of Indians," passed April 22, 1850, in *The Statutes of California passed at the First Session of the Legislature* (San Jose, 1850). KFC25.A213 1st 1849 (LC-USZ62-116681). Law Library.

The act reveals a continuing effort to regulate Indian affairs and provide some protection to Indians. Section 2 contains provisions to guarantee Indians continued occupation of their traditional homes. Sections 3 and 4 establish procedures to be followed by those seeking custody of Indian children, and providing penalties for improper treatment of these children. Since 1978, the Indian Child Welfare Act has established a preference for adoptive and foster care placement of Indian children with their extended families or tribes. Unless otherwise provided by federal law, the Indian tribes have exclusive jurisdiction over child custody proceedings involving Indian children from their respective reservations.

"Bill No. 16, Resolution. Authorizing the principal chief to take legal steps to recover the value of timber unlawfully cut from public domain of the Choctaw Nation" in *Acts and Resolutions of General Council of the Choctaw Nation*, 1905; LLAB Case Indian Nations Choctaw Acts and Resolutions 1905 (LC-USZ62-116679). Law Library.

This bill is included in a two-part collection of the original Acts and Resolutions of the Choctaw General Council passed at its Extraordinary and Regular Session in 1905. These acts and resolutions also included measures authorizing disbursement of funds, directing actions on impeachment resolutions, and vesting authority in the Principal Chief to take particular action or to respond to a given concern. Still others dealt with land transactions or the appointment of a committee to attend a separate statehood meeting. Some, like Bill No. 16, reflect action by President Theodore Roosevelt approving or disapproving action taken by the General Council of the Choctaw Nation.

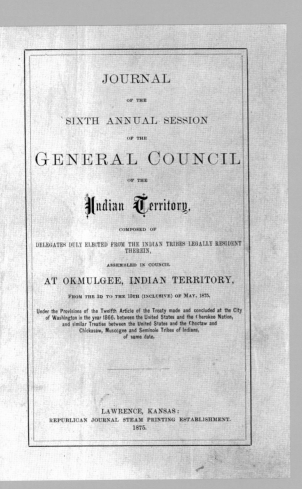

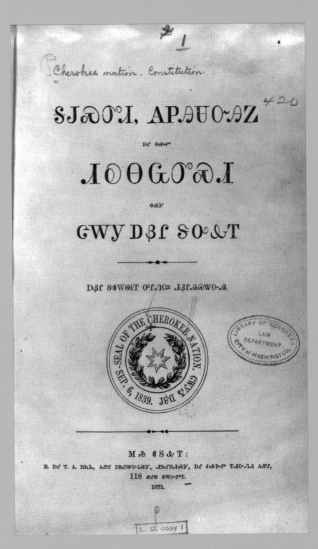

Title page, *Journal of the Sixth Annual Session of the General Council of the Indian Territory*. Lawrence, Kansas, 1875; LLAB Case Indian Territory, 1875 (LC-USZ62-116680). Law Library.

This pamphlet is an example of the kind of surprise a legal resource can contain. This journal is the record of the 6th Annual General Council of the Indian Territory. The Council was composed of elected delegates from the Cherokee Nation and the Choctaw, Chickasaw, Muskogee and Seminole tribes of Indians assembled under the provisions of a series of 1866 treaties. Speeches by delegates are filled with progress reports and comments on acculturation progress. The appendices consist of status reports for each tribe, a report by the Education Committee, the text of the Constitution of the Indian Territory, and the Declaration of Rights.

Title page, *Constitution and Laws of the Cherokee Nation* (in Cherokee), originally published by the authority of the National Council of the Cherokee Nation in 1839. (St. Louis, Mo., 1875). Law Office (LC-USZ62-61141). Law Library.

One of the treasures of the Law Library Rare Book Collection, this volume is one of the most important in the field of Cherokee law and history. A Cherokee publication authorized by the National Council, it shows the advanced state of legal structure and organization among the nineteenth-century Southeastern tribes.

Handbook of BLACKFEET TRIBAL LAW

Blackfeet Heritage Program

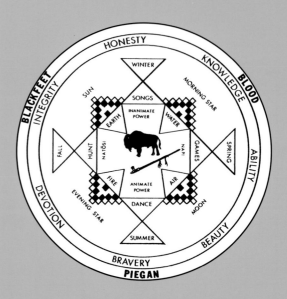

Title page, *Handbook of Blackfeet Tribal Law* by Dan Gilham, Sr. (Browning, Mont.: Blackfeet Heritage Program, 1979). KF8228.S54 copy 2 1979 (LC-USZ62-116682, left, and LC-USZ62-116683, detail). Law Library.

Today, many tribes are publishing legal materials. This handbook provided information to tribal members about their legal rights and obligations as reflected in Tribal Court decisions. Not yet officially recognized by the Blackfeet Tribal Business Council at the time of its publication, it was written by an enrolled member of the Blackfeet Tribe who was serving as a judge for the tribe.

CONSTITUTION AND BY-LAWS OF THE ANGOON COMMUNITY ASSOCIATION

PREAMBLE

We, the Indians having a common bond of residence in the neighborhood of Angoon, Territory of Alaska, do ordain and establish this constitution and by-laws in accordance with and by authority of, the Acts of Congress of June 18, 1934 (48 Stat. 984), and May 1, 1936 (49 Stat. 1250).

ARTICLE I—NAME

The name of this organization shall be the Angoon Community Association, hereinafter called the Community:

ARTICLE II—MEMBERSHIP

SECTION 1. The membership of this Community shall be as follows:

(*a*) All persons whose names appear on the roll of those entitled to vote on the adoption of this constitution and by-laws. Within one year from the approval of this constitution, the council elected under this constitution may make corrections in this roll.

(*b*) All children both of whose parents are enrolled members of the Community.

(*c*) All children one of whose parents is an enrolled member of the Community and has a permanent home in Angoon.

(*d*) All other persons of Indian blood who make a permanent home in Angoon and are adopted by the Council.

SEC. 2. All members and their minor children who cease to make a permanent home in Angoon shall cease to be members of this Community until they resume their residence.

SEC. 3. The Council may make rules and regulations governing the enrollment and adoption of members and the conditions under which a member may abandon his membership, or having abandoned it, be readmitted to membership.

SEC. 4. *Definition of Residence.*—Any person shall be considered a resident of the neighborhood of Angoon who maintains a home within the town of Angoon or in any area in the vicinity of Angoon which may be reserved or otherwise acquired for the use of the Indians of the Community.

ARTICLE III—GOVERNING BODY

SECTION 1. The governing body of this Community shall be a Council composed of seven members elected by the adult membership of the Community.

SEC. 2. The membership of the Community shall meet on the first Tuesday in November and the first Monday in March of each year. At the regular membership meeting in November the adult members

236426—40   (1)

Constitution and By-Laws of the Angoon Community Association [Alaska] (ratified November 15, 1939). (Washington, D.C., 1940). Law Office. Indian Tribes—Angoon Community Assoc. (LC-USZ62-116684). Law Library.

The Law Library Collection contains a large number of tribal corporate charters, tribal constitutions, and by-laws drawn up under the Indian Reorganization Act of 1934. They address issues such as tribal or community membership; governing structure; elections; powers and duties of officers or governing body; qualifications, installation, and removal of officers; rights of tribal or community members; and procedures for ratification of the constitution and by-laws.

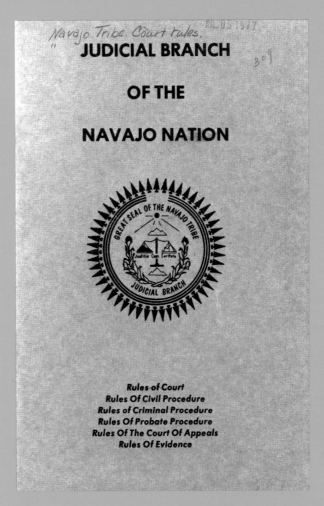

Navajo Tribe. Court rules.

JUDICIAL BRANCH

OF THE

NAVAJO NATION

Rules of Court
Rules Of Civil Procedure
Rules of Criminal Procedure
Rules Of Probate Procedure
Rules Of The Court Of Appeals
Rules Of Evidence

Front cover, *Judicial Branch of the Navajo Nation;* KF8228.N3 A5 1977 (LC-USZ62-116685). Law Library.

The Navajo Nation has one of the most developed of all Native American governments. Among the rules included in this volume are the Rules of Court, Rules of Civil Procedure, Rules of Criminal Procedure, Rules of Probate Procedure, Rules of the Court of Appeals, and Rules of Evidence.

PRINTS AND PHOTOGRAPHS DIVISION

INTRODUCTION

Since their first encounter with European culture, North American Indians have been the subject of countless prints, drawings, and photographs. The Library of Congress Prints and Photographs Division preserves and makes available thousands of pictorial records of Indian people, in the form of drawings, woodcuts, engravings, etchings, lithographs, posters, and photographs, made chiefly by European and Euro-American artists and photographers since the seventeenth century. Most of these have documentary importance; some are also important to the artistic development of graphic art and photography.

Many of these pictorial records came to the Library through copyright. Other pictorial works have been obtained through gift, purchase, transfer from other federal agencies, and exchange, contributing to a total of nearly fifteen thousand pictorial documents pertaining to Native Americans, more than three-quarters of which are photographs.

While pictorial material relating to American Indians was produced as early as the fifteenth century, the Prints and Photographs Division's holdings in this area are strongest for the period 1860 to 1940. Currently the division has little material from the period after the late 1970s.

The division's holdings document several major aspects of Indian history and life, and the conventions of their depiction:

- Indian Delegations and Government Relations
- Federal Government Surveys and Other Expeditions
- Indian Wars and Confrontations
- The Frontier, Villages, and Reservation Life
- Education

- Expositions, World's Fairs, and Wild West Shows
- Pictorialist Photographs
- Allegories, Satires, Stereotypes, and Polemical Representations

These categories provide the organizing principle for the Selected Collections section of the Prints and Photographs Division chapter.

Among the earliest true portraits of Native Americans are those made of tribal leaders or delegates who, beginning in the seventeenth century, travelled to European capitals for diplomatic purposes. These visits were often memorialized in such works as Wenceslaus Hollar's 1645 etching of an Algonquian from Virginia, which is considered to be the earliest printed portrait of a Native American taken from life. This practice continued in the United States as Indian emissaries visited Washington to negotiate treaties or disputes. Once photography was introduced in the 1840s, a trip to the photographic studio became customary on these missions.

Some of the most important portrayals of Indians and Indian life were produced by artists and photographers accompanying exploration teams into the western parts of the United States, Canada, and Alaska. During the nineteenth century prints and photographs were produced as records of several such excursions.

Wars and confrontations between Indians and the U.S. military were rendered for posterity in prints, drawings, and in illustrations for books and magazines. Many, if not most, of these are highly interpretive or even wholly fanciful portrayals; few are based on firsthand observation. The many lithographs of William Henry Harrison and Richard M. Johnson's fabled exploits during the Indian Wars of the 1810s, produced by American publishers of popular prints, are notable examples of this genre.

In the age of photography the recording of Indian life was limited initially by the bulky size and fragility of the early photographic equipment and by the long exposure times required by the glass negative process. Consequently, from the Civil War period to the end of the century, photographs afford the historian largely static views of military figures, installations, prisoners of war, and the sites and tragic aftermaths of battles, rather than glimpses of these violent encounters themselves. With time the medium's capabilities were enlarged.

During the nineteenth century, as Indian tribes were relocated to reservations, artists, photographers, journalists, and others journeyed to frontier towns and reservations to record Native American lifestyles that were increasingly being altered by assimilation. The thousands of resulting images document the domestic life, homes, ceremonies, games, and work of tribal people and their families. Photographs such as those by Frances Benjamin Johnston of the Indian School at Carlisle, Pennsylvania, show life in the boarding schools where young Native Americans recruited from reservations learned to read, write, and practice white cultural traditions.

Later, newspaper, magazine, and wire-service photographers captured the realities of reservation life and the economic challenges resulting from the federal government's self-determination policies and the Indian rights movement. Posters, used to advance the often acrimonious struggle to redress past Indian grievances against federal and state governments, also survive as records of these activities and of the varying issues and viewpoints which drove them.

Both anthropologists and showmen had an interest in recording threatened tribal cultures. During the late nineteenth and early twentieth centuries, anthropological organizations sponsored a number of world's fair exhibits featuring representatives from many different tribes. Photographers documented these "living exhibits" and also produced hundreds of studio portraits of the Indians.

The spectacle of wild west show performances featuring "real Indians" also attracted photographers and artists who produced often dramatic records of such performances as well as dynamic and colorful advertising posters promoting them.

Aside from being the objects of historical record and scientific study, Native Americans have since the end of the nineteenth century frequently aroused in artists and photographers the vision of a simple, exotic existence, appealing in its stark contrast to the rapid urbanization and industrialization of American society after the Civil War. During the late nineteenth and early twentieth century, several photographers of the Pictorialist school (a movement in American photography well represented in the division's holdings) created soft-focus and often highly romanticized images of Indians and of tribal life. Works in this vein held by the division range from the photographs of Edward S. Curtis, who employed props, costumes, and various staging devices to construct his idealized portrayals, to the masterful portrait studies of Gertrude Käsebier.

The Indian figure has also been widely used as the allegorical symbol of America in political cartoons and on bank note engravings and certificates. Generalized or fictionalized Indians often appeared on labels for tobacco and herbal medicines, on music covers, and in the popular prints of Currier and Ives and others.

The next section of this chapter describes access, arrangement, and guides to the Prints and Photographs Division's incomparable holdings. The final section highlights notable collections in each of the major areas of Native American representation.

USING THE COLLECTIONS

PRINTS AND PHOTOGRAPHS READING ROOM

LOCATION: Madison Building, 3rd floor, LM 337; telephone (202) 707-6394

HOURS: Monday through Friday, 8:30 A.M. to 5:00 P.M.

To make full use of the collections, a personal visit is recommended. Limited service by mail and telephone is also available. Advanced research guidance relating to the Library's pictorial collections is provided. In addition to presenting the mandatory Library of Congress photo ID card, researchers are required to register on arrival in the reading room. Photographic copies of works in the division's collections may be obtained from the Library's Photoduplication Service (telephone (202) 707-5640).

LOTS

The pictorial materials described in the Prints and Photographs Division section of this guide may be viewed in the division's reading room. A major portion of this material has been organized as "LOTS." Often referred to as a collection, a LOT is a cohesive body of material, maintained and cataloged as a group to preserve unity of subject, provenance, or format. A LOT can consist of a few items, an album containing photographs or prints, or a large number of loose items. More than five hundred LOTS pertaining to American Indians are described in *Indians of North America: A Guide to LOTS*, available in the Prints and Photographs Reading Room. Many of the LOT descriptions are also available on-line in the Library's bibliographic database and throughout the world on Internet. LOTS are stored in areas adjacent to the reading room and can be retrieved by the reference staff using call slips filled out by the researcher.

Browsing Files

Another significant portion of the Native American related material is stored in self-serve "browsing files" in the reading room. These files, which provide easy and immediate access to researchers, contain original photographs and prints as well as reference copies of originals housed in other parts of the division. Four important browsing files related to American Indians include the following: A *Biographical File* contains photographs, lithographs, engravings, photomechanical reproductions of paintings, and other kinds of portraits filed alphabetically by surname, Indian name, or translated name such as Rain-in-the-Face. Although not complete, a corresponding card file, the "Indian Biographical Index," lists more than 3,000 names and provides a brief description, name of photographer, creator, or publisher, and the original source of the image within the Library. In the *Specific Subjects File*, photographs of Indians are organized by the heading "Indians of North America" with subdivisions by subjects such as "Government relations," "Education," and "Domestic life." Similarly, the *Stereograph Subjects File*, which holds approximately five hundred stereos, is organized under the main subject heading "Indians of North America," further subdivided by geographic region, and then by tribe. Stereographs consist of two almost identical photographic images mounted on a card. When viewed through a binocular-type device called a stereoscope, the images produce a three-dimensional effect.

Graphic material related to Native Americans can be found in a separate *Specific Subjects Graphics File*, a major source for reproductions of drawings and paintings, and photocopies of many of the original historical prints, drawings, posters, and book and magazine illustrations in the Library's collections. The images are filed by broad topics such as "Discovery and exploration," "Colonial life and settlement," "Indians and Indian life," and the "Seminole Indian War." In addition, there are a few images of Indians under headings such as "American Revolution," "War of 1812," "Advertising," "Symbolism," and "Political cartoons." The file also includes sections, organized alphabetically by state name, that often include views of settlements and forts, the earliest of which frequently show Indian dwellings and people. (Many of the images in the Graphics File are, of course, recreated scenes rather than depictions based on actual observation.)

Native Americans and related subjects are also treated in original popular graphic art, posters, panoramic photographs, cartoon drawings, newspaper and magazine photographic collections, fine prints, master photographs, and architectural drawings and photographs. Organized in "filing series," this material can be identified and accessed by consulting specific card catalogs, an on-line public access catalog, reference aids, and other electronic imaging devices, all available in the division's reading room. Notable collections representing many of these diverse formats are discussed in the final section.

Major Reference Works

Useful publications that specifically address American Indian-related collections in the Prints and Photographs Division include the following:

American Political Prints, 1766–1876: A Catalog of the Collections in the Library of Congress. Bernard F. Reilly, Jr. Boston, Mass.: G.K. Hall, 1991; E183.3.R45 1991

Native American-related political prints comprise a small but significant percentage of the hundreds discussed in Reilly's illustrated catalog.

GATEWAYS

Since the 1960s, the struggle for Native American self-determination has dominated Indian affairs. The threat of termination from the previous decade, combined with the sweeping civil rights movement, fostered inter-tribal unification and resulted in a resurgence of pan-Indian organizations demanding tribal control over their governance. The first major instance of pan-Indian militancy—focusing on cultural revitalization and self-determination—was the occupation of Alcatraz Island in San Francisco Bay in November 1969 by a group of armed Indians calling themselves Indians of All Tribes. Renaming the island "Indian land," the activists sought to establish an Indian cultural center, a college, a museum, and a center for ecology. After nineteen months, federal marshalls halted what they considered an invasion of federal land.

Indian activism accelerated during the Johnson and Nixon administrations when the American Indian Movement (AIM) was founded in Minneapolis by a group of urban Indians that included Dennis Banks and Russell Means. Court action was also an important source of political mobilization. Rapidly expanding to national status after their active participation in the Alcatraz protest, AIM next mobilized the November 1972 "Trail of Broken Treaties" caravan of more than two thousand people representing one hundred reservations. Begun as an effort to draw attention to Indian issues just prior to the presidential elections, the peaceful march ended in a six-day takeover of the Bureau of Indian Affairs offices in Washington, D.C.

Perhaps the protest of greatest symbolic impact, stunning both militant and moderate Indian factions, was the confrontation between AIM activists and a heavily armed force of federal agents at the site of the famous 1890 Sioux Wounded Knee massacre on the Pine Ridge Reservation in South Dakota. Two Indians were killed and a U.S. marshall was paralyzed. The final unified national action undertaken by AIM was the 1978 "Longest Walk," a six-month cross-country trek from San Francisco to Washington, D.C., intended to increase Indian cultural awareness and stimulate political activism.

Three factors persuaded Congress to adopt a policy of Indian self-sufficiency: the Indian rights movement and the well-established National Congress of American Indians; national task force investigations documenting abject impoverishment on most reservations, and underscoring the inadequacy of past federal assistance; and White House endorsement of self-determination from presidents Kennedy, Johnson and Nixon, including the latter's 1970 "self-determination without termination" message to Congress. The keystone legislation to emerge was the Indian Self-Determination and Education Assistance Act of 1975, which recognized that "prolonged federal domination of Indian service programs has served to retard rather than enhance the progress of Indian people." Supported by statutory authority and increases in federal expenditures, tribes began administering their own programs and contracting directly with the Bureau of Indian Affairs and Indian Health Services. The trend toward self-determination was further supported by important Supreme Court decisions during the 1980s, such as *Mississippi Choctaw* v. *Holyfield*, and congressional actions. These reaffirmed tribal sovereignty and broadened Indian rights to control land, natural resources, economic development, law and order, education, and health within reservation boundaries. Today Indian tribes continue to seek greater self-determination and reversal of injustices. Primary concerns which have been addressed by legislative action include child welfare, religious freedom, fishing rights, and repatriation of ancestral remains and objects.

WHERE TO LOOK: The General Collections (including Microform), Law Library, Prints and Photographs Division, and Motion Picture, Broadcasting and Recorded Sound Division.

We Remember Wounded Knee, 1890–1973. Poster based on a woodcut by Bruce Carter (New York: Akwesasne Notes, 1973). POS 6-U.S.361. Yanker Poster Collection (LC-USZC4-4819, color; LC-USZ62-111941, black and white). Prints and Photographs Division.

During the 1960s and '70s, Indian activists often referred to the massacre at Wounded Knee as a reminder to policy makers that injustices toward American Indians still existed.

The caricatures, allegories, campaign banners, and other visual political commentary from the Prints and Photographs Division of the Library of Congress, reflect public debate on government policy toward Indians during the early years of the nation.

The First Americans: Photographs from the Library of Congress. William H. Goetzmann. Washington, D.C.: Starwood Publishers, 1991; E89.L53 1991

Historian William H. Goetzmann offers social commentary on about one hundred fifty images of Native Americans from the Prints and Photographs Division, most of which were taken by turn-of-the-century commercial photographers. Investigating the photographers themselves, Goetzmann questions how their perceptions of American Indians, as well as what was marketable, influenced the visual records they made.

Indians of North America: A Guide to LOTS. Jennifer Brathovde with Arden Alexander and Sarah Rouse. Washington, D.C.: Library of Congress, 1995; Available from Prints and Photographs Division.

A comprehensive, annotated list and subject/creator index of American Indian related collections (LOTS) in the Prints and Photographs Division of the Library of Congress. Entries, which number more than five hundred, generally include a descriptive summary noting tribe, geographic location, activity, photographer, creator, or copyright claimant, dates, and number of items.

The North American Indian. Edward S. Curtis. 20 vols. and 20 portfolios in 4 vols. Cambridge, Mass.: Harvard University Press, 1907–30; New York: Johnson Reprint Corp., 1970; E77.C98

Curtis spent nearly thirty years compiling twenty volumes and twenty portfolios of photographs and text describing Indians of the Plains, the Central Plateau, the Northwest Coast, the Southwest, California, and Alaska. More than eighty tribes are pictured in nearly every facet of native life including portraits, dwellings, ceremonies, domestic activities, hunting, fishing, and battle. The 1970 reprint of this work is available in the division's reading room.

Prints of the West: Prints from the Library of Congress. Ron Tyler. Golden, Colo.: Fulcrum Publishing, 1994; NE962.W48 T96 1994

Tracing the illustrated history of the West among the holdings in the Library of Congress, Tyler also examines the portrayal of Native Americans from the earliest depictions by expeditionary artists to Frederic Remington's popular cowboy and Indian compositions. Tyler's lavishly illustrated work surveys the historical formats and genres in which Indians were presented, and analyzes art works as embodiments of values and beliefs, reflecting as well as shaping, widely-held attitudes toward the American Indian.

❏ SELECTED COLLECTIONS

The Prints and Photographs Division collections selected for description are grouped within the subject categories described in the introduction to this chapter, as follows:

Indian Delegations and Government Relations

During the seventeenth and eighteenth centuries, English monarchs anxious to win the allegiance of powerful tribal leaders invited many of them to visit London to establish or cement diplomatic relations. During these friendly political missions, chiefs and other prominent Native Americans would often have their portraits painted. Such was the case with the four sachems presented at Queen Anne's court in April 1710, whose portraits were painted by John Verelst, and engraved and published as prints (Fine Prints, John Simon).

Indian delegates visiting Washington, D.C., during the first half of the nineteenth century continued this tradition, sitting for such artists as Charles Balthazar Julien Fevret de St. Memin, and Charles Bird King. As in earlier centuries, such likenesses were disseminated through inexpensive prints. Eventually, photography supplanted painting and drawing as the preferred means of documenting delegation trips to the capital. The Library's collection is rich in both the earlier, European-produced portrayals (included in the Fine Prints and Popular Graphic Art filing series) and the printed and photographic representations of Native American leaders of the nineteenth and twentieth centuries, as noted below:

McKenney & Hall Lithographs (PGA Filing Series and LOT 7802).

Thomas McKenney, a long-time key administrator of federal Indian policy and the first director of the Bureau of Indian Affairs, maintained an active interest in preserving the historical record of American Indians. He established the Indian Portrait Gallery in Washington, D.C., and commissioned artists such as Charles Bird King and James Otto Lewis to paint the portraits of Indian delegates in their traditional clothing. Lithographs of the portraits, with accompanying text by James Hall, were published in the *History of the Indian Tribes of North America* between 1836 and 1844, and are held by the Rare Book and Special Collections Division. About one hundred twenty large prints and twenty-five smaller lithographed plates from McKenney and Hall's publication are held by the Prints and Photographs Division. These prints, many of which are hand-colored, represent leaders from the Iroquois, Creek, Sioux, Shawnee, Winnebago, Sauk (Sac) and Fox, Chippewa, Pawnee, Seminole, and Cherokee tribes.

A. Zeno Shindler (LOT 12894).

This small, extraordinary collection of studio portraits was produced in 1868 by A. Zeno Shindler, a leading delegation photographer. Two images feature Chief Keokuk, Jr., wearing ceremonial clothing, and his fourteen-year-old son Charles, in a modern suit. These descendants of Keokuk—a noted Sac and Fox leader whose daguerreotype portrait was taken twenty years earlier—reportedly came to Washington as members of an unofficial delegation to complain about the agent assigned to oversee their tribal affairs. A number of the Indian delegates were arrested on the journey between Kansas and D.C. Other noteworthy photographs in the collection include oval albumen print portraits of two unidentified Montauk Indians from New York, in stiff poses, wearing the white man's conventional, formal attire, and of O-Tan-Dan, a prisoner-of-war from Minnesota.

Alexander Gardner (LOTS 11790 and 12935).

Many of Alexander Gardner's studio portraits of Sioux Indians visiting Washington, D.C., were commissioned by William Blackmore of the Blackmore Museum in Salisbury, England. Blackmore pursued his avid interest in American Indians and the West by publishing photographic booklets of prominent leaders and their relatives. The Library's thirty-eight albumen prints of the Sioux, taken in 1872, include portraits of Big Foot, Lone Wolf, Red Cloud (pictured shaking hands with Blackmore), and others.

C. M. Bell Studio Collection (LOTS 12262, 12552, 12566, 12567, and 13008).

One of Washington's leading portrait photographers during the latter part of the nineteenth century, Charles Milton Bell is well known for his photographs of Native Americans. Under the auspices of Ferdinand Hayden, a director of the U.S. Geological Survey, Bell produced several hundred portraits of Indian delegates who came east to negotiate treaties. Bell also photographed Indians for the Department of the Interior and the Bureau of American Ethnology.

Of the more than six hundred Indian photographs produced by Bell, nearly one hundred photographic prints and original glass plate negatives, dating from 1873 to 1892, are held by the division. Most of these are individual or group portraits of Sioux leaders, although Fox, Nez Perce, Pawnee, Comanche, and Navajo tribes are also represented. These range in format from cabinet cards to larger (twenty by twenty-four inch) mounted photographs. Many present tribal groups wearing modern, Euro-American clothing, seated or standing against a prosaic studio backdrop. More elaborate portraits feature men (and a few women) in ceremonial dress, holding peace pipes, feathers, or war clubs, against a painted wilderness backdrop.

National Photo Company Collection (LOTS 12282, 12283, 12286, 12291, 12293–12299, and 12337).

The National Photo Company operated as a service to newspapers, news distributors, and other photo agencies by supplying photographs of current political and social events in Washington, D.C. The collection of loose images and chronological albums, covering activities from 1909 to 1932, includes about two hundred and fifty Indian-related photographs documenting Indian delegates from more than twenty tribes from Washington, Oregon, Idaho, Arizona, the Dakotas, Oklahoma, and Montana. Some of the representatives are posed with presidents Harding or Coolidge. Prominent leaders, pictured either in studio portraits or informally on the Capitol grounds, include the famous Chief Plenty Coups who traveled to Washington many times to lobby for Crow Indian land claims. Various activities on Capitol Hill such as ceremonial dancing, mock battles, and a tribute to the unknown soldier, also feature Indian participation.

New York World-Telegram & Sun Collection (finding aid in Prints and Photographs Reading Room).

A small number of images from this vast photo morgue document newsworthy Indian events between 1920 to 1967, including incidents in the history of tribal rights activism among the Chippewa, Creek, Iroquois, Seminole, Yakima, and Blackfeet, and a 1962 meeting between President John F. Kennedy and tribal delegates.

U.S. News & World Report Magazine Collection (Prints and Photographs Reading Room).

The magazine's archive of photographs, covering the years 1952 to 1986, includes visual documentation of relatively recent social, cultural, and political events concerning American Indians. A few photographs record the 1972 pan-Indian occupation of the Bureau of Indian Affairs in Washington, D.C., and the 1978 "Longest Walk" demonstration that included tipi encampments on the Washington Monument grounds and at Patapsco Park in Maryland.

Federal Government Surveys and Other Expeditions

Beginning in the early 1800s, the federal government and various private sponsors sent a number of survey teams and other exploring expeditions to the western U.S. to map territory, document natural resources, and identify potential travel routes. Artists and photographers were frequently among the geologists, zoologists, botanists, biologists, entomologists, and other scientists who composed these parties, and their visual documentation of American Indians was often incorporated in the surveys' published reports. The earliest photographic record of Indian life held by the division, in fact, originated with such a survey: a daguerreotype, made by Solomon Nunes Carvalho on the 1853 government expedition led by John Charles Fremont, pictures a Plains Indian tipi encampment and meat drying racks in the Kansas Territory. Important collections in this genre include the following:

Pacific Railroad Reports (LOT 3986).

The findings of the U.S. government-sponsored enterprise to determine the best railroad route from the Midwest to the West Coast were published in the massive twelve-volume *Reports of Explorations and Surveys, to Ascertain the Most Practicable and Economical Route for a Railroad from the Mississippi River to the Pacific Ocean*, (1855–61), commonly known as the Pacific Railroad Reports. More than seven hundred lithographs and engravings by about a dozen artists illustrate the work. Many loose plates from the publication, fifty of which feature American Indians from California, Colorado, Oregon, Utah, and Washington, are held in the Prints and Photographs Division. The lithographs, some colored and others uncolored, show native people in their natural environments, surrounded by mountain ranges, valleys, rivers, or canyons, and often conversing with the surveyors. Scenes from the tribal life of Blackfeet, Nez Perce, Salish, Assiniboine, Zuni, Navajo, Mohave, and Gros Ventre Indians, including the convening of treaty councils, the distribution of government goods, and the tribes' villages and encampments near military forts, are also portrayed.

Wheeler, Hayden, and Powell Surveys (LOTS 3193, 3427, 3960, 4677, 11557, and 12975).

These major geographical and geological surveys, conducted over large areas of the West between 1867 and 1879, were undertaken by the U.S. Army Corps of Engineers. Named after the expedition leaders, the Wheeler, Hayden, and Powell surveys were published in well-illustrated reports.

Timothy H. O'Sullivan, an official photographer for the Wheeler Survey, documented Apache, Mohave, Navajo, Zuni, and Paiute Indians primarily in Arizona, New Mexico, Colorado, and Nevada, between 1870 and 1879 (LOTS 3427 and 4677). Many of the nearly seventy stereographs and photographic prints picture Indian scouts posed with expedition crew members. Others show homes, portraits, and daily life. Two stereographs taken by William Henry Jackson on the Hayden Survey (LOT 3960) depict a Nez Percé Indian tipi encampment in Montana around 1871 and traditional food preparation by a tribal woman.

Chief photographer of the Powell Survey, John K. Hillers, often posed the Zuni, Hopi, Ute, and Paiute Indians he encountered, perhaps to obscure the grim realities of their impoverished existence. Taken between 1871 and 1879, more than forty of Hillers' images document tribal activity in Arizona, New Mexico, Utah, and Wyoming (LOTS 3193, 11557, and 12975).

Harriman Expedition to Alaska, 1899 (LOT 4841).

One of the last major surveys of the nineteenth century, the Harriman Expedition was undertaken to explore potential routes for a trans-Alaskan railroad. Twenty-three of America's leading authorities in various fields, led by C. Hart Merriam (see entry in Manuscript Division chapter), accompanied the expedition to document botanical, anthropological, geological, and other scientific findings. Edward S. Curtis, one of the party's chief photographers, recorded the daily life of the Native Alaskans among other subjects, and this early experience greatly influenced his eventual commitment to a thirty-year photographic study of North American Indians. Close to one hundred photographic prints from the expedition show native dwellings, campsites, small family groups, seal hunting, basketry, and totem poles.

Indian Wars and Confrontations

To a large extent, Indian-white relations were marked by hostility and violence for hundreds of years after the first encounters, causing the term "Indian wars" to gain wide currency. Artists portrayed the bloody conflicts, sometimes literally and sometimes imaginatively, in paintings, drawings, prints, and in illustrations for popular newspapers and magazines. Until the twentieth century, photographic technology was not sufficiently developed to effectively capture the action of a military battle or skirmish. As a result, nineteenth-century photographers usually confined themselves to documenting the sites of battles (rather than the action itself), leaders and other participants, peace negotiations, and such stationary subjects as forts, equipment, ordinance, and terrain. The division's holdings reflect the full range of this sort of graphic and photographic documentation, with notable areas of concentration as follows:

Gray and James Publishers (PGA Filing Series).

Nine hand-colored lithographs issued by the printing firm of Gray and James illustrate the Second Seminole War in Florida (1835–42). Scenes include U.S. soldiers in camp at Tampa Bay; Seminole Indians attacking a block house; a military detachment fording Lake Ocklawah in central Florida; troops burning a Seminole village; and other significant sites. Most of the Seminoles were driven from Florida after the war.

Louis H. Heller (LOT 11480).

One of two photographers to document the military camps, battlefields, and participants in the 1872–73 Modoc War in California, Louis H. Heller alone produced images of the Modoc pris-

oners of war. These rare portraits show the Indian militants, some of whom are chained together, shortly before their execution. Others, sentenced to life imprisonment, are also pictured. The Modoc Indians, originally residing in California, had been relocated to a reservation in Oregon in 1864. After several peaceful attempts to return to their homeland, fighting finally broke out in 1872 and resulted in the deaths of many white officers, soldiers, civilians, and Indians. Key insurgents, whose portraits appear in this collection, included Captain Jack, Schonchin Jim, and Curley Headed Doctor.

C. S. (Camillus S.) Fly (LOT 7449).

Although he operated a thriving photography studio in Tombstone, Arizona, for more than twenty years, C. S. Fly is best known for the documentary images he produced during the March 25, 1886, peace conference between General George C. Crook and Apache leader Geronimo. Fly boldly invited himself to join Crook's expedition to the Canyon de los Embudos in the Sierre Madre Mountains, where Crook planned to confer with the Apaches about ending their frequent raids on settlers and restricting their tribal domicile to the San Carlos Reservation. The resultant documentation, which shows both leaders, Geronimo's camp, Apache and U.S. troops, and the council meetings, includes the only known photographs taken inside a hostile Indian camp.

George E. Trager (LOT 11347).

Although no photographs of the actual massacre at Wounded Knee, South Dakota, exist, George E. Trager was the first photographer on the scene to record the grim aftermath. Soon after, he formed the Northwestern Photographic Company to speed the commercial circulation of those haunting images. Five of Trager's 1891 photographic prints, showing the frozen corpses of Sioux Indians and their burial, are in the division's collection.

Indian Prisoners of War (LOTS 5635 and 7106).

Four photographs (ca. 1895) document villages of relocated Apache prisoners of war near Fort Sill, Oklahoma, including one showing Geronimo with his wife and children holding watermelons grown in their garden (LOT 5635). Stereographs were produced of Sitting Bull and other Sioux Indian prisoners of war about 1881, at a campsite near Fort Randall, South Dakota, where they were held for two years. Published by Bailey, Dix & Mead as a series, these works show daily life and dwellings in the camp during the winter and summer months; Sitting Bull and others; issuance of annuity supplies and rations; and the daily roll call of prisoners. The collection also includes a portrait of a photographer reportedly taken by Sitting Bull (LOT 7106).

Charles Schreyvogel (LOT 4655).

Among the most popular western artists and illustrators, Charles Schreyvogel is best remembered for his late nineteenth and early twentieth-century oil paintings of military scenes. After a brief tour of the West during which he made studies of Ute Indians, army life, and cowboys, Schreyvogel returned to his New Jersey studio with the gear he had collected, to create the painstakingly detailed works for which he is known. Prints and Photographs Division has forty-four black-and-white photographs of Schreyvogel's paintings which are action-filled, often graphically violent portrayals of battles between American Indians and U.S. troops.

The Frontier, Villages, and Reservation Life

Away from the confines of the studio, a number of frontier photographers endured substantial hardships and surmounted great obstacles to capture the daily life of Indian people. A few settled among tribal communities, on or near reservations, and began long-standing careers. Visiting photographers, eager to satisfy the curious (or prurient) interests of the mass market, wanted pictures of these "exotic" people for commercial use. Others, inspired by more altruistic motives, sought to expose injustices or merely to record the peoples that fascinated them. While hundreds of graphic and photographic images of American Indian life and culture are scattered throughout the division, descriptions of several notable collections follow.

Charles Gentile (LOT 13024).

Among the earliest pictorial records of Mohave, Yuma, Maricopa, Yavapai, Pima, and Apache Indian people are forty-one albumen photographs taken between 1870 and 1872 by Charles Gentile. Contained in an apparently unique album titled, "Series of Photographic Views and Portraits of Arizona and Arizona Indian Tribes," the images show various reservations, military camps, and "the first Indian school in Arizona," with students posed in front of the building. Some captioned studio portraits suggest Gentile's preoccupation with an exotic presentation of native people.

Ben Wittick (LOTS 12910 and 12949).

George Ben Wittick produced photographs for early railroad enterprises and independently for his own commercial purposes. An ardent recorder of Southwestern Indian life, Wittick is noted for his images of the Hopi Snake Dances, taken shortly before the tribe outlawed the photographing of sacred ceremonies. Some of these reveal a profaned, commercialized spectacle in which the dancers are surrounded, and even crowded, by fashionably dressed tourists, photographers, and other curious onlookers. In

GATEWAYS

Under current federal law, Indian reservations are lands reserved by Indian tribes for themselves, often out of larger areas ceded to the federal government, wherein tribes exercise self-government within limits set by federal law.

The concept of defined land areas for Indian groups dates from early in the colonial period. The concept usually acknowledged inherent native land claims but chiefly sought to confine Indian activities within recognized boundaries while attempting to prevent colonial encroachment. After independence, the United States included in its Indian treaties the concept of tribes reserving lands for themselves, but the government also used the idea of general boundary lines beyond which non-Indians could not settle. Indian removal beyond the Mississippi in the 1830s and 1840s can be seen as an intensification of the boundary-line concept. By the mid-nineteenth century, however, non-Indian pressure for land west of the Mississippi led the federal government to establish defined reservations for individual tribes or bands or for groups of tribes.

On these reservations, political authority was gradually taken from tribal leaders by U.S. government officials—Indian agents—who pressed the assimilation policy and made major decisions involving reservation life. Indian agents were political appointees (until 1908). They and other reservation employees were regularly accused of corruption or incompetence throughout the nineteenth century, and were frequently the objects of congressional investigation. Like most non-Indians, many agents came to their jobs with little knowledge of Indian culture.

As problems on Indian reservations became publicized, and as land pressure continued unabated, Indian sympathizers ("friends of the Indians") and non-sympathizers, who generally favored assimilation, concluded that reservations themselves were a hindrance to that assimilation as well as to non-Indian expansion. Collective tribal ownership should be ended, they felt, and reservation land allotted to Indian families and the surplus opened to homesteading. This policy found expression in the General Allotment Act (Dawes Severalty Act) of 1887.

Allotment and the sale of surplus land, while it did not occur on all reservations, deprived Indians of some 60 percent of their lands between 1887 and 1934, when allotment was ended. Like reservations, allotment exerted further pressure on Indian autonomy and culture. Since 1934, legislation and tribal litigation have restored some of the lands lost in treaty cessions and under the allotment policy. At present about 115 million acres lie within Indian reservations and Alaska Native lands, nearly 57 million acres of which are held in trust by the federal government for the benefit of Indian people.

WHERE TO LOOK: The General Collections, the Law Library, and the Rare Book and Special Collections, Manuscript, Geography and Map, and Prints and Photographs Divisions.

"An Indian agency—distributing rations," wood engraving from *Harper's Weekly*, November 13, 1875. AP2.H32. LOT 4391-B (LC-USZ62-38020). General Collections (Microform) and Prints and Photographs Division.

The engraving represents the distribution of rations at the Red Cloud Agency in Nebraska (now part of the Pine Ridge Sioux Reservation). Home of the Oglala chief Red Cloud, this agency was one of several under investigation during that year for suspected fraud on the part of contractors and suppliers.

addition, the division's holdings include about fifty photographic prints and stereographs produced between 1879 and 1899, which show Apache, Mohave, Pueblo, Hopi, and Havasupai people, pueblos, and ceremonies in Arizona and New Mexico.

John C. H. Grabill (LOT 3076).

Thought to be the largest surviving collection of this early Western photographer's work, the division's holdings of John C. H. Grabill's photographs document frontier life in Colorado, South Dakota, and Wyoming. Grabill had studios in Deadwood and Lead City, South Dakota, not far from the Pine Ridge Indian Reservation. About fifty large sepia-toned prints (ca. 1891) in the division's collection concern Sioux Indian life on and near the reservation. Although a few picturesque views of Indian villages are included, most of the images are straightforward and unsentimental. Grabill recorded the Sioux people in contact with white culture, primarily with government beef issue activities, but also with Buffalo Bill (William F.) Cody, who visited the reservation to recruit performers. Other images show community dwellings, tipi encampments, an Indian school, ceremonial dancing, and members of the Sioux nation.

Charles F. Lummis (LOT 2840).

A journalist, photographer, and pioneer in the study of the American Southwest, Charles F. Lummis was among the first photographers to live near the Pueblo Indians, learn their language, and record their history. Nearly one hundred photographs by Lummis in the division portray the daily life of many Southwestern tribes between 1888 and 1894 and combine a journalistic objectivity with a marked sensitivity to the Indian people. Some of Lummis's photographs portray individuals at work in farming, hunting, weaving, making pottery, and baking, and at play in foot races, swinging lassos,

and gaming. Others show ceremonial dancing, homes, prayer sticks, and a mission school.

Lloyd Winter and Percy Pond (LOT 2291-A).

Lloyd Winter and Percy Pond operated a commercial photography studio in Juneau, Alaska, from 1893 to 1943. During that time they produced a relatively small number of photographs (about four hundred in all) depicting Tlingit and Haida Indian life, which are nonetheless quite valuable as records for historians today. Although they were commercial photographers, Winter and Pond differed from most of their fellow professionals in many ways. First, they did not present an anachronistic view of Native Alaskan culture. Modern western influence in clothing, dwellings, tools, utensils, and economic conditions is in evidence in most of their works. Second, as year-round residents of Alaska they were able to document everyday activities and conveniently visit obscure native communities which surrounded the more populated areas. Some works show a summer fishing encampment, remote Indian villages, women weaving baskets, individuals and small groups in front of their homes, children on the beach, and Indian prisoners hauling water in wagons. Finally, Winter and Pond had been formally initiated into a Tlingit tribe and were allowed to explore areas prohibited to others. Interiors of highly respected tribal leaders' homes, potlatch dancers, and other ceremonials are represented. The division's collection of seventy-five Winter and Pond photographs, taken between 1894 and 1905, also picture totem poles, grave houses, ceremonial masks, and other beautifully and intricately carved objects.

Katherine Taylor Dodge (LOT 12768).

Katherine Taylor Dodge's small collection of photographs document harsh life on the San Carlos Apache Reservation in Arizona around 1899 and includes reservation Indians crowded in line to receive government provisions.

John Alvin Anderson (LOTS 3328, 3398, and 12984).

John Alvin Anderson, a Swedish immigrant, lived with his family on the Rosebud Reservation in South Dakota for nearly half a century beginning in 1880. While photography was his primary career, Anderson also worked as a clerk in a trading post and in both capacities developed a close relationship with the Brulé Sioux people whose lives he recorded. Anderson's photographic approach ranged from starkly literal documentation to dramatic staging of his subjects. The division's collection of seventy-five photographs includes portraits of prominent Indian leaders such as Hollow Horn Bear, He Dog, Crow Dog, and others; everyday scenes such as Sioux camps, councils with government leaders, dances, and beef issues; and staged recreations of traditional activities, such as a scaffold burial, a man making arrows, and hunting and fishing.

Adam Clark Vroman (LOTS 3273 and 3333).

A Pasadena, California, book dealer and former railroad worker, Adam Clark Vroman began traveling to the Southwest to photograph Indians, their homes, rituals, and handicrafts about 1894. His portrayals of Pueblo, Hopi, Zuni, and Navajo people are simple, genuine, and unromanticized. Vroman lectured publicly about the mistreatment of Indians and offered his evocative images, many of which feature young children in street scenes, as documentation. The division's collection of forty photographs also depict tribal officials and other individuals, families, a Snake Dance, and daily cultural activities.

Frank Bennett Fiske (LOT 4810).

Born in Dakota Territory in 1883, Frank Bennett Fiske spent most of his life in the Fort Yates (or Standing Rock Sioux) Reservation area where he gained an uncommon familiarity with his photographic subjects. The more than six hundred photographic prints by Fiske included in the division's holdings were produced between 1900 and 1931. Both studio and plein air portraits, they depict Standing Rock Sioux adults, children, and families, primarily in traditional dress, and non-Indian community members such as government agents and interpreters. Among these are also group portraits of tribal police and the tribal council, images of dwellings and other structures including tipi camps, a medicine lodge, cabins, Indian schools, and the Fort Yates agency buildings. Traditional dancing, drumming, rodeos, ranching, farming, and church activities are also shown.

Simeon Schwemberger (LOTS 5026, 11497, 11498, 11891, and 11892).

Simeon Schwemberger, a Franciscan brother, arrived at St. Michael's Mission in Arizona in 1901 and began taking pictures of the native population a year later. A self-taught amateur, Schwemberger was undoubtedly influenced by the many professional photographers who traveled to the Southwest to record Indian life at the turn of the century. Brother Schwemberger's images of the Navajo, Jemez, Hopi, and Zuni Indians from surrounding reservations are marked at times by the formality characteristic of studio photography in the period and at times by a candid realism evidently born of his vocational empathy with his subjects. More than two hundred photographic prints held by the division include intimate individual, family, and other group portraits, and views of daily reservation life, ceremonial dancing, dwellings, Navajo prisoners and scouts, and military activity at Fort Defiance, Arizona. An extraordinary series chronicles a Navajo Yebichai (Nightway or Night Chant), a nine-day healing ceremony which involved construction of a medicine lodge and sweat lodge. Aspects portrayed include sand painting, various stages of the ceremony itself, and portraits of the patient and participants. That Brother Schwemberger was permitted to attend and photograph the ceremony was a testament to the trust he earned among the tribal members. His work is an important contribution to the photographic history of Navajo people.

Frederic Remington (Prints & Photographs Reference Aid #79).

One of the best-known illustrators of the American West, Frederic Remington was born in New York in 1861 and first visited Montana when he was nineteen years old. He later pursued occupations as a gold prospector, cowboy, sheepherder, and salonkeeper, and also traveled with the U.S. Army as a civilian scout on several military campaigns. These diverse frontier experiences provided material for Remington's vast body of artwork and writings. The division holds nearly one hundred reproductions of paintings, drawings, and etchings by Remington. These include portraits and illustrations of daily life among Ute, Blackfeet, Apache, Cheyenne, Sioux, and Crow tribes. Many of the works portray battles with pioneers and U.S. military troops, including the surrender of Chief Joseph, Custer's last stand, and a defiant Geronimo. Others depict buffalo hunting, the Sun Dance and Ghost Dance, picture-writing, prayer and worship, and lodges.

Historic American Buildings Survey (HABS) (Prints and Photographs Reading Room).

The largest and most widely used architectural collection in the division, HABS includes photographs, measured drawings, and written historical documentation on nearly thirty thousand structures. Created under this ongoing project, more than fifty surveys currently relate to American Indians. Those made in the Southwest, such as the Acoma pueblo in New Mexico, are the most extensive. Aside from pueblos, structures documented include missions, churches, government agency buildings, military forts, trading posts, and Indian schools. The surveys

can be identified by consulting a subject card catalog.

Farm Security Administration/Office of War Information Collection (Various microfilmed LOTS and Prints and Photographs Reading Room).

The photographs produced under these federally-sponsored projects form an extensive pictorial record of American life between 1935 and 1943. An estimated three hundred images concern American Indians. Photographers Marion Post Wolcott, Dorothea Lange, and Arthur Rothstein recorded daily activity and living conditions in Indian communities and on reservations in Montana, Oregon, Nevada, and New Mexico. Russell Lee's documentation of Cherokee tenant farmers and day laborers in Oklahoma and the families of migrant Indian blueberry pickers in Minnesota tent camps convey a vivid sense of the hard times of the Great Depression.

Photographs of signs in Midwestern taverns warning "No beer sold to Indians" also reflect the discriminatory practices of the era. John Collier, Jr.'s photographs of a local Indian fair in Connecticut suggest the commercialization and stereotyping of Indian lore and image. This series by Collier includes images of a medicine show featuring "Paw Maw—the Great American Indian Psychic" and photographs of "Indian braves" teaching white customers how to use a bow and arrow.

U.S. News & World Report Magazine Collection (Prints and Photographs Reading Room).

About three hundred photographs of Indian subjects in this collection examine substandard living conditions and tribal efforts to combat poverty during the 1960s and 1970s on the Navajo, Northern Cheyenne, and Rosebud Sioux reservations. Images include portraits, scenes from Indian business, government, mining, manufacturing, farming, ranching, and construction activities, and scenes from everyday life.

Education

As part of the federal government's assimilation efforts, many Indian children were taken from their reservations and enrolled in boarding schools run by non-Indians. "Before and after" photographs of the students were often used to demonstrate and publicize this "civilizing" process. Many such documents are found among the late nineteenth- and early twentieth-century commercially produced photographs deposited in the division's LOT holdings. Numerous single images of Indian schools, their students, and group portraits of their football teams and musical bands can also be found in the division's collections. Extensive photographic documentation of two institutions which earned considerable regard as model schools are noted below.

Hampton Normal & Agricultural Institute, Hampton, Virginia (LOT 11051).

Founded in 1868 to educate newly freed blacks, the Hampton Normal & Agricultural Institute accepted its first American Indian students (former prisoners of war) ten years later. Over a fifty-year period more than thirteen hundred Indian students from sixty-five tribes enrolled in the Hampton program, which was designed to assimilate Indians into the dominant white culture. Housed in "wigwam" dormitories and dressed in military uniforms, the Indian students were encouraged to master the cultural ways of mainstream America through academic coursework, vocational training, and a Christian education. In Frances Benjamin Johnston's photographs of the school taken between 1899 and 1900, Indian students appear among the predominantly black population in classroom scenes; farming, carpentry, bricklaying, and sewing instruction; orchestra and band group portraits; and related school activities. Some boys and girls are shown wearing traditional Indian clothing.

Carlisle Indian Industrial School, Carlisle, Pennsylvania (LOTS 6818, 12369, 12764, and 13016).

Established in 1879 by Richard Henry Pratt, the military officer who first placed Indian students at Hampton, the Carlisle Indian School was initially set up in abandoned army cavalry barracks. Similar to Hampton, the program at Carlisle offered reading, writing, and mathematics, as well as vocational and farming trades for the boys and housework for the girls. Pratt advocated the students' complete severance from their tribes, and promoted this strict approach to Indian education through lectures, pamphlets, and "before and after" photographs of transformed students. The local, semi-official school photographer John N. Choate recorded early student life at Carlisle and also produced studio portraits of well-known visiting Indian leaders (LOTS 6818, 12764 and 13016). More than one hundred photographs by Frances Benjamin Johnston also document student activity between 1901 and 1903 (LOT 12369).

Panoramic Photographs of Indian Schools (On-line Public Access Catalog).

Campus-wide views of Indian government schools, student group portraits, school parades, and the 1905 Carlisle Indian Industrial School football team are pictured in this unique collection of large photographic prints, most exceeding 28 inches in length. Taken between 1905 and 1914, the panoramas represent schools in Arizona, Kansas, Michigan, North Carolina, Pennsylvania, and South Dakota.

Expositions, World's Fairs, and Wild West Shows

Some of America's early anthropologists produced educational "living exhibits" of Native American homes, traditional dress, ceremonials, and daily life, which were shown at expositions and world's fairs. Photographers often documented these staged tableaux and performances, and memorialized many of the Indian participants in studio portraits. Wild West shows, on the other hand, appealed less to the educational interests than to the imaginations of middle class Americans, and became a popular form of entertainment during the late nineteenth and early twentieth centuries. Because of the offer of employment and the opportunity to escape the desperate conditions of reservation life, many Native Americans appeared in the purportedly "historical" depictions of frontier events featured in such shows. Indian performers are particularly well documented in studio portraits while the actual shows are represented in photographs and in posters advertising such attractions. Of particular note are the following collections:

Frank A. Rinehart and Adolph Muhr (LOT 12841).

In 1885 Rinehart opened his own photographic studio in Omaha, Nebraska. Thirteen years later he became the official photographer for the Trans-Mississippi International Exposition held in Omaha, which established his renown. In addition to the fair buildings, Rinehart photographed many of the living exhibits of the Plains Indians, particularly the sham battle extravaganzas performed by the "Indian Congress." Originally intended as educational demonstrations of traditional culture, "Indian Congress" activities quickly degenerated into pure, and extremely popular, entertainment. A notable image in this collection is an outdoor group portrait depicting several hundred Indian Congress performers, spectators, scouts on horses, and onlookers. The scene typifies the circus-like atmosphere of the performances. Also pictured is a constructed Indian encampment on the exposition grounds featuring Pueblo men making bricks and Cheyenne and Arapaho Indians reenacting the Ghost Dance.

Adolph Muhr, a Rinehart employee, took the studio portraits of Indian participants, including Sioux chiefs Hollow Horn Bear and American Horse, and Apache leader Geronimo. More than sixty portraits of Sioux, Assiniboine, Kiowa, Tonkawa, Arapaho, Pueblo, Sac and Fox, and Blackfeet tribal representatives make up the major portion of the Rinehart-Muhr collection.

Herman Heyn and James Matzen (LOT 3401).

Heyn and Matzen, of Omaha, Nebraska, probably took their striking, finely-crafted studio portraits at the Trans-Mississippi International Exposition in 1898. Five hundred and fifty images came to the Library between 1899 and 1900. This portrait collection depicts primarily Sioux Indian men, women, and children, most of whom appear in elaborate ceremonial garb. Group portraits of families and individuals are also included as well as evidently staged outdoor portrayals of hunting, stalking, dancing, and tribal council meetings.

C. D. Arnold (LOT 4654).

Charles Dudley Arnold was the official photographer for the 1893 Chicago World's Fair and in 1901 he also documented the Pan-American Exposition held in Buffalo, New York. Of the division's extensive holdings of Arnold photographs, nearly fifty depict American Indians. The most notable of these are the images of the "Indian Congress" mock battles between whites and Indians. Three years after the initial presentation at the Trans-Mississippi Fair, the theatrics seemed perfected. At the New York site, an enormous stadium was constructed to stage the battles which featured "real war whoops," Geronimo, the "human tiger," and Winona, a Sioux woman touted as the "most phenomenal rifle shot in the world." After the battles, Indian women appeared on the field and pretended to mutilate the "dead" bodies. Arnold's photographs vividly document these performances and the American Indians on the fair grounds and in the studio.

The Gerhard Sisters (LOTS 3796, 4863, and 13007).

At the 1904 St. Louis World's Fair, American Indians were featured in living anthropological exhibits (along with villagers from the Philippines) that showed indigenous peoples from various parts of the world in their daily activities. The "least civilized" and "advanced people" section of the fairgrounds juxtaposed tableaux of Indian reservation dwellings occupied by Indian people in traditional clothing with a neighboring exhibit in which their grandchildren learned white ways in a model government Indian school.

The Gerhard Sisters, Mamie and Emma, about whom little is known, produced sensitive and dynamic portraits of the Indian people, taken in their St. Louis studio, revealing dignified, unique individuals, often interacting warmly or playfully with each other. Cheyenne, Osage, Pueblo, Apache, Inuit, and Sioux people, including the well-known Geronimo, American Horse, Hollow Horn Bear, and Wolf Robe, are pictured in forty elegant compositions. Family group portraits, mothers with babies, young children and their pet dogs, and individual men and women clothed in fine, traditional attire, are pictured as well. In sharp contrast, a small number of images, taken in the exposition, document exhibit performances and mock ceremonials such as the Snake Dance. Overwhelmingly, however, the Gerhard Sisters chose to portray the Indians as people, rather than as curiosities or exhibits.

William H. Rau (LOT 11045).

Rau began his career as a government survey photographer, working briefly with William Henry Jackson, but established his reputation by producing scenic landscape views for railroads. In 1904 he also photographed the anthropological Indian exhibits at the St. Louis World's Fair, documenting the diverse activities of the Hopi, Wichita, Pawnee, Cheyenne, and Sioux tribes. Thirteen stereographic prints, taken outdoors on the fair grounds, capture the hustle and bustle of the exposition, unlike the sedentary views of studio images. They include "Indian braves" riding horses, Pueblo women selling pottery, a "rainmaker" in conversation, a Hopi "squaw" weaving a blanket, Wichita men building an enormous grass lodge, and "medicine men" wearing face paint with squirming rattlesnakes at their feet. A staid Geronimo is also shown demonstrating how to use a bow and arrow.

Buffalo Bill's Wild West Show and Congress of Rough Riders of the World (LOTS 3424 and 6337).

Pony Express rider, Indian scout, buffalo hunter, and showman William F. Cody produced the most famous touring Wild West show in the United States and Europe. "Buffalo Bill" Cody mounted and toured his namesake extravaganzas between 1883 and 1916. Cody employed thousands of Indians (and cowboys) to perform in spectacular mock battles, war dances, fancy horseback riding, acts of markmanship, and other western theatrics. Photographs of Cody and his shows are documented in two notable collections.

Napoleon Sarony, a photographer known for masterful portraits of actors, actresses, and other famed personalities, chronicled a New York performance of Buffalo Bill's Wild West Show in 1886 (LOT 6337). Departing from posed studio compositions, Sarony's unusual images capture the animation of an Indian attack, charging wild horses and stage coaches, and a mass retreat by the defeated Indians, performed in an outdoor stadium. Additional photographs show a performance group of Native American men, women, and children, informally gathered around tipis on the arena backlot, sharing a watermelon. Two

GATEWAYS

"Lo, the poor Indian."   "Indian giver."
"Drunken Indian."   "Noble savage."
"The only good Indian is a dead Indian."
"Squaw."   "On the warpath."
"Bloodthirsty warrior."
"Vanishing American."   "Redskin."

Images, stereotypes, and myths have profoundly affected the way Native Americans were traditionally viewed. Most depictions, whether presented in dime novels, motion pictures, paintings, federal policies, advertising, photographs, or museum exhibits, have not been based on a thorough knowledge of Indian people but rather have reflected non-Indian political, religious, economic, or moral attitudes.

Since Columbus's first encounter, misconceptions about Indians have persisted. The basic notions of "discovery" and "new world" have been sharply challenged as millions of inhabitants, comprising hundreds of distinct cultural societies, had already discovered America. Characterizing these native inhabitants as exotic, primitive, wild, and heathenish, Columbus and other newcomers applied the doctrine of conquest and, later, intent to "civilize." Depictions of savage-like creatures flourished in historical accounts and drawings.

Images of American Indians changed through time to mirror particular political or social trends. Manifest destiny justified forcing the "good," submissive natives onto reservations for assimilation purposes, while battling the recalcitrant, "bad" hostiles advanced settlement of the last frontier. The cowboys and Indians of the West became indelible symbols of a moral struggle in the public's imagination. Traveling wild west shows featuring Buffalo Bill and Sitting Bull brought these myths to life with reenactments of battle scenes played against wilderness backdrops. Some non-Indian sympathizers tended to view native people as a "vanishing race," doomed to extinction. Many nineteenth and twentieth-century anthropologists rushed to document tribal customs while photographers such as Edward S. Curtis and Joseph K. Dixon recreated romantic scenes of pristine native culture before encroachment. Museums also attempted to preserve traditional lifestyles by presenting a static image of the American Indian, frozen in time, surrounded by artifacts. Years later, the youthful counter-culture embraced Native Americans with nostalgia and guilt-ridden sympathy. Ironically, many Indian people in cities and on reservations were disparaged for not being "real Indians," although government, church, boarding schools, and other social institutions had relentlessly urged tribal communities to cease being Indian. Despite centuries of change since contact, many picture the "real" Indian as the one created by non-Indian image makers in art, literature, films, photography, and other media.

WHERE TO LOOK: Images, stereotypes, and myths of the American Indian are pervasive throughout the collections, most particularly in the General Collections and in the collections of the Rare Book and Special Collections, Prints and Photographs, Motion Picture, Broadcasting and Recorded Sound, and Music Divisions.

Lo the poor Indian. Lithograph by Vance, Parsloe and Co. Publishers, New York, 1875. PGA—Vance & Parsloe (A size). (LC-USZ62-92901). Prints and Photographs Division.

Awkwardly holding the white man's weapon while inadvertently spilling his liquor, this dazed and inept Indian is among the many historic caricatures devised by non-Indian artists.

particularly rare photographs in this group, taken on board a ship by the company Merritt and Van Wagner, picture the Indian performers, Cody, and other troupe hands departing from New York for London. The collection also includes a studio portrait of Sitting Bull with Cody. Sitting Bull, who toured briefly with the show, was prominently featured in the "Custer's Last Stand" dramatizations.

Buffalo Bill's Wild West Show troupe also visited many European cities where their performances were equally popular. Thirty-six images provide a pictorial record of the 1903 presentation at the Olympia Stadium in London, England (LOT 3424).

Pawnee Bill's Wild West (LOT 12898).

Gordon W. Lillie, another famous showman and entrepreneur, billed this rival Wild West show "Pawnee Bill's." Sixteen studio photographs, copyrighted in 1905 by the Chicago-based Siegel, Cooper, and Company, picture reenactments of "The Death of Custer," "Pocahontas [saving] John Smith," "The Departure of Minnehaha," and other stereotypical dramas. A group portrait of Lillie with the Indian performers includes Princess Winona, who had also been featured at the New York World's Fair in 1901.

Wild West Show Posters (Poster Collection).

With the promise to present "actual scenes, genuine characters" from the West, posters marketing the Wild West performances helped bring to life images of American Indians in popular culture. Showing attacks on the Deadwood stage, covered wagons, forts, settlements, and troops, and the defeat of General George Custer at Little Big Horn, these colorful images of Indians lured audiences into the stadiums and arenas where the shows were performed. Other posters, focussing on the exotic and lurid "peculiarities of the wily dusky warriors" and their "weird war dances," attracted the curious, who were anxious to see real Indians for the first time.

More than twenty lithographic posters promoting Buffalo Bill's and Pawnee Bill's Wild West shows are held in the division's poster collection.

Pictorialist Photographs

The Pictorialist movement in photography, which flourished in the United States between the 1890s and about 1910 and resurged again briefly during the 1920s, was founded upon the belief in photography as a fine art, comparable to drawing and painting. Pictorialist photographers tended to compose their images carefully, and often manipulated the optical qualities and printing processes of the medium, and cropped their final prints to produce photographs intended to be viewed as artistic objects. Photographers working in this vein created beautiful, idealized portraits of Native Americans and Indian life. The division holds an extensive collection of American pictorialist works:

Edward S. Curtis (LOTS 12310 through 12331).

America's leading photographer of Indian people, Edward S. Curtis produced over forty thousand negatives of more than eighty tribes during his lifetime. Begun in 1898, Curtis's major work, *The North American Indian*, was published in a twenty-volume set of photogravure prints with ethnographic text. Financed in part by J. Pierpont Morgan and encouraged by President Theodore Roosevelt, the thirty-year project was an attempt to photograph all of the Indian tribes, as noted by Curtis in his introduction, that "still retain to a considerable degree their primitive customs and traditions." However, by the turn of the century, virtually all native people had changed radically and tribal life incorporated elements of both traditional and contemporary European culture. Nevertheless, Curtis was determined to produce a record of Indians as they supposedly looked and lived prior to contact with whites. To this end he masterfully manipulated his subjects and their surroundings to create an artistically beautiful but artificial past, often obliterating traces of the modern, such as product labels, alarm clocks, and Euro-American attire. Still Curtis's photographs, albeit nostalgic and sentimental, today epitomize for many the archetypal Native American.

The division's Curtis holdings number more than 2,800 contact prints made from the original large-format negatives, arranged in twenty-two LOTS and organized by tribe. More than half of the photographs were not published in *The North American Indian*. They include variant views of the same people and places represented in many of those that were published, and are a valuable, but little known, source of documentation.

Gertrude Käsebier (LOT 10136).

Trained as an artist, Gertrude Käsebier was a founding member of the Photo-Secession Club and a leading figure in the Pictorialist movement. In 1964 the Library acquired fifty-two of the original glass negatives for Käsebier's studio portraits of Sioux Indians who were members of Buffalo Bill's Wild West Show. Taken in New York in 1901, most of these beautifully composed and technically superior images show the performers wearing ceremonial clothing and feathered headdresses, and holding such implements as peace pipes, war clubs, and bows and arrows. A number of poignant double portraits, of Mr. and Mrs. Samuel Horse and Mr. and Mrs. Charging Thunder, are included along with an unusual and delightful photograph of Charging Thunder with his collie dog.

Roland Reed (LOTS 12840 and 13022).

During his childhood years in Wisconsin, Roland Reed was drawn to the Native Americans he encountered, and throughout his life he befriended many Indians from numerous tribes. As a photographer, Reed made American Indians the exclusive subject of his images. Shunning commercial success, Reed slowly and arduously produced his technically advanced, and meticulously and artistically composed photographic studies. The division holds about thirty of Reed's photographs of Blackfeet, Chippewa, Navajo, and Hopi Indians, many of them portraits and views of fishing, scouting, traveling, and other aspects of village life, from about 1907 to 1913.

Joseph Kossuth Dixon (LOTS 11687-1 and 12916).

Guilt-ridden and concerned about the plight of Native Americans, Rodman Wanamaker launched a privately-funded, national campaign to focus attention on saving Indian populations from extinction by promoting U.S. citizenship for them. Joseph Kossuth Dixon was commissioned to organize and document three Wanamaker Expeditions to several tribal communities including the Apache, Blackfeet, Cheyenne, Umatilla, and Sioux, between 1908 and 1913. The division's holdings of Dixon's contrived yet starkly alluring images, some of which were published in his 1913 book *The Vanishing Race*, show reenactments of battles, romantic tipi camps at twilight, bands of warriors on horseback, mock scenes of peace treaty signings, "the last great Indian council," U.S. flag raising ceremonies, and individual portraits of chiefs in ceremonial dress. Dixon's sentimentalized pictorial recreations of the past were designed to convince the public and government officials that Indians were worthy of citizenship and worthy of saving.

Laura Gilpin (LOT 4522 and PH Filing Series).

The soft-focus quality and impeccable craftsmanship evident in Laura Gilpin's early images of Pueblo and Navajo Indians reflect the influence of her photographic training at the school of Clarence H. White. (White was a formative influence on many American pictorialist photographers.) Gilpin was engaged in documenting the lives and environment of the Southwest Indians for over sixty years, and published two books which combined social commentary with her art. The division's holdings include twenty master photographs produced by Gilpin between 1925 and 1930, mostly portraits and views of dwellings and landscapes. A group of about twenty-five platinum prints, produced by Gilpin in 1939 (LOT 4522), shows Acoma Pueblo Indian men, women and families, dwellings, street scenes, church interiors and exteriors, a woman spinning wool, and a Navajo silversmith.

Allegories, Satires, Stereotypes, and Polemical Representations

The image of the Native North American has, since the Age of Discovery, served a number of imaginative and symbolic purposes for artists of Europe and America. The Indian has appeared in allegories and political satires to represent the virgin domain of the American continent, the rebellious actions of the early colonists, and, in the late eighteenth and early nineteenth centuries, the emerging United States itself. Many of these are scattered among the Library's outstanding collection of British and American satirical prints. The division's extensive holdings of American Indian-related advertising prints and labels, posters, and photographs, moreover, exemplify the many ways in which pictorial images have conveyed and disseminated powerful and influential ideas, both favorable and unfavorable to Native Americans. Significant concentrations of such works are described below.

American Political Prints (PC / US and PGA Filing Series).

Nearly thirty cartoons, caricatures, patriotic allegories, campaign banners, and other individually issued prints, provide a visual record of political debate on federal policies affecting Native Americans during the early years of the nation. Several images, for instance, vilify Presidents Andrew Jackson and Martin Van Buren,

both of whom established government treaties under which thousands of Cherokee, Seminole, and other eastern tribes were displaced and deprived of their lands. Van Buren is further criticized for his directive to use bloodhounds to hunt fugitive Indians during the Second Seminole War in Florida. The country's ninth president, William Henry Harrison, successfully exploited his zealous military record of Indian-fighting in his 1840 presidential campaign banners.

Indians were also a frequent motif in prints promoting the nativist "Know Nothing" movement's prejudice against the foreign-born. They also appear as symbols in an elaborate martial allegory of the U.S. titled "Arms of the United States of America." *American Political Prints, 1766–1876: A Catalog of the Collections in the Library of Congress* (Boston: G.K. Hall, 1991) by Bernard Reilly, Jr., is a chronological illustrated guide to this material.

Currier and Ives Lithographs (PGA Filing Series).

Currier and Ives, one of America's best-known lithographic printing and publishing firms, may be the richest single source of nineteenth-century American popular imagery. Between 1835 and about 1900, the New York firm produced more than seven thousand different prints illustrating nearly every aspect of American life and culture. The inexpensive prints were primarily used as decorative pieces, "works of art to brighten the home within the reach of all." The Library's holdings of approximately 3,600 Currier & Ives lithographs are the most extensive held by any public institution. *Currier & Ives: A Catalogue Raisonné* (Detroit: Gale Research Company, 1983; NE2312.C8 A4 1983a), a comprehensive, illustrated catalog, lists the individual lithographs.

The American Indian is prominently featured in more than thirty works by Currier & Ives, many of which are hand-colored, and as incidental figures in numerous others. Typical of Currier

& Ives' style, the images are often sentimental and conventionalized, appealing to the romantic notions of the era. Indian males are stereotypically rendered as warriors (bare-chested and holding tomahawks), hunters, or as noble primitives settled in idyllic wilderness villages. More dramatic are two representations of Longfellow's poem "Hiawatha," one illustrating Minnehaha on her deathbed, the other showing a preternatural Hiawatha entering the kingdom of heaven—in a canoe. Deviations from Currier & Ives' familiar stylized approach include George Catlin's relatively realistic portrayals of Wi-jun-jon, an Assiniboine Indian delegate visiting Washington, D.C., in 1831, and a Mandan (?) Snow-Shoe Dance. Originally issued as part of Catlin's *North American Indian Portfolio,* these prints were reissued by Currier & Ives, probably in the late 1840s or early 1850s.

Bank Note Engravings (LOTS 11344, 12592-12595, and 12601).

During the first half of the nineteenth century, paper currency was issued by state and local banks, rather than by the federal treasury. The vignette illustrations used on these engraved bank notes often incorporated images of Indians, especially in symbolic representations mapping the progress of the United States and of the virtues of "civilization." Nearly thirty-five proofs for these engravings, scattered among various LOTS, picture Native Americans witnessing the encroachment of ships, colonists, the Christian ministry, and urban industry on the American wilderness. Other scenes featuring Indians show confrontational and peaceful encounters with frontiersmen, the arms of Ohio, Kentucky, and New York states, and hunting and fishing scenes.

Tobacco Labels (LOT 10618-48).

Images of American Indians were widely used by the tobacco industry on their nineteenth-century advertisements and labels, per-

haps because of the widely-held belief that tobacco use originated with native people. More than twenty-five richly colored labels, designed to attract the attention of consumers and increase sales, picture Indians in a wide range of settings. Many feature the bare-breasted Indian "princess," variously holding tobacco leaves, gingerly crossing a stream, or walking on a river bank. A few show women in more active roles, such as hunting and canoeing. Many labels promoting brand names of famous chiefs offer bold and dynamic likenesses of Black Hawk, Sequoyah, Red Cloud, and Massasoit. Others show scenes from frontier life in which Indians hunt animals or sit peacefully in tipi camps.

Patent Medicine and Other Advertising Labels (LOT 10632-22 and LOTS 10692-10771).

Nineteenth-century advertisers, invoking native culture's traditional knowledge of herbs and plants, often used images of Indians to sell medicinal concoctions. Focusing on famous individuals such as Joseph Brant and Red Jacket, or incorporating general tribal names, patent medicine labels promoted "Indian" expectorant, stomach bitters, Cherokee liniment, Seminole cough balsam, and wigwam tonic. In many of the nearly twenty illustrative, engraved medicine labels in the collection, Indian men and women are pictured heroically curing an ailing white population. Depictions of Native Americans hunting, greeting colonists, or communing with nature are also found on miscellaneous advertisements for fertilizers and manures, insurance, paint, fur garments, and perfume.

Music Covers (LOT 10615).

A small number of decorative covers for sheet music of popular songs from the nineteenth century feature images of Indians and Indian life. Frontier and tipi encampment scenes adorn editions of songs such as "Sacajawea's Papoose Waltz," "Indian Hunter Quick Step," and

"Indian's Lament," while images of first encounters between Native Americans and Europeans illustrate "The Pilgrim's Legacy" and "My New England Home."

Cabinet of American Illustration (Videodisc in Prints and Photographs Reading Room).

Among this collection of original drawings by American book, magazine, and newspaper illustrators from the period 1850 to 1930 are about twenty-five works which depict the American Indian, primarily in sentimental wilderness scenes, as a hostile threat to settlers in the West, or as a spiritual force in nature. Four drawings by F. O. C. Darley, a noted illustrator of Indian life, picture an Indian on horseback, a tribal council, a War of 1812 battle, and a white hunter befriending an Indian brave.

Caroline and Erwin Swann Collection of Caricature and Cartoon (Online Public Access Catalog—One Box and Swann Collection Finding Aid).

The Swann Collection, spanning the years 1780 to 1975, contains drawings, prints, and paintings for caricatures, cartoons, and book and magazine illustrations. American Indians are caricatured as wilderness guides, "Indian givers," deft ax-throwers, users of wampum, and the nemesis of cowboys, in more than thirty images, primarily from the period 1910 to 1950.

Work Projects Administration Posters (Poster Collection—POS WPA Filing Series).

Silkscreen posters generated by this 1930s New Deal program were used to publicize exhibits, community activities, theatrical productions, and health and educational programs. Noteworthy posters related to American Indians incorporate symbols and images from various tribes, some of which were created by Indian artists. These vibrant color posters include those advertising a Museum of Modern Art exhibit on Indian art in the U.S., Index of American Design exhibitions featuring craft and folk arts, and U.S. Travel Bureau promotions to "See America."

New York World-Telegram & Sun Newspaper Photograph Collection (Finding aid in Prints and Photographs Reading Room).

Covering mainly the period from 1920 to 1967, this collection contains about two hundred photographs that are American Indian-related. As images captured for news and human interest events that represented the fare of newspaper journalism, some of these photos reflect, especially in their captions, a contemporaneous, stereotypical view of Indian people. Derisive commentary, often facetious in intent, frequently accompanies pictures of Native Americans eating hot dogs, watching television, using soap and toothbrushes, and inspecting a Cadillac.

Yanker Collection of Posters (Videodisc in reading room and POS 6 Filing Series).

Native American-related political, propaganda, and social issue posters in this collection reflect the emergence of pan-Indian national organizations and the tribal rights movement. Spanning the years 1960 to 1980, many of the posters concern American Indian Movement (AIM) demonstrations, native women's liberation, and Indian self-determination. Another focus of several posters is the non-Indian counterculture's rediscovery of the traditional Native American, whose image illustrates ecological awareness, spirituality, and worldly wisdom. About forty posters pertain to American Indians.

ABOVE: *Villa of Brulé*. Albumen silver print by John C. H. Grabill, 1891. LOT 3076. (LC-USZ62-19725). Prints and Photographs Division.

This tranquil view of a Brulé Sioux camp near Pine Ridge documents the vicinity of the Wounded Knee shortly after the massacre. Grabill, an early Western photographer, created some of the more detailed images of frontier life in the Dakota territory, including Indians and Indian life.

RIGHT: *View of a Plains Indian Camp*. Daguerreotype, half plate, possibly by Solomon Carvalho, 1853. DAG no. 251. (LC-USZ62-9065). Prints and Photographs Division.

This daguerretoype, possibly taken on the John C. Frémont expedition of 1853, is the earliest photographic view of Indian life in the Library's collections. The tipis and drying racks are typical of those created by the Plains buffalo culture.

LEFT: *Pigeon's Egg Head (the Light) going into and return-ing from Washington.* Lithograph by Currier and Ives after George Catlin, 1837-39. PGA -Currier & Ives—Wi-Jun-Jon (B size). (LC-USZC2-3313). Prints and Photographs Division.

In late 1831, Wi-jun-jon, or Pigeon's Egg Head, travelled with a small delegation of his Assiniboine tribesmen to Washington to meet President Andrew Jackson. Along the way he met the artist George Catlin, who followed the im-pressionable young man's journey from a Western wigwam to the nation's capital. At Washington, Wi-jun-jon imbibed the sights, sounds and, unfortunately, spirits he found there. Back home in the West he affected the dress, man-ners, and vices of a white man with tragic results: three years after his return he was murdered by tribesmen suspi-cious of his Eastern ways.

RIGHT TOP: *A Scene on the Frontiers as Practiced by the Humane British and their Worthy Allies.* Etching with wa-tercolor by William Charles, 1812. PGA—Charles (W.)—Scene (A size). (LC-USZC4-4820, color; LC-USZ62-5800, black and white). Prints and Photographs Division.

Scottish-born caricaturist William Charles emigrated to America about 1805 and soon established himself as one of the country's leading political cartoonists. During the War of 1812, he produced a memorable series of satires against the British, including this image in which an En-glish officer offers money and weapons to mercenary Indi-ans in return for scalps taken from American troops.

RIGHT BOTTOM: *The Grand National Caravan Moving East.* Lithograph drawn by Hassan Straitshanks [attributed to David Claypool Johnston], 1833. PC/US−1833.E567, no. 1 (A size). (LC-USZ62-9646). Prints and Photographs Division.

Two events of 1832, the election of President Andrew Jack-son to a second term and the arrest of militant Sac Indian leader Black Hawk, converge in this caustic political satire. The cartoonist portrays Jackson at the head of a motley vic-tory parade which includes Vice-President Martin Van Bu-ren, the Devil, a prostrate drunkard, an army officer, and a barred wagon bearing the captured Sac chief and other Native Americans.

A Scene on the FRONTIERS as Practiced by the HUMANE BRITISH and their WORTHY ALLIES

Bring me the Scalps
and the King our master
will reward you—

Reward for
Sixteen
Scalps

Arise Columbia's Sons and forward press,
Your Country's wrongs call loudly for redress;
The Savage Indian with his Scalping knife,
Or Tomahawk may seek to take your life,

By bravery aw'd they'll in a dreadful Fright,
Shrink back for Refuge to the Woods in Flight;
Their British leaders then will quickly shake,
And for those wrongs shall restitution make.

FAR LEFT: *OSCEOLA, of Florida*. Lithograph by George Catlin, 1838. PGA–Catlin—Osceola (D size). (LC-USZ62-7747). Prints and Photographs Division.

Osceola (ca. 1804–38), born a member of the Creek nation, first distinguished himself in the defense of the Florida territories against federal troops under Andrew Jackson in the first phase of the Seminole Wars. In 1837, after leading the Seminole Indians in their long and costly campaign of guerilla resistance against U.S. government efforts to relocate them to the Arkansas Territory, Osceola was tricked into captivity under a flag of truce by Gen. Thomas Jesup. He was imprisoned at Fort Moultrie near Charleston, South Carolina, and died the following year. Catlin's large-scale and sympathetic life portrait of the great leader was issued within a few weeks of Osceola's death.

RIGHT: *Joseph Fayadaneega, Called the Brant, The Great Captain of the Six Nations*. Mezzotint (proof before letters) by John Raphael Smith, after a painting by George Romney, circa 1776. PGA–Anonymous—Joseph (B size). (LC-USZ62-20488). Prints and Photographs Division.

Joseph Brant (1742–1807), or Thayendanegea, was an influential Mohawk chief and staunch supporter of the British Army during the French and Indian War and the American Revolution. Raised in the Mohawk Valley, he was educated at Eleazer Wheelock's Indian Charity School in Lebanon, Connecticut, where he became a convert to Christianity. He first fought for the British against the French at Lake George in 1755 and by the mid-1770s had become prominent in the Iroquois League. In 1776, Brant traveled to London with a delegation of British and Mohawk leaders, where this likeness was captured by the fashionable English painter George Romney.

LEFT: Unus Americanus ex Virginia. Aetat: 23. Engraving by Wenceslaus Hollar, 1645. FP–XVII–H733, no. 2009 (A size). (LC-USZ62-114953). Prints and Photographs Division.

This work is apparently the earliest engraved portrait made from life of a Native American. Drawn and engraved by the Czech printmaker Wenceslaus Hollar, it depicts a twenty-three-year-old Algonquian Indian of Virginia, presumably seen by the artist in England during his prolonged tenure as artist in residence to the Earl of Arundel. Hollar's sensitive and detailed eyewitness rendering is surprisingly free of the caricature and conjecture found in most Native American portraits from the seventeenth and eighteenth centuries.

COPYRIGHT G.H. FARNUM
10307 - 1924 OKEMAH OKLA.

LEFT TOP: *Native American stickball players*. Silver gelatin print, copyrighted by G. H. Farnum, 1924. LOT 13001 (LC-USZ62-114959). Prints and Photographs Division.

An Oklahoma team of Creek or Cherokee Indian stickball players, wearing ribbon work loincloths and holding hand-crafted racquets. Stickball, a more vigorous and rougher version of modern lacrosse, was a standard part of ceremonial events and an occasional means of settling disputes among Southeastern tribes.

LEFT BOTTOM: *Under the salmon row*. Silver gelatin print by Frank H. Nowell, 1906. LOT 12779 (LC-USZ62-114925). Prints and Photographs Division.

In Nome, Alaska, on the Bering Sea, Frank Nowell photographed these Inuit children posing in the bright summer sun, under a tribal community fish drying rack. More than seventy views by Nowell reveal daily life among the Tlingit and Inuit people between 1904 and 1910.

BELOW: The patient on the sand painting. Silver printing out paper print by Simeon Schwemberger, 1906. LOT 11891 (LC-USZ62-103650). Prints and Photographs Division.

In this rare image of a healing ritual inside a Navajo hogan in Arizona, the patient is seated on a sand painting while a masked participant in the ritual, a Yebichai, sits on a nearby blanket. Such healing ceremonies, still practiced today, took as long as nine days, requiring sweat baths, memorized chants, and intricate sand paintings such as the one pictured here.

Hopi artists. Albumen stereographic print, copyrighted by Underwood & Underwood, 1903. Stereo file (LC-USZ62-57189, full stereograph; LC-USZ62-46918, single image). Prints and Photographs Division.

In this stereograph, two women look on as the potters decorate their wares inside a pueblo room on the Hopi Reservation in Arizona. The traditional squash blossom hairstyles of the two young women standing in this photograph denote their unmarried status.

Full delegation of Sioux Indians in Washington, 1891. Albumen print by C. M. Bell, 1891. LOT 12566 (LC-USZ62-4536). Prints and Photographs Division.

Photographs of Indian delegations to Washington are among the earliest and most extensive historical records of Native American diplomacy. This Sioux delegation of prominent tribal leaders came to Washington, D.C., in an effort to hold the government to the terms of existing treaties. The names of the individuals shown are printed on the studio mount.

Mathematics class, Carlisle Indian School. Cyanotype print by Frances Benjamin Johnston, 1903. LOT 12369 (LC-USZ62-72450). Prints and Photographs Division.

As part of the U.S. government's late nineteenth and early twentieth century assimilation policy, Indian children were frequently enrolled in boarding schools away from their reservations. Photographs documenting student life at the highly regimented institutions often portray Indian children wearing clothing and hair styles of the dominant white culture. Such images were used to publicize this "civilizing" or "transformation" process advocated by school officials.

Images of Indians in Advertising. [LEFT:] "Cleveland Cycles." Color lithographic poster by Jean de Paleologue, Paris, c. 1897. POS-U.S. P349, no. 6 (D size). (LC-USZC4-3893, color; LC-USZ62-80342, black and white). [RIGHT:] "Harris, Beebe & Company—The Pocahontas Chewing Tobacco." Color lithograph by the Hatch Lithograph Co., New York City, 1868. LOT 10618-48 (LC-USZC4-1071). Prints and Photographs Division.

Invoking native culture's traditional use of herbs and plants, nineteenth century tobacco and patent medicine industries incorporated images of famous Indians into graphic designs on labels (such as Pocahontas, right). Fictionalized depictions of Indians also appeared in product advertisements, often with seemingly little or misconstrued link to native cultures, such as this poster of a hatchet-waving Plains Indian on a bicycle.

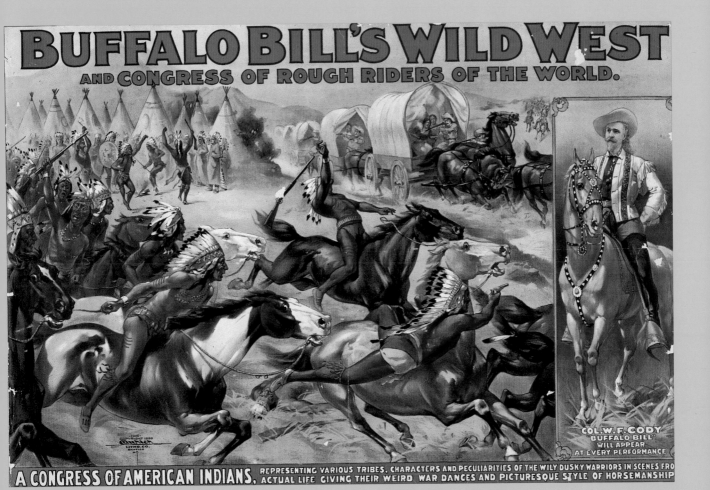

Buffalo Bill's Wild West and Congress of Rough Riders of the World. Color lithograph by Courier Lithographic Company, 1899. Poster Collection, POS–CIRCUS–Buff.Bill. 1899, no. 3 (C size). (LC-USZ62-1164, black and white, and LC-USZC4-778, color). Prints and Photographs Division.

The Wild West Show became a popular entertainment for people east of the Mississippi and in Europe. Freed from the confines of their reservations, the Indian performers helped recreate wagon attacks and sham battles and performed traditional dances in the productions. The Poster Collection in the Prints and Photographs Division houses several of the lithographs used to advertise these extravaganzas.

FAR LEFT: *Old Woman, Acoma Pueblo.* Platinum print by Laura Gilpin, 1939. LOT 4522 (LC-USZ62-36220). Prints and Photographs Division.

Laura Gilpin, an acclaimed Southwestern photographer, is noted for both her intimate portraits and monumental landscapes. This woman of the Acoma Pueblo wears several strands of beads and a Navajo silver necklace with squash blossoms. The traditional woven black manta and strip woven belt is worn over a cotton print blouse and covered with a check cloth apron. The eclectic style is typical of the clothing worn by the Pueblo women during the first years of the twentieth century.

LEFT: *Joe Black Fox, a Sioux Indian from Buffalo Bill's Wild West Show.* Silver gelatin print from original glass negative by Gertrude Käsebier, 1901. LOT 10136 (LC-K2-65). Prints and Photographs Division.

Gertrude Käsebier, a leading figure in the Pictorialist movement in photography, created this sensitive portrait in her New York City studio. Pictorialist photographers tended to create artistically pleasing or idealized images of Indian life. Works by many American pictorialists are included in the Library's photography collections.

RIGHT: *Navajo smile.* Silver gelatin print by Edward S. Curtis, c. 1904. LOT 12311 (LC-USZ62-46943). Prints and Photographs Division.

Edward S. Curtis, the best-known photographer of Indians and Indian life, was a master at presenting the stoic, vanishing American in his romantic images. This distinctive, atypical portrait of a young Navajo woman, smiling and unreserved, is among the many Curtis photographs held by the division that were not published by him.

Schonchin Jim and Captain Jack (Kintpuash). Albumen print by Louis Heller, 1873. LOT 11480 (LC-USZ62-45903). Prints and Photographs Division.

After an aggressive two-year struggle to reclaim their ancestral lands from the U.S. government, the Modoc Indians of California finally surrendered to military officers in 1873. Modoc leaders of the rebellion, Schonchin (left) and Captain Jack, are pictured here chained together at the ankles, shortly before their execution by hanging.

Signs behind the bar, Birney, Montana. Silver gelatin print by Marion Post Wolcott, 1941. Farm Security Administration Collection (LC-USF34-58504-D). Prints and Photographs Division.

The federal government restricted the sale of alcohol to Indian people, in varying degrees, until 1953. Although intended to enforce such legislation, signs in taverns often reinforced discrimination against Indians. The sentimental banner "God Bless America—Life, Liberty and Justice for all," pictured here on the left, is an ironic juxtaposition.

Mitchell Red Cloud, Congressional Medal of Honor recipient. Silver gelatin print, U.S. Army, c. 1940. New York World-Telegram and Sun Collection (LC-USZ62-109610). Prints and Photographs Division.

Mitchell Red Cloud, a Winnebago Indian from Wisconsin, posed for this portrait when he was a World War II Marine sergeant. After heroic service in the Korean War, Red Cloud was posthumously awarded the medal of honor. Distinguished military veterans are highly honored by their family tribes in traditional ceremonies, usually during pow-wows held on their reservations.

GEOGRAPHY AND MAP DIVISION

INTRODUCTION

Land and environment are fundamental to American Indian culture and history and also central to Indian/non-Indian relations. As the primary means of storing geographical knowledge and experience and communicating locational and spatial information, maps are links between landscape and history, and although often overlooked, they are potentially rich sources of historical information for Indian studies. Maps provide a graphic representation of an almost five hundred-year historical record of the physical and cultural landscape of America. As such they reflect the changes set in motion by the arrival of Europeans in America and the subsequent competition for control of the land. In many cases the maps most valuable for the study of Indian history are those that are not specifically devoted to Indian matters but include such Indian-related geographic data as place names, settlement sites, trails, and tribal range as part of recording the known geographic landscape. In addition to their historical value, maps are tools for portraying the present-day physical environment and natural resources of Indian lands.

Maps are not, however, only neutral and impartial mirrors of nature. What is depicted and what is omitted from the cartographic record, either inadvertently or intentionally, reveal aspects of the cultural values and attitudes of the map-maker and the social and political climate in which the map was constructed. Since maps of North America are almost exclusively Euro-American in origin, the cartographic depiction of Indian cultures and environments is primarily a reflection of the non-Indian population's perceptions of, and attitudes toward, indigenous peoples and their lands. These attitudes are also revealed in the imagery of the title cartouche and vignettes that appear on a variety of continental, national, and regional maps. The imagery may depict either noble or ignoble stereotypes, aspects of Indian culture and environment, the interaction of Indians and whites (often depicting trade relationships), and the Indian as a symbolic representation for the continent of North America.

In the contest over land rights, maps and mapping can be seen as tools for defining power relationships and symbolizing authority. As a means for documenting as well as legitimizing the transfer of land rights from Indian to non-Indian control, maps were tools for promoting and promulgating the Euro-American appropriation of territory. In particular, as tools for identifying and publicizing information about the existence and location of valuable natural resources, maps had a direct effect on Indian groups' use and control of their environment. Even maps specifically of established and recognized Indian lands were often not intended to portray Indian affairs, but rather reflected the interest of others in acquiring rights to those lands.

The Library's cartographic holdings relating to Indian studies are neither comprehensive nor easily identified, but the coverage is broad and embraces those aspects of Indian society and culture that have been traditionally mapped. Emphasis has been on mappable characteristics associated with the Indians' physical world and historical distribution. Little cartographic attention has been given to social or political issues affecting Indian lives.

Cartographic works, including reproductions of historical maps, are frequently illustrative supplements to textual works. Consequently, significant maps can be found in most parts of the Library's diverse collections. The majority of the Library's cartographic holdings are, however, held in the Geography and Map Division, and the focus of this chapter is on that division's collections.

USING THE COLLECTIONS

GEOGRAPHY AND MAP READING ROOM

LOCATION: Madison Building, Basement, Room B01; telephone (202) 707-6277

HOURS: Monday to Friday, 8:30 A.M.–5:00 P.M.

Access to collections is restricted. Reference service is available by mail and telephone, but to make full use of the Geography and Map Division's collections and reference services a personal visit is recommended. Limited "quick-copy" photocopying facilities are available in the Reading Room and a variety of other photoreproduction services can be ordered from the Library's Photoduplication Service.

The Geography and Map Division has custody of a cartographic collection of over 4.5 million items. Unfortunately, there is neither a comprehensive catalog of the division's holdings nor a guide to its resources for Indian studies. The division's Indian-related cartographic holdings are composed primarily of governmental (federal) and commercial printed materials. The division also has a number of manuscript maps and a valuable collection of photostatic reproductions of maps from European archives and libraries which primarily supplement its coverage of the colonial period.

The Geography and Map Division maintains a number of organizational and filing schemes for its cartographic materials and, because of this variety, researchers must consult with the division's reference staff. The following are the major collections which contain cartographic material of value for Indian studies:

MARC Maps Collection

Maps acquired since 1968 have been cataloged in the Library's MARC Maps format and are searchable through the computer catalog in the same way one would search for textual records.

Computer-based searches on MUMS can be limited to map records by appending the term ";file=maps" to the search entry. SCORPIO searches can be limited to the maps file by entering "bgns gmap."

Uncataloged/Titled Collection

The majority of maps received prior to 1968, including most of the maps of interest for Indian studies, are uncataloged and unclassified and will remain uncataloged for the foreseeable future. This Uncataloged / Titled collection is organized primarily by geographic area and date. The geographic areas of concern for this resource study are North America, United States, and the individual states. These geographic areas are further subdivided by: a) subjects, b) miscellaneous geographic regions, c) first order administrative divisions (county maps), and d) city plans. Since Indian-related maps fall within a great number of geographic areas, there are numerous possible filing locations for pertinent material. There are, however, two key filing locations under each geographic heading where most of the material on American Indians will be found. The first and most important is in the "subject" files under the heading "Indians," and the second, which will contain fewer items of interest, is in the "miscellaneous geographic regions" files under the name of individual tribes. Other subject files, such as archaeology, history, military, linguistics, and wars, may also contain items of interest.

Atlas Collection

The majority of atlases are cataloged and searchable in the Library's computer catalog. In addition, the Library's nine-volume *A List of Geographical Atlases in the Library of Congress* by Philip L. Phillips and Clara Egli LeGear contains a fairly complete index to individual maps bound into atlases published prior to 1968.

Vault Collection

The division's rare globes, atlases, and maps, including all manuscript maps, are housed in a separate secure room. The "Vault" collection contains a combination of cataloged and uncataloged material. Most of the separate maps included in the Vault collection are described in a preliminary vault shelflist which is available for examination in the division's reading room.

The division's Vault collection holds two small manuscript collections which contain some Indian-related material. The Lewis and Clark Collection contains thirteen maps which belonged to the explorer William Clark. The maps were transferred to the Library by the Office of Indian Affairs in 1925. Several of the maps pertain to Clark's years as superintendent of Indian affairs. The Andrew Jackson Collection of eleven maps relates chiefly to General Jackson's operations in the South during the War of 1812 and his campaign against the Creek Indians in 1813 and 1814.

❏ SELECTED COLLECTIONS

Although the maps of value for Indian studies are scattered geographically throughout the division's collections, they fall in general within a number of subject categories related to the Indians' physical and cultural environment. Some maps overlap into more than one category, but the following thematic structure provides a guide to the various Indian-related subjects for which the Library's cartographic collections offer research resources:

- General Reference and Bibliographic Resources

- Indian Maps, Mapping, and Geographic Knowledge
- Indian Lands, Village Sites, Tribal Range, Place Names, and Communication Routes
- Treaty Boundaries and Cessions
- Indian Territory
- Reservations and Allotments
- Indian Wars
- Ethnography, Linguistics, Distribution, and Archaeology
- Historical Maps
- Natural Resources

Following topical introductions are brief descriptions of selected cartographic resources, which are listed in chronological order. All items cited are in the Geography and Map Division, unless noted otherwise.

General Reference and Bibliographic Resources

General coverage in a cartographic format of a variety of historical and cultural aspects of American Indian studies is found in the following works:

Comparative Studies of North American Indians. Harold E. Driver and William C. Massey. In *Transactions of the American Philosophical Society* (New Series, Vol. 47, part 2). Philadelphia: The American Philosophical Society, 1957; Q11.P6— General Collections

Contains 163 maps illustrating broad generalizations about the geographic distribution of aspects of the subsistence, material culture, economics, and social organization of North American Indians.

Atlas of the North American Indian. Carl Waldman. New York: Facts on File Publications, 1985;

E77.W195 1985—General Collections and Geography and Map Reading Room

Contains ninety-six maps dealing with cultural distribution, migrations, wars, settlement sites, and aspects of social issues.

Atlas of Ancient America. Michael Coe, Dean Snow, and Elizabeth Benson. New York: Facts on File Publications, 1986; E61.C66 1986—General Collections and Geography and Map Reading Room

Although primarily text, this work contains several maps illustrating the climate, physical environment, and cultural groupings of pre-contact American Indians.

Atlas of Great Lakes Indian History. Edited by Helen Hornbeck Tanner. Norman, Oklahoma: Published for the Newberry Library by the University of Oklahoma Press, 1987; E78.G7A87 1987—General Collections and Geography and Map Reading Room

Contains thirty-three maps showing Indian battle sites, land cessions, and disease epidemics, and also a series of maps showing the changes in village sites and tribal distribution between the late prehistoric period and 1870.

Atlas of American Indian Affairs. Francis Paul Prucha. Lincoln, Nebraska: University of Nebraska Press, 1990; G1201.E1P7 1990—General Collections and Geography and Map Reading Room

Contains 109 maps. In addition to the historical coverage of land cessions, reservations, removal, and military engagements, it includes coverage of modern social issues and population distribution.

The following bibliographic works, all of which can be found in the Geography and Map

Reading Room, list maps and atlases within the Library's collections, some of which will be of value for Indian studies:

A List of Maps of America in the Library of Congress. P. Lee Phillips. Washington, D.C.: Library of Congress, 1901; Z881.U5

Published in 1901, this bibliography is a valuable, but not a comprehensive, guide to the maps of America in the Library's collections.

United States Atlases: A List of National, State, County, City, and Regional Atlases in the Library of Congress. Compiled by Clara Egli LeGear. Washington, D.C.: GPO, 1950; Z881.U5 1950

Contains bibliographic descriptions of some 1,400 county atlases dating from the late nineteenth century, some of which will include detailed coverage of Indian lands

Land Ownership Maps: A Checklist of Nineteenth Century United States County Maps in the Library of Congress. Compiled by Richard W. Stephenson. Washington, D.C.: GPO, 1967; Z6027.U5U54 1967

Contains bibliographic descriptions of nearly 1,500 county landownership maps, some of which will include coverage of Indian lands.

Maps and Charts of North America and the West Indies. 1750–1759: A Guide to the Collections in the Library of Congress. Compiled by John R. Sellers and Patricia Molen van Ee. Washington, D.C.: Library of Congress, 1981; Z6027.N68U54 1981

The American Revolution in Drawings and Prints; a Checklist of 1765–1790 Graphics in the Library of Congress. Compiled by Donald H. Cresswell. Washington, D.C.: GPO, 1975; E209.U54 1975

Within this extensive work are reproductions as well as bibliographic descriptions of Indian imagery appearing in map cartouches and vignettes.

A List of Geographical Atlases in the Library of Congress. 9 vols. Compiled by Philip Lee Phillips and Clara Egli LeGear. Washington, D.C.: Library of Congress, 1909–1992; Z6028.U56

An extensive listing of atlases with a thorough index to the maps within the atlases.

The following are additional reference resources and bibliographic works which identify Indian-related cartographic works. All can be examined in the Geography and Map Reading Room:

Mapping the Transmississippi West, 1540–1861. Carl I. Wheat. 5 vols. in 6. San Francisco: The Institute of Historical Cartography, 1957–1963; GA405.W5

Monumental history and bibliographic study of the mapping of the American West.

The Bibliography of Cartography. Library of Congress, Geography and Map Division. 5 vols. Boston: G.K. Hall & Co., 1973; Z6028.U49 1973

Two-volume supplement published in 1980. Contains citations to a few Indian-related maps and articles under the headings "Indians" and "Maps, primitive."

Cartographic Records of the Bureau of Indian Affairs. Compiled by Laura E. Kelsay. Washington, D.C.: National Archives and Records Service, 1977; Z1209.2.U5U53 1977

This is a revised edition of a bibliography by Kelsay published in 1954 under the title *List of Cartographic Records of the Bureau of Indian Affairs.*

Indianische Karten Nordamerikas, Beitrage zur historischen Kartographie vom 16. bis zum 19. Jahrhun-

dert. Rainer Vollmar. Berlin: Dietrich Reimer Verlag, [1981]; E98.C17V64 1981

Reproduces and describes many Indian-drawn cartographic works.

U.S. Serial Set Index, Part XIV, Index and Carto-Bibliography of Maps, 1789–1969. Edited by Donna P. Koepp. Bethesda, Md.: Congressional Information Service, 1996; Z1223.Z9C65 1975

Multi-volume work containing a comprehensive index to, and complete bibliographic descriptions of, more than fifty thousand maps bound in the reports and documents comprising the Congressional Serial Set. Included are descriptions of maps depicting Indian ceded lands, migrations, reservations, village locations, battle sites, and burial grounds.

Indian Maps, Mapping, and Geographic Knowledge

Maps drawn by Indians and Indian mapping abilities have been documented in a number of sources, but because of their ephemeral nature, relatively few Indian-produced maps exist today. The indigenous population was often sought out by European explorers to guide or provide geographical information about unknown lands, and Indian guides were also often enlisted to provide reconnaissance data for military activities. Responses to solicitations for geographic information were sometimes given in a cartographic format. The cartographic and geographic information provided by Indians could appear in the explorer's report and might eventually be incorporated into published maps. Maps drawn by Indians, as well as evidence of their contributions to European-produced maps, are valuable and rare documents for studying Indian peoples' geographical knowledge and spatial understanding. They complement the oral record, and they also help establish and clarify the Indians' role as guides and informants in furthering European explorations in North America. The Geography and Map Division does not have original examples of Indian cartography which pre-date European contact, but it has two eighteenth-century manuscripts created by Indians for use by Europeans and a few reproductions and facsimiles of other maps drawn by Indians.

Pintura que por Mandado de D[on] Fran[cisco] Balverde de Mercado factor de S.Mag[estad] hizo Miguel yndio natural de la provincias de Nuevo Méxi[co]. . . . [1602?] Photocopy from original manuscript in Archivo de las Indias, Seville. Map 21 x 28 cm. Scale not given; New Mexico—1602?

Drawn by the Indian Miguel, this map of New Mexico is the earliest known example of Indian cartography in the United States.

Virginia. Discovered and Described by Captain John Smith, 1606. Graven by William Hole. [London? 1624?] Map 32 x 41 cm. Scale ca. 1:1,290,000; G3880 1624 .S51 Vault, and Rare Book and Special Collections (see p. 58)

Symbols on the Smith map distinguish the portions of the map which are based on information supplied by Indian informants.

This Map describing the Scituation of the Several Nations of Indians to the NW. of South Carolina was Coppyed from a Draught drawn & painted on a Deer Skin by an Indian Cacique and Presented to Francis Nicholson Esqr., Governour of Carolina. . . . [ca. 1721] Photocopy, original manuscript in the British Museum, London. Col. map 81 x 118 cm. Scale not given; U.S.—South—Indians—1721?

This Catawba deerskin map shows an interconnected network of tribes located on the South Carolina piedmont. It includes an inset of Charleston with its rectangular street grid pattern (p. 215).

Copy of a sketch of the Monongahela, with the field of battle, done by an Indian. [1755?] Manuscript map on sheet 26 x 27 cm. Scale not given; G3824.P6S26 1755 .C6 Vault (see p. 215)

Based on information provided by an unidentified Indian scout, this map depicts the site of the battle between English forces and the French and Indians near Fort Duquesne (Pittsburgh) on July 9, 1755.

Map of the country about the Mississippi. Drawn by Chegeree (the Indian) who says he has travelled through the country. [1755?] Manuscript map on sheet 34 x 42 cm. Scale not given; G3300 1755 .C5 Vault

Shows Indian settlements in the area from Lake Erie to the mouth of the Ohio River.

A New Map of the Cherokee Nation with the Names of the Towns & Rivers They are Situated on, No. Lat. from 34 to 36. Engrav'd from an Indian Draught by T. Kitchin. For the *London Magazine.* [London, 1760] Map 18 x 23 cm. Scale ca. 1:1,100,000; G3865 1760 .K Vault

Shows area between the head of the Savannah River and the Mississippi River.

An Indian Map of the Upper-Missouri. 1801. Map 19 x 50 cm. Scale not given; Kohl Collection 243

Manuscript redrawing of a map by a Blackfeet Chief, which was given to the Hudson Bay Company fur trader Peter Fidler in 1801. It shows the tributaries of the Upper Missouri River and supplies the Indian name for each branch.

Wayishkee's Map of the Source of the Taquymenon and Maniste Rivers. 1826 [possibly 1820]. Manuscript map on sheet 41 x 35 cm. Scale not given; Henry Rowe Schoolcraft Papers (Oversized material container 91). Manuscript Division

This manuscript map shows headwaters of the Manistique and Tahquanmenon Rivers in the Upper Peninsula of Michigan.

[*Map copied from one drawn by the Tassel, and some other head-men of the Cherokees, to describe their territorial claims. 1785*] Photocopy from Misc. U.S. Congressional Doc. no. 25, 33d Congress, 2d. Session. 1855. Map on sheet 36 x 28 cm. Scale not given; Tennessee—Indians—1785

Shows area between Savannah River and Mississippi River.

[*Map of New Archangel (Sitka, 1841?) Made by a Native during the Russian occupancy, 1841?*]. Facsimile printed in 1977? Col. map on sheet 42 x 50 cm. Scale not given; G4374.S5A5 1841 .M3 1977

Drawn by an unknown Indian, this map shows native and Russian settlements at Novo-Arkangel'sk (New Archangel), Alaska.

[*Lean Wolf's map from Fort Berthold to Fort Buford, Dakota, along the Missouri River.* 1878] Redrawing from 4th annual *Report of the Bureau of American Ethnology,* 1885. Map on sheet 14 x 20 cm. Scale not given; U.S.—Indians—1878

Shows footprints of Lean Wolf's route to Fort Buford to steal a horse; his return route is shown by hoof prints.

Sketch of the Akularak Slough from the Catholic Mission to near the Yukon River, drawn by a native. Copied from original in possession of Father Barnum, March 1899 . . . Blueprint map on sheet 32 x 20 cm. Scale not given; Alaska—Akularak Slough—1899

Depicts watercourse in the Yukon River Delta and shows village locations.

The Archive of North American Indian Maps on CD-ROM. Edited by Sona Andrews, David Tilton, and Mark Warhus. Milwaukee: University of Wisconsin-Milwaukee, Department of Geography; forthcoming.

Contains high resolution reproductions accompanied by bibliographic and textual descriptions of over 400 maps of areas of the United States and Canada drawn by Indians.

Indian Lands, Village Sites, Tribal Range, Place Names, and Communication Routes

The Geography and Map Division holds a very large group of maps, both historic and current, which in most cases were not intended to specifically describe the Indian environment, but which nevertheless record such cultural data as village locations and tribal range. A large component of this category, and one of value for anthropological and archaeological studies, is the series of maps that portray the landscape at the time of Euro-American contact and exploration. Since exploration of North America was an evolutionary process that began with maritime expeditions and continued almost four hundred years, maps illustrating the contact period for a coastal area may differ greatly in date from those of interior regions of the continent.

With the advancement of Euro-American settlement, much of the Indian cultural data recorded on early maps was replaced by depictions of the evidence of non-Indian occupancy. When these maps are studied over time, they can provide insight into tribal migrations as well as intertribal and Indian/non-Indian relations.

This category encompasses thousands of maps dating from the time of first European contacts to the present. It includes small-scale maps of North America, general maps of the United States, early state maps, regional maps, county maps, and even some city plans. For example, large-scale county landownership maps and atlases published from the mid-nineteenth century to the present may provide information about Indian landownership and the sale of reservation lands. Even large-scale nineteenth century hydrographic charts of the Pacific coast published by the United States, Great Britain, and Russia often include the location of, and sometimes significant detail about, coastal Indian settlements.

The maps in this category are also valuable resources for tracing Indian place names. When correctly deciphered, indigenous place names are linguistic artifacts containing environmental and historical meaning. In addition, early maps may record the trails and communication routes of aboriginal people, routes which have in many cases determined the course of modern roads and influenced the location of American cities and towns.

Modern mapping continues, at larger scales, to depict settlements, roads, names, and other cultural features of Indian reservations. The 1:24,000 scale and 1:100,000 scale topographic mapping of the United States by the U.S. Geological Survey, for example, portrays the current physical and cultural landscape of Indian reservations.

Descripsion des costs, pts., rades, illes de la Nouuele France faict selon son vray méridien . . . Samuel de Champlain, 1607. Manuscript map on vellum 37 x 55 cm. Scale ca. 1:1,500,000; Vellum Chart Collection no. 15

Based on Champlain's explorations and observations and his interviews with Indians, this map locates a number of French and Indian settlements on the northeast coast of North America.

Manatus, Gelegen op de Noot Riuier. [Johannes Vingboons] 1639. Col. manuscript map 45 x 67 cm. Scale ca. 1:170,000; Harrisse Collection—Vingboons Atlas, vol. 3, map 12 (see p. 213)

Copied between 1665 and 1670 from Vingboons' original 1639 manuscript, this map shows Manhattan Island and vicinity and locates and names Indian villages on Long Island.

This represents the Charecke Nation by Col. Herberts map & my own observations with the path to Charles Town . . . , Certified by me, George Hunter, May 21, 1730. Manuscript map 42 x 66 cm. Scale ca. 1:1,500,000; G3860 1730 .H8 Faden 6 Vault

GATEWAYS

Continued non-Indian population expansion after the American Revolution led to conflicts with Indian tribes east of the Mississippi River. By the early nineteenth century the United States government attitude toward Indians moved into a new phase. The post-1780s policy of gradual, controlled expansion of white settlement and the acculturation (called "civilization") of Indians had not met its supporters' hopes. After the War of 1812 the idea of removing all eastern tribes across the Mississippi was urged more and more strongly. Proponents argued that the tribes obstructed settlement and could be preserved only by separation from the undesirable influences of their non-Indian neighbors. Under President Andrew Jackson, Indian removal became federal policy, although Congress only narrowly approved the Indian Removal Act (1830) authorizing negotiation of removal treaties.

Many tribes and some of their non-Indian supporters, however, saw the many U.S.-Indian land treaties as inviolable agreements between sovereign nations, and attempted to fight removal on these grounds. These conceptions were dealt a blow by the Supreme Court in *Cherokee Nation v. Georgia* (1831), which deemed the Indian tribes "domestic dependent nations." Although the Supreme Court later barred application of Georgia law on Cherokee Nation lands (*Worcester v. Georgia*, 1831), President Jackson refused to enforce the Court's order.

Of the voluntary and involuntary tribal movements west of the Mississippi, few were as traumatic as those of the so-called "Five Civilized Tribes." The coercion of Cherokee, Chickasaw, Choctaw, Creek, and Seminole tribes into abandoning their homelands for Indian Territory was ironic because many had adopted the larger American culture. Several families were more educated, cultured, industrious, and wealthy than their non-Indian neighbors. The Cherokee had constitutional government by 1827, practiced non-Indian agriculture, sought white education, and published a tribal newspaper facilitated by Sequoyah's Cherokee syllabary.

Tribes varied in their reaction to federal insistence on agreement to removal, and not all factions within tribes accepted removal. These divisions sometimes led to bloodshed. In addition, some of the moves were harsh journeys that resulted in disease and death for significant numbers; in the case of the Cherokee, this gave rise to the appellation of the path westward as "the Trail of Tears."

WHERE TO LOOK: Material on Indian removal across the Mississippi can be found in the General Collections, the Local History and Genealogy Reading Room, the Law Library, and Manuscript, Rare Book and Special Collections, and Geography and Map Divisions.

John Currin's bid of August 4, 1836, addressed to Capt. John Page, Superintendent of Creek Emigration. Thomas S. Jesup Papers (LCMS-27771-1). Manuscript Division

One of forty bids submitted during July and August 1836 for the removal of the Creek Indians from Georgia and Alabama to "homes west of the Mississippi," Currin's price of "twenty four dollars per head" for subsistence and transportation was at the low end of the bidding. His bid was rejected, however, because he failed to appear.

Irwinton Ala, 4th August 1836?

Capt. John Page,

I will remove a party of Indians of from 1000 to 5.000, from their Camps in the Creek Country, to their homes west of the Mississippi at twenty four dollars per head, and will furnish every thing required by your advertisement.

My securities are John L. Hunter, Isaac Bunch, Daniel McKenzie and Jacob Jackson, all of Barbour County Ala.

If my bid is accepted I shall expect to be advised of the fact as early as may be convenient.

Respectfully

John Currin

No 24 Currd

Shows path from Charleston, South Carolina to the Mississippi River and includes names of Indian villages.

Descripcion Geographica, de la parte que los Españoles poseen Actualmente en el Continente de la Florida . . . 1670 . . . Drawn in 1742 by Antonio de Arredondo. Col. manuscript map 41 x 70 cm. Scale ca. 1:4,750,00; G3860 1742 .A7 1914 Vault

Copied in 1914 from the original in Archivo General de Indies, Seville, Spain, this map shows the route through the southeastern United States of Hernando de Soto (1539–43) and the Indian villages he visited. Another manuscript copy of this map is in the Manuscript Division, Hans P. Kraus Collection of Hispanic American Manuscripts, #156.

Plan du Fort des Sauvages Natchez Blocqué par les François le 20 Janvier 1731 . . . Photocopy. Map 25 x 38 cm. Scale ca. 1:3,000; Louisiana—Sicily Island—1731

Copied from an original manuscript in Bibliothèque Nationale, Paris, the map shows the French attack on the Natchez settlement at Sicily Island, Louisiana. In addition to the military data, it shows the settlement pattern of a Natchez community.

Carte Particulière du Fleuve Saint Louis [Mississippi River], *Dressée sur les Lieux avex les Noms des Sauvages du Pais,* . . . [Henry Abraham Chatelain. 1732] Map 37 x 46 cm. Scale ca. 1:11,500,00; U.S.—Great Lakes—1732

Shows Indian settlements in the Great Lakes region; it also includes legends listing Indian tribes and languages.

[*A trader's map of the Ohio country before 1753.* John Patten. 1753?] Col. manuscript map 52 x 74 cm. Scale ca. 1:1,270,000; G3707.O5 1753 .P3 Vault

Attributed to the English fur trader John Patten, this map covers the area from Lake Erie to Virginia and shows Indian towns, trails, and portages.

A Map of the British and French Dominions in North America, . . . John Mitchell. [London]: Sold by And: Miller, 1755. Col. map 136 x 195 cm. Scale ca. 1:2,000,000; G3300 1755 .M5 Vault Shelf

One of the most important and complete cartographic documents in American history, this map shows roads, frontier settlements, routes of exploration, and Indian settlements, fortifications, and deserted villages.

Mapa que comprende la Frontera de los Dominios del Rey en la America Septentrional . . . Joseph de Urrutia and Nicolas de LaFora. 1769. Col. manuscript map in four parts, each 64 x 163 cm. Scale ca. 1:1,350,000; G4410 1769 .V Vault

Based on surveys conducted by Joseph de Urrutia and Nicolas de LaFora, this map shows the border areas of northern Mexico and the southwestern United States from the Gulf of Mexico to the eastern frontier of Texas. Pictorial symbols designate various Spanish and Indian settlements.

Map of Alabama Constructed from the Surveys in the General Land Office and other Documents. John Melish. Philadelphia, 1819. Col. map 69 x 49 cm. Scale ca. 1:950,000; G3970 1819 .M4 Vault

Shows Indian village sites, tribal territories, Indian battle sites, and Indian paths.

A Map of Fox River and that part of Winnebagoe Lake as contained within the limits of the cession of 1821 by the Menominie and Winnebago Indians to the New York Tribes . . . Anonymous. 1832. Col. manuscript map on sheet 52 x 72 cm. Scale not given; G4122.F7 1832 .M Vault

Detailed plan of the town of Statesburgh established by Munsee and Stockbridge Indians on the Fox River in Wisconsin.

[*Map of the western United States, from 91° to 119° West longitude and 36° to 50° North latitude*] Respectfully presented to Col. D. D. Mitchell by P. J. De Smet, Soc. Jes., 1851. Col. manuscript map 89 x 168 cm. Scale 1:2,200,000; G4050 1851 .S Vault Oversize (see p. 219)

Drawn by Father P. J. De Smet, a Jesuit missionary to the western Indians, this map shows tribal lands. Some scholars believe it was made in conjunction with the Treaty of Fort Laramie concluded in 1851 between the United States and several Plains Indian tribes.

Map of the Territory of the United States from the Mississippi to the Pacific Ocean; . . . Lieut. G. K. Warren. Office of R.R. Surveys, War Dept. [Washington, D.C.: War Dept., 1857] Col. map 108 x 118 cm. Scale 1:3,000,000; G4050 1857 .W32 Vault

Displays tribal territories and some Indian villages.

U.S. Geographical Surveys West of the 100th Meridian. Lieut. Geo. M. Wheeler, U.S. Army in charge. [Washington, D.C.: U.S. Government Printing Office, 1873–89] Map sheets 45 x 53 cm. Scales 1:253,440 and 1:506,880; G1380.U56 1873 Vault

Wheeler produced nearly one hundred medium-scale topographic maps of much of the southwestern United States based on field surveys conducted between 1871 and 1879. These detailed maps include Indian names and show the locations of Indian settlements, trails, and ruins.

Standard Atlas of Becker County, Minnesota . . . Compiled and published by Geo. A. Ogle & Co. Chicago, 1911; G1428.B2O3 1911

This atlas shows detailed physical, cultural, and cadastral information about Becker County, including coverage of a portion of the White Earth Indian Reservation. Like many other late nineteenth- and early twentieth-century county maps and atlases, this work contains landownership information, including references to Indian landownership.

Map of the Navajo Country: Arizona, New Mexico, and Utah. U.S. Geological Survey Professional Paper 93, plate 1. [Washington, D.C.], 1916. Col. map 61 x 76 cm. Scale 1:500,000; U.S.—Indians—1916

Shows roads, trails, schools, missions, ruins, and routes of scientific explorations between 1853 and 1906.

Indian Villages of the Illinois Country. Compiled by Sara Jones Tucker. Volume II, Scientific Papers, Illinois State Museum, part 1, Atlas. Springfield: Illinois State Library, 1942; G1406.E1T8 1942

Contains reproductions of fifty-four maps relating to the Indian occupation of the central United States. In 1975, Tucker's atlas was reprinted with a supplement of thirty-nine additional maps compiled by Wayne C. Temple.

Treaty Boundaries and Cessions

The first permanent Euro-American settlements began a pattern of Indian displacement and land appropriation that continued until the twentieth century. The agreements and treaties which resulted in the progressive extinguishing of Indian title and the cession and surrender of Indian lands were often accompanied, or soon followed, by surveys of the boundaries of the ceded lands. The Geography and Map Division has only a few surveys of individual cessions in the United States. As records of official governmental decisions and actions, most boundary and cession maps will be found in the National Archives and Records Administration. In addition to the surveys of individual cessions, there have been a number of maps which depict the history of the cession of Indian lands. As documentation of tribal land use and occupancy, cession and treaty boundary maps have been important legal sources for Indian land claims.

A Map of the Lands Ceded by the Cherokee Indians to the State of South Carolina at a Congress held in May, A.D. 1777; containing about 1,697,700 acres [1777?]. Col. manuscript map 51 x 60 cm. Scale ca. 1:250,000; G3910 1777 .M3 Vault (see p. 217)

Shows the lands ceded to the states of South Carolina and Georgia by the Cherokee following their defeat during the American Revolutionary War.

Sketch of the coast of which the Creek Indians have been deprived by the Americans on both sides of the River Apalachicola. Anonymous. 1814? Col. manuscript map 49 x 60 cm. Scale ca. 1:1,900,000; G3941.E1 1814 .M Vault

Shows the tribal areas of the southeastern United States. In what is now Alabama, a large area is labeled "Lands which the Americans obliged the Indians to cede lately by which means their communication is cut off from the Sea."

Map by which the Creek Indians gave their Statement at Fort Strother on the 22nd. Jany. 1816. John Coffee. Manuscript map 25 x 39 cm. Scale note given; Andrew Jackson Collection no. 4

Covering the Creek lands in Alabama and Georgia, this map was apparently drawn by John Coffee, one of the commissioners appointed in 1816 to survey the boundary of the lands ceded by the Creek following their defeat in 1814 at the Battle of Horseshoe Bend. Prior to beginning this survey, Coffee interviewed some of the Creek headmen regarding the boundaries of the Creek Nation. A note on the verso of the map contains "Spokehajo's [spelling unclear] Statement" of the extent of Creek lands.

Plat of the Survey of the Delaware Lands and Outlet, north of Kanzas River (on sheet No. 1, No. 2, and No. 3), according to the Treaty of September 24, 1829, ratified by the Senate of the U.S., May 29, 1830. Isaac McCoy, Surveyor. December 30, 1830. Col. manuscript map 33 x 118 cm. Scale ca. 1:320,000; G4200 1830 .M Vault Oversize

Shows the strip of land in northeastern Kansas granted to the Delaware in 1829, which was later surrendered by treaties.

A Map of the Choctaw Territory in Alabama, from the United States Surveys. Shewing each Section & Fraction Section. John La Tourrette. Mobile: 1833. Col. map 62 x 27 cm. Scale ca. 1:280,000; Alabama—Choctaw Territory—1833

The Choctaw were the first of the "Five Civilized Tribes" to relocate on western lands, moving across the Mississippi between 1830 and 1833. This map depicts the former Choctaw Territory as it was being opened for white settlement.

Map Exhibiting the position of the Lands occupied by Indian Tribes in Amity with the United States; and also the Lands ceded to the United States by Treaty with various Indian Tribes. Compiled in the Bureau of Topographical Engineers, from the Maps of Capt. Wash. Hood; C.T.E. and I. McCoy, Esq. with additions in compliance with a Resolution of the Senate, 1839. J. Goldsborough Bruff, Del. Col. map 115 x 192 cm. Scale 1:2,000,000; G3701 .G5 1839 .B Vault

The base map is a commercially published 1839 map of the United States which has been heavily annotated to illustrate cession boundaries. The map also includes legends detailing Indian land cessions. Twelve copies of this map were produced by the War Department.

Map of the Mineral Lands upon Lake Superior ceded to the United States Government by treaty of 1842 with the Chippeway Indians. Drawn by A. B. Gray.

Col. manuscript map 70 x 96 cm. Scale ca. 1:455,000; G4112.U6H1 1845 .G Vault

Shows lands adjacent to Lake Superior in Michigan, Wisconsin, and Minnesota, and locations of U.S. Mineral Land Agency, Methodist and Catholic missions, and American Fur Company posts.

Map of the State of Indiana, Exhibiting the Lands ceded by the Indian Tribes to the United States. C. C. Royce. [Washington, D.C.] Bureau of Ethnology, 188–?] Col. map 81 x 58 cm. Scale 1:633,600; Indiana—Indians—188–?

Delineates Indian land cessions and locates Indian towns and villages.

Map of the Former Territorial Limits of the Cherokee "Nation of" Indians. Exhibiting the Boundaries of the Various Cessions of Land Made by Them to the Colonies and to the United States . . . C. C. Royce. U.S. Bureau of Ethnology, 5th Annual Report, pl. VIII. Washington, D.C.: Bureau of Ethnology, 1884. Col. map 72 x 80 cm. Scale ca. 1:1,000,000; U.S.—Indians—1884

Includes portions of Virginia, West Virginia, North Carolina, South Carolina, Georgia, Alabama, Tennessee, and Kentucky and shows Indian place names, paths, and villages.

Indian Land Cessions in the United States. Comp. by Charles C. Royce. U.S. Bureau of American Ethnology. 18th Annual Report, 1896–97. Washington, D.C., 1899; G1201.G6R7 1899

Contains sixty-seven maps illustrating the history of Indian land cessions. A comprehensive study of Indian land cessions, it was used as the geographical basis for land claims litigation heard by the Indian Claims Commission.

Indian Land Cessions. Sam B. Hilliard. Map supplement no. 16, *Annals* of the Association of American Geographers, vol. 62, no. 2, June 1972. New York: Association of American Geogra-

phers, 1972. Col. map 114 x 86 cm. Scale ca. 1:10,000,000; G3701.E1 1972 .H5

Seven maps on one sheet, five show the extent of Indian land cessions for the periods 1784–1819, 1820–39, 1840–59, 1860–79, and 1880–1972; the others show "Land Claim by Tribe" and "Present Indian Reservations."

Garland American Indian Ethnohistory Series. Compiled and edited by David Agree Horr. New York: Garland Publishing Inc. The individual volumes are filed in the Library's General Collections under each tribe's unique classification number. See also the *Indian Claims Commission* in the Microform Reading Room section of this guide.

Published in the 1970s, the multi-volume *Garland American Indian Ethnohistory* series contains historical and anthropological documents that were presented as evidence before the Indian Claims Commission in the 1950s, 60s, and 70s. Map reproductions were often included in the volumes of this series to illustrate the claims of various tribes to certain geographical regions.

Indian Land Areas Judicially Established. Prepared under the direction of the Indian Claims Commission as part of its final report. Reston, Virginia: U.S. Geological Survey, 1978. Col. map 89 x 123 cm. Scale 1:4,000,000; G3701.E1 1978 .U5

Portrays the results of cases before the U.S. Indian Claims Commission or U.S. Court of Claims, in which an American Indian tribe proved their original tribal land occupancy.

Indian Territory

A movement began in the United States in the early nineteenth century to remove Indian tribes from their ancestral lands in the rapidly developing eastern states and settle them in the newly acquired and largely uninhabited western lands. The Indian Removal Act of 1830 established the government policy of relocating the eastern tribes to a separate, reserved "Indian Territory" west of the Mississippi. A chronology of contemporaneous maps of the Indian Territory reveals the continuous loss of portions of this reserved land due to the pressure from non-Indian settlers and commercial interests to open Indian lands for non-Indian use. By the 1870s, Indian Territory—which had once extended from the present Texas-Oklahoma border to the Nebraska-Dakota border—had shrunk to encompass only what is today most of the state of Oklahoma. The Geography and Map Division has a good collection of maps, both federal and commercial publications, which document the diminishing of Indian Territory. There is also good coverage of Indian and Oklahoma Territories from the post-Civil War period to 1907 (when the remaining portions of Indian Territory were incorporated into the newly formed state of Oklahoma), and maps of individual parcels of land, such as the "Cherokee Outlet," which were ceded to the United States and opened for non-Indian settlement.

A Map of a Portion of the Indian Country Lying East and West of the Mississippi River . . . Constructed for the Topographical Bureau by G. W. F[eatherstonehaugh]. [Washington, D.C.?], 1835. Map 67 x 96 cm. Scale ca. 1:1,000,000; U.S.—North Central States—1835

Map of the northern Mississippi River basin showing Indian occupied lands, lands ceded to the federal government, and lands assigned to Indians removed from the eastern United States.

Map Showing the Lands assigned to Emigrant Indians West of Arkansas & Missouri. Prepared at the [U.S. Army] Topographical Bureau. [Washington, D.C.] 1836. Col. map 49 x 46 cm. Scale ca. 1:2,534,000; U.S.—Indians—1836 (see p. 220)

Shows boundaries of lands assigned to individual tribes, and includes legends listing the population of various Indian tribes and size of their land holdings.

Plat of the Survey of the Ioway and Sauk Lands. W. S. Donahoe, Surveyor, 1837. Col. manuscript map on sheet 53 x 82 cm. Scale ca. 1:31,680; Lewis and Clark Collection "g"—Vault

Shows Iowa and Sauk (Sac) lands in Kansas. One of several manuscript maps belonging to William Clark which were found in the Office of Indian Affairs in 1916.

Map of the Nebraska and Kansas Territories. Showing the Location of the Indian Reserves, according to the Treaties of 1854. Compiled by S[eth] Eastman, Captain, U.S.A. Philadelphia: Lippincott, Grambo & Co., 1854. Col. map 61 x 91 cm. Scale ca. 1:1,200,000; Nebraska—Indians—1854

Map of Eastern Kansas. E. B. Whitman & A. D. Searl, General Land Agents, Lawrence, Kansas. Boston: J. P. Jewett and Co., 1856. Col. map 69 x 53 cm. Scale ca. 1:515,000; Kansas—1856

Features the Indian reservations in Kansas and also locates trading posts, missions, post offices, forts, Indian villages, roads, and trails. Includes inset of the federal government reservation at Fort Riley.

Map of the Shawnee & Wyandott Lands in the Territory of Kansas. Compiled from the U.S. Surveys by Robt. J. Lawrence. Pittsburgh: Wm. Schuchman & Bros., 1857. Col. map 68 x 71 cm. Scale ca. 1:85,000; Kansas—Indians—1857

Shows roads, missions, Indian agencies, and names of selected settlers.

Boundary of the Creek Country. Surveyed under the Direction of the Bureau of Topl. Engs. I. C. Woodruff, 1st Lieut., Topl. Engs. [1858] From: House Exec. Doc. No. 104, 35th Cong., 1st Sess. Map 61 x 94 cm. Scale 1:600,000; Oklahoma—Indians—1858

Shows trails and Indian villages of the Creek lands in Oklahoma.

Indian Territory with part of the adjoining State of Kansas &c. U.S. Engineer Bureau, War Dept., [Washington, D.C.] 1866. Col. map 50 x 63 cm. Scale 1:1,500,000; Oklahoma—1866

Annotated to illustrate reduction of Cherokee, Seminole, Choctaw, and Creek tribal territories resulting from Indian involvement in the Civil War on behalf of the Confederate cause.

Indian Territory. Compiled from the official records of the General Land Office and other sources under supervision of Geo. U. Mayo. New York: U.S. General Land Office, 1887. From the papers of President Benjamin Harrison. Col. map 61 x 82 cm. Scale ca. 1:760,000; G4020 1887 .U Vault

This map contains extensive cultural detail relating to the reservations composing Indian Territory. It has also been annotated to illustrate the boundaries of the formation of Oklahoma Territory within Indian Territory.

Indian Territory. Compiled under the direction of the Hon. John H. Oberly, Commissioner of Indian Affairs, by C. A. Maxwell. Baltimore, 1889. Col. map 62 x 81 cm. Scale ca. 1:760,000; Oklahoma—1889

Shows the lands occupied by the various tribes and includes details about land transfers and cessions.

Map of the Indian and Oklahoma Territories. Chicago: Rand McNally & Co., 1892. Col. map 62 x 82 cm. Scale ca. 1:760,000; Oklahoma—1892

Rand, McNally & Co's New Sectional Map of the Cherokee Outlet, to be opened to settlers at High Noon (Central Standard Time), Saturday, September 16, 1893. [Chicago]: Rand, McNally & Co., 1893.

Col. map 49 x 112 cm. Scale ca. 1:310,000; Oklahoma—Cherokee Outlet—1893

One of several real estate promotional maps illustrating lands ceded to the United States and opened for white settlement.

Trout & Wall's Map of the Ft. Sill Country. Duncan, I.T.: Trout & Wall, 1894. Col. map 87 x 57 cm. Scale ca. 1:250,000; Oklahoma—Indians—1894

Shows the Cheyenne, Arapaho, Wichita, Kiowa, Comanche, and Apache lands which were scheduled to be opened to homesteading.

Tahlequah, Cherokee Nation, Ind. Terr. June 1896 [New York]: Sanborn-Perris Map Com., 1896. Col. map 64 x 54 cm. Scale ca. 1:600; Sanborn Fire Insurance Map Collection (see p. 220)

This 1896 set of three sheets is the second of nine editions of Sanborn fire insurance maps of Tahlequah published between 1894 and 1949. The Sanborn fire insurance maps provide detailed information about buildings in urban areas. This edition of the Tahlequah series depicts such structures as the Cherokee Male and Female Seminaries, the Cherokee National Capitol, and the Cherokee National Penitentiary.

Map of the Choctaw Nation, Indian Territory. Compiled and drawn by R. L. McAlpine. [Washington, D.C.]: Department of the Interior, Commission to the Five Civilized Tribes, 1903. Col. map 96 x 84 cm. Scale ca. 1:250,000; Oklahoma—Indians—1903

Showing progress of land allotments and selections and the coal and asphalt regions, it is one of several maps appearing in the annual reports of the Commission to the Five Civilized Tribes.

Proposed State of Oklahoma, Act of June 16, 1906. Compiled from official records in the General Land Office and other sources under the direction of Frank Bond, Chief of Drafting Division,

General Land Office. Washington, D.C.: General Land Office, 1906. Col. map 56 x 108 cm. Scale ca. 1:760,000; Oklahoma—1906

The Osage Nation's lands are shown as the only remaining tribal reserve.

[*Township Maps of the Cherokee Nation*]. Muskogee, Oklahoma: Indian Territory Map Company [1909]; G1365.I5 1909 (see p. 222)

This atlas shows cadastral and landownership information for the Cherokee Nation lands.

Trail of Tears National Historic Trail. Comprehensive Management and Use Plan, Map Supplement, September 1992. Denver: U.S. National Park Service, 1992; G1282.T7U5 1992

Set of maps illustrating the water route and the three principal overland routes used during the forcible removal of the Cherokee people in 1838–39.

Reservations and Allotments

By the mid-nineteenth century the policy of removal to one large Indian territory was replaced by a policy of isolating Indians on reservations. Maps of individual reserves make up a large part of the items included in the Geography and Map Division's subject files under the heading "Indians" and in the miscellaneous geographic regions file under the names of the individual tribes. The reservation maps date from the 1850s to the present, but most of the division's coverage is in the 1890–1950 time period.

Many of the individual reservation maps were produced by the Office of Indian Affairs during the 1920s, 1930s, and 1940s. The Geography and Map Division does not, however, have coverage of all reservations. The larger tribes with major land holdings are normally represented by the greatest number of maps, while there may be no separate maps of smaller reservations. The cultural information contained on the maps varies, but generally includes such features as roads, trails, boundaries, schools, wells, fences, and buildings. Since the 1970s, the U.S. Bureau of Indian Affairs has published a series of single and multi-sheet "Highway System Maps" for some 175 reservations. These maps and map series provide detailed coverage of the current physical and cultural features of reservations. In addition to the individual reservation maps, there is a rather extensive collection of small-scale maps of the United States dating from the early 1880s to the present which illustrate the Indian reservation system.

Within the collection of individual reservation maps there is a category which relates to the General Allotment or Dawes Severalty Act of 1887, and subsequent provisions to that act, which allowed for the allotment of tribal lands on certain reservations to individual Indians and the sale of unassigned lands to non-Indians (see pp. 156–7). The allotment policy led to the breakup of tribal land ownership and eventually resulted in the loss of over half of the Indian tribal lands before the termination of this policy in the 1930s. These allotment maps were primarily commercial publications prepared as promotional tools to advance the sale of unassigned lands. Because of their promotional character, they often contained information about the adaptability of the reservation lands for agricultural purposes. Another interesting feature of a few of the allotment maps is that, in the process of distinguishing allotted lands from unassigned lands, they included the names of Indian allottees, a feature of value for genealogical research.

A Map of Allegany Reservation. Anonymous. [18–?] Col. manuscript map 22 x 30 cm. Scale ca. 1:158,400; G3801.E2 18— .M Vault

Shows the Seneca Nation's Allegany Reservation in Cattaraugus County, New York.

Diagram of Indian Reservation on the Minnesota River. By Treaties with the Dakota or Sioux Indians

of 23d. July & 5th Augt. 1855. U.S. Surveyor Generals Office, St. Paul, 1859. Col. manuscript map 40 x 48 cm. Scale ca. 1:510,000; G4141.E1 1855 .U Vault

Shows alternate survey lines for the Sioux reservation adjacent to the Minnesota River. These reserved lands were ceded to the federal government in the 1860s.

Territory of Arizona. Compiled from the official records of the General Land Office and other sources by C. Roeser. [Washington, D.C.]: General Land Office, 1876. Col. map 59 x 73 cm. Scale ca. 1:1,150,000; Arizona—1876

This is one of several editions of the General Land Office map of Arizona published in the late nineteenth and early twentieth centuries. Viewed together, they illustrate the development of the reservation system in the state. Similar maps were produced for all the other western states.

Map of Tuscarora Indian Reservation, Located and Platted A.D. 1890. Henry B. Carrington, U.S. Army, Special Agent, Indian Statistics, 11th U.S. Census. Washington, D.C.: GPO, 1894. Col. map 25 x 27 cm. Scale not given; New York—Indians—1890

This map of the Tuscarora Reservation in Niagara County, New York, is one of several maps appearing in the *Report on Indians Taxed and Indians Not Taxed in the United States (Except Alaska) at the Eleventh Census, 1890* (U.S. Congressional Serial Set #3016).

Map Showing Indian Reservations within the Limits of the United States. Compiled under the direction of the Hon. T. J. Morgan, Commissioner of Indian Affairs. Washington, D.C., 1892. Col. map 59 x 73 cm. Scale ca. 1:1,150,000; U.S.—Indians—1892

One of numerous maps which indicate the location of Indian reservations.

Allotment Map of the Oto and Missouri Indian Reservation, O. T. R. S. Steele. 1902. Col. map 47 x 70 cm. Scale ca. 1:42,000; Oklahoma—Indians—1902

Names Indian allottees.

Map of the Spokane Indian Reservation, Stevens County, Washington Showing Indian Allotments, with the Name of the Allotters, Lands to be opened to Homestead Entry marked "Agricultural Lands," Lands not Allotted or to be opened to Homestead Entry shown blank. Spokane, Washington: W. M. Manning, 1910. Col. map 46 x 89 cm. Scale ca. 1:63,360; Washington—Spokane Indian Reservation—1910

Mescalero Indian Reservation, New Mexico. Compiled from aerial photographic mosaics, with corrections from the field. [Washington, D.C.] Department of the Interior, Office of Indian Affairs, 1938. Col. map 82 x 117 cm. Scale ca. 1:63,000; New Mexico—Indians, Mescalero Reservation—1938

Similar to many other maps of individual reservations published by the Office (Bureau) of Indian Affairs, it shows roads, trails, telephone lines, water sources, schools, and fire lookout stations.

The Navajo Atlas: Environments, Resources, People, and History of the Diné Bikeyah. James M. Goodman. Norman: University of Oklahoma Press, 1982; G1497.N3G6 1982

Contains forty-eight maps dealing with the physical environment, history, population, livelihood, and resources of the Navajo, and includes a section on the Navajo-Hopi land dispute.

A Zuni Atlas. T. J. Ferguson and E. Richard Hart. Norman: University of Oklahoma Press, 1985; G1496.E1F4 1985

Contains forty-four maps illustrating the physical environment, history, natural resources, and culture of the Zuni.

GATEWAYS

There are several different kinds of Indian claims, broadly considered, and a number of different venues in which the claims have been pursued. Indian claims can be for land, water rights, hunting and fishing rights, mineral rights, or other financial or resource losses. Indian claims have been based on allegations of fraud, theft, duress, unconscionably low compensation, breach of contract, statutory violations, mismanagement, and erroneous actions, among other reasons, by federal, state, or private agents. Indian claims have been pursued in federal trial and appellate courts, U.S. claims courts, the Indian Claims Commission, state and local courts, the U.S. Congress, and state legislatures. Indian claims have been brought both by tribes, federally recognized and unrecognized, and by individuals.

Land claims comprise the best known and longest lived claims. From 1863 to 1946, Indian claims against the U.S. needed an act from Congress granting jurisdiction to the U.S. Court of Claims to be heard. Congress created the Indian Claims Commission (1946–78) to try to answer all Indian claims against the U.S. The Commission received over six hundred claims and created a large body of ethnographic, ethno-historical, and legal records. Tribes continue to file claims in the U.S. Claims Court. Claims under the Indian Trade and Intercourse Act of 1790, involving state acquisitions of Indian land without federal approval, have required action by both federal courts and Congress, as well as states. Settlements of Indian water rights claims have also required congressional action.

The evidence brought forward in pursuing Indian claims has come from Indian and non-Indian sources. The former group includes tribal representatives, delegates sent to petition the federal government, and tribal members. The latter group includes, among others, travelers, missionaries, soldiers, traders, and settlers; federal employees such as Bureau of Indian Affairs agents and U.S. Army officers; and anthropologists, ethnohistorians, economists, and other scientists.

WHERE TO LOOK: Library collections bearing on Indian claims include the Law Library, the General Collections, Microform Reading Room, Local History and Genealogy Reading Room, and the Manuscript and Geography and Map Divisions.

President Harry S. Truman is congratulated by representatives of the Oklahoma Choctaw and the Uncompahgre and Uintah Utes of Utah, after signing the Indian Claims Commission Act, August 13, 1946. Collections of Encyclopedia Britannica. PRES FILE—Truman, Harry S.—Misc. political and social activities. (LC-USZ62-105437). Prints and Photographs Division.

The Choctaw were one of the first tribes to win a claim under the Act, while the Ute tribes later won several large awards.

Indian Land Areas. Compiled by the *Handbook of North American Indians* (Smithsonian Institution) in cooperation with the Bureau of Indian Affairs. Prepared by the U.S. Geological Survey. Reston Va., 1989. Col. map 65 x 105 cm. Scale ca. 1 : 5,000,000; G3701.G6 1989 .S6

Shows federal and state reservations, Alaskan regional corporation lands, and federal Indian groups without reservations.

Federal-aid Indian Road System Atlas. Bureau of Indian Affairs, Division of Indian Affairs. [Albuquerque, N.M.]: Bureau of Indian Affairs, 1974-; G1201.P2U46 1974

This atlas contains modern 1:63,360 scale maps which, in addition to portraying road and other transportation information, also show relief, drainage, administrative divisions, and building locations and usage within many Indian reservations.

Indian Wars

Cartography has long been a valuable resource for illustrating and studying military events within their topographic and environmental context. Although there is no large collection of Indian battle maps in the Geography and Map Division, the existing examples are useful tools for depicting the hostilities between Indians and non-Indians. Many of the Indian-related military maps in the Geography and Map Division were issued by the federal government to illustrate the results of specific battles, but there are also example of maps depicting military campaigns, maps of the "seat of war," and reconnaissance maps. There are also numerous maps that simply give the locations of battle sites. No examples were located of maps portraying conflicts exclusively between rival Indian groups.

Most of the Indian battle maps are filed in the Uncataloged/Titled collection under the heading "United States—Wars, Indian." Within this file of miscellaneous battle maps, the largest group relates to the French and Indian War. The maps of this war as well as those of the Revolutionary War contain very little data about the involvement or impact of the Indian participants. This file also contains a good collection of maps of the Seminole Wars in Florida, with particular emphasis on maps of the Second Seminole War from 1835–42. The single engagement most often represented is the Battle of the Little Big Horn.

A Prospective View of the Battle fought near Lake George, on the 8th of Sepr. 1755, between 2000 English, with 250 Mohawks, under the command of Genl. Johnson: & 2500 French & Indians under the command of Genl. Dieskau. . . . Samuel Blodget, delin. T. Jefferys, sculp. London: Thomas Jefferys, 1756. In *A General Topography of North America and the West Indies . . . 1768* by Thomas Jefferys. Col. map 29 x 51 cm. Scales differ; G1105.J4 1768 Vault, map no. 37 (see p. 217)

Contains map of Hudson River and views of the two engagements between New Englanders and their Mohawk allies, and French troops and their Iroqois allies.

Map of Gen. Sullivan's march from Easton to the Senaca & Cayuga countries. [1779] Col. manuscript map 76 x 75 cm. Scale ca. 1:350,000; G3791.S3 1779 .M3 Vault

Shows the route of Gen. Sullivan's 1779 expedition against the Indians of the Finger Lakes region of New York. Indian villages are located and engagements shown.

Battle of Tehoo [peka]. Anonymous. Manuscript map on sheet 21 x 13 cm. Scale not given; G3972.H6S42 1814 .B Vault

Shows the decisive 1814 battle at Tohopeka or Horseshoe Bend on the Tallapoosa River, Alabama between U.S. regular army troops led by Andrew Jackson and Creek forces led by Red Eagle (William Weatherford).

[*Battle of Okeechobee, Florida, 1837*] Anonymous. Col. manuscript map 32 x 40 cm. Scale ca. 1:17,000; G3931.S1 1837 .B Vault

General map of the Tampa Bay to Lake Okeechobee region during the Second Seminole War; it includes an inset of the troop positions at the Lake Okeechobee battle site.

Map of the Seat of War in East Florida. Compiled from various data in the U.S. Topl. Bureau under the direction of Col: John J. Abert, U.S. Top. Engr., by Wash: Hood. Washington, D.C., 1837. Col. map 118 x 69 cm. Scale ca. 1:350,000; U.S.—Wars, Indian—Florida—1837

Shows roads, Indian trails, fortifications, and battle sites for the 1835–37 campaign.

Sketch of the Blue Water Creek embracing the field of action of the force under the command of Bvt. Brig. Genl. W. S. Harney in the attack of the 3rd Sept. 1855, on the "Brule" Band of the Indian Chief Little Thunder. Made by Lieut G. K. Warren, Topl. Engr. of the Expedition. Sen. Ex. Doc. 76, 1st Sess., 34th Cong. [Washington, D.C.: 1855?]. Col. map 23 x 15 cm. Scale ca. 1:85,000; U.S.–Wars, Indian—Nebraska—1855 (see p. 216)

The sketch llustrates the surprise attack by federal forces on the Brulé Sioux band at Blue Water Creek, Nebraska.

Custer's Battle-Field (June 25th, 1876). Surveyed and drawn under the personal supervision of Lieut. Edward Maguire, Corps of Engineers, U.S.A., by Sergeant Charles Becker. From *Report of the Secretary of War . . .* vol. II, part III. Washington, D.C., [1876?]. Col. map 39 x 45 cm. Scale ca. 1:21,000; U.S.—Wars, Indian—Montana—1876

Topographic plan of the battlefield showing locations of the officers' graves.

Map of the Nez Percé Indian Campaign. Brig. Gen. O. O. Howard, U.S.A., Commanding. Compiled & prepared by Robt. H. Fletcher, 1st Lieut. Washington, D.C., [1877?]. Col. map 55 x 117 cm. Scale ca. 1:2,000,000; U.S.—Wars, Indian—1877?

Coverage extends from the Pacific coast to the Dakota Territory. Shows Chief Joseph's route through Idaho, Wyoming, and Montana and includes detailed insets of each of the major engagements.

Sketch of Scene of Action with Hostile Apache Indians on Big Dry Fork, A.T. July 17th, 1882. Drawn by Thomas Cruse, 2nd. Lieut, 6th Cav. Blueprint. Col. map 45 x 33 cm. Scale ca. 1:7,200; Arizona—Indians—1882

Shows positions of U.S. and Indian forces, rifle pits, and route of Apache retreat.

Outline Map of the Field of Operations against Hostile Chiricahua Indians showing operations from April 12th 1886 to the date of their Surrender September 4th 1886. Compiled and Drawn by direction of Brigadier General Nelson A. Miles, commanding the Department of Arizona, in the Office of First Lieut. E. J. Spencer, Corps of Engineers. [1886?] Blueprint. Col. map 95 x 110 cm. Scale ca. 1:633,000; U.S.—Wars, Indian—Arizona—1886

Covers portions of southern Arizona and New Mexico and northern Mexico, illustrating scene of final organized Indian resistance (led by Geronimo) against the United States.

Map of Custer Battlefield. Birdseye view of the Little Big Horn country and a portion of Davis creek—a tributary of the Rosebud—showing where Custer and his men traversed—June 25, 1876. Compiled and drawn by Russell White Bear. [Crow Agency, Montana], 1925. Col. map 28 x 31 cm. Scale not given; U.S.—Wars, Indian—Montana—1876

Includes inset: "Birdseye view of Custer's last stand hill." (see p. 222)

Battle of the Bear's Paw Between General Miles and Chief Joseph, Sept. 30 to Oct. 5, 1877. Surveyed by

C. R. Noyes. [1935?]. Col. map 51 x 37 cm. Scale ca. 1:2,400; U.S.—Wars, Indians—Montana—1877

Detailed survey of the battlefield at the Bear Paw, Montana portraying the final engagement of the Nez Perce campaign.

Civil War in Indian Territory, 1861–1865. Prepared by the Oklahoma Department of Transportation, Planning Division. [Oklahoma City: 1979?]. Col. map 44 x 62 cm. Scale ca. 1:1,375,000; G4021.S5 1979 .O4

Shows location of twenty-seven battle sites in Oklahoma.

Ethnography, Linguistics, Distribution, and Archaeology

Maps are tools for portraying the organization and distribution of American Indian cultures. Ethnographic maps depict the distribution of Indian tribes with common ethnic affinities, and linguistic maps group them by common language characteristics. As noted earlier, indications of tribal range appear on a number of early maps, but the first systematic efforts to map the geographic distribution of Indian cultural groups did not begin to appear until the early nineteenth century. Most ethnographic and linguistic maps focus on cultural and language associations at the time of European contact and often do not reflect the migrations and adaptations that occurred either prior to or after the contact period.

Portrayals of other aspects of Indian distribution appear primarily on recent maps, including items illustrating Indian land occupancy and use in relationship to Indian land claims; population maps which are usually based on federal census data and illustrate the distribution of individuals rather than tribes; and archaeological maps which portray the locations and distribution patterns of prehistoric Indian culture and habita-

tion. The Geography and Map Division contains maps illustrating all these aspects of the cultural and ethnic distribution of North American Indians.

Locations and Wandering of the Aboriginal Tribes, Introductory Map to Accompany Willard's History of the United States. Emma Hart Willard. In *A Series of Maps to Willard's History of the United States, . . .* New York: White, Gallaher, & White, 1828. Col. map 25 x 29 cm. Scale ca. 1:9,000,000; G1201. S1W5 1828 Vault (see p. 220)

One of the first attempts to graphically illustrate the distribution and migrations of Indian tribes in the eastern United States.

Map of the Indian Tribes of North America, about 1600 A.D. along the Atlantic; and about 1800 A.D. westwardly. Published by the Amer: Antiq: Soc: from a drawing by Hon: A. Gallatin. [1836] From American Antiquarian Society, *Transactions and Collections,* vol. 2.,1836. Col. map 39 x 43 cm. Scale ca. 1:15,000,000; G3301.E1 1800 .G Vault

Gallatin, the founder of the American Ethnological Society, was a recognized authority on Indian languages. This map of Indian tribal distribution appeared in his study of Indian languages, *A Synopsis of the Indian Tribes within the United States East of the Rocky Mountains. . . .*

A Map of the Ancient Indian Towns on the Pickaway Plain, Illustrating a sketch of the country. Felix Renick. Cincinnati: Doolittle & Munson, [1844]. Col. map 47 x 53 cm. Scale not given; Ohio—Indians—1846 (see p. 221)

Shows Shawnee villages and earthworks in central Ohio.

Plan of Indian Mounds at "Gideon's Farm," Excelsior, Hennepin Co., Minnesota, 1879. Frank H. Nutter, Topographical Engineer. Col. manuscript map 57 x 91 cm. Scale ca. 1:96,000,000; G4141.E1 1879 .N Vault

Shows location and height of over seventy Indian mounds at Gideon Bay and Lake Park near the shore of Lake Minnetonka, Minnesota.

Map of Alaska and Adjoining Regions . . . Showing the Distribution of Native Tribes. Compiled by Ivan Petroff, Special Agent, Tenth Census, 1880. Drawn by Harry King. [New York, 1880?] From Ivan Petroff, *Report on the Population, Industries, and Resources of Alaska*, 1884. Col. map 62 x 78 cm. Scale ca. 1:3,500,000; Alaska—Indians—1880

Shows distribution of Indian, Aleut, and Eskimo tribes.

Map of the Linguistic Stocks of American Indians chiefly within the present limits of the United States. J. W. Powell. From *Eleventh Census of the United States.* Washington, D.C.: [1890]. Col. map 52 x 45 cm. Scale ca. 1:13,000,000; North America—Indians—1890

Powell, the founder of the Bureau of Ethnology, conducted numerous archaeological, linguistic, and ethnographic studies of American Indians.

Chart of Central Settlements of Quivira and Harahey, Kansas Valley, North America. Drawn for Robert Henderson, by J. V. Brower. 1902. Col. map 21 x 34 cm. Scale ca. 1:350,000; Kansas—Indians—1902

Shows locations of Quivira, Harahey, and Kaw village sites and burial mounds in the vicinity of Manhattan, Kansas.

Archeological Atlas of Ohio, Showing the Distribution of the various Classes of Prehistoric Remains in the State, with a Map of the Principal Indian Trails and Towns. William C. Mills. Columbus: Ohio State Archeological and Historical Society, 1914; G1396.E15M5 1914

Contains a separate map of each county showing locations of mounds, enclosures, village sites, burial grounds, petroglyphs, and flint quarries.

Archaeological Atlas of Michigan. Wilbert B. Hinsdale (Michigan Handbook Series No. 4). Ann Arbor: University of Michigan Press, 1931; G1411 .E8H55 1931.

Contains twenty maps showing locations of mounds, enclosures, earthworks, villages, burial grounds, gardens, trails, and copper excavations.

The North American Indians, 1950 Distribution of Descendants of the Aboriginal Population of Alaska, Canada and the United States. A map prepared under the direction of Sol Tax, Department of Anthropology, University of Chicago. 4th Edition. Chicago: University of Chicago, 1961?. Col. map 63 x 71 cm. Scale ca. 1:10,000,000; North America—Indians—1950

Locates and gives the population of all self-identified Indian communities as of 1950.

Maps of Tribal Locations and Indian Agencies. In *Report with Respect to the House Resolution Authorizing the Committee on Indian and Insular Affairs to Conduct an Investigation of the Bureau of Indian Affairs.* Washington, D.C.: GPO, 1953. 82d Cong. 2d. Sess. House Report no. 2503; U.S. Congressional Serial Set no. 11582, Law Library

Contains 157 maps illustrating the location of various Indian groups as of 1950 and depicts approximations of the original range occupied by these groups.

Tribal Distribution in North America, 1500–1600. Robin F. Wells. [Toledo, Ohio], 1971. Col. map 122 x 105 cm. Scale ca. 1:6,336,000; G3301.E1 1600 .W4

Depicts the migrations of various tribes and links between tribes. There are five additional "Tribal Distribution" maps by Wells, filed under different classification numbers, covering the time periods 1600–50, 1650–1715, 1715–60, 1760–1810, and 1810–40.

North America Before Columbus. Produced by the Cartographic Division, National Geographic Society. Washington, D.C.: National Geographic Society, 1973. Col. map 92 x 80 cm. Scale ca. 1:10,610,000; G3301.E1 1973 .N3

Shows Indian occupation sites at four time periods: before 8000 B.C., 8000–1000 B.C., 1000 B.C.–A.D. 1000, and A.D. 1000-contact with Europeans. Verso of map contains map entitled "Indians of North America" which illustrates cultural and tribal divisions.

Number of American Indians by Counties of the United States: 1970. Prepared by Geography Division in cooperation with Population Division, Bureau of the Census. United States Maps, GE-50, no 49. Washington, D.C.: U.S. Government Printing Office, 1973. Col. map 70 x 99 cm. Scale ca. 1:5,000,000; G3701.E1 1970 .U5

Shows population density by county.

Native Languages of the Northwest Coast. Wayne Suttles. [Portland, Oregon:] The Press of the Oregon Historical Society, 1985. Col. map 70 x 101 cm. Scale ca. 1:3,000,000; G4371.E3 1985 .S9

Illustrates language families and relationships for the region from Kodiak Island, Alaska, to Northern California.

We the People: An Atlas of America's Ethnic Diversity. James Paul Allen and Eugene James Turner. New York: Macmillan Publishing Co., 1988; G1201.E1A4 1988

Contains chapter titled "People of Early North American Origin" which discusses and illustrates modern distribution and migration issues relating to Indians, Eskimos, and Aleut.

Atlante: Le civiltá indigene delle Americhe. Introduzione di Aurelio Rigoli, a curi di Anna-maria Amitrano. Genoa: Edizioni Colombo, 1992; G1101.E1A8 1992.

Shows the territorial distribution and habitat of Indian groups in the 1692–1728 time period.

Historical Maps

In general there has been little effort to produce historical cartography portraying the wide range of social, political, economic, and cultural themes of Indian life. Historical coverage is usually limited to depicting ethnographic or linguistic distribution, battle sites, and the locations of villages and reservations. Exceptions are found in *Comparative Studies of North American Indians* (1957), *Atlas of the North American Indian* (1985), *Atlas of Great Lakes Indian History* (1987), and *Atlas of American Indian Affairs* (1990), all of which include historical coverage of a broader spectrum of Indian matters, and which are cited in the "General Reference and Bibliographic Resources" section at the beginning of this chapter. General coverage of Indian history is usually included in thematic and historical atlases of the United States and in individual state atlases. Historical maps are valuable resources not only for their recreation of past events and their documentation of tribal distribution and habitation sites, but also for what they reveal about the perceptions and cultural values of the time in which they were produced.

Atlas of the Historical Geography of the United States. Charles O. Paullin. [Washington, D.C.]: Published jointly by Carnegie Institution of Washington and the American Geographical Society of New York, 1932; G1201.S1P3 1932

Contains coverage of Indian distribution, wars, reservations, and missions.

Hearne Brothers Indian History Series. Detroit, Hearne Brothers. Maps are filed individually under each state.

In the early 1960s, Hearne Brothers published a separate large wall map for each state illustrating pre-contact tribal ranges, settlements, historic sites, and reservation boundaries. Textual information about the tribes within the state is included on the verso of each map.

Atlas of Early American History, The Revolutionary Era, 1760–1790. Edited by Lester J. Cappon. Chicago: Published for the Newberry Library and the Institute of Early American History and Culture by Princeton University Press, 1976; G1201.S3A8. 1976

Contains maps of Indian villages located in the eastern U.S. in the 1760–94 time period.

Atlas of Native History. Jack D. Forbes. Davis, California: D-Q University Press, [1981]; G1201 .E1F6 1981

Contains seventeen maps showing tribal migrations and distribution.

Historical Atlas of the United States, Centennial Edition. Washington, D.C.: National Geographic Society, 1988; G1201.S1N3 1988

Includes coverage of a number of aspects of Indian culture, politics, lands, and wars.

Historical Atlas of Oklahoma. John W. Morris, Charles R. Goins, and Edwin C. McReynolds. Third Edition. Norman: University of Oklahoma Press, 1986; G1366.S1M6 1986

Contains twenty-seven maps relating to Indian affairs in Oklahoma, including coverage of tribal lands and location of missions and battle sites.

Natural Resources

Natural resources have always been key factors influencing the choice of settlement sites, the level of subsistence, and the survival of a region's inhabitants. Historically, the identification and mapping of resources of economic value on In-dian lands often have had the effect of promoting non-Indian encroachment and the removal of the native inhabitants. The demand for agricultural lands and the search for mineral deposits are the most obvious examples, but other resources, such as timber, water, and grazing lands, were also often sought on Indian lands and occasionally depicted on maps. The natural resources of present-day reservations have been, in many cases, the principal means of tribal income, and modern maps of the soils, geology, mineral deposits, water, climate, energy, timber, and agriculture potential of reservation lands are all aids to decision-making regarding issues of land use, economic development, and conservation.

The extent of thematic mapping of the natural resources varies for each reservation, but in general there is little coverage for most reservations in the Geography and Map Division. Some pertinent earth sciences maps will, however, be included with scientific publications and can be found in the Library's General Collections rather than the Geography and Map Division.

A Map of that Part of Georgia Occupied by the Cherokee Indians Taken from an Actual Survey made during the present year, 1831 in Pursuance of an Act of the General Assembly of the State. John Bethune, Surveyor Genl. of the State of Georgia. [Milledgeville, George: 1831]. Col. map 74 x 55 cm. Scale ca. 1:2,200,000; G3921.E1 1831 .B Vault

Shows roads, towns, villages, and gold mining sites in northwestern Georgia, an area occupied by the Cherokee Indians. The map also includes the following note: "This interesting Tract of country contains four millions . . . Acres, many rich Gold Mines & many delightful Situations & though in some parts mountainous, Some of the richest Land belonging to the state."

Sketch of Public Surveys in New Mexico & Arizona to accompany the Annual Report of the Commissioner of the General Land Office for 1866.

[Washington, D.C.]: Department of the Interior, General Land Office, 1866. Col. map 54 x 71 cm. Scale ca. 1:1,850,000; New Mexico—1866

Shows gold, silver, and copper deposits situated within the lands occupied by Indian nations.

Classification Map of Creek and Seminole Nations. Ricksecker, Hackbush and Patton, Civil Engineers. Muskegee, I.T.: Bradley Real Estate Co., [189–?]. Col. map 68 x 63 cm. Scale ca. 1:250,000; Oklahoma—Indians—189–? (see p. 223)

Lands of the Creek and Seminole Nations in Indian Territory are classified according to potential agricultural use.

Map of the Blackfeet Indian Reservation Showing the Mountainous Region Proposed to be ceded to the U.S. Government, also a part of Flathead and Deer Lodge Counties. Made by Ross Cartee. 1896. Col. map 56 x 62 cm. Scale ca. 1:126,000; Montana—Indians—1896

Includes text entitled "Opening of the Ceded Mineral Strip of the Blackfeet Reservation," which describes the mineral potential of the land ceded in 1895 to the federal government.

The Rosebud Indian Reservation of South Dakota: Map and Guide to Quality of the Soil. Omaha: C. J. Conner, 1903. Col. map 65 x 56 cm. Scale ca. 1:90,000; South Dakota—Indians—1903

In addition to coverage of soil and vegetation types, this map designates lands allotted to the Indians.

Part of Uinta Indian Reservation, Utah, To be disposed of under Act of March 3, 1905 and President's Proclamation dated July 14, 1905. I. P. Berthrong. Washington, D.C.: U.S. General Land Office, [1905]. Col. map 65 x 115 cm. Scale ca. 1:130,000; Utah—Indians—1905

Shows grazing lands, proposed Indian timber reserve, allotments, mining claims, water re-served for Indian irrigation, and water reserved by the U.S. Geological Survey for irrigation.

Graphic Summary of the Tewa Basin Study. By the Indian Land Research Unit in Cooperation with United States Forest Service, Soil Conservation Service. Prepared under direction of Mark W. Radcliffe. [Albuquerque]: U.S. Department of the Interior, Office of Indian Affairs, Land Division, 1935; G1507.T4U5 1935

Contains fifty-eight maps, accompanied by aerial photographs illustrating the soil types, soil erosion, vegetation, geology, timber, population, endemic diseases, and ownership of cultivated lands in the Tewa Basin of New Mexico.

Land Resources of Southeast Alaska Native Villages: An Inventory of Lands Withdrawn for Native Selection in Southeast Alaska under the Alaska Native Claims Settlement Act. Juneau: Sealaska Corporation, 1973; G1531.G1S4 1973

Includes coverage of timber, water, mineral, soils, and man-made resources.

Soil Survey of Colorado River Indian Reservation Arizona-California. U.S. Department of Agriculture, Soil Conservation Service; in cooperation with the U.S. Bureau of Indian Affairs, Arizona Agriculture Experiment Station, and California Agricultural Experiment Station. [Washington, D.C.?]: Soil Conservation Service, [1986]; S599. A7N45 1986—General Collections

Contains twenty-six 1:20,000 scale maps detailing the location of various soil types.

Northern Cheyenne Integrated Resource Management Plan: Atlas. [Billings, Montana: U.S. Bureau of Indian Affairs, Billings Area Office, 1988?]; G1472.N6G4U5 1988

Contains fifteen maps illustrating forest, agricultural, mineral, oil and gas, rangeland, and recreation resources.

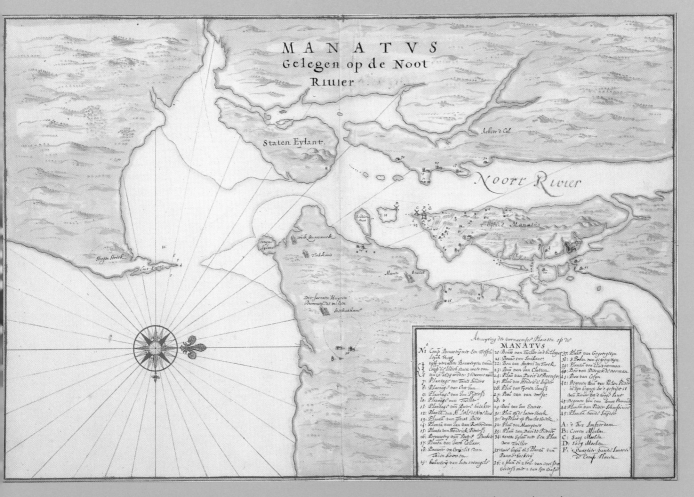

Manatus, Gelegen op de Noot Riuier. [Johannes Vingboons]. 1639 [ca. 1665] Harrisse Collection, Vingboons Atlas, vol. 3, map 12 (LCG&M-2086.1 CT). Geography and Map Division.

This manuscript map of Manhattan and vicinity was drawn in ca. 1665 after a 1639 work by the Dutch cartographer, Johannes Vingboons. In addition to the evidence of Dutch settlement in Manhattan, the map features in the Brooklyn area four longhouses representing the Indian villages Wichquawank, Techkonis, Mareckewich, and Keskachauc. One of the settlements contains the note: "This is the type of houses the Indians live in." This is typical of the unexpected evidence of Indian settlement and culture that can appear on cartographic documents not normally considered resources for American Indian studies.

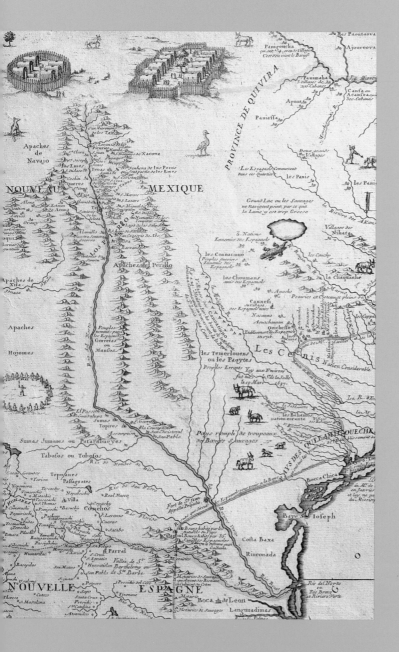

Detail from *La France Occidentale Dans l'Amérique Septentrional . . . / La Cours du Mississippi ou de St. Louis Fameuse Rivière de l'Amérique Septentrionale ux Environs de laquelle se trouve le Pais appellé Louisiane.* Nicolas De Fer. 1718. G3300 1718 .F Vault (LCG&M-283 CT). Geography and Map Division.

Illustrated is the portion of De Fer's map of North America showing the Rio Grande Valley with its Spanish settlements and Indian villages and pueblos. The two illustrations of Indian settlements at the top of this map also appeared on other early maps of North America and likely depict settlement patterns of Eastern Indians, rather than those of the Southwest. The map is typical of the many general maps that may also include information pertinent for Indian studies.

RIGHT: *This Map describing the Scituation of the Several Nations of Indians to the NW. of South Carolina was Coppyed from a Draught drawn & painted on a Deer Skin by an Indian Cacique and Presented to Francis Nicholson Esqr., Governor of Carolina . . . ca. 1721.* Photocopy from original manuscript in the British Museum, London. North America—Indians—1721? (LCG&M-4290 CT). Geography and Map Division

Given to the governor of South Carolina, Francis Nicholson, in ca. 1721, this map was drawn on a deerskin, probably by a Catawba chief. It features thirteen circles representing the Indian tribes in the South Carolina piedmont. The tribes are connected by a network of double lines representing paths. Along the left side of the map is a portrayal of the city of Charlestown, with its rectangular street grid and a ship in the harbor. Although the map may appear to be rather schematic, it accurately reflects the spatial relationships of the Indian groups and their interconnecting trails.

Copy of a Sketch of the Monongahela , with the field of battle, done by an Indian. 1755. G3824.P6S26 1755 .C6 Vault (LCG&M-780). Geography and Map Division.

Drawn by an unidentified Indian scout, this sketch is one of two original manuscript maps by an Indian in the Geography and Map Division. It depicts the battle near Ft. Duquesne between Gen. Edward Braddock's British forces and the French and their Indian allies on July 9, 1755. With a sizable force of Indian allies and the advantage of fighting from the protection of natural cover, the French destroyed over half of the British force.

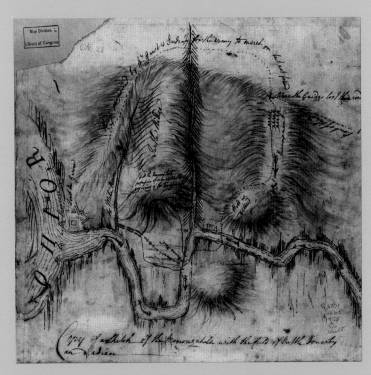

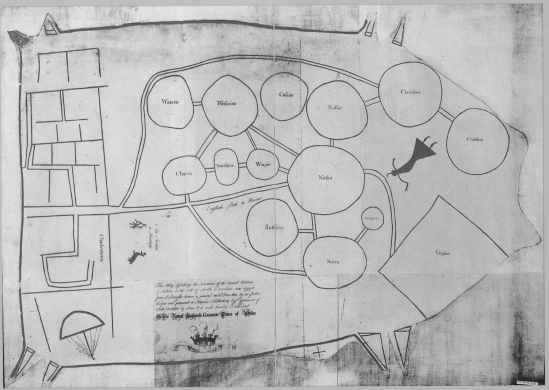

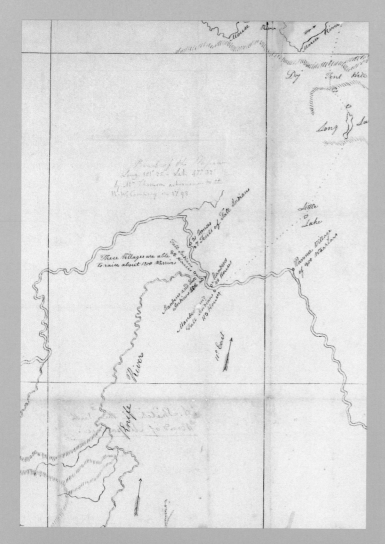

Detail from *A Sketch of the North Bend of Missouri*. Attributed to David Thompson, copied by Meriwether Lewis. 1798? Lewis and Clark Collection, map j (LCG&M-4289). Geography and Map Division.

In preparation for the Lewis and Clark Expedition, Lewis copied David Thompson's 1798 sketch of the Great Bend of the Missouri River. The portion of the map shown here locates a number of Mandan and Pawnee settlements near the confluence of the Knife and Missouri Rivers and includes notations on the number of warriors, houses, and tents of each village.

Sketch of the Blue Water Creek embracing the field of action of the force under the command of Bvt. Brig. Genl. W.S. Harney in the attack of the 3rd Sept. 1855, on the Brule Band of the Indian Chief Little Thunder. Lieut. G.K. Warren. [1855] U.S. Wars, Indian—Nebraska—1855 (LCG&M-4288 CT). Geography and Map Division.

One of the numerous engagements between the Sioux and the U.S. military over nearly fifty years, the Battle of Blue Water Creek (Nebraska) was precipitated by earlier conflicts, including the Sioux destruction of a detachment of U.S. infantrymen in 1854. In retaliation in 1855 a force of 600 troops from Fort Kearny conducted a surprise attack on a Brulé village at Blue Water Creek, killing or capturing half of its 250 inhabitants.

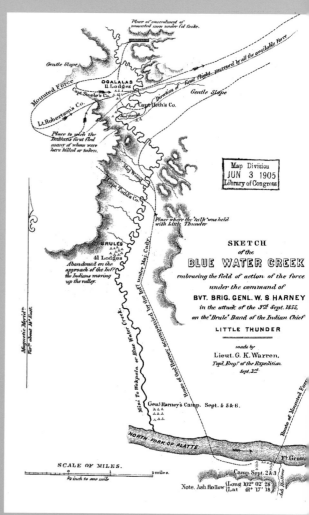

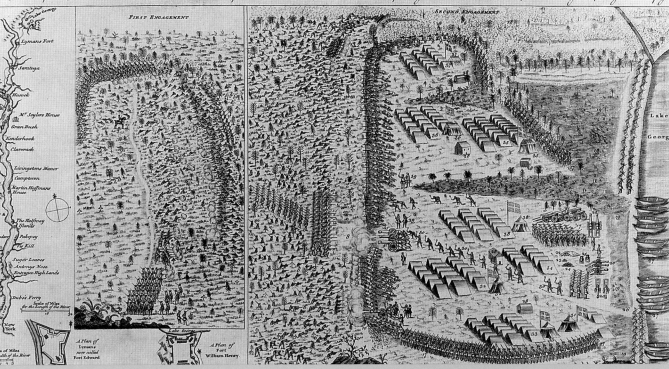

A Prospective View of the Battle fought near Lake George, on the 8th of Sepr. 1755, between 2000 English, with 250 Mohawks, under the command of Genl. Johnson: & 2500 French & Indians under the command of Genl. Dieskau. . . . Thomas Jefferys. 1756. G1105.J4 1768 Vault, no. 37 (LCG&M-4287). Geography and Map Division.

This map illustrates the two stages of the battle in 1755 between a force of New Englanders with their Mohawk allies and French troops and their Iroquois supporters, part of the long series of battles between the French and British for control of North America that often involved Indian participants. Ambushed in the initial engagement near Crown Point on Lake George, the New Englanders retreated south where they repelled another French attack. Although the English and Mohawk could claim victory, the success was bitter for the Mohawk, who had fought their fellow Iroquois.

A Map of the Lands Ceded by the Cherokee Indians to the State of South-Carolina at a congress held in May, A.D. 1777; containing about 1,697,700 acres. [1777?] G3910 1777 .M3 Vault (LCG&M-4286). Geography and Map Division.

This manuscript map shows the land ceded by the Cherokee Indians to South Carolina and Georgia by a treaty signed on May 20, 1777. The Cherokee entered the American Revolutionary War against the Americans in 1776, but a counterattack by southern militia forced the Cherokee to sue for peace. This treaty and a later one with Virginia and North Carolina ceded over two and a half million acres of Cherokee territory to the southern colonies or states.

Cartouche from *A Map of the Inhabited Part of Canada from the French Surveys; with the Frontiers of New York and New England.* William Faden. 1777. G3401.F2 1777 .F3 Vault (LCG&M-4291 CT). Geography and Map Division.

As with many map title cartouches, this one of a map of Canada and New England reflects elements of the economic interests of the region depicted on the map. In this case the cartouche symbolizes the economic importance of the North American fur trade and the significance of the America Indian in the promulgation of that trade.

Frontispiece from *Colton's American Atlas.* George W. Colton. 1855. G1019.C548 1855 vol. 1, copy 2 (LCG&M-4292 CT). Geography and Map Division.

This frontispiece symbolizes elements of the attitude of manifest destiny, the divine sanctioning of the westward expansion of the United States. In the foreground, Indians are depicted as part of the natural environment observing the advance of the population, agriculture, commerce, and industry of Western civilization.

RIGHT: *[Map of the western United States, from 91° to 119° West longitude and 36° to 50° North latitude]* Pierre Jean De Smet. 1851. G4050 1851 .S Vault (LCG&M-653). Geography and Map Division.

De Smet, a Jesuit missionary to the Indians of the American west, travelled widely and wrote extensively about the Western Indians. This manuscript map attests to his extensive knowledge of the geography and tribal lands of the American West. De Smet was present at the 1851 Treaty of Laramie and his map may have been produced to illustrate the lands of the Western Indians at the time of the treaty. A portrait of a signer of the treaty, the Crow Chief Big Robber, appears at the center top margin.

Vignette from *A Map of the State of Kentucky, ...* Luke Munsell. 1818. G3950 1818 .M8 Vault, copy 2 (LCG&M-1427.1 CT). Geography and Map Division.

This allegorical vignette expresses the Euro-American view of the legitimacy of Indian removal and also depicts the role that surveying and cartography played in that removal process. The surveyors in the foreground with their tools and cadastral surveys have measured and divided the land for sale and settlement. Justice stands above, appearing to legitimize and sanction the legality of the proceedings. In the background the native inhabitants leave their homeland.

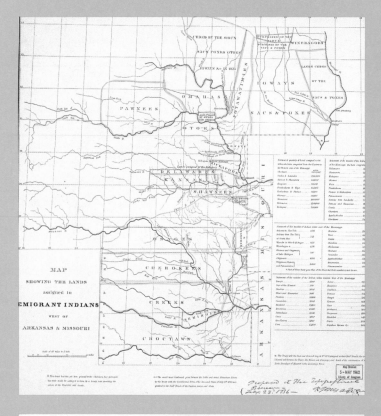

Map Showing the Lands assigned to Emigrant Indians west of Arkansas & Missouri. U.S. Topographical Bureau. 1836. United States—Indians—1836 (LCG&M-683 CT). Geography and Map Division.

Indian policy in the early nineteenth century favored the formation of an Indian Territory west of the Mississippi River which would alleviate the continuing clash of opposing cultures and open eastern Indian lands to white settlement. Indian Territory included both local tribes and those removed from east of the Mississippi. Beginning in the 1850s a series of land appropriations reduced this supposedly inviolate Indian reserve until the last Indian lands were incorporated into the State of Oklahoma.

LEFT: *Locations and Wanderings of the Aboriginal Tribes.* Emma Willard. From *A Series of Maps to Willard's History of the United States.* 1828. G1201.S1W52 1839 Vault (LCG&M-429 CT). Geography and Map Division.

Emma Willard, an early nineteenth century American publisher, author, and educator, published this early graphic depiction of the distribution and migrations of Indian tribes in the eastern United States. Rather than employing the Western tradition of delineating precise geopolitical boundaries separating the Indian nations, the map portrays a loose affiliation of independent groups.

RIGHT: *A Map of the Ancient Indian Towns on the Pickaway Plain Illustrating a Sketch of the Country.* Felix Renick. ca 1844. Ohio—Indians—1844? (LCG&M-4295 CT) Geography and Map Division.

Renick's map illustrates the Shawnee villages located on the Pickaway Plains of Ohio after the Shawnee had moved there in the mid-1700s. The map locates Indian mounds and the important sites of Lord Dunsmore's battles with the Shawnee Chief Cornstalk. It also illustrates the route of the escape of John Slover from the Shawnee at Cornstalks Town.

Tahlequah, Cherokee Nation, Ind. Terr. Sanborn-Perris Map Company. June 1896. Sanborn Fire Insurance Map Collection (LCG&M-4294 CT). Geography and Map Division.

Sanborn fire insurance maps provide detailed coverage of cities and towns in the United States. Illustrated here is sheet one of a four-map series of Tahlequah, the capital of the Cherokee Nation. It depicts specific Indian institutions, such as the Cherokee Female and Male Seminaries shown here, and the Cherokee National Penitentiary and Capitol shown on another sheet. This 1896 edition is one of nine editions issued between 1894 and 1949 that provide a unique graphic history of the development of Tahlequah.

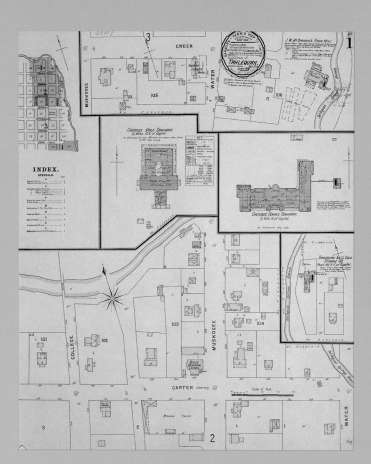

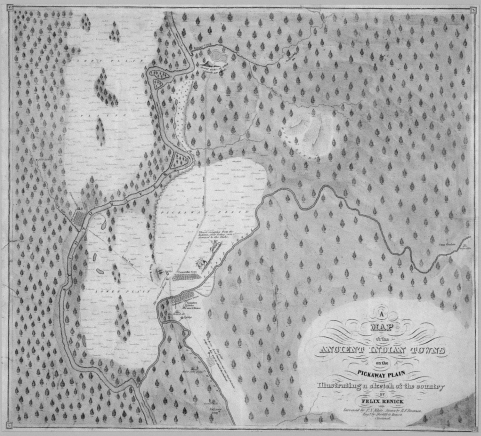

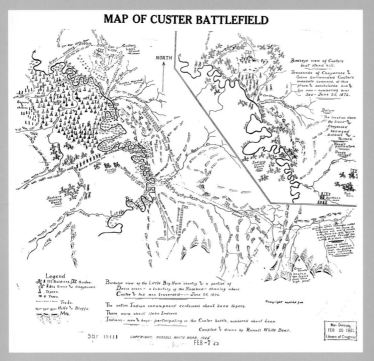

Map of Custer Battlefield. Birdseye view of the Little Big Horn country and a portion of Davis Creek—a tributary of the Rosebud—showing where Custer and his men traversed June 25, 1876. Russell White Bear. 1925. U.S.—Wars, Indian—Montana—1876 (LCG&M-4284). Geography and Map Division.

The Battle of the Little Big Horn was precipitated by the effort of the United States to gain control of the Black Hills and further subdue the Plains tribes. Drawn in 1925 by Russell White Bear of the Crow Agency, Montana, this view depicts the annihilation of a force of some three hundred cavalry troops under the command of Gen. George A. Custer by a combined force of Sioux, Cheyenne, and Arapahoe. Although a major defeat for the U.S. military, the loss served to rally the United States to advance its conquest of the Sioux and its allies.

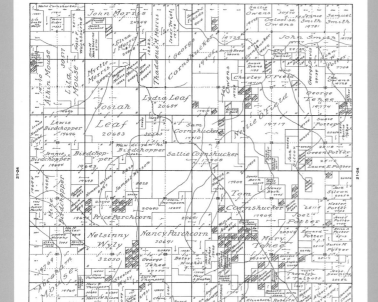

Cherokee Nation, Township 21 North, Range 24 East. From: [Township Maps of the Cherokee Nation] Indian Territory Map Company. [1909] G1305.I5 1909 (LCG&M-4296). Geography and Map Division.

Illustrated is one plate (one township) of a 237-plate atlas depicting the cadastral division and landowners of the lands of the former Cherokee Nation. Under a policy of assimilation and land allotment, federal legislation promoted the break-up of tribal lands and the allotment of 160-acre parcels to the heads of Indian families. Unassigned property could be purchased or leased to non-Indians. The Cherokee refused to participate in the allotment program, but in 1898 Congress dissolved their tribal government and extended the policy to them. The inclusion of numerous Indian names on this plate attest to the landownership by individual Cherokee Indians.

Classification Map of Creek and Seminole Nations. Rich-secker, Hackbush and Patton, Civil Engineers. [189–?] Oklahoma—Indians—189–? (LCG&M-4297 CT) Geography and Map Division.

The discovery and mapping of economic resources of Indian lands often promoted non-Indian encroachment on native lands. This map, prepared for the Bradley Real Estate Co., classifies the agricultural potential of the lands of the Creek and Seminole Nations, indentifying the prime lands that the allotment system would possibly make available for white settlement.

Kaibab Indian Reservation, Arizona, 1944. Department of the Interior, Office of Indian Affairs. Arizona—Indians—Kaibab Reservation—1944 (LCG&M-4285). Geography and Map Division.

Located in northern Arizona, between the Utah border and the Grand Canyon of the Colorado River, the 120,000-acre Kaibab Reservation is the homeland of the Southern Paiute. This 1944 map of the reservation locates roads, trails, pipelines, telephone lines, fences, corrals, springs, reservoirs, and streams. The map is similar in content to many other reservation maps produced by the Office of Indian Affairs.

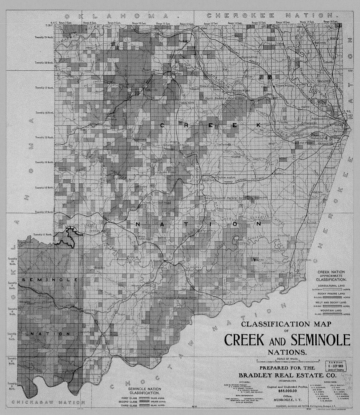

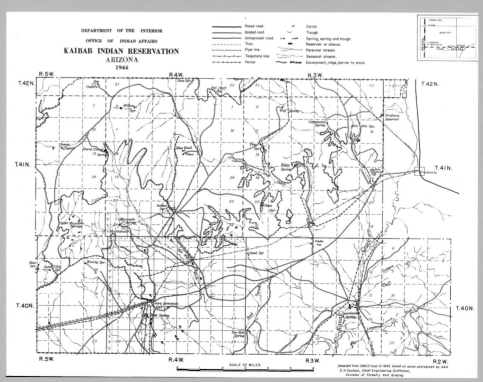

MOTION PICTURE, BROADCASTING AND RECORDED SOUND DIVISION

INTRODUCTION

The Motion Picture, Broadcasting and Recorded Sound Division (MBRS) of the Library of Congress houses more than 275,000 motion picture and video recordings in all formats and genres, including educational films, documentaries, newsreels, television programs, and feature films, making this the largest and most diverse repository of its kind in the United States. The division's extensive holdings of moving images provide a formidable historical record of the changing perceptions of Indian people in society on both the large and small screens.

Whether motion pictures reflect or shape popular attitudes is a question social critics continue to debate. But there is little doubt that for Americans in the eastern half of the country, who had little or no contact with Indian people after the mid-nineteenth century, movies—like the dime novels before them—shaped perceptions (or misperceptions) of America's native peoples.

The first motion pictures to feature Native Americans documented ceremonial dances of Sioux and Hopi tribes at the 1893 World's Columbian Exposition. Shown at vaudeville theaters on Thomas Alva Edison's kinetoscopic devices, these 90-second films provided entertainment to an audience eager to view "exotic" subjects. During the silent film era, Indians quickly became a mainstay in the classic western, a genre which grew enormously in popularity after the introduction of sound.

Stereotypical portrayals of American Indians and formulaic story patterns established during the early development of the movie industry persisted for several decades. In the descriptions of the fiction films that follow, one also sees the era's social strata, mores, prejudices, and even the sense of fair play reflected in the dramas. It is striking in the silent films, for example, to see how frequently the tensions of cross-ethnic love were played out on the screen. The usual images—good and bad—of Indian people appear, sometimes in the same film: the treacherous savage or the noble savage; the doomed victim of Euro-American society or the honorable avenger of that society's wrongdoers; the faithful companion or the faithless heathen. Even some of the early documentaries emphasized the stereotypes. Yet, more than occasionally, the screenwriter's or director's thrust appears intentionally to prick America's conscience about the real condition of its first peoples.

Strong and positive characterizations, as well as recognition of diverse and complex native cultures, however, were usually neglected until the 1970s. With the continuing pressure of the civil rights movement, the film industry began to address cultural sensitivity. Tribal consultants and Indian actors were hired; scripts attempted to reflect historical accuracy and a native viewpoint; and stereotypes were countered by more humane representations of Indian people. Documentary film makers, especially independents, became the most powerful force in transforming images of American Indians, both in commercial and public broadcast arenas.

Native-American-produced documentary films, television programs, and videos have flourished, as have supporting professional organizations, such as the Film and Video Center of the National Museum of the American Indian, the American Indian Film Institute, and the Native American Public Broadcasting Consortium. The National Film and Video Center maintains a comprehensive database of documentary films and videotapes about American Indians, many of which concern tribal cultures, history, art, and political and social issues presented from a Native American perspective. Most of these recent works are among the division's vast holdings which chronicle the history of the American Indian in film and video to the present.

USING THE COLLECTIONS

MOTION PICTURE AND TELEVISION READING ROOM

LOCATION: Madison Building, 3rd floor, Room LM 336; telephone (202) 707-8572

HOURS: Monday to Friday 8:30 A.M.–5:00 P.M.

Viewing facilities, available without charge, are provided for those doing research of a specific nature leading toward a publicly available work such as a dissertation, publication, or film-television production. All viewing is by advance appointment and viewing lists (arranged in alphabetical order) must be received at least three days in advance of appointments. Long lists require one week for preparation. Three consecutive weeks of viewing time may be reserved. Upon request, the division will send out copies of its viewing guidelines.

Films currently protected by copyright cannot be reproduced. Preservation status, special donor restrictions, and the uniqueness of the film material are other factors affecting availability for reproduction. To inquire about individual titles, contact the division's Public Services Office, which handles requests for duplication and provides information on costs and procedures. The majority of films and television programs within the division's collections are copyright deposits (that is, films deposited in the Copyright Office at the time of registration and housed within the film archive). Early copyright deposits consisted of photographs printed on strips of paper. The division holds viewing copies of three thousand of these paper print titles, dating from 1894 to 1915. Currently, more than ten thousand titles are added annually to the collection through copyright deposit. The division also acquires materials by purchase, gift, and exchange.

Access to much of the archival material within the division is *by title only.* Thus the patron will not often find subject headings such as "American Indian," specific tribal names, or genres such as "Indian dance" in the card and computer catalogs. The division does, however, maintain a small vertical subject file for "Indians of North America" that includes catalogs of American and Canadian films, flyers, lists, reviews, and so on.

Major Reference Works

Also useful for determining relevant educational and documentary titles are basic reference works such as the *Educational Film & Video Locator* and the *Video Source Book*, as well as the audiovisual records found on MUMS; note, however, that an earlier method used in coding such titles on the Library's computer may result in an erroneous "Not in LC Collection" message. The reference staff can help the researcher assess the information.

For information on television program titles, see *Three Decades of Television: A Catalog of Television Programs Acquired by the Library of Congress 1949–1979* by Sarah Rouse and Katharine Loughney (Washington, D.C.: Library of Congress, 1989; PN1992.9.L53 1989). Broad content descriptors help lead the researcher to programs listed by title. For more recent acquisitions, see the title card catalog and MUMS.

The reading room also contains reference books on its shelves and in its subject file with specific relevance for Indian-related searches; a few titles are:

The American Indian in Film. Michael Hilger. Metuchen, N.J., and London: Scarecrow Press Inc., 1986; PN1995.9.I48H54 1986

Descriptions and synopses of a broad range of fictional films from the silent era to the 1980s.

Images of American Indians on Film: An Annotated Bibliography. Gretchen Bataille and Charles Silet. New York and London: Garland Publishing Co., 1985; Z5784.M9B388 1985

"Meanwhile Back on the Reservation: 'Good' and 'Bad' Indians in Television Westerns" in *Riding the Video Range: The Rise and Fall of the Western on Television.* Gary A. Yoggy. Jefferson, N.C.: McFarland & Company, Inc., 1995; PN1992.8.W4 Y64 1995

Native Americans on Film and Video. Vols. 1 and 2, plus supplement. Elizabeth Weatherford and Emelia Seubert. New York: Museum of the American Indian/Heye Foundation, 1981, 1988, and 1993; PN1995.9.I48N37 1981

Lists approximately 800 films by title with production information and short synopses.

There are also guides to educational films and videos about Indians in the subject file and clippings for individual titles in the review files.

Once titles have been identified, the next step is to find out whether MBRS has the films themselves or only other documentation. The division stopped entering new acquisitions in the reading room card catalogs in 1986; thus the cards should be consulted primarily for older materials. For additional and more recent information, patrons use computer searches, using the command "find t [title of film or program]; f=av". Some titles in which a patron is interested may be listed in a separate nitrate film database. Check with the reference staff if there are questions concerning specific Indian-related titles.

The division also holds a limited selection of movie stills, while film posters are held by the Prints and Photographs Division.

❏ SELECTED FILMS, TELEVISION, AND DOCUMENTARY VIDEOS

The following lists of film, documentaries, and videos are only representative selections of visual media on Indian themes in the division's collections. They are extracted from two guides available in the Reading Room: *American Indians on Film and Video: Documentaries in the Library of Congress* by Jennifer Brathovde and *American Indians in Silent Film: Motion Pictures in the Library of Congress* by Karen Lund. Each lists selected films and videos from the division's holdings. For this guide, theatrical films from the 1930s to the 1990s and television programs have been added. Titles are in black and white unless otherwise stated.

Silent Films: Non-Fiction

The American Indian: Government Education. Harmon Foundation (FAA 5999). Harmon Foundation, [1933]; 1 reel, 15 min., 16mm ref. print.

Surveys provisions made by the government for citizenship training of American Indians.

The American Indian: How he earns a living. Harmon Foundation (FAA 6010). Harmon Foundation, [1933]; 1 reel, 15 min., 16mm ref. print.

Discusses the Indians' adaptation of ancient crafts to modern farming, fishing, cattle ranching, carving, and jewelry-making; and points out that Indian peoples are also working in the learned professions.

Buffalo Bill's Wild West and Pawnee Bill's Far East. Ernst Collection (FLA 1402). Buffalo Bill and Pawnee Bill Film Co., 1910; 1 reel (inc.), 436 ft., 16mm ref. print.

In this wild west show, Indians and cowboys are shown parading by on horses, and wild horse riding and trick riding are exhibited among other acts. This copy is missing reels 2 and 3.

Carrying out the Snakes. Paper Print Collection (FLA 4120). Edison, 1901; Cameraman: James H. White (?); 1 reel, 31 ft., 16mm ref. print.

Hopi Indians of Walpi village perform a tribal ceremony in which they carry snakes. One of a series of five short films. [See also: *Line-up and Teasing the Snakes, The March of Prayer and Entrance of the Dancers, Panoramic View of Moki-land,* and *Parade of Snake Dancers Before the Dance.*]

A Century of Progress Exposition: Indian Village. Herford T. Cowling Film Collection (FLA 236). Burton Holmes Films, 1933; 1 reel, 114 ft., 16mm ref. print.

Shows scenes of Navajo from New Mexico, Hopi from Arizona, Sioux from North Dakota, and Winnebago from Wisconsin at Chicago's Century of Progress International Exposition in replicas of their native surroundings, dressed in traditional costumes, performing dances unique to their tribes, and working with tribal crafts.

Esquimaux Game of Snap-the-Whip. Paper Print Collection (FLA 3759). Edison, 1901; Cameramen: Edwin S. Porter, Arthur White; 1 reel, 17 ft., 16mm ref. print.

In front of a large tent of animal skins, two spectators watch two participants perform a game of skill. Each participant holds a long whip with which he attempts to snare his opponent's whip. Filmed at the Pan-American Exposition in Buffalo, N.Y.

Ford Educational Weekly, No. 232: The Wards of a Nation. AFI/Nichol Collection (FEB 3995). Ford

GATEWAYS

Native American economies ranged from hunting-and-gathering societies to agricultural and urbanized ones, and by the time of European contact included whale and sea-mammal hunting in the Arctic; caribou and moose hunting across the forests of Alaska and northern Canada; intensive fishing by many groups along the coasts of Alaska, the Pacific Northwest, southern California, and Florida; buffalo and large-game hunting on the Great Plains and in the Rocky Mountains; intensive gathering in California and the Great Basin, supplemented by small-game hunting; and farming of maize (corn), beans, squash, and other plants in the eastern United States and the Southwest.

Native American economies chiefly utilized stone, wood, plant fibers, bone, shells, animal skin and fur, and pottery, although metals were used in parts of North America. (Indians near Lake Superior cold-hammered native copper, starting as early as 3000–2500 B.C.; the copper tools and ornaments they made were traded far and wide across the United States. Eastern Inuit in the far north also cold-hammered meteoric iron.) Trade in other materials had begun to increase during the Archaic period (6000–700 B.C.). The earliest pottery currently known in North America dates to 2500 B.C., but pottery only became widespread with the intensification of agriculture after about 700 B.C.

Maize, squash, and beans were domesticated in Mesoamerica before 5000 B.C. Maize first ar-rived in the Southwest some time between 1500 and 1000 B.C. In eastern North America, meanwhile, gourds (perhaps from Mesoamerica) were cultivated before 2000 B.C., and local plants such as sumpweed, goosefoot, and sunflowers began to be domesticated around 2000–1500 B.C. Another Mesoamerican import, squash, was being cultivated in Kentucky by 1000 B.C. The elaborate North American mound-building traditions called Adena and Hopewell (700 B.C.–400 A.D.) were based on an intensified pre-maize agriculture using local domesticates and squash. Maize cultivation arrived in the Southeast soon after 200 A.D., but it was not until new, cold-adapted forms of maize appeared, after about 700 A.D., that the plant became the major eastern North American crop. A new tradition called the Mississippian, boasting towns, early urban centers, and renewed mound-building, was based largely on these new maize strains. Cities arose, such as Cahokia, the largest prehistoric city north of Mexico, which flourished between 1050 and 1250 A.D. and was the center of a transcontinental trading network.

WHERE TO LOOK: Readers interested in pre-contact Indian economies and technology should explore the General Collections and Rare Book and Special Collections, Manuscript, Prints and Photographs, Motion Picture, Broadcasting, and Geography and Map Divisions.

In Indian languages, there is not always a generic

"Mode of tilling and planting," from *La Floride française, scènes de la vie indienne, peintes en 1564* by Theodor de Bry and Charles de la Roncière (Paris: Les editions nationales, 1928). F314.L33 (LC-USZC4-4821, color; LC-USZ62-31869, black and white). Rare Book and Special Collections Division.

Timucua Indians of northeast Florida are shown planting beans or maize in a print made from a watercolor by Jacques Le Moyne de Morgues (ca. 1533–88). Le Moyne observed the Timucua during an abortive French Huguenot settlement in 1564–65. While his illustrations of the Timucua are considered less reliable ethnographically than his explanatory descriptions, they are the only pictures of the tribe to have survived.

Motion Picture Laboratories, 1920; 1 reel, 675 ft., 35mm ref. print.

Newsreel footage of American Indian delegates from more than one hundred churches attending fiftieth annual Christian conference, site unknown. Includes scenes of Indians attending church, tent life, and a confirmation service.

Hopi Indians Dance for TR at [Walpi, Ariz.] 1913. The Theodore Roosevelt Association Film Collection (FAB 1134). Producer unknown, Aug. 1913; 1 reel, 103 ft., 16mm ref. print.

On Aug. 20, 1913, Theodore Roosevelt, numerous visitors, and Hopi Indians observed the performance of the ritual Hopi snake dance on the Hopi Reservation at Walpi, Arizona.

[Ickes, Harold L. Home Movies: Indian Family and Community Life]. Ickes Collection (VBK 2101). [193–?]; 1 videocassette, ca. 13 min., 3/4″ viewing copy.

Contents include Indians rolling dough; baking bread; cooking; shearing sheep; washing, carding, spinning and weaving wool; working metal; views of pueblos; Indian ruins; Indian children playing; and people posing for the camera.

In the Land of the War Canoes: Kwakiutl Indian Life on the Northwest Coast. Copyright Collection (FDA 2741). Burke Museum, University of Washington, 1973; 1 reel, 44 min., 16mm ref. print.

Bill Holm and George I. Quimby's re-edited version of the Edward S. Curtis 1914 film originally entitled *In the Land of the Headhunters*, a saga of romantic love among the Kwakiutl Indians on Vancouver Island. The added soundtrack includes authentic tribal singing, chants, spoken parts, and instrumental music.

Nanook of the North. The Copyright Collection (FCA 9828–29). U. S. Pathe, 1922; Direction, scenario, photography, and editing: Robert Flaherty; 2 reels, 64 min., sd., 16mm ref. print.

Flaherty seeks to show man's struggle to live against the forces of nature by portraying scenes from the life of Nanook and his family, Eskimos in the Hudson Bay area. Restored version by David H. Shepard, with music by Stanley Silverman.

Serving Rations to the Indians, No. 1. Paper Print Collection (FLA 4383). Edison, 1898; 1 reel, 27 ft., 16mm ref. print.

Indians come out of a door of a log cabin carrying flour or grain sacks in their arms. The location is possibly New Mexico or Colorado.

Sham Battle at the Pan-American Exposition. Paper Print Collection (FLA 5203). Edison, 1901; 1 reel, 128 ft., 16mm ref. print.

Some American Indians on horseback wearing feathers, warpaint, and carrying frontier rifles ride across a field. Men dressed as U.S. Army troops in battle regalia are lined up in the position of skirmishers. They fire at the Indians, who gallop by and then circle them. The location is Buffalo, N.Y.

A Vanishing Race. The George Kleine Collection (FLA 1897). Edison, 1917; 1 reel, 168 ft., 16mm ref. print.

Scenes of daily life of the Blackfeet Indians on a reservation in northwestern Montana. Shows maps which indicate the empire of the Blackfeet in the early part of the nineteenth century, and shows the Indians demonstrating sign language, taking down a tipi when they break camp, and fording a river.

The Zuni Kicking Race. Ickes Collection (VBJ 9309). Outing-Chester Pictures, 1918; Producer: C. L. Chester; 1 videocassette, ca. 11 min., 3/4″ viewing copy.

The Zuni are shown making pottery and participating in the kicking race, an Indian sport where players kick a stick for twenty-five miles with their bare feet across the desert.

Silent Films: Fiction

The Aborigine's Devotion. AFI/Post Collection (FEA 9790). World Film Mfg. Co., 1909; 1 reel, 429 ft., 35mm ref. print

A trapper leaves his small child in his Indian friend's care. A trader attacks the child, but the Indian tracks him down and kills him.

The Call of the Wild. Paper Print Collection (FLA 5273). American Mutoscope & Biograph, 1908; Director: D. W. Griffith; Camera: Arthur Marvin, G. W. Bitzer; Cast: Florence Lawrence, Charles Inslee, Mack Sennett; 1 reel, 376 ft., 16mm ref. print.

An Indian proposes to a white woman. She declines, and the Indian angrily returns to his tribe. Later, the heroine is captured by Indians while in the woods, but is saved by the intervention of her rejected suitor. She returns home, while the Indian rides off sadly.

The Chief's Daughter. MOMA Collection (FAB 2670). Biograph, 1911; Director: D. W. Griffith; Camera: Billy Bitzer; Cast: Frank Grandon, Stephanie Longfellow, Jack Dillon; 1 reel, 408 ft., 16mm ref. print.

A prospector wins the love of the Indian chief's daughter and cruelly casts her aside when his Eastern fiancee arrives unexpectedly. The Indian girl has the opportunity to show his unfaithfulness, and he loses both his fiancee and the Indian girl.

Comata, the Sioux. Paper Print Collection (FLA 5228). Biograph, 1909; Director: D. W. Griffith; Camera: G. W. Bitzer; Cast: James Kirkwood, Marion Leonard, Arthur Johnson, Florence Lawrence, Linda Arvidson, Verner Clarges; 1 reel, 360 ft., 16mm ref. print.

An Indian maiden leaves her village to live with a white man, and they have a child. After the man abandons her for a white woman, she goes off toward the Black Hills with an Indian man who has loved and guarded her from the beginning.

The Girl and the Outlaw. Paper Print Collection (FLA 5407). American Mutoscope & Biograph, 1908; Director: D. W. Griffith; Camera: Arthur Marvin; Cast: Florence Lawrence, Charles Inslee; 1 reel, 316 ft., 16mm ref. print.

The chief of a band of renegade Indians leaves his girlfriend beside the road after severely beating her. She is found and revived by the daughter of a local settler. The two start out for the settlement, but they are captured by the outlaw band. The Indian girl dies after helping her rescuer to escape.

Her Indian Mother. AFI/New Zealand Film Archive Collection (FEB 8630). Kalem, 1910; Cast: Alice Joyce, Jane Wolfe; 1 reel, 995 ft., 35mm ref. print.

A man in the Hudson Bay country takes an Indian wife, and they have a daughter, but he leaves them to return to Montreal. When he sees his daughter years later on an inspection trip, he decides to take her back to Montreal to educate her. Missing her tribe, she returns to her village, and her heartbroken father finds her in the tipi of a young brave whose wife she has become.

Hiawatha. AFI/Ohio Historical Society Collection (FBC 5871). Fort Defiance Film Co., Gaumont, 1913; Producer: Frank E. Moore; Camera: Victor Milner; Based on the poem "The Song of Hiawatha" by Henry Wadsworth Longfellow; Cast: Soon-goot; 1 reel, 16mm ref. print.

Years after Gitche Manito proclaims that a prophet will come to unite the Indian warriors, Hiawatha is born and is later declared to be the long-awaited prophet. Hiawatha marries and lives happily until famine strikes the village. When white men arrive, Hiawatha greets the

Black Robe and proclaims that the real prophet has finally arrived.

His Last Game. AFI / Miller Collection (FAB 0434). Imp, 1909; 1 reel (incomplete?), 354 ft., 16mm ref. print.

Two gamblers attempt to fix a baseball game by bribing the Indian pitcher. When he refuses, they try to poison him, and he kills one of the gamblers. The Indian is about to be shot for his crime when the sheriff grants him a respite to pitch in the game, which he wins. The Indian is shot the moment before a reprieve for him reaches the sheriff.

Just Squaw. Public Archives of Canada / Dawson City Collection (FEB 8387–90). Superior Pictures, 1919; Director / Producer: George E. Middleton; Writer: Earle Snell; Cast: Beatriz Michelena, William Pike, Andrew Robson, Albert Morrison, D. Mitsoras, Jeff Williams, Katherine Angus; 4 reels (inc.; reels 1–3 and 5 of 5 only), 2,127 ft., 35mm ref. print.

A mixed blood woman named Fawn falls in love with a white stranger. Her brother, a fugitive known as the Phantom, saves Fawn from the man who stole her from her white father. Her father later kills the kidnapper who confesses that Fawn is white, thus making it possible for Fawn and the stranger to marry.

Kentuckian. Paper Print Collection (FLA 5513). American Mutoscope & Biograph, 1908; Director: Wallace McCutcheon; Scenario: Stanner E. V. Taylor from the play by Augustus Thomas; Camera: G. W. Bitzer, Arthur Marvin; Cast: Eddie Dillon, Robert Vignola, John Adolfi, Florence Auer, Wallace McCutcheon, Jr., D. W. Griffith; 1 reel, 311 ft., 16mm ref. print.

An Indian woman saves the life of a card player robbed by Indians and left for dead. They marry and have a child. As he is struggling to de-

cide whether to return East for his inheritance, his Indian wife commits suicide.

Leather Stocking. Paper Print Collection (FLA 5524). Biograph, 1909; Director: D. W. Griffith; Camera: G. W. Bitzer, Arthur Marvin; Cast: James Kirkwood, Linda Arvidson, Mack Sennett, Billy Quirk, George Nicholls, Owen Moore, Henry B. Walthall; 1 reel, 372 ft., 16mm ref. print.

Based on James Fenimore Cooper's story, the movie begins as a party of settlers led by a friendly Indian and escorted by a British soldier set out out on a journey. En route they are stalked and attacked by Indians. At the crucial moment, soldiers from the fort arrive and beat off the unfriendly Indian tribe.

The Little Indian Weaver. AFI / Casselton-Larson Collection (FEB 8579). Madeline Brandeis Productions, Pathe, 1929; 1 reel, 1,015 ft., 35mm ref. print.

Based on the book of the same title by Madeline Brandeis, the movie tells the story of a Navajo girl who wants the doll of a white child, so she weaves a blanket to exchange for one at the trading post. The trader refuses to take the blanket, but the trader's son buys the girl a doll with his savings. Because of this act of kindness, the Navajo accept the white boy as their friend.

The Mended Lute. Paper Print Collection (FLA 5568). Biograph, 1909; Director: D. W. Griffith; Camera: G. W. Bitzer; Cast: James Kirkwood, Florence Lawrence, Owen Moore, Mack Sennett, Arthur Johnson, James Young Deer, Princess Red Wing; 1 reel, 375 ft., 16mm ref. print.

Little Bear and Standing Rock are vying for the Sioux chief's daughter, and the chief gives her to the highest bidder, Standing Rock, the man she does not love. After she leaves her new husband for Little Bear whom she loves, the two are captured by Standing Rock and his tribe and are about to be burned at the stake when, impressed by his rival's bravery, he sets them both free.

A Midnight Phantasy. Paper Print Collection (FLA 3256). American Mutoscope & Biograph, 1903; Camera: F. S. Armitage; 1 reel, 15 ft., 16mm ref. print.

A cigar-store Indian is standing in front of a picket fence and next to it is a poster of a ballerina. A man appears, steals the cigar from the Indian and escorts away the ballerina who steps out of the poster. The Indian scalps him and hands the scalp to the astonished ballerina.

A Mohawk's Way. Paper Print Collection (FLA 5584). Biograph, 1910; Director: D. W. Griffith; Camera: G. W. Bitzer; Cast: Dorothy Davenport, George Nicholls, Alfred Paget, Mack Sennett, Claire McDowell, W. J. Butler; 1 reel, 398 ft., 16mm ref. print.

A white doctor refuses to treat a sick Indian child, so his wife ministers in his stead. Later, the Indians take to the warpath and kill the settlers except for the wife, who is spared because of her earlier kindness to the ailing Indian child.

The Paleface. Copyright Collection (FBA 3635). Comique Film Co., First National, 1921; Director/Writer: Buster Keaton, Eddie Cline; Cast: Buster Keaton, Joe Roberts; 1 reel, 800 ft., 16mm ref. print.

Indians capture Buster Keaton, and his asbestos clothing saves him from burning. They think he is a god and take him into the tribe under the name of Little Chief Paleface. Then he saves the tribe from being cheated by crooked oilmen.

Ramona. Paper Print Collection (FLA 5651). Biograph, 1910; Director: D. W. Griffith; Camera: G.

W. Bitzer; Cast: Mary Pickford, Henry B. Walthall, Frank Grandon, Kate Bruce; 1 reel, 432 ft., 16mm ref. print.

The movie is based on the story by Helen Hunt Jackson of an orphan from a great Spanish household who falls in love with an Indian, Alessandro, but her foster mother tries to thwart the romance. Upon hearing that she has Indian blood, Ramona renounces the white world to be with Alessandro, but they are driven away from Alessandro's home by white men until he finally dies.

The Redman and the Child. Paper Print Collection (FLA 5657). American Mutoscope & Biograph, 1908; Director: D. W. Griffith; Camera: Arthur Marvin; Cast: Charles Inslee, John Tansy, Harry Salter, Linda Arvidson; 1 reel, 328 ft., 16mm ref. print.

Outlaws kill an old miner and kidnap his grandchild while their Indian friend is away. Upon his return, the Indian rescues the child and avenges the death of his old friend by killing the outlaws.

Redskin. AFI/Paramount Collection (FCA 6983–84). Paramount, 1929; Director: Victor Schertzinger; Story & Screenplay: Elizabeth Pickett; Photography: Edward Cronjager; Color Photography: Ray Rennahan and Edward Estabrook; Musical Score: J. S. Zamecnik; Cast: Richard Dix, Gladys Belmont, Tully Marshall, George Rigas, Noble Johnson, Jane Novak, Larry Steers, Augustina Lopez; 2 reels, 2,927 ft., 16mm color, ref. print.

The son of a Navajo chief returns from college and finds it difficult to assimilate into his tribe. When his father dies, he refuses to take his place and is exiled. He goes to a fellow student he loves, Corn Blossom, a member of an enemy tribe, the Pueblos, but is discovered in her camp and escapes into the desert where he discovers oil. He returns to his people, informing them they are rich now and marries Corn Blossom, who had been hiding from her people in his village.

The Silent Enemy. AFI/Paramount Collection (FEA 8085–92). Paramount, 1930; Director: H. P. Carver; Cast: Chief Yellow Robe, Chief Long Lance, Chief Akawanush, Spotted Elk, Cheeka; 8 reels, 7,548 ft., 35mm ref. print.

With winter approaching and food scarce for the Ojibwa tribe, Baluk attempts to lead the tribe in search of food, but is opposed by his rival, Dagwan, who tries to have him killed.

Strongheart. Paper Print Collection (FLA 5902). Klaw & Erlanger, 1914; Supervisor: D. W. Griffith; Director: James Kirkwood; Cast: Henry B. Walthall, Lionel Barrymore, Alan Hale, Antonio Moreno, Blanche Sweet, Gertrude Robinson; 1 reel, 1,144 ft., 16mm ref. print.

Based on the play by William C. DeMille, the movie tells the story of Strongheart who leaves his tribe, goes to college in the East, becomes a football star, gets in trouble for lying to help a white friend who has cheated, and falls in love with a white woman. When he finds out that his tribe needs him because of the death of his father, he respects his duty and, leaving his sweetheart behind, sadly returns to his people.

The Vanishing American. AFI/Paramount Film Collection (FGC 1728–32). Paramount, 1925; Director: George B. Seitz; Screenplay: Ethel Doherty; Adaptation: Lucien Hubbard; Photographers: Edgar Schoenbaum, Harry Perry; Cast: Richard Dix, Lois Wilson, Noah Beery, Malcolm MacGregor; 10 reels, 9,816 ft., 110 min., 35mm ref. print.

Based on the serial story by Zane Grey, the injustices suffered by reservation Indians are dramatized in the story of Nophaie who falls in love with a white school teacher on the reservation. He and other Indians return from World War I to find their lands taken and their people starving.

Sound Feature Films

Across the Wide Missouri. Copyright Collection (FGA 66–73). Metro-Goldwyn-Mayer, 1951; Director: William A. Wellman; Producer: Robert Sisk; Screenplay: Talbot Jennings; Story: Talbot Jennings, Frank Cavett; Music: David Raksin; Film editor: John Dunning; Cast: Clark Gable, Ricardo Montalban, John Hodiak, Adolph Menjou, J. Carrol Naish, Maria Elena Marques; 8 reels, 7,020 ft., color, 35mm ref. print.

A beaver trapper marries a Blackfeet girl in the hope that their union will give him and his fellow hunters ready access to unexplored Indian country.

Apache. Copyright Collection (FGA 435–444). Linden Productions, 1954; released by United Artists; Director: Robert Aldrich; Producer: Harold Hecht; Screenplay: James R. Webb; Music: David Raksin; Editorial supervisor: Alan Crosland, Jr.; Based on the novel *Broncho Apache* by Paul I. Wellman; Cast: Burt Lancaster, Jean Peters, John McIntire, Charles Buchinsky, John Dehner; 10 reels, 8,190 ft., color, 35mm ref. print.

Embittered by the surrender of Geronimo, by threats of imprisonment, and by betrayal by fellow tribesmen, the fierce Apache warrior Massai wages a one-man war against the U.S. Army.

Billy Jack. Copyright Collection (FGC 8046–8051). National Student Film Corporation, 1972 (originally released by Warner Bros., 1971); Director: T. C. Frank; Producer: Mary Rose Solti; Screenplay: T. C. Frank, Terean Christin; Camera: Fred Koenekamp, John Stephens; Cast: Tom Laughlin, Delores Taylor, Clark Howat, Bert

Freed, Julie Webb; 12 reels on 6, 9,900 ft., color, 35mm ref. print.

A mixed blood Vietnam veteran resorts to violence to protect a freedom school for runaway teenagers on an Indian reservation when it is threatened by local townspeople.

Broken Arrow. Copyright Collection (FGA 1545–1553). Twentieth Century-Fox, 1950; Director: Delmer Daves; Producer: Julian Blaustein; Screenplay: Michael Blankfort; Music director: Alfred Newman; Music author: Hugo Friedhofer; Film editor: J. Watson Webb; Based on the novel *Blood Brother* by Elliott Arnold; Cast: James Stewart, Jeff Chandler, Debra Paget, Basil Ruysdael, Will Geer; 9 reels, 8,370 ft., color, 35mm ref. print.

In a courageous effort to make peace between the white man and the Indian, a former army officer turned prospector goes into the Apache stronghold. He negotiates a peace with Cochise, the Apache leader, and marries an Indian woman, who is killed later when renegade whites attack the tribe.

Broken Lance. Copyright Collection (FGA 1554–1564). Twentieth Century-Fox, 1954; Director: Edward Dymtryk; Producer: Sol C. Siegel; Story: Philip Yordan; Screenplay: Richard Murphy; Music: Leigh Harline; Music conductor: Lionel Newman; Film editor: Dorothy Spencer; Cast: Spencer Tracy, Robert Wagner, Jean Peters, Richard Widmark, Katy Jurado; 11 reels, 8,700 ft., color, 35mm ref. print.

An imperious cattle baron's empire is threatened by his three weakling sons who resent their father's domination, his defiance of the law and society, his marriage to an Indian princess after their mother's death, and his favoritism to their mixed blood brother.

Cheyenne Autumn. Copyright Collection (FGB 9357–9366). Ford-Smith Productions, 1964; re-leased by Warner Bros.; Director: John Ford; Producer: Bernard Smith; Screenplay: James R. Webb; Music: Alex North; Director of photography: William Clothier; Film editor: Otho Lovering; Cast: Richard Widmark, Carroll Baker, Karl Malden, Sal Mineo, Dolores Del Rio; 10 reels, 13,300 ft., color, 35mm ref. print.

A small, heroic band of Cheyenne escape from a wretched Oklahoma reservation in 1878 and fight their way back to their homeland in the Yellowstone River country fifteen hundred miles away.

Chief Crazy Horse. Copyright Collection (FGA 2034–2043). Universal, 1955; Director: George Sherman; Producer: William Alland; Story: Gerald Drayson Adams; Music: Frank Skinner; Music supervisor: Joseph Gershenson; Film editor: Al Clark; Cast: Victor Mature, Suzan Ball, John Lund, Ray Danton, Keith Larson; 10 reels, 7,800 ft., color, 35mm ref. print.

Crazy Horse believes that he is the warrior who will defeat the whites, as promised by a Sioux prophecy. After uniting the Dakota tribes and leading them in their struggle to defend their territory against invading white men, Chief Crazy Horse is killed by a jealous tribesman while visiting an Army fort on a peaceful mission.

Dances with Wolves. Copyright Collection (CGB 7454–7463). Tig Productions, 1990; released by Orion Pictures; Director: Kevin Costner; Producers: Jim Wilson and Kevin Costner; Screenplay: Michael Blake; Based on the novel by Michael Blake; Cast: Kevin Costner, Mary McDonnell, Graham Greene; 19 reels on 10, ca. 17,420 ft., color, 35mm ref. print.

An army lieutenant is stationed at a deserted outpost where he becomes friendly with the local Sioux. He joins them in fighting their enemies and marries a white woman who has become part of their tribe. When captured by soldiers, he

GATEWAYS

By the mid-1920s it was widely held that the allotment policy had not succeeded and that conditions on Indian reservations were deplorable. Many of the criticisms of federal Indian policy were summarized in the 1928 Meriam report, *The Problem of Indian Administration*. The debate over federal Indian policy shifted to the idea of maintaining tribal cultures and encouraging tribal self-government and reservation development. Support for these ideas led to a major change in policy, called the reform era or the "Indian New Deal." Many of the reforms were carried through during John Collier's term as commissioner of Indian affairs (1933–1945). Congress enacted a number of new laws, including (1) the Indian Reorganization Act (Wheeler-Howard Act) of 1934, which ended allotment, authorized tribes to create their own business councils and governments, and promoted reservation land acquisition and economic development; (2) the Johnson-O'Malley Act of 1934, which authorized the contracting of BIA programs by States and, later, by other entities, including tribes; and (3) the Indian Arts and Crafts Board Act of 1935, which promoted nationwide marketing of Indian crafts. The reform policy also led, indirectly, to the beginning of modern national Indian political activism.

While the Indian New Deal era ended allotment, it did not end the debate over assimilation.

Proponents of assimilation inside and outside Congress attacked the reform policy and, after World War II, succeeded in moving federal Indian policy back toward assimilation. This began the termination era of Indian policy, whose eventual goal was to terminate the trust relationship between the federal government and every Indian tribe, in order to free tribes and individual Indians from federal control. Termination found its general expression in a 1953 congressional resolution and its specific expression both in Public Law 83-280, which granted to five states criminal and most civil jurisdiction over most reservations within their borders, and in statutes terminating the federal relationship with about 120 tribes or bands, such as the Menominee and the Klamath. The opposition of Indian political organizations, and the unhappy experience of the terminated tribes, led Congress to cease terminating tribes in 1962. By the end of 1994, Congress had restored federal recognition to almost all terminated tribes.

WHERE TO LOOK: Library collections with materials on federal Indian policies include the General Collections, the Microform Reading Room, the Law Library, and the Manuscript, Geography and Map, and Prints and Photographs, and Motion Picture, Broadcasting Divisions.

Representatives of the Confederated Salish and Kootenai Tribes of the Flathead Reservation, Montana, receiving their just-approved constitution and bylaws from Secretary of the Interior Harold L. Ickes, October 28, 1935. LOT 12363-1-C. (LC-USZ62-115958). Prints and Photographs Division.

The Salish and Kootenai constitution was the first approved under the Indian Reorganization Act, which was the brainchild of Commissioner of Indian Affairs John Collier but had the whole-hearted support of Secretary Ickes.

is rescued by the Sioux. Knowing that the army will pursue him, he leaves the tribe with his wife to protect the Sioux.

Drums Along the Mohawk. AFI / Anonymous 6 (FCA 9509–9512). Darryl F. Zanuck production, 1939; presented by Twentieth Century-Fox; Director: John Ford; Associate Producer: Raymond Griffith; Scenario: Lamar Trotti, Sonya Levien; Photography: Bert Glennon, Ray Rennahan; Music: Alfred Newman; Art director: Richard Day; Based on the novel by Walter D. Edmonds; Cast: Claudette Colbert, Henry Fonda, Edna May Oliver, Eddie Collins, John Carradine, Doris Bowdon, Jessie Ralph, Arthur Shields; 4 reels, 3,727 ft., color, 16mm ref. print.

A young couple moves to the Mohawk Valley at the start of the Revolutionary War where they are subject to Indian attacks by the Iroquois. They have a loyal Indian friend, Blue Back, who is a Christian.

The Exiles. LC Purchase (FCA 9398–9399). A Mackenzie Production, 1961; distributed by Pathe Contemporary Films; Director, producer, writer: Kent Mackenzie; Producers: Ronald Austin, Sam Farnsworth, John Morrill, Erik Daarstad, Robert Kaufman, Beth Patrick, Sven Walnum, Paula Powers; Photography: Erik Daarstad, Robert Kaufman, John Merrill; Archive photographs: Edward Curtis; Cast: Yvonne Williams, Homer Nish, Tommy Reynolds, Rico Rodriguez, Clifford Ray Sam; 2 reels, 2,604 ft., 16mm ref. print.

Three young Indians leave the reservation and go to Los Angeles where they eventually discover that they are caught between cultures and do not belong in city life. They go to a hilltop near the freeway where they beat drums and sing and dance in the traditional ways.

Flap. Copyright Collection (FGD 495–500). Warner Bros., a Kinney National Company, 1970;

Director: Carol Reed; Screenplay: Clair Huffaker; Based on the novel *Nobody Loves a Drunken Indian* by Clair Huffaker; Cast: Anthony Quinn, Shelley Winters, Claude Akins, Victor Jory; 12 reels on 6, 9,450 ft., color, 35mm ref. print.

An Indian war hero tries to claim the city of Phoenix for his tribe.

Fort Apache. AFI / RKO Collection (FEA 8289–8301). Argosy Pictures, 1948; released by RKO Radio Pictures; Director: John Ford; Presenters: John Ford and Merian C. Cooper; Cinematographer: Archie Stout; Screenplay: Frank S. Nugent from the story "Massacre" by James Warner Bellah; Cast: John Wayne, Henry Fonda, Shirley Temple; 13 reels, 11,492 ft., 35mm ref. print.

A Civil War general is demoted to lieutenant colonel and is sent west to fight Indians. In his search for glory he follows Cochise into Mexico with his men and sends his captain, whom Cochise trusts, to arrange a meeting. The colonel double-crosses his captain and Cochise and sends troops to force Cochise's people to return to their appointed lands. The Indians slaughter the colonel's troops, with the exception of the captain's small squad.

Geronimo, an American Legend. Copyright Collection (CGB 9897–9903). A Walter Hill / Neil Canton production, 1993; released by Columbia Pictures; Director: Walter Hill; Producers: Walter Hill and Neil Canton; Screenplay: John Milius and Larry Gross; Cast: Wes Studi, Jason Patric, Gene Hackman, Robert Duvall; 14 reels on 7, ca. 10,350 ft., color, 35mm ref. print.

Geronimo is taken into custody by the U.S. Army, but he and some followers escape and go on a rampage through the settlements. An army lieutenant, Gatewood, is ordered to capture Geronimo.

The Great Sioux Massacre. Copyright Collection (FGB 9182–9187). F. & F. Productions, 1965; released by Columbia Pictures; Director: Sidney Salkow; Producer: Leon Fromkess; Story: Sidney Salkow, Marvin Gluck; Screenplay: Fred C. Dobbs; Music: Emil Newman, Edward B. Powell; Director of Photography: Irving Lippman; Editor: William Austin; Cast: Joseph Cotten, Darren McGavin, Philip Carey, Julie Sommars, Nancy Kovack; 12 reels on 6, 8,200 ft., color, 35mm ref. print.

General Custer, a sadistic, ambition-plagued man, is persuaded by a group of political lobbyists to kill off the Sioux tribes so that their lands may be confiscated.

Hiawatha. Copyright Collection (FGA 4966– 4973). Monogram Pictures Corp., 1952; Director: Kurt Neumann; Producer: Walter Mirisch; Screenplay: Arthur Strawn, Dan Ullman; Music: Marlin Skiles; Film editor: Walter Hanneman; Based on the poem "The Song of Hiawatha" by Henry Wadsworth Longfellow; Cast: Vincent Edwards, Yvette Dugay, Keith Larsen, Gene Iglesias, Armando Silvestre; 8 reels, 8,000 ft., color, 35mm ref. print.

After his marriage to Minnehaha, a Dakota maiden, Hiawatha thwarts the plot of Pau Puk Keewis, a villainous young brave who seeks to instigate a war between the peaceful Ojibwa and the hostile Dakota.

Hondo. Copyright Collection (FGA 5129–5138). Wayne-Fellows Productions, 1953; released by Warner Bros.; Director: John Farrow; Producer: Robert Fellows; Screenplay: James Edward Grant; Music: Emil Newman, Hugo Friedhofer; Film editor: Ralph Dawson; Based on a story by Louis L'Amour; Cast: John Wayne, Geraldine Page, Ward Bond, Michael Pate, James Arness; 10 reels, 7,500 ft., color, 3-D, 35mm ref. print.

In 1874, Hondo, a cavalry dispatch rider who is part Indian, escapes from execution by the Apache and saves a band of settlers and a cavalry patrol from warring Indians.

Igloo. AFI/Universal Collection (FEB 0916– 0921). Universal, 1932; Carl Laemmle presents; Director and story: Ewing Scott; Producer: Edward Small; Photography: Roy H. Klaffki; Film editor: Richard Cahoon; Narrative by Edward T. Lowe and Wilfred Lucas; Narration by Gayne Whitman; Cast: Chee-Ak, Kyatuk, Toyuk, Lanak, Nahshook, and other Eskimo villagers and huntsmen of the Nuwuk tribe in the Arctic; 6 reels, 5,277 ft., 35mm ref. print.

In the area above Pt. Barrow, Alaska, the Nuwuk, an Eskimo tribe, emerge from their igloos at the end of winter. Chee-ak, a member of a neighboring tribe who hopes to win Kyatuk, the daughter of the chief, arrives with food. After a storm occurs and they run out of food, Chee-ak leads them on an arduous journey in search of food.

Jeremiah Johnson. Copyright Collection (FGC 8086–8092). Warner Bros, Inc. & Sanford Productions, Inc., 1972; Director: Sidney Pollack; Producer: Joe Wizan; Screenplay: John Milius, Edward Anhalt; Cast: Robert Redford, Will Geer, Stefan Gierasch, Allyn Ann McLerie; Based upon the novel *Mountain Man* by Vardis Fisher; 14 reels on 7, ca. 10,890 ft., color, 35mm ref. print.

An ex-soldier, Jeremiah Johnson, retreats to the wilderness to become a fur trapper. He becomes friends with the Flathead and marries the chief's daughter. Later, the cavalry desecrates a Crow burial ground against Jeremiah's wishes when he acts as their guide. The Crow seek revenge by killing Jeremiah's family, and he retaliates by killing Crows.

The Last of the Mohicans. AFI/Small Collection (FEB 0306–0315). Reliance Pictures, 1936; released through United Artists; Director: George B. Seitz; Producer: Edward Small; Screenplay: Philip Dunne; Based on the novel *The Last of the Mohicans* by James Fenimore Cooper; Cast:

Randolph Scott, Binnie Barnes, Henry Wilcoxon; 10 reels, 8,225 ft., b&w, 35mm ref. print.

During the French and Indian War, Hawkeye, a white man raised by Indians, comes to the aid of the two daughters of a British colonel, Alice and Cora. They have been kidnapped by an Indian scout named Magua. With the help of the Mohicans, Uncas and Chingachgook, Hawkeye rescues them and falls in love with Alice. The two women are captured by Magua again after an Indian attack on the fort. Uncas falls in love with Cora and dies trying to save her. Cora leaps off a cliff to join Uncas in death. Hawkeye is captured attempting to save Alice, but is rescued by the army.

The division also has the 1992 Twentieth Century-Fox version of this title.

The Legend of the Lone Ranger. Copyright Collection (FGE 4157–4162). A Martin Starger production, 1981; distributed by Universal; Director: William A. Fraker; Producer: Walter Coblenz; Screenplay: Ivan Goff, Ben Roberts, Michael Kane & William Roberts; Adaptation by Jerry Derloshon; Cast: Klinton Spilsbury, Michael Horse, Christopher Lloyd; 6 reels, 8,820 ft., color, 35mm ref. print.

John Reid assumes the identity of the Lone Ranger to avenge his family's deaths and is aided by his childhood Indian friend, Tonto.

Little Big Man. Copyright Collection (FGC 6480–6487). National General, 1970; Hiller Productions, Ltd. & Stockbridge Productions, Inc., released by Cinema Center Films; Director: Arthur Penn; Producer: Stuart Millar; Screenplay: Calder Willingham; Music: John Hammond; Camera: Harry Stradling, Jr.; Based on the novel by Thomas Berger; Cast: Dustin Hoffman, Faye Dunaway, Martin Balsam, Richard Mulligan, Chief Dan George, Jeff Corey; 15 reels on 8, 13,230 ft., color, 35mm ref. print.

An elderly white man recounts his life story, which includes being raised by Indians as a Cheyenne brave. He is captured by the army and rejoins white civilization, but later meets a woman from his old tribe and marries her. General Custer attacks the Indian camp where they live, killing the man's wife and child. He is later made a scout and is present at the Little Big Horn massacre, where his life is saved by a Cheyenne friend.

A Man Called Horse. Copyright Collection (FGC 4545–4550). National General, 1970; Sandy Howard Productions Corp.; Director: Elliot Silverstein; Producer: Sandy Howard; Story: Dorothy M. Johnson; Screenplay: Jack DeWitt; Music: Leonard Roseman, Lloyd One Star; Cast: Richard Harris, Dame Judith Anderson, Jean Gascon, Manu Tupou, Corinna Tsopei; 12 reels on 6, 10,260 ft., color, 35mm ref. print.

A British man is captured by Sioux. He adapts to their way of life and marries the daughter of the chief after enduring the torture of being hung by the skin of his chest. His wife and the chief die in confrontations with a rival tribe, and he becomes the tribe's new chief, before later deciding to return to England.

Massacre. United Artists Collection (FEB 1616–1623). First National Pictures, 1934; Director: Alan Crosland; Story: Robert Gessner; Screenplay: Ralph Block, Sheridan Gibney; Photography: George Barnes; Cast: Richard Barthelmess, Ann Dvorak, Dudley Digges, Claire Dodd, Henry O'Neill, Sidney Toler; 8 reels, 6,289 ft., 35mm ref. print.

An Indian who makes a living as a stunt rider, Joe Thunder Horse, returns to the reservation to see his sick father and learns that the reservation is run by corrupt officials. When he avenges the rape of his sister, he is arrested for attempted murder, but escapes to Washington, D.C., where he pleads his case to the head of the Bureau of Indian Affairs. The Indian agent's corruption is eventually revealed, and Joe is offered a job by the Bureau.

Navajo. Copyright Collection (FGA 7964–7971). B-F Productions, 1951; released by Lippert Pictures; Director and writer: Norman Foster; Producer: Hall Bartlett; Music: Leith Stevens; Editor: Lloyd Nosler; Cast: Francis Kee Teller, John Mitchell, Mrs. Teller, Billy Draper, Hall Bartlett; 8 reels, 6,300 ft., 35mm ref. print.

A seven-year-old Navajo boy determines to remain free of the white man and the reservation school by escaping to a canyon.

The Outsider. Copyright Collection (FGB 5711–5716). Universal, 1961; Director: Delbert Mann; Producer: Sy Bartlett; Screenplay: Stewart Stern; Composer and conductor: Leonard Rosenman; Photographer: Joseph LaShelle; Film editor: Marjorie Fowler; Based on the book *The Hero of Iwo Jima* by William Bradford Huie; Cast: Tony Curtis, James Franciscus, Gregory Walcott, Bruce Bennett, Vivian Nathan; 11 reels on 6, 9,500 ft., b&w, 35mm ref. print.

The tragic career of Ira Hamilton Hayes, a Pima youth who lived on a reservation and was thrust into national fame as one of the six Marines who raised the American flag on Iwo Jima during World War II, is traced, from his enlistment in the Marines in 1944 to his death in 1955 of alcoholism and exposure.

The Paleface. Copyright Collection (FBA 3632–3634). Paramount, 1948; Director: Norman Z. McLeod; Producer: Robert A. Welsh; Screenplay: Edmund Hartman; Music score: Victor Young; Film editor: Ellsworth Hoagland; Cast: Bob Hope, Jane Russell, Robert Armstrong, Iris Adrian, Robert Watson; 10 reels, 8,180 ft., 35mm ref. print.

A timid, traveling dentist, mistaken for a federal agent, despite gun duels and attempted burning at the stake, escapes the Indians on the war path, outwits the outlaws, and wins the love of a gun-toting cowgirl.

Rio Conchos. AFI/20th Century-Fox Collection (FGD 2002–2007). Twentieth Century-Fox, 1964; Director: Gordon Douglas; Cast: Richard Boone, Stuart Whitman, Tony Franciosa; 12 reels on 6, 9,630 ft., color, 35mm ref. print

An Indian-hating white man leads the U.S. cavalry to a gun runner who is planning to give rifles to Apaches. When he finds the Indian that killed his family, he tries to attack him, but is imprisoned by the colonel. An Indian woman named Sally frees him, and he and a sergeant destroy the camp, killing everyone except for Sally and a captain. Note: Film is English language with Spanish subtitles.

Sitting Bull. Copyright Collection (FEB 6983–6994). W. R. Frank production, 1954; Director: Sidney Salkow; Mexican director: Rene Cardona; Cast: Dale Robertson, Mary Murphy, J. Carol Naish; 12 reels, 9,630 ft., color, 35mm ref. print

A pro-Indian soldier tries to make peace with the Sioux, led by Sitting Bull. He is accused of aiding the enemy when Custer attempts to destroy the Indians. At the end, President Grant and Sitting Bull meet to discuss peaceful coexistence between the two races.

Tell Them Willie Boy is Here. Copyright Collection (FGC 5708–5712). Universal, 1969; Director and writer: Abraham Polonsky; Producer: Philip A. Waxman; Presented by Jennings Lang; Photographer: Conrad Hall; Cast: Robert Redford, Katharine Ross, Robert Blake, Susan Clark; 10 reels, 8,575 ft., color, 35mm ref. print.

Willie Boy, a Paiute Indian, returns to his reservation in 1909. He attempts to meet his love, Lola, in the woods, which leads to a fight between him and her father and brothers, resulting in the father's death. Willie and Lola run away and are pursued reluctantly by the sheriff at the head of a bloodthirsty posse. Willie kills a member of the posse, which intensifies the pursuit. Lola is found dead, and the sheriff is forced to kill Willie only to discover that Willie's gun has no bullets.

Thunderheart. Copyright Collection (CGB 6173–6179). Tribeca-Waterhorse, 1992; released by TriStar Pictures; Director: Michael Apted; Producers: Robert De Niro, Jane Rosenthal, John Fusco; Screenplay: John Fusco; Cast: Val Kilmer, Graham Greene, Sam Shepard; 13 reels on 7, ca. 10,620 ft., color, 35mm ref. print.

A federal agent who is part Indian is sent to investigate a murder on a Sioux reservation in the late 1970s. Even though he is disdainful of his Indian heritage initially, during the course of the investigation he becomes attuned to his Indian self.

The Unforgiven. Copyright Collection (FGB 6887–6893). James Productions, Inc., 1960; released by United Artists; Director: John Huston; Producer: James Hill; Screenplay: Ben Maddow; Music: Dimitri Tiomkin; Cast: Burt Lancaster, Audrey Hepburn, Audie Murphy, John Saxon, Charles Bickford, Albert Salmi, Lillian Gish; 7 reels, 11,000 ft., color, 35mm ref. print.

Rachel, a girl raised by whites in Texas in the 1870s, is discovered to be Kiowa. She is subjected to racism, and the Indians attempt to claim her back through battle. When the Indians attack her foster home, the girl is forced to kill her Indian brother. After the Indians are defeated, Rachel and her foster brother, Ben, decide to marry.

Valley of the Sun. AFI Collection (FBA 8386–8389). RKO Radio Pictures, 1942; Director: George Marshall; Producer: Graham Baker; Screenplay: Horace McCoy; Music: Paul Sawtell; Photographer: Harry Wild; Editor: Desmond Marquette; Based on the story of the same title by Clarence B. Kelland; Cast: Cedric Hardwicke, Dean Jagger, Lucille Ball, James Craig, Peter Whitney, Billy Gilbert, Tom Tyler; 4 reels, 2,795 ft., 16mm ref. print.

An Indian scout averts a massacre by preventing a crooked Indian agent from swindling food from his people.

The White Dawn. Copyright Collection (FGD 529–535). Paramount, 1974; Director: Philip Kaufman; Screenplay: James Huston and Tom Rickman; Based on the book *An Eskimo Saga* by James Huston; Cast: Warren Oates, Timothy Bottoms, Lou Gossett, Simonie Kopapik; 14 reels on 7, 9,810 ft., color, 35mm ref. print.

In 1896, three whalers stranded in the Arctic are rescued by Eskimos and bring havoc to the Eskimos' lives.

Windwalker. Copyright Collection (FGE 0074–0078). A Santa Fe International production, 1980; distributed by Pacific International Enterprises; Director: Keith Merrill; Producers: Thomas E. Ballard, Arthur R. Dubs; Screenplay: Ray Goldrup; Director of photography: Reed Smoot; Based on the novel by Blaine M. Yorgason; Cast: Trevor Howard, Nick Ramus, James Remar, Serene Hedin, Dusty Iron Wing McCrea, Silvana Gallardo; 10 reels on 5, ca. 9,000 ft., color, 35mm ref. print.

In the eighteenth century, a Cheyenne comes back to life to protect his tribe from their enemies, the Crow, one of whom is his son, who was stolen from his tribe. Note: Soundtrack is in Cheyenne and Crow languages with English subtitles and narration.

Television Programs

Broken Arrow. Copyright Collection (FBB 7728–7747; FBB 8731–8743, 8745, 8747; FBB 9635, 9960; FCA 9956–60). Twentieth Century-Fox; telecast on ABC-TV, 1956–1958; Cast: John Lupton, Michael Ansara; 42 episodes on 42 reels, ca. 936 ft. each, 16mm ref. print.

Cochise and Indian agent Tom Jeffords fight renegades and evil men together.

The Broken Chain. Copyright Collection (VBN 2509–2510). A VonZerneck-Sertner production, 1993; released by Turner Pictures, Inc.; telecast on cable TV channel TNT; Director: Lamont Johnson; Producers: Cleve Landsberg, Lamont Johnson, Hanay Geigamah, Phill Lucas, Richard Hill; Writer: Earl W. Wallace; Camera: William Wages; Cast: Eric Schweig, Buffy Saint-Marie, Pierce Brosnan, J. C. White Shirt; 2 videocassettes, color, 3/4" viewing copy.

In the mid-eighteenth century, a young Mohawk is sent away by an Englishman to be educated. When he returns, he finds himself torn between his loyalties to the Indian world and the British world. A boyhood friend spurns the Indian's adoption of white ways, and a conflict ensues.

Centennial. Copyright Collection (FDA 5324–48). A John Wilder Production in association with Universal, 1978; telecast on NBC-TV; Director: Virgil W. Vogel; Producers: Howard Alston; Writers: John Wilder; From the novel by James A. Michener; Cast: Robert Conrad, Raymond Burr, Richard Chamberlain, Sally Kellerman, Michael Ansara, Clint Walker, Barbara Carrera, Gregory Harrison, Donald Pleasence, Christina Raines, Richard Crenna, Mark Harmon, Cliff De Young, Dennis Weaver, Timothy Dalton, Lynn Redgrave, Brian Keith, David Janssen, Andy Griffith, Robert Vaughn, Sharon Gless, Merle Haggard; 12-part mini-series; 26 reels, 56,160 ft., color, 16mm ref. print.

The settlement of a piece of land in the Rocky Mountain region is chronicled from the white man's first contact with Pawnee and Cheyenne to the present day. During this history, the white inhabitants clash with the Indians, even though some wish to coexist peacefully with them.

Geronimo. Copyright Collection (VTB 1332–1333). Yorktown production, 1993; released by Turner Pictures, Inc.; telecast on cable TV channel TNT; Director: Roger Young; Producer: Ira Marvin; Writer: J. T. Allen; Camera: Donald M. Morgan; Cast: Joseph Runningfox, Nick Ramus, Michelle St. John, Michael Greyeyes; 2 videocassettes, 1/2" viewing copy.

The life of Apache warrior Geronimo is depicted through the various stages of his life: his youth, his middle years, and old age. He battles Mexican and, later, American soldiers, and ultimately witnesses the destruction of his way of life.

Hawkeye and the Last of the Mohicans. Copyright Collection (FCA 565). Normadie Productions; telecast on syndicated TV, 1957; Director: Sam Newfield; Producer: Sigmund Neufeld; Story and teleplay: Bob Bailey and Hugh King; Cast: John Hart, Lon Chaney, Jr., Daryl Masters, Bonar Stuart; 1 episode, "Snake tatoo," 30 min., 1,100 ft., 16mm ref. print.

Hawkeye and his Indian friend Chingachgook have adventures on the frontier in the 1750s. In this episode, the son of a Cree chieftain is stolen and raised by a reformed white man. A former accomplice of the white man returns with the idea of using the child to learn the secret of the Cree silver wealth.

The Last of His Tribe. Copyright Collection (VBN 2507–2508). A River City production, 1992;

released by Home Box Office, Inc.; Director: Harry Hook; Cast: Jon Voight, Graham Greene, David Ogden Stiers, Anne Archer; 2 videocassettes, color, 3/4" viewing copy.

In 1911, an anthropologist discovers the last living member of the Yahi tribe, Ishi. Ishi becomes an object of study for the remainder of his life.

The Legend of Walks Far Woman. Copyright Collection (FDA 5877–5878). A Roger Gimbel Productions for EMI Television Programs, Inc., 1982; telecast on NBC-TV; Director: Mel Damski; Producer: William S. Gilmore; Cast: Raquel Welch, Bradford Dillman, George Clutesi; 2 reels, 4,320 ft., color, 16mm ref. print.

The life story of a Sioux woman is told from her youth to old age.

The Lone Ranger. Copyright Collection (FCA 0717, FCA 0718, FCA 0720, FCA 0975, FCA 0719). Lone Ranger or Range Rider Productions; telecast on ABC-TV, 1949–1957; 5 episodes, 30 min., 16mm ref. print.

A masked man fights crime on the frontier with the help of his Indian friend, Tonto.

The Mystic Warrior. Copyright Collection (FDA 7275–7277, FDA 7284–7285). A David L. Wolper/Stan Margulies production in association with Warner Brothers Television, 1984; telecast on ABC-TV; Director: Richard T. Heffron; Producer: Paul Freeman; Based on the novel *Hanta Yo* by Ruth Beebe Hill; Cast: Robert Beltran, Devon Ericson, Rion Hunter; 2-part miniseries; 5 reels, 12,800 ft., color, 16mm ref. print.

In the early 1800s, a young Sioux warrior becomes the leader of his tribe.

Documentaries

Aghveghniighmi: At the Time of Whaling. Copyright Collection (FCA 9421). Alaska Native Heritage Film Project, 1974; Director: Leonard Kamerling and Sarah Elder; 1 reel, 38 min., color, 16mm ref. print; In Eskimo with English subtitles.

Documents the extreme danger and exacting coordination of a modern Inuit community whale hunt.

The American Indian Speaks. Copyright Collection (FBB 2887). Encyclopedia Britannica Educational Corporation, 1973; 1 reel, 23 min., color, 16mm ref. print.

Members of three Indian tribes articulate past injustices and present concerns. A Muskogee Creek remembers the "Trail of Tears;" Nisqually Indians discuss fishing rights; and a Dakota Rosebud Sioux explains the significance of the massacre at Wounded Knee.

And Woman Wove it in a Basket. Copyright Collection (VBH 6652). Bushra Azzouz, Marlene Farnum, Nettie Jackson Kuneki, 1989; Director: Bushra Azzouz; 1 videocassette, 70 min., color, 3/4" viewing copy.

While focusing on the life of Nettie Kuneki, a Klickitat and master basketweaver, this film presents the history of the Klickitat of Oregon and their life along the Columbia River. Archival footage and current interviews document fishing methods, legends and beliefs, and the intricate art of basketmaking.

Another Wind is Moving: The Off-Reservation Indian Boarding School. Copyright Collection (VBF 5418). Summit Street Productions/Kickapoo Nation School, 1985; Director: David M. Kendall; 1 videocassette, 59 min., color, 3/4" viewing copy.

Examining the history of Indian boarding schools which were once intended to foster assimilation of Indian children into white culture, the documentary shows the impact of the schools on tribal survival.

Beyond Tradition: Contemporary Indian Art and its Evolution. Copyright Collection (VAB 9471). Jacka Photography Video Presentation, 1989; 1 videocassette, 45 min., color, 1/2" viewing copy.

Based on the award-winning book of the same title, this video presents more than three hundred examples of prehistoric, historic, and contemporary American Indian art. The evolution of Indian art is traced through the centuries, including carvings, paintings, sculptures, baskets, rugs, jewelry, and pottery.

Broken Rainbow. Copyright Collection (FDA 8448). Earthwork Films, Inc., 1986; Director: Victoria Mudd; Narrator: Martin Sheen; 1 reel, 69 min., color, 16mm ref. print.

This Academy-award winning (1985) documentary examines the controversial Hopi-Navajo land dispute which resulted in the dramatic relocation of ten thousand Navajo from their hogans in northern Arizona to distant tract housing.

Broken Treaty at Battle Mountain. Copyright Collection (FDA 9513). Cinnamon Productions, Inc., 1974; Director: Joel L. Freedman; Narrator: Robert Redford; 1 reel, 60 min., color, 16mm ref. print.

The struggle of the Western Shoshone to keep 24 million acres of land in Nevada—which they say is guaranteed in a treaty—is shown by contrasting differing viewpoints within the tribe between traditionalists and those who are willing to sell the land to the government.

Buckeyes: Food of the California Indians. Copyright Collection (FBA 110). Department of Anthropology, University of California, 1961; 1 reel, 14 min., color, 16mm ref. print; From the *University of California American Indian Film Series.*

The ancient methods used to purify the poiso-nous buckeye, or horse chestnut, and prepare it as food, are demonstrated by Nisenan Indians.

Calumet, Pipe of Peace. Copyright Collection (FBA 4339). Department of Anthropology, University of California, 1964; 1 reel, 23 min., color, 16mm ref. print; From the *University of California American Indian Film Series.*

This film presents the traditional use of the calumet, or peace pipe, among the Plains Indians. Rituals, legends, history, and powers of the calumet peace pipe are described.

The Chaco Legacy. Copyright Collection (VBB 4198). Public Broadcasting Associates, Inc. 1980; Director and producer: Graham Chedd; narrated by Stacy Keach; 1 videocassette, 59 min., color, 3/4" viewing copy.; from the *Odyssey* series.

Examines archaeological theories about the rise and fall of Chacoan culture, which flourished between 1,000 and 1,400 years ago in the area of Chaco Canyon, New Mexico.

Children of Wind River. Copyright Collection (VBH 7063). Wyoming Public Television, 1989; Director: Victress Hitchcock; 1 videocassette, 30 min., color, 3/4" viewing copy.

Filmed on the Wind River Reservation in Wyoming, this documentary takes a critical look at the problems facing Indian families. Through interviews with tribal leaders, health and child care providers, social service workers, and tribal members, solutions to teenage suicide, alcoholism, and poverty are sought.

A Conversation with Vine Deloria, Jr. Copyright Collection (VBD 3748). University of Arizona and KUAT-TV, 1978; 1 videocassette, 29 min., color, 3/4" viewing copy; From the *Words and Place: Native Literature of the American Southwest* series.

GATEWAYS

Always part of American Indian life, artistic expression involves religious, mythological, natural, and economic influences. North American archaeological excavations have abundantly demonstrated that indigenous people often created objects—functional or not—for their artistic value. Since Columbus's arrival, Indian artists and craftspeople have incorporated European tools and materials into their workmanship and developed new art forms. Navajo silverwork, for example, was not a native craft, but one encouraged by Mexican influences.

In the non-Indian world, until about sixty years ago, most Indian art and craft was appreciated largely by museums or by the savant. The intense drive toward acculturation during the late nineteenth and early twentieth centuries subdued Indian art, craft, and design. This condition started changing in the 1920s and 1930s with exhibitions of Indian work presented for its artistic merit. Key artisans and artists who sparked the renaissance were San Ildefonso potter Maria Martinez and her artist husband Julian, artists Fred Kabotie (Hopi), Harrison Begay (Navajo), Allan Houser (Apache), and others.

In 1935, the federal government established the Indian Arts and Crafts Board to promote Indian creativity and broaden markets. The Santa Fe Indian School devoted a studio to Indian art; from this seed developed today's Institute of American Indian and Alaska Native Culture and Arts Development. As appreciation and demand grew, Indian artists and artisans began tailoring or modifying styles and designs to accommodate public tastes. Over time, traders and merchants also convinced them to sign their works, a concept that was alien to people with a communal rather than an individualistic view of their efforts.

By the 1960s and 1970s cultural and economic appreciation of Indian work began achieving unprecedented heights. Artistic spillover and the economic attraction, meanwhile, revived arts and crafts among other individuals and tribes. Artists began—and continue—innovating traditional Indian motifs, establishing individual styles within the context of American Indian experience. Navajo rugs and silverwork, Zuni jewelry and fetish carving, Pueblo pottery, Hopi kachinas, Pomo basketry, Kiowa beadwork and painting, Haida and Iroquois wood sculpture, and individual creations in all media by Indian artists from many tribal affiliations command worldwide respect and appropriate prices.

This worldwide popularity has also, however, attracted cheap imitation, mass production, stylistic copying, and outright forgery of Indian creations, here and abroad. As with any art vogue, this may saturate interest and affect the Indian art market. But the distinctiveness and originality of the true American Indian artist appears to be set permanently on the landscape.

WHERE TO LOOK: The General Collections, Microform Reading Room, Rare Book and Special Collections, Manuscript (Vincent Price Papers), Prints and Photographs, and Motion Picture, Broadcasting and Recorded Sound Divisions, and the American Folklife Center.

"Navajo Weavers." Gelatin silver print by William J. Carpenter, copyrighted in 1914. LOT 11442. (LC-USZ62-99569). Prints and Photographs Division.

Recognized as fine weavers since the eighteenth century, Navajos by the late nineteenth century had largely turned from weaving blankets for their own use to weaving rugs for the retail trade. Nontraditional textiles, dyes, and designs emerged to satisfy the public taste. Today, as with most Indian art and craft, Navajo rugs command high prices in the marketplace.

The noted Native American author discusses the unique role of the Indian writer.

Discovering American Indian Music. Copyright Collection (FBA 7268). BFA Educational Media, 1971; Director: Bernard Wilets; 1 reel, 24 min., color, 16mm ref. print.

Introduces traditional native customs, costumes, dances, and music still practiced by eleven Indian tribes, principally of the Plains and Southwest. Dances include the Kiowa Victory War Dance, the Tesuque Pueblo Bow and Arrow Dance, and the Tlingit Death Dance.

The Divided Trail: A Native American Odyssey. Copyright Collection (FCA 8923). Phoenix Films, 1977; Director: Jerry Aronson; 1 reel, 33 min., color, 16mm ref. print.

Documents eight years of urban living for three Chippewa Indians who were encouraged to move from the reservation by the Bureau of Indian Affairs. Michael Chosa, his sister Betty Chosa Jack, and their friend Carol Warrington confront poverty, discrimination, alcohol abuse, and, finally, rehabilitation.

The Drummaker. Copyright Collection (FCA 1689). Smithsonian Institution-Folklife Programs, 1978; 1 reel, 38 min., 16mm ref. print; from *Smithsonian Folklife Studies.*

William Bineshi Baker, Jr., an Ojibwa living on the Lac Courte Oreilles Reservation in northern Wisconsin constructs a drum, step-by-step according to tradition.

Franz Boas, 1858–1942. Copyright Collection (VBB 3407). Public Broadcasting Associates, Inc., 1980; Director: T. W. Timreck; 1 videocassette, 58 min., color, 3/4" viewing copy; from the *Odyssey* series.

Franz Boas was one of the most important influences in American anthropology. This film explores his life and ideas through interviews with modern anthropologists, Native American people, and Boas himself.

Fritz Scholder: An American Portrait. Off-Air Collection (VAA 1145). Oklahoma Summer Arts Institute, 1983; Director: Mary Y. Frates; 1 videocassette, 29 min., color, 1/2" viewing copy.

Fritz Scholder, Native American artist, takes the viewer from his studio, where painting is a solitary, private activity, to the public world of a gallery opening.

Geronimo: The Final Campaign. Copyright Collection (VBG 7342). KUAT-TV, 1988; Directors: Hector Gonzalez and Fran Sherlock; 1 videocassette, 30 min., color, 3/4" viewing copy.

Narrated by Will Rogers, Jr., the film presents the history of the Chiricahua Apache of the Southwest from the Spanish introduction of cattle and horses into their society until their eventual confinement to reservations.

Home for the Weekend. Copyright Collection (FAB 370). Davidson Films, Inc., 1972; 1 reel, 13 min., color, 16mm ref. print.

Indians from the Sac and Fox tribes talk about their dances, way of life, and the differences between them and the white people who watch them perform during a weekend powwow.

Hopi Indian Arts and Crafts. Copyright Collection (FAB 1280). Coronet Instructional Media, 1975; 1 reel, 10 min., color, 16mm ref. print.

Hopi Indians demonstrate basket weaving, pottery making, silverwork, and weaving using traditional tools.

Hopi: Songs of the Fourth World. Copyright Collection (FDA 9402). Ferrero Films, 1983; Director: Pat Ferrero; 1 reel, 58 min., color, 16mm ref. print.

An in-depth look at the Hopi way, a philosophy of living in balance with nature, the film describes the Hopi meaning of life, death, and renewal as revealed in the interweaving life cycle of humans and corn plants.

Huteetl: Koyukon Memorial Potlach. Copyright Collection (VBD 6069). Yukon Koyukuk School District, 1983; Director: Curt Madison; 1 video-cassette, 55 min., color, 3/4" viewing copy; in Koyukon and English.

Documents a traditional Koyukon Athabas-kan memorial potlatch held in Hughes, Alaska, in June 1982.

The Image Maker and the Indians: E. S. Curtis and his 1914 Kwakiutl Movie. NEA/Burke Museum Collection (FBA 6681). Burke Memorial Museum, University of Washington, Seattle, 1979; Director: David Gerth; 1 reel, 16 min., b&w & color, 16mm ref. print.

Investigates how the famous photographer Edward S. Curtis made the first full-length documentary film on Native Americans. Provides background and methods, as well as previously unpublished photos and testimony of Indians who were actors or spectators during the filming. (See also *In the Land of the War Canoes: Kwakiutl Indian Life on the Northwest Coast* in the Silent Films—Non-Fiction section).

Indian Country. Copyright Collection (VBF 9914). WGBH Educational Foundation, 1988; 1 video-cassette, 60 min., color, 3/4" viewing copy; from the PBS series, *Frontline.*

Close-up look at life on the Pacific coast Quinault Reservation—one of the largest in Washington state. Through interviews with the tribal chair and other members, the film traces the largely "white influenced" economic and environmental demise of the tribe and then focuses on current efforts to rebuild the community.

Inuqqaanin: From the First People. Copyright Collection (FDA 6285). Leonard Kamerling and the village of Shungnak, Alaska, 1976; Directors: Sarah Elder and Leonard Kamerling; 1 reel, 45 min., color, 16mm ref. print.

A community-produced film which presents the Inuit village of Shungnak through early winter subsistence activities in temperatures of −47 degrees and short three-hour days.

Ishi: the Last Yahi. LC Off-Air Taping Collection (VBL 6649). Rattlesnake Productions, 1992; telecast on PBS-TV as part of *The American Experience* in 1994; Director and producer: Jed Riffe and Pamela Roberts; Writer: Anne Makepeace; 1 videocassette, color, 3/4" viewing copy.

The life of Ishi is recounted from his emergence in the white man's world in 1911 to his death from tuberculosis. Emphasis is given to anthropologist Alfred Kroeber's study of Ishi and his friendship with him.

Keep Your Heart Strong. Copyright Collection (VAB 3907). Prairie Public TV, 1986; 1 video-cassette, 58 min., color, 1/2" viewing copy.

Documents a series of Indian powwows during the summer of 1986 in Bismark, Fargo, Fort Totten, and Twin Buttes, North Dakota.

Lakota Quillwork: Art and Legend. Copyright Collection (FBC 2032). Nauman Films, Inc., 1985; Director: H. Jane Nauman; Narrator: Alice Blue Legs and H. Jane Nauman; 1 reel, 27 min., color, 16mm ref. print; in Lakota and English.

Explores the spiritual origins of porcupine quillwork through the legend of Double Woman, who brought the art from the spirit world to the Lakota Sioux. Contrasts the original method of handwork with some modern adaptations used by nationally recognized artist Alice Blue Legs.

Lenape: The Original People. Copyright Collection (FBC 1937). Agnello Films, 1986; Director: Thomas Agnello; 1 reel, 22 min., color, 16mm ref. print.

Two full-blooded Lenape (Delaware) Indians recall their tribe's history and customs and reflect on their own loneliness and fears for the tribe as their numbers dwindle. Includes art reproductions, archival photographs, and scenes from the first reunion of Lenape from all parts of the U.S. which was held in 1983.

Make my People Live: The Crisis in Indian Health Care. Copyright Collection (VBD 6522). WGBH Educational Foundation, 1984; Director: Linda Harrar; Narrator: Lee Grant; 1 videocassette, 60 min., color, 3/4" viewing copy; from the PBS series, *Nova*.

Examines the health problems of Native Americans and the quality of care they receive, particularly among four tribes (Sioux, Tlingit, Navajo, Creek). The film also explores the reasons why American Indians suffer from diseases such as diabetes, tuberculosis, and alcoholism at rates far exceeding the national averages.

Mohawk Basketmaking: A Cultural Profile. Copyright Collection (VBB 5813). Frank Semmens, 1980; Director: Frank Semmens; Narrator: Larry Richardson; 1 videocassette, 28 min., color, 3/4" viewing copy.

Photographed on the St. Regis Reservation in upstate New York, this film documents the art of basketmaking as practiced by Mary Adams, a nationally recognized Mohawk artist. During the intricate process, she narrates the story of her youth and her people's struggle to survive. The paintings of Iroquois artist Ernest Smith illustrate the historical use of Indian baskets.

More than Bows and Arrows. Copyright Collection (FBB 8012–8013). Cinema Associates, Inc., 1978; Director: Roy Williams; Narrator: N. Scott Momaday; 2 reels, 58 min., color, 16mm ref. print.

This award-winning film demonstrates the impact of Native American culture on American society in areas of medicine, architecture, agri-culture, science, urban development, and environmental planning, among others.

My Hands are the Tools of My Soul. Copyright Collection (FDA 6215). Swann Films, Inc., 1975; Directors: Arthur Barron and Zina Voynov; Narrator: Gerald Vizenor; 1 reel, 54 min., color, 16mm ref. print.

Vignettes of Indian artists with their work stress that "the process of artistic creation, the doing, is as important as the end product." A Navajo woman weaving an original design, Pueblo basketmasters and potters, a Hopi Kachina doll carver, and various musicians are included.

Myths and the Moundbuilders. Copyright Collection (VBB 1561). Public Broadcasting Associates, Inc., 1981; Director, producer, and writer: Graham Chedd; 1 videocassette, 58 min., color, 3/4" viewing copy; from the *Odyssey* series.

Reconstructs the myths and theories of the huge earthen mounds scattered throughout the central United States. Until the late 1800s it was believed that these were built by a lost civilization, but it is now known that the mound-building cultures were American Indians.

Native American Myths. Copyright Collection (FBA 7370). Encyclopedia Britannica Educational Corporation, 1977; 1 reel, 24 min., color, 16mm ref. print.

Collaborators Alfonso Ortiz, Stephen S. Jones, Hazel John, Frank Collison, Barbara Bravo, and Mary Lou Byler helped create this animated presentation of American Indian myths of the Seneca, Haida, Klamath, Cherokee, and Hopi tribes.

Navajo Code Talkers. Copyright Collection (VBC 4789). New Mexico Film & Video, 1981; Director: Tom McCarthy; 1 videocassette, 27 min., color, 3/4" viewing copy.

This film documents the participation of Navajo Indians in the Marine Corps during World War II. A code for military communications was invented based on the Navajo language; the Navajos interviewed in the film were the radio operators.

Navajo: The Last Red Indians. L.C. Purchase (VBA 7956). BBC TV / Time-Life Films, 1972; Director: Michael Barnes; 1 videocassette, 35 min., color, 3/4" viewing copy; from the BBC series, *Horizon*.

Depicts efforts by the largest tribe in America to preserve traditional culture while synthesizing it with selected features of modern American life. Filmed on their reservation in northern Arizona and New Mexico, many uncensored scenes of Navajo rituals, ceremonies, and healing practices are presented.

Neshnabek: The People. Copyright Collection (FCA 9813). Donald David Stull and University of Kansas, 1979; Director: Gene Bernofsky; Narrator: Kirby Kemble and James Carothers; 1 reel, 30 min., 16mm ref. print.

Using original footage made of the Prairie Band Potawatomi by amateur anthropologist Floyd Schultz between 1927 and 1941, this film was edited and supplied with a soundtrack based on recent interviews with elderly Potawatomi.

The New American Indian Wars: Without Arrows and Bullets. Copyright Collection (VAB 0071). Rodman-Downs, Ltd., 1987; 1 videocassette, 30 min., color, 1/2" viewing copy.

David Hartman interviews tribal members from various reservations about current political and economic concerns. The Lummi tribe in Washington state discuss fishing rights; the Flathead in Montana battle for land; the Mohawk Nation confronts gambling; and the Navajo pursue entrepreneurial interests.

No Turning Back. Copyright Collection (VBF 4584). KNME-TV, 1984; Director: Dale Sonnenberg; 1 videocassette, 58 min., b&w & color, 3/4" viewing copy.

Examines the recent phenomenon of a fundamental Christian movement on Navajo reservations—which includes tent revivals, speaking in tongues, and healings—and the opposition by traditional tribal members. Much of the documentary, which was filmed in part by hidden cameras, focuses on the personal crusade of evangelist Boots Wagner, himself a Navajo.

Origin of the Crown Dance and Ba'ts'oosee: An Apache Trickster Cycle. Copyright Collection (VBD 3743). University of Arizona and KUAT-TV, 1978; 1 videocassette, 40 min., color, 3/4" viewing copy; in Apache with English subtitles; from the *Words and Place: Native Literature of the American Southwest* series.

Apache storyteller Rudolph Kane relates "stories of long ago" to a group which includes his children, grandchildren, and great-grandchildren.

Our Sacred Land. Copyright Collection (VBE 9793). Chris Spotted Eagle, 1984; Director: Chris Spotted Eagle; 1 videocassette, 28 min., color, 3/4" viewing copy.

Explores the contemporary issue of Native American religious freedom by focusing on the continuing struggle of the Sioux to regain the Black Hills of South Dakota. Many spokesmen with key roles in the dispute are interviewed.

People of the Klamath: Preserving a Way of Life. Copyright Collection (VBH 1397). James Culp Productions, 1989; Director: James Culp; Narrator: Ed Asner; 1 videocassette, 28 min., b&w & color, 3/4" viewing copy.

Shows how the Karuk (Karok) of Northern California preserve their culture by teaching the younger generation traditions such as basket-making, salmon fishing, language, and crafts.

Return to Sovereignty: Self-Determination and the Kansas Kickapoo. Copyright Collection (VBI 6635). Donald D. Stull and David M. Kendall, 1982; Director: David Kendall; 1 videocassette, 46 min., color, 3/4″ viewing copy.

Examines how the Indian Self-Determination and Education Assistance Act of 1975 has been implemented among the Kansas Kickapoo. Commentary from tribal administrators and elders, local BIA representatives, specialists in Indian law, and anthropologists reveals success on some levels and failure on others.

Seeking the First Americans. Copyright Collection (VBB 3406). Public Broadcasting Associates, Inc., 1980; Director: Graham Chedd; 1 videocassette, 60 min., color, 3/4″ viewing copy; from the *Odyssey* series.

Investigates the work of archaeologists who are trying to determine when the earliest American Indians lived on this continent.

The 21st Annual World Eskimo-Indian Olympics. Copyright Collection (VBD 4387). Skip Blumberg, 1983; Director: Skip Blumberg; 1 videocassette, 27 min., color, 3/4″ viewing copy.

More than ten thousand fans gathered to observe the 1982 Eskimo-Indian Olympics in Fairbanks, Alaska. Contests include two-foot and one-foot high kicks, seal-skinning, knuckle hop, and blanket toss.

Vision Dance [Ihanbla Waktoglag Wacipi]. Copyright Collection (VBB 8957). Solaris Dance Theatre, Inc., 1982; Director: Skip Sweeney; 1 videocassette, 60 min., color, 3/4″ viewing copy; in Lakota with English subtitles.

Solaris, a modern dance theater company, and Sioux dancers from nine reservations of the Lakota Nation in South Dakota perform sacred and traditional powwow dances.

Warriors. Copyright Collection (VAB 3903). Prairie Public Broadcasting, 1987; 1 videocassette, 60 min., color, 1/2″ viewing copy.

Examines the active role of Native Americans in the Vietnam war.

Motion picture frames sent to the Library of Congress as part of the copyright deposit for the film *In the Land of the Head-hunters* (Seattle Film Co., 1914). Motion Picture

This film, which was directed by Edward S. Curtis, was rereleased as part of a preservation effort by the Burke Museum in 1973 under the title In the Land of the War Canoes: Kwakiutl Indian Life on the Northwest Coast. *Curtis, a celebrated photographer of Indians, attempted to recreate the lifestyle of the Kwakiutl Indians before their contact with white men, using Kwakiutl actors. Even though it has been criticized for its romanticism, the film remains one of the most important early films to depict Indian life.*

FORM NO. 1352   BULLETIN No. 182. RELEASED October 27, 1908

THE CALL OF THE WILD

Sad Plight of the Civilized Redman

LENGTH, 988 FEET.   PRICE, 14 CENTS PER FOOT.

"Gild the farthing if you will, but it is a farthing still." So it is with the Redman. Civilization and education cannot bleach his tawny epidermis, and that will always prove an unsurmountable barrier to social distinction. He may be lauded and even lionized for deeds of valor and heroism, or excellence in scientifics, but when it comes to the social circle—never. "Lo the poor Indian", and well we may say it, for his condition is indeed deplorable; elevated to intellectual supremacy, only to more fully realize his extreme commonalty. Such was the plight of George Redfeather, the hero of this Biograph subject, upon his return from Carlisle, where he not only graduated with high honors, but was also the star of the college football team. At a reception given in his honor by Lieut. Penrose, and Indian Agent, the civilized brave meets Gladys, the Lieutenant's daughter, and falls desperately in love with her. You may be sure he is indignantly repulsed by Gladys and ordered from the house for his presumption by her father. With pique he leaves, and we next find him in his own room, crushed and disappointed, for he realizes the truth: "Good enough as a hero, but not as a husband". What was the use of his struggle? As he reasons, his long suppressed nature asserts itself and he hears the call of the wild: "Out there is your sphere, on the boundless plains, careless and free, among your kind and kin, where all is truth". Here he sits; this nostalgic fever growing more intense every second, until in a fury he tears off the conventional clothes he wears, donning in their stead his suit of leather, with blanket and feathered headgear. Thus garbed, and with a bottle of whiskey, he makes his way back to his former associates in the wilds. He plans vengeance and the opportunity presents itself, when he surprises Gladys out horseback riding. He captures her after a spirited chase and intended holding her captive, but she appeals to him, calling to his mind the presence of the All Powerful Master above, who knows and sees all things, and who is even now calling to him to do right. He listens to the call of this Higher Voice and helping her to her saddle, sadly watches her ride off homeward. The film is most thrilling in situations, beautiful in photography and superbly acted.

No. 3482   CODE WORD—Revezado

Produced and Controlled Exclusively by the
American Mutoscope ℞ Biograph Co.
11 East 14th Street, New York City.

PACIFIC COAST BRANCH, 312 California Street
Los Angeles. Cal

Licensees { Kleine Optical Co.   American Mutoscope ℞ Biograph Co.
Great Northern Film Co   Williams, Brown ℞ Earle.
We will protect our customers and those of our licensees against patent litigation in the use of our licensed films.

Biograph Bulletin no. 3482 for The Call of the Wild *(AM&B), released October 27, 1908 (LC-USZ62-116691). Motion Picture*

This company advertised its product to exhibitors on handbills such as this one, which typically contained florid, melodramatic synopses, but did not mention the names of the actors because they were considered to be unimportant. The Call of the Wild, *one of several films D. W. Griffith made concerning Indians, focuses on the love of an Indian man for a white woman.*

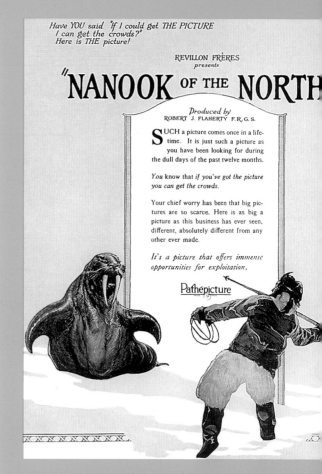

Advertisement from Motion Picture News, *June 17, 1922, for* Nanook of the North *(U.S. Pathé, 1922). (LC-USZ62-116710) Motion Picture*

One of the most famous documentaries ever made, Nanook of the North *was initially turned down for distribution by several film companies before Pathé agreed to distribute it. The film was both a critical and box-office success. In what has been termed "salvage ethnography," Flaherty chose to focus on a hunter of the Itivimuit tribe, Nanook, asking him and the others to recreate the Inuit lifestyle before exposure to white men.*

Advertisement from *Exhibitor's Trade Review*, May 3, 1919, for *Just Squaw* (Superior Pictures, 1919), featuring Beatriz Michelena (LC-USZC4-4822). Motion Picture

---

Fiction films about Indians often focused on the subject of interracial love. Many of these films would posit race as a barrier to love—a barrier which is removed when one of the protaganists discovers that he or she is in reality white, a typical example of which is the film Just Squaw.

Still from *Igloo* (Universal, 1932), featuring Eskimo villagers and huntsmen of the Nuwuk tribe in the Arctic. Motion Picture. Copyright © 1932 by Universal City Studios, Inc. Courtesy of MCA Publishing Rights, a Division of MCA Inc. (LC-USZ62-116692). All rights reserved.

Director Ewing Scott shot this film using an all-native cast while living with the tribe in the Arctic region of Alaska. The film was supposedly based on authentic incidents in the lives of the Eskimos.

Still from *Across the Wide Missouri* (MGM, 1951), featuring Ricardo Montalban (LC-USZ62-116693). Motion Picture. Copyright © 1951 Turner Entertainment Co. All Rights Reserved.

Although Across the Wide Missouri *attempted to follow the trend of sympathetic Indian portrayals started by films such as* Broken Arrow, *it still featured the standard film battle scenes between Indians and whites and a stereotypical Indian princess who died for her white man.*

Still from *Ramona* (Biograph, 1910), featuring Mary Pickford, Kate Bruce, and Henry B. Walthall (LC-USZ62-116711). Motion Picture

The first of several film versions of Helen Hunt Jackson's novel Ramona, *this film attempted to dramatize the white man's injustice to the Indian. Jackson loosely based the character of Ramona upon a Cahuilla woman named Ramona Lubo, or Lugo.*

Still from *Navajo* (Lippert Pictures, 1951), featuring Francis Kee Teller and John Mitchell (LC-USZ62-116694). Motion Picture

In a story far removed from the typical dramas of Indian warfare and interracial romances, a young Navajo boy resists going to a white-run reservation school.

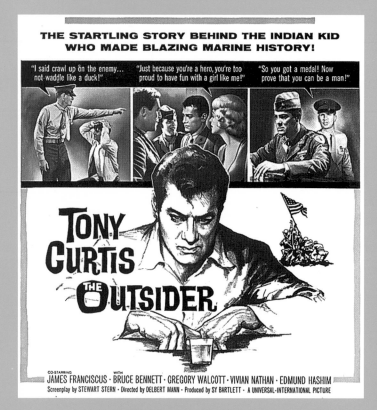

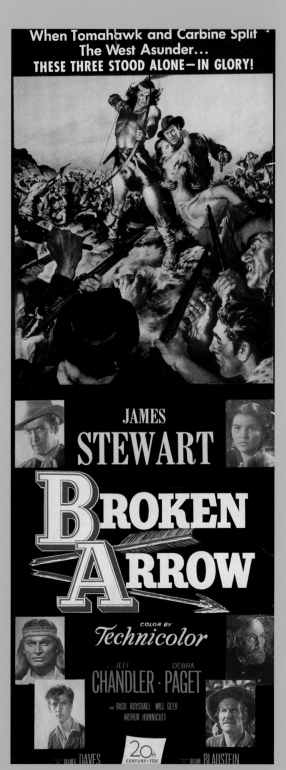

Advertisement for *The Outsider* (Universal, 1961), featuring Tony Curtis, from *Universal International Showman's Manual* (LC-USZ62-116695). Motion Picture. Copyright © 1961 by Universal City Studios, Inc. Courtesy of MCA Publishing Rights, a Division of MCA Inc. All Rights Reserved.

This biographical film illustrated the difficulties of being an Indian in U.S. society through the tragic life of World War II hero Ira Hamilton Hayes, a Pima Indian who died from alcoholism.

Motion picture poster from *Broken Arrow* (20th Century-Fox, 1950), featuring James Stewart, Jeff Chandler, and Debra Paget. C Mot. Pic. B 843 1 (LC-USZC4-3931). Prints and Photographs Division. Copyright 1950 20th Century-Fox Film Corporation. All Rights Reserved.

Broken Arrow *was the most influential of a wave of films in the 1950s which attempted to depict Indians in a more positive and sympathetic vein. In this film, Cochise is portrayed as a man of integrity, Indian society is portrayed as cultured, and an interracial marriage is condoned, although it ends with the death of the Indian woman and the return of the white man to "civilization."*

Motion picture poster from *Chief Crazy Horse* (Universal, 1955), featuring Victor Mature, Suzan Ball, and John Lund. C Mot. Pic. 1955 C55 1 (LC-USZC4-3932). Prints and Photographs Division. Copyright © 1955 by Universal City Studios, Inc. Courtesy of MCA Publishing Rights, a Division of MCA Inc. All rights reserved.

Although films in the 1950s, such as Chief Crazy Horse, *portrayed Indians sympathetically, they still continued to use non-Indian actors in the major Indian roles.*

Still from *Apache* (United Artists, 1954), featuring Burt Lancaster and Jean Peters (LC-USZ62-116696). Motion Picture Copyright 1954. United Artists Corporation. All Rights Reserved.

In an effort to show the Indian's point of view about white civilization, this film focused on one of Geronimo's braves who refused to surrender. This attempt by Hollywood to be sympathetic to the Indian cause was mitigated by an ending which showed the Indians conforming to a white lifestyle.

Still from *Little Big Man* (National General, 1970), featuring Dustin Hoffman and Robert Little Star (LC-USZ62-116697). Motion Picture. Courtesy of CBS, Inc.

Several feature films in the 1970s attempted to reverse stereotypes of Indians by portraying the atrocities of white soldiers, and by featuring Indian actors. Little Big Man *was told from a white man's viewpoint and, as such, served more as an allegory for what was happening in Vietnam at the time.*

Still from *A Man Called Horse* (National General, 1970), featuring Richard Harris and Dame Judith Anderson (LC-USZ62-116698). Motion Picture. Courtesy of CBS, Inc.

Promotion for this film stressed the authenticity of the Indian rituals portrayed and the language used, but critics charged that the film was highly inaccurate and that it was another depiction of the supposed superiority of white men.

MUSIC DIVISION AND RECORDED SOUND REFERENCE CENTER OF MOTION PICTURE, BROADCASTING AND RECORDED SOUND DIVISION

INTRODUCTION

Patrons come into contact with two large special collections when they enter the Performing Arts Reading Room. The Music Division holds some seven million items; the Recorded Sound Reference Center of the Motion Picture, Broadcasting and Recorded Sound Division is the access point for more than two million audio recordings. Given the size of these two collections and the knowledge that oral traditions such as songs and stories are major elements of cultural expression in tribal communities, the patron might expect that this reading room would be a major resource. The history of scholarship, documentation, and copyright, as well as of the institution itself, however, have made this presumption somewhat problematic.

Spoken language was transcribed according to varying phonetic schemes from the time Europeans made contact with native people. Until the late nineteenth century, however, very few Europeans and Americans wrote down more than brief impressions (usually critical) of Indian songs and dances. But with the growing belief that Indian cultures were dying, there was a move to document as much as could be found. With the invention of the cylinder recorder, ethnologists, folklorists, and linguists had a tool with which to capture the actual sounds of those cultures. By and large, however, the linguistic materials continued to be documented by phonetic transcription, and since most of the researchers had little experience with music, they typically chose to leave the analysis of song recordings to others. The field recordings themselves were not often gathered with the intention of actual publication. (The earliest published recordings of Indian songs were Berliner discs recorded in Washington, D.C., in July 1894; the singer was not an Indian, but rather the anthropologist Charles Mooney, or possibly his brother

James, singing Ghost Dance songs from five tribes.)

Turn-of-the-century Euro-American composers who wanted to evoke or create uniquely American sounds, however, sought out field recordings—or made their own—and used the melodic materials as well as general impressions of "Indian-ness" as resources for their own works. It is these compositions, rather than transcriptions of the actual recordings, for the most part, which ended up on sheet music decorated with generalized "Indian" motifs.

Sound recordings themselves could not be copyrighted until 1972. Before that, only transcriptions of music could be registered by the composer. Given that Indian people themselves did not generally think of songs as being composed as much as being received, that few songs were transcribed, and that few Native Americans were regular participants in the copyright process, the Indian-related material that has found its way to the Music Division is typically the work of non-Indian composers.

The same is true for the earliest commercial recordings accessed through the Recorded Sound Reference Center; these, even if recorded by Indian people, are directed primarily to non-Indian audiences. Working with these materials, we perhaps learn more about the audience's expectations and perceptions than about the cultures from which the musical motifs and iconography were derived. But this is important documentation in its own right of Indian and non-Indian history.

As time has passed, there have been more and more commercial recordings pertaining to Indian America. Some were recorded by scholars primarily for non-Indian audiences, others are on labels that sell principally to native people. A substantial number of these recordings can be accessed through the Recorded Sound Reference Center. But a tradition of privately-made recordings marketed solely at Indian events and occasionally by mail has also grown up in the past few decades. Producers of these relatively "homemade" recordings rarely send copies to the Library, so unless Library staff are aware of these publications and specifically order them, it is unlikely that the Library would have them. There is no mechanism to assess what may be missing from this category of publication.

The original unpublished ethnographic field recordings that came to the Library of Congress were placed in the Archive of Folk Song, initially part of the Music Division but transferred to the American Folklife Center after its creation in 1976. Those in search of primary sound-recording documentation will, therefore, need to visit the Folklife Reading Room.

USING THE COLLECTIONS

PERFORMING ARTS
READING ROOM

LOCATION: Madison Building, LM 113; telephone (202) 707-5507

HOURS: Monday through Friday, 8:30 A.M. to 5:00 P.M. (Listening service is also accessible on Saturdays, if appointments are made in person during the week).

MUSIC DIVISION

Only a small percentage of the Library's music holdings of more than seven million items is included in published book or computer catalogs distributed by the Library. The remainder is either uncataloged or can be accessed through catalog cards found only in the division itself or on-line at Library computer terminals. Readers should, therefore, first consult the reading room's reference staff for orientation in use of the collections.

Catalogs

The reading room contains several sets of card files for works cataloged up to 1980: the names catalog of composers, arrangers, and editors of musical scores; the title catalog for musical scores; the classed catalog scores (all entries for a specific call number); the catalog of literature about music (works for which the call number begins with "ML"); the catalog of instruction and study books (the "MT" entries); and special files and indexes. The periodical index cards include entries for many articles published from the 1880s to the 1940s.

The basic call number for American Indian music is M1669. Under this number will be found published collections that have been classified as music (as opposed to books *on* American Indian music in which the transcriptions are considered as illustrations rather than as the books' main purpose). M1669 includes much published music by the late nineteenth- and early twentieth-century Indianists—non-Indian composers who used American Indian melodies, mostly in simple voice-and-piano arrangements. Some Indianists, such as Charles Wakefield Cadman and Thurlow Lieurance, conducted their own fieldwork in American Indian communities to gather musical materials. Specific tribal sources and transcriptions of the Indian melodies are sometimes found in the printed music.

More ambitious Indianist compositions—those symphonies, suites, and string quartets "on Indian themes," for example, or songs "based on an Indian melody"—are classified not in M1669 but by their musical genre (symphony, M1001; orchestral suite, M1003; piano suite, M24; string quartet, M452; song with piano, M1621). Works in the larger forms can almost always be found in the Music Division's catalogs under composer and title; songs and piano pieces may have to be searched by classification

and composer within the collections themselves.

There is no subject approach to music on American Indian subjects, a category of work that could be of interest to those studying the image of Native Americans in works of other cultures. (A useful list of operas [but not musicals] on American Indian subjects may be found in H. Earle Johnson's *Operas on American Subjects* [New York: Coleman-Ross, 1964]; ML128.O4J6) Nor is there any subject access to works by individual American Indian composers.

"M2132.I5" is the heading for Indian language hymnals of North America. According to the classed catalog scores index, these include Apache, Cherokee, Cree, Dakota, Flathead/Kalispel/Spokane, Iroquois, and Narragansett material.

The "ML" catalog includes the subject heading "Indians of North America" and lists standard ethnomusicological texts with cross-references to anthropological and ethnographic sources in the "E," "GN," and "Q" areas of the General Collections; some of the references are linked as well to disc recordings. In addition, readers will find references to period pieces such as Saidee Knowland Coe's *Melodrama of Hiawatha* (1905).

Some other guides to the collection are available at the circulation desk and may be consulted with the help of the reference staff on duty. These include a card file for the division's special collections as well as ring binders containing Music Division and Archive of Folk Culture finding aids and bibliographies, and brief descriptions of the special collections.

❏ SELECTED COLLECTIONS

Frances Densmore Collection

Frances Densmore, a prominent collector of American Indian recordings (see the American

Folklife Center/Archive of Folk Culture entries), deposited important materials with the Music Division. Nineteen archival boxes contain nine annotated scrapbooks documenting her career; some correspondence and lectures; a typed chronology of her work; a few photographs, glass negatives, and lantern slides; and papers pertaining to an analysis by physicist Dayton C. Miller (see below) of samples of her Ute recordings. This collection is not as yet fully processed; until it is, it will be available to Library patrons only by prior appointment with the acquisitions and processing staff of the Music Division.

Natalie Curtis Burlin Collection

Material relating to the author of *The Indians' Book* includes four boxes containing handwritten transcriptions of mostly American Indian songs with some translations and other notes documenting use and ownership. Organized primarily by tribe, the collection has separate folios for Acoma, Apache, Arapaho, Cheyenne, Cocopa, Dakota, Hopi, Isleta, Kiowa, Kwakiutl, Laguna, Mohave/Apache, Navajo, Pawnee, Pima, San Juan, Seneca, Sioux, Wabanaki (including Maliseet, Passamaquoddy, and Penobscot), Winnebago, Yuma, and Zuni, in addition to miscellaneous non-Indian compositions. A few songs of other tribes are also found in the notebooks in some of the folios.

Miscellaneous Manuscript Collections

Special collections also include a fragile music manuscript underlaid with Micmac or Maliseet-Passamaquoddy texts for parts of the Catholic liturgy. The provenance of the manuscript is unclear, but it probably dates back to the nineteenth century.

Several other collections also pertain to gatherers of American Indian material (e.g., Charles Wakefield Cadman, Willard Rhodes, the Lieurance correspondence in the Taubeneck collection) but do not necessarily focus on that part of their careers.

The Dayton C. Miller Flute Collection

Dayton C. Miller (1866–1941), a professor of astronomy and physics at the Case School of Applied Science in Cleveland, Ohio, spent much of his life collecting flutes and primary material concerning the instrument's history and development. Hoping to establish a national archive for scholarly studies of the flute at the Library of Congress, he bequeathed his collection to the nation. He died before these plans could be realized, but the instruments, books, and related materials were moved to the Library.

Of the more than 1,600 flutes in Miller's collection, approximately 120 are American Indian. While Miller's books on flutes and flute music are available in the Performing Arts Reading Room, the instruments themselves may be viewed only by appointment. Inquiries should be directed to the Curator, Dayton C. Miller Collection, Library of Congress, Music Division, Washington, D.C. 20540. Patrons may also call (202) 707-9083 to arrange a time.

In 1961 the Music Division published a checklist of the instruments. Compiled by Laura E. Gilliam and William Lichtenwanger, *The Dayton C. Miller Flute Collection* follows the numbering assigned by Dr. Miller, roughly chronological by date of acquisition. The index for "Primitive, Folk, and Oriental Instruments," on pages 114–15, lists most of the North American Indian flutes by tribal source, where that is known. Note, however, that Miller purchased many of the Indian flutes from curio stores and dealers around the country, especially N. E. Carter of Elkhorn, Wisconsin. Confirmation of the Indian source is available in relatively few cases: see, for example, the

GATEWAYS

In Indian languages, there is not always a generic word for "music" as Euro-Americans usually think of the term (encompassing both vocal and instrumental expression). Instead, there are words for "song"—for texted melodies. Even in cases where the only audible sound is instrumental, as in flute melodies, there is usually an underlying text of which the player is conscious. The texts, however, are frequently not words found in the singer's spoken language, but are instead vocables—"nonlexical" syllables, such as "hey" or "na," that are not randomly chosen but fall into patterns shaped by linguistic, song genre, and musical considerations.

Studies of Indian musical expression typically divide the area north of Mexico into "culture areas," such as Woodlands, Plains (Northern and Southern), Southwest, California, Great Basin, Plateau, Northwest, Subarctic, and Arctic. Each area has different musical characteristics and song genres not found elsewhere. The style that has come to typify pantribal "Indian" music—characterized by songs that start high (men in falsetto) and descend, by a tense vocal style, and by the use of a large drum around which a group of singers clusters—is Northern Plains in origin. Songs from other regions have different forms and melodic shapes, different characteristic rhythms, and use other kinds of drums or no drums at all. But the Hollywood Indian "BOOM boom boom boom" drum rhythm is rarely, if ever, heard.

Songs constitute property in many areas. Songs often originate in dreams and may be conveyed from person to person by formal rites of transfer. Song performance often includes the telling of the song's origin.

Over the course of time, some song genres have declined as the occasions for their use have passed, while new ones have arisen and others have been adapted in response to changing contexts. The tradition of war dance songs, for example, once used to commemorate intertribal conflict, now honors the experiences of Indian members of the armed forces in the World Wars, in Korea, in Vietnam, and in the Persian Gulf.

Like song, dance permeates Indian cultures and is manifested in different ways depending on function and context, whether social, ceremonial, or courtship. Filled with meaning and rich symbolism, dances take different forms in different areas—from the counterclockwise circles typical of Iroquoian dances, to the clockwise Sun Dance circuits of the Plains, to the straight lines of Great Basin Bear Dances, to the individual exhibitions of competitive powwow "fancy dancers." In many cases, events called dances are ceremonial complexes that include not only movements to song, but also specific roles, prayers, site preparation, regalia, timing, and food.

WHERE TO LOOK: American Folklife Center, Music Division, Recorded Sound Reference Center of the Motion Picture, Broadcasting and Recorded Sound Division, Prints and Photographs Division, and the General Collections.

Dance contestants and drum arbor in the center of the arena, Omaha powwow, Macy, Nebraska, 1986. Photograph by Dorothy Sara Lee (Federal Cylinder Project; FCP/0-86-DSL-2-13). American Folklife Center.

Dance contests are part of many current powwows. Here three men in the Men's Traditional (or Straight Dance) category await the judges. Several drum groups are under the arbor—one identified as the Host Drum, the others invited guests. The drums take turns providing the songs for the dance competitors.

Winnebago flute (#242 in Miller's collection) made by John Spear; the Ute instrument (#205) made by Henry Johnson especially for the collection, and purchased through Frances Densmore; the Quapaw flute (#480) made by Red Fox, a gift to Miller from Thurlow Lieurance [this last flute is not listed in the index].

The checklist identifies flutes from the following communities (using Miller's or his agents' names for the tribes): Apache, Arapaho, Blackfeet, Cheyenne, Chippewa/Ojibwa/Pillager, Crow, Haida, Iroquois, Kickapoo, "Kichai," Kwakiutl, Mandan, "Moki" (Hopi), Omaha, Osage, Pawnee, Potowatomi, Pueblo, Quapaw, Sac and Fox, Seminole, Shoshone, Sioux, Ute, Umatilla, "Utsehta or Little Osage," Winnebago, Yuki, Yuman, and Yurok. About twenty-five flutes are of unknown tribal origin.

RECORDED SOUND REFERENCE CENTER OF THE MOTION PICTURE, BROADCASTING AND RECORDED SOUND DIVISION

The Performing Arts Reading Room is also the point of access—through the Recorded Sound Reference Center—to the approximately three million sound recordings and radio broadcasts of the Motion Picture, Broadcasting and Recorded Sound Division (whose film collections are described in the preceding section of this guide).

Commercial recordings have been cataloged by the Library since 1951 and are accessible through computer databases and separate card catalogs. However, only 10–20 percent of the Library's collection of commercial recordings has been cataloged to date. The pre-MARC database contains materials cataloged between 1951 and 1984; post-1984 cataloging is found in MUMS. In addition, copyrighted sound recordings released since 1978 are listed in the copyright computer

catalog (COHM) by title, performer, and copyright claimant; perhaps 10 percent of these receive full Library cataloging. Another place to search is the OCLC CD-ROM database which gives subject access and, unlike MUMS, will also index by record company. The Recorded Sound Reference Center staff provides assistance in searching the different catalogs.

A patron should begin by checking the card files and computers, but because such a small percentage of the Library's sound recording holdings has been fully cataloged, the failure to find a listing does not automatically mean that a recording is not in the Library. Further, in pre-MARC listings, the method that was used for coding sound recordings may cause the computer to give an erroneous "Not in LC Collection" message. The reference staff will assist the researcher in assessing such messages and choosing various means of locating material.

Most commercial releases are shelved numerically by recording company. Among the best guides to the collections, therefore, are the many record manufacturers' or other trade catalogs on file in the reference center, or listed there and filed in the Music Division. Once a label and number are located, a search can be made for the recording. Note, however, that the presence of a manufacturer's catalog does not indicate that all of those recordings will be in the Library's collection.

The card catalog in the reference center is searchable by album title, performer or ensemble, and subject. It provides some listings of American Indian recordings following the heading "Indians of North America" as well as after individual tribal names and some song genres ("sun dance" and "chicken scratch," for example, but not "ghost dance" or "stomp dance"). There are also some materials *about* Indians, found in entries such as "Indians—Lectures" or "Indians—Treatment of." The subject cataloging may be based partially on song or composition titles, for sometimes a Euro-American orchestral piece with a tribal name in its title is found among that tribe's entries.

Note as well the segment of the card catalog labeled "Recorded Sound Catalog Supplement: Index of Uncataloged Items." Many Indian entries here are for items in the American Folklife Center's Archive of Folk Culture or for performances of Indianist compositions like the "Indian Love Call," but there are also a few cassettes of Indian languages.

The Library acquires commercial recordings through the copyright process, through gifts, and through purchase. Unfortunately for the researcher, as noted in the introduction, many American Indian recordings were and are released by small independent producers who do not necessarily copyright their materials or distribute them nationally. While Library staff are making efforts to locate such recordings, many releases may not find their way into this national repository. Larger labels such as Canyon, Indian House, and Folkways, however, are better represented.

Researchers may wish to consult volume five of Richard K. Spottswood's *Ethnic Music on Records: A Discography of Ethnic Recordings Produced in the United States, 1893 to 1942* (University of Illinois Press, 1990; ML156.4.F5 S69). Pages 2927–34 describe a variety of commercial disc releases, some authentic Indian songs, others the works of Indianist composers like Carlos Troyer and Thurlow Lieurance. Another useful source is the *Rigler and Deutsch Index*, a union catalog of the 78rpm discs in five U.S. libraries (Syracuse, Stanford, and Yale Universities; the New York Public Library; and the Library of Congress). This index is based on literal transcriptions from the recording labels, so users should anticipate the need to search for variant forms and spellings of names and titles. The index provides no subject access.

Other resources in the Recorded Sound Reference Center include the microfiche indices and databases for major radio broadcasting collections. National Public Radio (NPR), Pacifica, and British Broadcasting Corporation (BBC) programs can be searched by subject on microfiche. The NPR index covering 1971 through 1983 includes over seven hundred entries under "Indians, America." Note, however, that while NPR transfers recordings of its cultural programming broadcasts to the Library (about five years after initial broadcast), its news and public affairs programs are housed at the National Archives. Many of the Indian topics appear to fall under the "news" heading and would not, therefore, be available in the Library. The Pacifica index identifies approximately one hundred fifty programs under "Indians of North America." To determine which of these are in the Library collections, patrons will need to consult the computer database, searching by title or subject. The BBC lists about thirty programs under "Red Indians;" those with a cataloging number beginning with "LP" may be in the Library's collections.

The Library also holds over 175,000 discs of National Broadcasting Company (NBC) radio broadcasts between 1935 and 1970. A rapidly growing database available on microcomputer in the Reference Center already provides subject access to more than 30,000 items. Among them, for example, are radio dramas and educational series ("The World is Yours," "Lands of the Free," "Music of the New World," etc.) that present various images of Indian societies.

There are additional collections accessed through the Recorded Sound Reference Center that include some Indian-related material. For example, the recordings in the Margaret Mead collection include two interviews with Atsugewi people in 1963 and a symposium, "On Indians and Anthropologists," held at the 1970 meeting of the American Anthropological Association.

Researchers should work with the reference staff to locate other published and unpublished indexes to sound recordings.

LISTENING FACILITIES

Performing Arts Reading Room multi-purpose rooms are available for listening to commercially-recorded materials, broadcasts, and field recordings for which there is as yet no reference tape. The Recorded Sound Reference Center staff will guide the patron through the procedures required to listen to such recordings and to see album covers or other documentation. Though the Recorded Sound Reference Center itself is closed on the weekend, patrons who visit the Library during the week may make listening appointments for Saturday. The materials they request will then be available through the Performing Arts Reading Room desk.

Recordings are heard through speakers in the listening rooms. A handout identifies guidelines for listening. Copying of recordings is not permitted; tape recordings or equipment may not be taken into the listening area. Patrons may purchase tape copies of recordings from the Library's Recording Laboratory after written authorization is acquired from those who possess legal rights.

Frances Densmore and Mountain Chief, member of the Blackfeet tribe, listening to a cylinder recording, 1916. Photograph by Harris and Ewing. (Similar to LC-USZ62-107289). Prints and Photographs Division.

Densmore, the well-known "collaborator" for the Smithsonian Institution's Bureau of American Ethnology, is shown here with Mountain Chief. They are listening to a recording, as is evident by the playback horn on the cylinder machine in front of Densmore (a recording horn is narrow and does not flare out at the end). Mountain Chief apparently was translating what he heard into sign language. It is possible that they were listening to cylinder recordings gathered by Walter McClintock in Montana in 1898, including words that Mountain Chief had recorded. The recordings Densmore herself made, as well as the McClintock Blackfeet collection, are presently in the American Folklife Center collections, while Densmore's scrapbooks are in the Music Division.

Flutes from the Dayton C. Miller collection: Flute #480–obtained from Red Fox, a Quapaw of Miami, Oklahoma in 1925. Gift of Thurlow Lieurance, a collector of cylinder recordings; Flute #205–made for the collection by Henry Johnson, a Ute, in 1921. Purchased from Frances Densmore, a collector of cylinder recordings; Flute #242–made for the collection by John Spear, a Nebraska Winnebago, in 1922. Purchased from Oliver La Mere, of the family included in the Paul Radin cylinder collection.

These flutes from the Music Division's Dayton C. Miller collection are related to sound recording collectors or performers whose materials are in the Archive of Folk Culture.

ABOVE: *Navajo War Dance* by Arthur Farwell (Newton Center, Mass.: The Wa-Wan Press, 1905). M1669 (LC-USZ62-116699). Music Division.

In this piano piece, Arthur Farwell, an Indianist composer, conveyed his impression of Navajo music through the use of the repeated single note in the left hand (imitating a drum) and a right-hand melody consisting primarily of skips rather than adjacent notes. See also his instructions on how to play the piece: "with severe precision of rhythm throughout, and savagely accented."

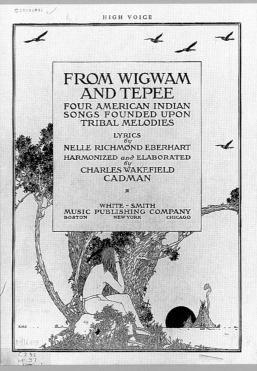

RIGHT: *Indian Songs* by Thurlow Lieurance (Philadelphia: Theodore Dresser Co., 19?) (LC-USZ62-116700); and *From Wigwam and Tepee* by Charles Wakefield Cadman (Boston: White-Smith Music Publishing Co., 19?) (LC-USZ62-116701). Both M1669. Music Division.

Sheet music covers for Indianist compositions by Thurlow Lieurance and Charles Wakefield Cadman (both collectors of Indian recordings—see the American Folklife Center entries). The design motifs—lone Indian males next to trees, tipis, the moon and setting sun, and a courting flute—convey a sense of closeness to nature as well as an impression, perhaps, that songs are individualistic expressions removed from the hustle and bustle of daily life.

Relocation by XIT. Canyon Record C-7121, 1977 (LC-USZC4-4823). Recorded Sound Center of Motion Picture, Broadcasting and Recorded Sound Division.

This album, released in 1977 by the intertribal group XIT, features rock songs that include historical commentary ("Christopher Columbus") or draw on elements of social dances such as the "49 (a genre in which songs often incorporate an English-language phrase or two).

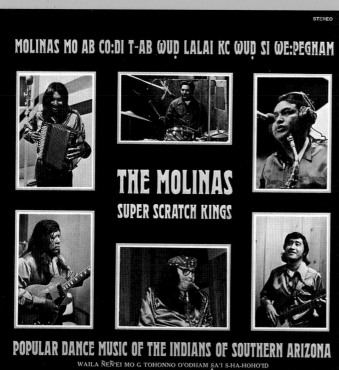

The Molinas: Super Scratch Kings: Popular Dance Music of the Indians of Southern Arizona. Canyon Record C-6128, 1975 (LC-USZ62-116702). Recorded Sound Center of Motion Picture, Broadcasting and Recorded Sound Division.

"Waila" or "chicken scratch" music is a popular dance tradition among the Tohono O'odham (Papago) people of southern Arizona. Evolving from an ensemble featuring fiddles to one composed of accordion, saxophone, electric (or amplified acoustic) guitar and bass, and drums, waila bands provide the music for dances such as the polka-like waila, the chota (schottische), and cumbia (a dance showing Hispanic influences).

Turtle Dance Songs of San Juan Pueblo. Indian House 1101, 1972 (LC-USZ62-116703). Recorded Sound Center of Motion Picture, Broadcasting and Recorded Sound Division.

The Turtle Dance, which takes place at the winter solstice, is a major public religious ceremony at San Juan. Named for the turtle (described as the first hibernating being that moves about after the beginning of a new annual cycle), the dance defines the end of one year and the beginning of the next. The dancers, all male, carry gourd rattles and evergreen branches. Turtle shell rattles are tied to their right knees.

Handgame of the Kiowa, Kiowa Apache, & Comanche: Carnegie Roadrunners vs. Billy Goat Hill. Indian House 2501, 1972 (LC-USZ62-116704). Recorded Sound Center of Motion Picture, Broadcasting and Recorded Sound Division.

Recorded live in Carnegie, Oklahoma, in 1968, this album (and its cover photo) demonstrate the excitement of such an event. Two teams face each other. Each team sings, in part to distract the other, whenever it has a turn to hide two plain and two marked sticks in the hands of two team members. The singing stops when the sticks are hidden. The opposition then guesses the location of the marked sticks, using gestures to signify the choices. The object, ultimately, is to win the set of sticks used for score-keeping. Handgames are occasions for vigorous socializing and sometimes gambling.

AMERICAN FOLKLIFE CENTER

INTRODUCTION

American Indian culture has been preserved over the centuries primarily by oral and physical rather than written means. Even today, the past is continually brought to life as parents and grandparents tell children the stories, sing the songs, and perform the dances that had been passed along to them. One of the Library's principal collections of unique American Indian materials, therefore, is the more than one thousand hours of ethnographic sound recordings located in the American Folklife Center. While the emphasis of these recordings is on oral traditions (both spoken and sung), they also document aspects of cultural expression such as dance and ceremonial complexes.

Established within the Library by an act of Congress in 1976, the center is charged with the preservation and presentation of American folklife, defined in Public Law 94-201 as the "traditional, expressive, shared culture of various groups in the United States." Serving a varied constituency, the center coordinates programs with other government agencies, academic organizations, and local groups; and offers a wide range of programs and services, such as reference and research facilities, archival preservation, field projects, publications, conferences, exhibitions, workshops, concerts, advisory assistance, and equipment loans.

The Archive of Folk Culture, established in 1928, became part of the Folklife Center in 1978. Originally called the Archive of American Folk-Song, it was renamed to reflect the subject breadth of its multiformat holdings. The Archive consists of more than forty thousand hours of recordings, two hundred thousand photographs, and more than six hundred thousand pages of manuscript material, as well as a number of video recordings, microfilms, material objects, and other formats. Acquisitions stem from fieldwork by staff members, donations of materials, and duplication of major collections from the United States and other nations.

The Library's acquisition of American Indian recordings began within a decade of the establishment of the Archive of Folk-Song. Starting in 1936, the noted ethnomusicologist Helen Heffron Roberts gave the Library her original cylinder recordings plus disc copies of California Indian songs as well as Blackfeet, Flathead, and Pacific Basin material collected by others. The Library also collaborated in field projects with outside agencies by supplying recording equipment, technical assistance, archiving facilities, and sometimes funding. Between 1944 and 1946, for example, Henrietta Yurchenco was engaged by the Library of Congress, the Inter-American Indian Institute, and the Department of Education of Mexico to document music of isolated Indian communities in Mexico and Guatemala. From 1940 to 1952, Willard Rhodes of Columbia University recorded the music of approximately fifty tribes in this country in the course of working for the Bureau of Indian Affairs, partly with Library-supplied equipment.

Most of the early recordings documenting American Indian traditions were made on wax cylinders by employees or contractees ("collaborators") of the Smithsonian Institution Bureau of American Ethnology (BAE). After a brief transfer from the Smithsonian to the National Archives, the BAE cylinders were moved to the Library of Congress, where they were preserved through duplication on disc and later on tape by staff of the Library's Recording Laboratory. In time, other institutions and individuals added their collections, making the Library currently the largest repository of such early recordings. In 1979, the American Folklife Center initiated the Federal Cylinder Project to further preserve and catalog the ten thousand ethnographic cylinders now in

the Archive. Part of this project was the dissemination of copies of the American Indian material to the communities of origin. To date, five catalog volumes have been published, and cassette copies of relevant cylinder collections have been given to more than one hundred Indian communities. The American Folklife Center also collaborated with the Omaha Tribal Council to produce an album of turn-of-the-century recordings of Omaha songs assembled by Fletcher and LaFlesche (see their collection description).

In the course of the Omaha project, Center staff recorded and photographed several annual powwows. Such contemporary documentation of Indian traditions has also been part of the center's field projects in Chicago (1977), Paradise Valley, Nevada (1978–82), and Montana (1979); a study of ethnic heritage and language schools (1982); and the ongoing work of the Federal Cylinder Project; as well as several concerts and lectures sponsored by the center at the Library. Visitors to the center may consult these files, photos, and recordings.

USING THE COLLECTIONS

FOLKLIFE READING ROOM

LOCATION: Jefferson Building, Ground floor, Room LJ G17 (temporary); telephone (202) 707-5510

HOURS: Monday through Friday, 8:30 A.M.– 5:00 P.M.

ACCESS AND USE: Appointments for more than three people are recommended. A Library of Congress photo I.D. card is required for registration. Permissions issues will arise for most phonoduplication and some photoduplication requests.

In addition to serving as the access point for the Archive of Folk Culture ethnographic collections, the center's reading room has several thousand books, indices, and periodicals pertaining to folk music and folklore—a sampling of the many relevant works in the Library's collections. Here readers may use standard publications as well as sizable collections of magazines, newsletters, posters and other ephemera, unpublished theses and dissertations, plus many bibliographic, subject, and collection-related files. More than two hundred bibliographies, directories, and finding aids describing the collections (some on American Indian groups or topics) have been prepared by staff members and are available to the public free of charge. As in other divisions, readers are encouraged to consult the reference staff for assistance in locating information on American Indian topics.

In addition, the Library has published eighty-six LP or cassette recordings from the Archive's collections; twenty contain samplings of American Indian materials recorded by Frances Densmore, William Fenton, Alice Fletcher and Francis LaFlesche, and Willard Rhodes. These recordings may be purchased in the Library's gift shop or by mail order.

Other relevant publications include the American Folklife Center's *Folklife Annual* for 1987, containing two richly illustrated articles on Indian powwows and community gatherings; the *Folklife Center News*, which occasionally features articles on Native American collections; and the ten issues of *American Folk Music and Folklore Recordings: A Selected List*, an annotated discography of thirty to forty releases annually from 1983 to 1992 that were judged by an independent panel of specialists to feature American folk and ethnic cultural traditions in a well-documented manner. American Indian recordings were among those listed.

Patrons may request copies of manuscript, photographic, and recorded materials in person or by mail. Order forms, billing information, and notification of necessary permissions will be provided. After permissions are obtained (where applicable), such orders are filled by the Library's Recording Laboratory and other duplicating services.

❏ SELECTED COLLECTIONS

Collections from the American Philosophical Society Library

In 1970 several ethnographic collections of wire and disc recordings were sent to the Library for preservation duplication. Among the North American Indian materials are Nootka and Makah stories gathered by Morris Swadesh, Tlingit recordings by Frederica de Laguna and Catherine McClellan, Tonawanda Seneca songs recorded by Martha Randle, and Northern and Southern Cheyenne material from Kenneth Croft.

The Laura Boulton Collections

Boulton (1899–1980) documented world music in the course of more than twenty expeditions on five continents. Her collections—over thirteen hundred discs and three hundred fifty tapes—also include some material recorded by others. Boulton's American Indian materials are primarily from the Southwest and from Canada.

Collections from the Bureau of American Ethnology (BAE)

The core of the ethnographic cylinder collections now at the Library of Congress, the thirty-five hundred BAE recordings were assembled by many people. Those who contributed most to the documentation process include:

Alice Cunningham Fletcher (1838–1923) An Office of Indian Affairs employee who assisted with the land allotment procedure on the Omaha and Nez Perce reservations, Fletcher is known primarily for her documentation of Omaha ceremonies in collaboration with her adopted son, Francis LaFlesche. Her home in Washington, apparently in the block where the Library of Congress's Madison Building now stands, was the site of many recordings made by members of visiting Indian delegations at the turn of the century. The Library has published the Alice Fletcher / Francis LaFlesche recording, *Omaha Indian Music* (AFS L71)

Francis LaFlesche (1857–1932) Son of Joseph LaFlesche (who, though half French, was one of the last traditional Omaha chiefs), Francis LaFlesche was the first American Indian professional anthropologist. His major work was the documentation of Osage rituals, the written portion of which is found in a series of BAE publications.

Frances Densmore (1867–1957) Most prolific of the cylinder collectors, Densmore gathered more than twenty-five hundred recordings from members of forty tribes between 1907 and the early 1940s; she also organized the cylinder collections of other BAE employees. Since she worked intensively with Library staff on the production of the published recordings drawn from her cylinder material, abundant correspondence is available, along with copies of the BAE bulletins in which she published her descriptions of dance, musical and other ceremonial events, commentaries, and musical analyses.

The Library has published sampler recordings drawn from the Frances Densmore collections. They are:

Songs of the Chippewa (AFS L22)
Songs of the Sioux (AFS L23)
Songs of the Yuma, Cocopa, and Yaqui (AFS L24)
Songs of the Pawnee and Northern Ute (AFS L25)
Songs of the Papago (AFS L31)
Songs of the Nootka and Quileute (AFS L32)
Songs of the Menominee, Mandan and Hidatsa (AFS L33)

John Peabody Harrington (1884–1961) An ethnologist and linguist, Harrington recorded primarily California Indian songs and speech on more than three hundred cylinders and one hundred discs. Voluminous documentation of his work is housed at the National Anthropological Archives in the Smithsonian Institution.

Indians for Indians Hour Collection

In 1988 the Western History Collection at the University of Oklahoma in Norman sent the Library a collection of discs for preservation duplication. The 121 discs contain WNAD radio broadcasts made between 1943 and 1950. Developed and emceed by Don Whistler, a Sac and Fox chief, the programs include songs by more than five hundred people from eighteen Oklahoma tribes.

Collections from the Peabody Museum of Harvard University

In 1970 the Peabody Museum presented the Library with more than two hundred fifty cylinders, including those from the first documented use of a phonograph for ethnological research: Jesse Walter Fewkes's recordings of two Passamaquoddy men in March 1890. Other American Indian collections include Fewkes's recordings of Zuni and Hopi, Benjamin Ives Gilman's recordings of Kwakiutl participants in the 1893 World's Columbian Exposition in Chicago, turn-of-the-century Navajo recordings collected by Washington Matthews, and Nez Perce cylinders made by Herbert Spinden.

The Willard Rhodes Collections

Through the transfer of material from the Bureau of Indian Affairs and a gift of Dr. Rhodes in 1964, the Library acquired approximately two hundred seventy original discs and fifty tapes of American

GATEWAYS

Despite years of vigorous suppression, and even prohibition, of sacred ceremonies by the Bureau of Indian Affairs and various Christian groups, many Native Americans have tenaciously retained their ancient spiritual beliefs and practices. Although surviving religions vary from tribe to tribe, commonalities exist. Spiritual beliefs form a cornerstone of tribal cultural identity. Native religion is reflected in virtually all areas of native societies from child-naming practices and medicinal approaches to hand-made objects used in daily life such as cradleboards, clothing, and utensils. Dances of all kinds usually involve some facet of religious belief.

Most American Indian religions include creation stories. They recount how the world, its people, and the complexities of the human condition came into being. These sacred oral histories differ among tribes, usually according to geographical tribal origin and historical patterns of subsistence such as gathering, hunting, fishing, and farming. Accordingly, an inextricable link between nature and religion often exists among Indian people, emphasizing reverence and harmony.

Many Native Americans experience spiritual guidance through sacred ceremonies such as fasting, sun dances, vision quests, and sweat lodges. At rituals and ceremonies, dance forms part of the complex celebrating the physical and spiritual worlds. In effect, dance serves as a connection between the natural and the spiritual world. Sacred objects, which include drums, medicine bundles, pipes, rattles, masks, feathers, and corn ears, to name a few, are often an integral part of religious practices. Many ceremonies are only conducted at specific natural locations such as mountains, lakes, and mounds, all of which may be ancient sacred sites of worship. In these traditional places, believers reverentially communicate with spiritual powers, ancestors, humans, plants and animals, and glean spiritual sustenance.

It was not until 1934 that the federal government ceased regulatory action—begun in the nineteenth century and inconsistently applied—to suppress the practice of traditional Indian religions. Today Native Americans are understandably concerned about protecting and preserving their religious freedom. Efforts to bolster the American Indian Religious Freedom Act of 1978 have increased as sacred sites throughout the country have been threatened or destroyed by logging, ski resorts, mining, hydroelectric plants, and careless land development. Unlike Judaeo-Christian worshippers, Indian practitioners of native religions do not always arbitrarily construct places of worship.

A 1994 amendment to the American Indian Religious Freedom Act, which legalizes the use of peyote by Indians for religious purposes, represents a major victory for Native American Church members, who for years have actively defended its use as a sacrament in their ceremonies. Tribal leaders are increasingly requesting that religious and funerary objects which are stored and displayed in non-Indian museums be returned to the tribes under the 1990 Native American Graves Protection and Repatriation Act. Drug and alcohol treatment programs, based on traditional spiritual principles, healing ceremonies, and tribal medicine, are also proliferating on reservations nationwide.

WHERE TO LOOK: Studies and evidence of Native American religions, or related legal statutes, can be found in General Collections, American Folklife Center, Law Library, and Rare Book and Special Collections, Manuscript, and Prints and Photographs Divisions.

Ponca Indian Sun Dance. Silver gelatin print by Thomas Croft, 1894. LOT 12831. (LC-USZ62-100432). Prints and Photographs Division.

During the sacred Sun Dance ceremonial, which is common among Plains Indian tribes, participants seek spiritual renewal through a series of rituals, some of which demand extraordinary physical endurance.

Indian songs from a series of field trips Rhodes made between 1940 and 1952. The ten LPs based on these collections that were released by the Library in cooperation with the Bureau of Indian Affairs and the Indian Arts and Crafts Board are listed below; Rhodes also edited two LPs for Folkways Records:

Northwest (Puget Sound) (AFS L34)
Kiowa (AFS L35)
Indian Songs of Today (AFS L36)
Delaware, Cherokee, Choctaw, Creek (AFS L37)
Great Basin: Paiute, Washo, Ute, Bannock, Shoshone (AFS L38)
Plains: Comanche, Cheyenne, Kiowa, Caddo, Wichita, Pawnee (AFS L39)
Sioux (AFS L40)
Navajo (AFS L41)
Apache (AFS L42)
Pueblo: Taos, San Ildefonso, Zuni, Hopi (AFS L43)

The Helen Heffron Roberts Collections

As noted above, Roberts (1888–1985) was the first to donate American Indian recordings to the Archive of Folk-Song. Beginning in 1936, she gave the Library approximately two hundred fifty cylinders and three hundred sixty disc copies of her own and other collectors' cylinder recordings of songs, together with extensive fieldnotes and transcriptions of her work.

Collections from the School of American Research

In 1979 this Santa Fe organization transferred several cylinder collections to the Library. Among them are Mescalero and Chiricahua Apache recordings made in 1931 by members of a field ethnology training school, Ernest Beaglehole's Hopi materials, Acoma rituals recorded by Bernhardt Reuter, and various Pueblo recordings made by Helen Roberts.

Collections from the Mary C. Wheelwright Museum

In 1972 the museum transferred southwestern Indian recordings to the Library of Congress. Most notable among the collections are the 1,285 cylinders documenting Navajo Creation and Hail chants, Beadway and Blessingway rituals, collected in 1929 and 1932 by George Herzog (1901–83). Herzog was the founder of ethnomusicological studies in American academic institutions and of the Archives of Folk and Primitive Music (now the Archives of Traditional Music at Indiana University).

Zuni Storytelling Collections

In 1991, the Archive of Folk Culture received over fifty hours of Zuni storytelling in the Zuni and English languages, accompanied by transcriptions and translations. This project, "Telapna:we—Zuni Verbal Art in Performance," was undertaken by the Pueblo of Zuni and funded by the Folk Arts Program of the National Endowment for the Arts. In the course of collecting this material from seven storytellers, project members located some four hundred fifty hours of storytelling tapes recorded by twenty-two Zunis in 1967 as part of the Doris Duke Oral History Project. The Library of Congress has agreed to purchase and conserve the 1967 tapes, which in due course will be added to the collection already here.

❏ AMERICAN INDIAN RECORDINGS

The table below provides information on collections of American Indian recordings in the Folklife Center's Archive of Folk Culture, arranged alphabetically by tribe.

Each entry identifies the relevant accession numbers, the collector (usually individuals but in some cases institutions), the known or approximate date(s) of the collection, and the estimated duration of the material. The Archive of Folk Culture labels American Indian collections according to the tribal affiliation of the performers: this means, for example, that songs of Sioux origin recorded by Frances Densmore from Chippewa singers are considered part of her Chippewa collection.

In some cases, the documentation for a collection does not completely specify the tribe; there are, for example, collections identified only as "Iroquois" or "Sioux," while others indicate which Iroquois and Siouan tribal or linguistic subgroups ("Mohawk," "Teton," or "Lakota," for example) are included. To help the reader locate all relevant collections, the list groups all "Iroquois" and "Sioux" recordings together, but points out (by means of parenthetical notes) whatever subgroups have been labeled. "N" and "S" are used to indicate northern and southern branches of tribes such as the Cheyenne and Ute. Since collectors usually identified specific pueblos, readers should look first for the particular pueblo names rather than to the general "Pueblo" category. In certain instances, such as the Puget Sound recordings of Willard Rhodes, decisions were made to group closely related communities under one heading. Readers seeking information on a tribe in close proximity to other groups (e.g., Mandan, Hidatsa, and Arikara) may also find relevant materials among the entries under the related names.

Tribal affiliations have tentatively been assigned to some collections based on the specific location(s) where the recordings were made, and are therefore followed by question marks. Other collections can only be listed as "Unidentified," with a general geographical reference if one is known.

Recordings in Archive of Folk Culture collections are located principally by their catalog numbers. Until 1991, each original recording or its preservation copy was assigned an "AFS" (originally meaning "Archive of Folk Song")

number—and those are the numbers listed in the table. Starting in 1991, the American Folklife Center staff has assigned accession numbers that begin with the year and the sequence in which the materials were processed—"1991/001" and so on. Several collections already in the Library to which the new numbering sequence has been applied are identified by the AFC designation in the "AFS Number" column.

Some AFS numbers are followed by an asterisk. This indicates that there are materials belonging to other tribes within the specified range of AFS numbers. Where it was feasible to be specific about the tape locations of materials from one group, this has been done, but in many instances, a collection contains recordings from several tribes or ethnic groups, and the material belonging to one community is scattered throughout; or a preservation tape contains materials from several locations or collections. This is particularly true for the Willard Rhodes and Laura Boulton collections, as well as for materials from some of Frances Densmore's field trips.

Some collections, especially of cylinders, came to the Library in increments over the years. Consequently these materials were not always transferred to preservation tape or assigned AFS numbers at the same time, so these collections as wholes are not numbered consecutively. In such cases, the AFS numbers for the first portion of each collection are noted, followed by a plus (+) sign to indicate that more numbers apply.

Collection dates can suggest the original recording medium and its typical characteristics. For example, with very few exceptions, the pre-1930s material was recorded on cylinders; such collections are often partially obscured by surface noise and broken into two-minute segments.

Many persons begin their searches by requesting information on materials from a particular tribe or gathered by a particular collector. Quite often, however, both visiting researchers and those who send inquiries by mail are looking for recordings of a particular singer or of a specific song or dance genre. The reference staff frequently can oblige with detailed information, but they are dependent on whatever documentation accompanied the collections. Sometimes there was no index with a collection, or the documentation is fragmentary and confusing. With the help of Indian consultants and knowledgeable persons, the American Folklife Center staff is clarifying the unidentified portions of American Indian collections.

While the following pages attempt to cover the materials currently available, given the dimensions of the collections the list is incomplete. Patrons should check further with the reference staff.

* includes materials belonging to other tribes   + additional AFS numbers apply   ? tentative tribal affiliations

AMERICAN INDIAN RECORDINGS IN ARCHIVE OF FOLK CULTURE

TRIBE	AFS NUMBERS	COLLECTOR	DATE	APPROXIMATE DURATION
Achumawi	10,501–10,502*	Jaime de Angulo	1949	50 min.
Acoma	10,712B–10,718; other versions: 21,268–21,270, 21,835–21,837	Stirling/Densmore	1928	3.2 hrs.
Acoma	14,069–14,071*	Robert Black	1957	5 hrs.
Acoma	19,471–19,501	Bernhardt Reuter	1929–30	62 hrs.
Acoma	19,502–19,508*	Helen H. Roberts	1929–30	1.3 hrs.
Alabama	10,736–10,739+	Frances Densmore	1932	1.7 hrs.
Aleut	15,414–15,419	J.P. Harrington	1941	6 hrs.
Apache	3314–3315*	M. Valiant (FSA)	1939	10 min.
Apache	9541B–9542A	Willard Rhodes	1941	20 min.
Apache	12,269–12,273*	Willard Rhodes	1949	30 min.
Apache	13,560	Russell Mosby	1949	8 min.
Apache	14,618–14,623*	Willard Rhodes	1951	2.6 hrs.
Apache	14,624B	Willard Rhodes	1952	4 min.
Apache	15,467	J.D. Robb	1949	<40 min.
Apache	16,800–16,815	Laura Boulton	1940	2 hrs.
Apache	19,183*, 19,185	Monroe Benton	ca. 1969	30 min.
Apache	19,509–19,513	Ethnology Training Group	1931	11 hrs.
Apache	19,728*, 19,730	Richard Spottswood	1976	40 min.
Apache	21,341–21,343	Ethnology Training Group	1931	6.3 hrs.
Apache	26,053, 26,086, 26,099	Indians for Indians Hour	1943–50	1.5 hrs.
Apache/Sioux	20,615	AFS/Chicago Ethnic Arts Project	1977	25 min.
Arapaho	10,094: A7	Willard Rhodes	1950	3 min.
Arapaho	14,034, 14,038–14,041, 14,045	Charles & James Mooney	1894	15 min.

TRIBE	AFS NUMBERS	COLLECTOR	DATE	APPROXIMATE DURATION
Arapaho	14,618–14,619*	Willard Rhodes	1951	55 min.
Arapaho	15,097	Frank Speck	1950	8 min.
Arapaho	20,308, 20,324*	Alice Fletcher	1895	30 min.
Arapaho	26,093+	Indians for Indians Hour	1943–50	2.5 hrs.
Arikara	14,624*	Willard Rhodes	1952	5 min.
Arikara	21,368: 10-16	Frances Densmore	1912–15	20 min.
Arikara	23,206-23,207*	Orin Grant Libby	1915	1 hr.
Arikara	AFC 1990/032	Sol Tax, et al.	1950–53	3.2 hrs.
Assiniboine? Gros Ventres?	9556–9557*	Willard Rhodes	1947	20 min.
Assiniboine	10,053–10,054*	Christian Leden	1911	5 min.
Assiniboine	12,149	Willard Rhodes	1942	4 min.
Atna Athabaskan	12,000*–12,003	De Laguna	1954	7.3 hrs.
Atna Athabaskan	12,066–12,073	De Laguna/McClellan	1960	8 hrs.
Athabaskan/Tlingit	10,498	Catherine McClellan	1950–51	1 hr.
Blackfeet	801–810; also on 11,316–11,320 and 20,327–20,329	Walter McClintock	1898	2.5 hrs.
Blackfeet	814–816	Clark Wissler	1904	30 min.
Blackfeet	9553–9556*	Willard Rhodes	1947	1.3 hrs.
Blackfeet	9847, 9853, 9864*	National Folk Festival	1938	20 min.
Blackfeet	10,879*	William Fenton	1950	<1 hr.
Blackfeet	17,999	Ralph McFadden	ca. 1950	1 hr.
Blackfeet	20,519–20,520	Truman Michelson	1910	1.3 hrs.
Blackfeet?	22,490–22,491	RCA (commercial)	1914	15 min.
Caddo	14,036, 14,042* 14,044	Charles & James Mooney	1894	8 min.
Caddo	9538B*	Willard Rhodes	1941	3 min.
Caddo	14,621B*	Willard Rhodes	1951	2 min.
Caddo	14,624B*	Willard Rhodes	1952	11 min.
Caddo	26,066+	Indians for Indians Hour	1943–50	1 hr.
Caddo	AFC 1988/024	Scott Tonemah	1962	4 hrs.
Cahuilla	11,098–11,099*+	Charles Lummis	1904	15 min.
Cahuilla	19,890: 12–17	Richard Lando	1969	20 min.
Cahuilla/Chemehuevi	21,284: 7	J.P. Harrington	?	5 min.
Carrier	10,693*	Frances Densmore	1926	3 min.
Carrier	16,587–16,599+	Laura Boulton	1942	1.7 hrs.
Catawba	21,352	Truman Michelson	1913	25 min.
Chehallis	10,093B*	Willard Rhodes	1950	5 min.
Cherokee	7957–7958	Artus Moser	1946	15 min.

TRIBE	AFS NUMBERS	COLLECTOR	DATE	APPROXIMATE DURATION
Cherokee	9811–9812	Gillespie/Moser	1949	15 min.
Cherokee	12,199B–12,200B	Willard Rhodes	1943	12 min.
Cherokee	14,622–14,623A*	Willard Rhodes	1951	20 min.
Cherokee	14,624: B14	Willard Rhodes	1952	4 min.
Cherokee	15,098–15,099	Frans Olbrechts	1927	2 hrs.
Cherokee	26,072+	Indians for Indians Hour	1943–50	25 min.
Cheyenne (S)	10,145*, 13,735: B3	Vincent McMullen	1940	5 min.
Cheyenne (N), (S)	14,358–14,367 [= 14,445B–14,449B]	Kenneth Croft	1948-49	9 hrs.
Cheyenne (S)	14,621B–14,622A*	Willard Rhodes	1951	25 min.
Cheyenne (N)	17,995*	Thurlow Lieurance	1911–12?	20 min.
Cheyenne	20,308, 20,324*	Alice Fletcher	1895–1900	10 min.
Cheyenne (N)	20,519–20,520*	Truman Michelson	1910	25 min.
Cheyenne (S)	21,262*	Frances Densmore	1935	3 min.
Cheyenne (S)	26,049–26,167*	Indians for Indians Hour	1943–50	7.5 hrs.
Chilkat	14,052, 16,878	J.P. Harrington	1929	3 min.
Chippewa	9700	[John Lufkins?]	1948	?
Chippewa	10,515–10,556+	Frances Densmore	1907–10	17.5 hrs.
Chippewa	16,568: A1	Laura Boulton	1942	2 min.
Chippewa	20,308*	Alice Fletcher	1899	10 min.
Chippewa	22,168	Laura M. Taylor	1915	30 min.
Chippewa	23,185–23,196	E. Oberholtzer	1946	7 hrs.
Chitimacha	18,472–18,473	Morris Swadesh	1931–34	2.5 hrs.
Choctaw	9522: B6–B7 9540B-9541: A7	Willard Rhodes	1941	30 min.
Choctaw	10,735+	Frances Densmore	1933	3 hrs.
Choctaw	12,201–12,202A	Willard Rhodes	1943	12 min.
Choctaw	14,625B	Willard Rhodes	1952	30 min.
Choctaw	26,072+	Indians for Indians Hour	1943–50	20 min.
Chumash	15,422	Henley/Bizzel	1912–14	ca. 1 hr.
Chumash	21,283–21,292+	J.P. Harrington	1912–19	7 hrs.
Clackamas Chinook	21,830–21,834	Melville Jacobs	1929–30	4.2 hrs.
Clayoquot	10,092: A9, A22	Willard Rhodes	1950	5 min.
Clayoquot	10,665–10,671+	Frances Densmore	1923–26	2.1 hrs.
Cochiti	9610–9611 (=15,463*)+	J.D. Robb	1948	24 min.
Cochiti	10,725–10,726*, 21,260*	Frances Densmore	1930	30 min.

TRIBE	AFS NUMBERS	COLLECTOR	DATE	APPROXIMATE DURATION
Cochiti	19,502–19,508*	Helen Roberts	1929–30	1.5 hrs.
Cochiti	21,317*	Inez Duddington	1927	24 min.
Cochiti/Taos/Navajo	21,317–21,323*	Arnold Barrington	1927	11.3 hrs.
Cocopa	10,642–10,645+	Frances Densmore	1922	1.7 hrs.
Cocopa (plus others?)	16,817–16,826?	Laura Boulton	1940	ca. 1 hr.
Comanche	9540A	Willard Rhodes	1941	10 min.
Comanche	14,035 (=18,051?)	Charles & James Mooney	1894	2 min.
Comanche	14,621–14,622*	Willard Rhodes	1951	15 min.
Comanche	20,616	AFC/Chicago Ethnic Arts Project	1977	45 min.
Comanche	21,250–21,254*	Harry H. St. Clair	1902	1.5 hrs.
Comanche	21,957–21,958*	Maurice Smith	1930	8 min.
Comanche	26,051–26,163*	Indians for Indians Hour	1943–50	7.5 hrs.
Comox	10,691–10,692+	Frances Densmore	1926	1 hr.
Costanoan	20,341–20,344	J.P. Harrington	1930	4 hrs.
Creek	12,197–12,203*	Willard Rhodes	1943	28 min.
Creek	14,622: B6–B17	Willard Rhodes	1951	15 min.
Creek	14,624: A10, B15–B18	Willard Rhodes	1952	10 min.
Creek	26,054+	Indians for Indians Hour	1943–50	2.7 hrs.
Crow	10,940	Oliver Lion Shows?	pre-1956	10 min.
Crow	12,271A	Willard Rhodes	1949	5 min.
Crow	17,995*	Thurlow Lieurance	1911–12?	30 min.
Crow	19,183*	Monroe Benton	1969	4 min.
Crow	20,261	Carter Inauguration	1977	10 min.
Crow	20,418–20,420	AFC/Montana Folklife Survey	1979	1.5 hrs.
Crow	23,206–23,207*	Orin Grant Libby	1915	10 min.
Delaware	14,621–14,622*	Willard Rhodes	1951	30 min.
Delaware	AFC 1991/045	Frank Speck	1928	45 min.
Diegueño	11,037–11,044*	Constance DuBois	1905	45 min.
(Fox: see Mesquakie, Sac and Fox)				
Flathead	11,024–11,026	Claude Schaeffer	1934	30 min.
Flathead	20,471–20,473, 20,475–20,476	AFC/Montana survey	1979	1.8 hrs.
Gabrielino	20,345–20,348	J.P. Harrington	1918–33	3.5 hrs.
Gros Ventre	17,995*	Thurlow Lieurance	1911–12?	10 min.
Haida	12,076–12,078	Ada Charlton	1963	1.5 hrs.
Haida	16,600–16,609+	Laura Boulton	1942	1.3 hrs.
Halkomelem?	10,093: B31–B32, B37–B38	Willard Rhodes	1950	8 min.

TRIBE	AFS NUMBERS	COLLECTOR	DATE	APPROXIMATE DURATION
Halkomelem	10,726–10,727+	Frances Densmore	1926	45 min.
Hare	12,298–12,302	Hiroko Sue	1962	4.5 hrs.
Havasupai	10,144	Alfred S. Whiting	1950	5 min.
Havasupai	12,278–12,280*	Willard Rhodes	1949	20 min.
Hidatsa: see also Mandan)				
Hidatsa	10,919–10,922	Voegelin/Harris	pre-1955	35 min.
Hidatsa	10,597–10,605+	Frances Densmore	1912–15	55 min.
Hidatsa	21,361–21,362+	Gilbert Wilson	1909–11	1.2 hrs.
Hidatsa	21,363–21,367*, 23,206*	Frances Densmore	1912–15	35 min.
Hidatsa	23,206*	Libby/Reid	1929	15 min.
Hopi	3314: B1–B2	M. Valiant (FSA)	1939	3 min.
Hopi	8691: A1	Austin Fife	1946	2 min.
Hopi	8900–8911*	Samuel Barrett	1911	4 hrs.
Hopi	9521A–9522A, 9542B	Willard Rhodes	1941	1 hr.
Hopi	11,093: A2–B2	Charles Lummis	1903–5	10 min.
Hopi	11,321–11,325 (14,046–14,051)	Jesse W. Fewkes	1926	20 min.
Hopi	12,279–12,295*	Willard Rhodes	1949	1 hr.
Hopi	14,059–14,077*	Robert A. Black	1957–66	28 hrs.
Hopi	14,737–14,738*	Jesse W. Fewkes	1890–91	15 min.
Hopi	16,235–16,256*	Laura Boulton	1933	2.5 hrs.
Hopi	19,183*	Monroe Benton	1969	4 min.
Hopi	19,502–19,508*	Helen Roberts	1929–30	1.7 hrs.
Hopi	19,503	Ernest Beaglehole	ca. 1930	30 min.
Hopi	19,976	Diana Cohen	1974	2 hrs.
Hopi	21,317–21,323*	Barrington	1927	?
Hopi	22,175	Natalie Curtis Burlin	1903	1 hr.
Hupa	11,104–11,105+	Charles Lummis	1904	15 min.
Hupa	19,886: 14–23	Frank Quinn	1956	15 min.
Ingalik	10,712*	John W. Chapman	1925	10 min.
Iowa	26,051*	Indians for Indians Hour	1943–50	10 min.
Iroquois: M=Mohawk O=Oneida Og=Onondaga C=Cayuga S=Seneca T=Tuscarora				
Iroquois (S/Og/C)	4556–4627	William Fenton	1941	9.5 hrs.
Iroquois	8042–8105	William Fenton	1941	11 hrs.
Iroquois (O)	8463–8465, 8468	Charles Hofmann	1946	30 min.
Iroquois	8906	Samuel Barrett?	ca. 1918	10 min.

TRIBE	AFS NUMBERS	COLLECTOR	DATE	APPROXIMATE DURATION
Iroquois	9596–9600	Rochester Museum/ William Fenton	1948	2 hrs.
Iroquois	9963–9973	William Fenton	1948	5.5 hrs.
Iroquois (M)	10,146–10,148	Martha Randle	pre-1945	25 min.
Iroquois	10,725	Frances Densmore	1932	6 min.
Iroquois (M)	10,898	Library of Congress	ca. 1954	1 hr.
Iroquois (T; maybe Og/S)	14,329–14,344 [= 14,434A–14,441A]	Anthony Wallace	1948–49	14 hrs.
Iroquois (O/Og)	14,345–14,357 [= 14,441A–14,445A]	Fred Lukoff	1948	8.5 hrs.
Iroquois (S)	14,387–14,414 [= 14,453A–14,456A]	Randle/Fenton	1936	5 hrs.
Iroquois (Og)	14,653–14,661	Harold Blau	1956–66	18 hrs.
Iroquois (S)	14,698–14,721	Dorothy Gaus	1962–63	48 hrs.
Iroquois (M)	15,335–15,345	Ann & Frank Warner	1940–41	40 min.
Iroquois (C/S/O/Og)	15,832–15,835, 16,929, 16,938	Laura Boulton, et al.	1930+	40 min.
Iroquois (S)	17,484	Merritt Malvern	1974	25 min.
Iroquois (Og)	19,871	National Folk Festival	1972	?
Iroquois (S)	20,617	AFC/Chicago Ethnic Arts Project	1977	20 min.
Isleta	6317–6327	Alan Lomax	1942	4 hrs.
Isleta	10,723–10,724*+	Frances Densmore	1930	50 min.
Isleta	11,082–11,093	Charles Lummis	1904–12	2 hrs.
Jemez	777–789	Bernice King	1933	2 hrs.
Jemez	9519A, 9520B	Willard Rhodes	1941	7 min.
Jemez	16,220A, 16,272–16,276	Laura Boulton	1933	30 min.
Jemez?	19,183*	Monroe Benton	1969	3 min.
Kalapuya	18,471*	Leo Frachtenberg	1915	45 min.
Karuk	19,874–19,882*	Helen Roberts	1926	7.5 hrs.
Karuk	19,880+	J.P. Harrington	1926–29	1.5 hrs.
Kaw	26,068*, 26,124*	Indians for Indians Hour	1943–50	10 min.
Kickapoo	15,090: A1, 15,092: B3	Omer C. Stewart	1938	10 min.
Kickapoo (Mexican)	20,513: 6–7	Truman Michelson	1910s	5 min.
Kiowa	9537B–9539	Willard Rhodes	1941	1 hr.
Kiowa	10,145*, 13,735*	Vincent McMullen	1940	10 min.
Kiowa	13,554–13,571*	Russell Mosby	1949	1.4 hrs.
Kiowa	14,037, 14,042–14,043	Charles & James Mooney	1894	6 min.
Kiowa	14,618–14,622*	Willard Rhodes	1951	25 min.
Kiowa	19,182–19,183*	Monroe Benton	1969	4 min.

TRIBE	AFS NUMBERS	COLLECTOR	DATE	APPROXIMATE DURATION
Kiowa	20,309*	Alice Fletcher	1896	5 min.
Kiowa	21,957–21,958*	Maurice Smith	1930	1.2 hrs.
Kiowa	26,052–26,168*	Indians for Indians Hour	1943–50	15.5 hrs.
Kiowa-Apache	9522–9543*	Willard Rhodes	1941	30 min.
Kiowa-Apache	13,573	Russell Mosby	1949	8 min.
Kiowa-Apache	14,621B*	Willard Rhodes	1951	8 min.
Kiowa-Apache	21,957–21,958*	Maurice Smith	1930	20 min.
Kitanemuk	20,335–20,336+	J.P. Harrington	1916–17	3 hrs.
Klallam (includes Lummi, Nooksack, Samish, Samiamo, Swinomish)	10,090–10,094*	Willard Rhodes	1950	1.1 hrs.
Klamath	11,131*	Samuel Barrett	1907	5 min.
Klamath	12,274–12,276*	Willard Rhodes	1949	5 min.
Konkow	11,027–11,028+	Helen Roberts	1926	20 min.
Konkow	14,315*	Frances Densmore	1937	15 min.
Konomihu	19,878–19,880*	Helen Roberts	1926	1.5 hrs.
Kwakiutl	10,092: B20, l0,093: A1	Willard Rhodes	1950	8 min.
Kwakiutl	14,741*	Benjamin I. Gilman	1893	40 min.
Kwakiutl	not yet assigned	Ida Halpern	1951–52	9.25 hrs.
Laguna	9520A*, 9523A*	Willard Rhodes	1941	4 min.
Laguna	14,069–14,071*	Robert Black	1957–66	45 min.
Laguna	19,182*	Monroe Benton	1969	3 min.
Luiseño	751–754	Helen Roberts	1926	40 min.
Luiseño	11,039–11,044*	Constance DuBois	1905	45 min.
Luiseño	11,100–11,101*+	Charles Lummis	1904	20 min.
Luiseño	15,403–15,413	J.P. Harrington	ca. 1933	11 hrs.
(Maidu: see Konkow)				
Makah	10,092–10,093*	Willard Rhodes	1950	1.7 hrs.
Makah	10,649–10,664+	Frances Densmore	1923–26	6.7 hrs.
Makah/Nootka	14,368–14,372* [= 14,450A–14,451A]	Morris Swadesh	pre-1950	2 hrs.
Mandan	8945	Library of Congress	1947	25 min.
Mandan	9556–9562*	Willard Rhodes	1947	50 min.
Mandan	10,597–10,605*	Frances Densmore	1912–15	3 hrs.
Mandan	20,613	AFC/Chicago Ethnic Arts Project	1977	15 min.
Mandan	21,363–21,370*, 23,206*	Frances Densmore	1912–15	7.2 hrs.
Maricopa	11,098*	Charles Lummis	1904	3 min.
Menominee	6801–6822	Alanson Skinner	1919	1.2 hrs.

TRIBE	AFS NUMBERS	COLLECTOR	DATE	APPROXIMATE DURATION
Menominee	10,676–10,687, etc.	Frances Densmore	1925–28	4 hrs.
Mesquakie	20,508–20,513+	Truman Michelson	1912–16	2 hrs.
Micmac	7184–7313*	Helen Creighton	1943–44	45 min.
Miwok	9573–9575	Edward W. Gifford	1914	1.2 hrs.
Miwok	10,502: B13–B18	Jaime de Angulo	1949	8 min.
Miwok	19,888: 17–21	unidentified	1948	10 min.
Modoc	10,502: B25–B26	Jaime de Angulo	1949	4 min.
Mohave	10,648: A1–A3	Frances Densmore	1922	7 min.
Mohave	11,132: A1	Alfred Kroeber	1908	3 min.
Mohave	16,816*	Laura Boulton	1940	8 min.
Mono	11,102–11,103*+	Charles Lummis	1904	10 min.
Mono	19,890: 1-5	Mrs. John Marvin	1961	5 min.
Navajo	6895B	Frances Densmore	1933	4 min.
Navajo	8691, 8699*	Austin Fife	1946	10 min.
Navajo	9519–9533A*	Willard Rhodes	1941	3.4 hrs.
Navajo	9545*	Willard Rhodes	1947	15 min.
Navajo	10,879*	William Fenton	1950	< 15 min.
Navajo	11,094B–11,096A	Charles Lummis	1903–4	20 min.
Navajo	12,081–12,086	David McAllester	1957	12 hrs.
Navajo	12,177–12,196	Willard Rhodes	1942	2.5 hrs.
Navajo	12,203*	Willard Rhodes	1943	2 min.
Navajo	12,265–12,294*	Willard Rhodes	1949	1.1 hrs.
Navajo	12,321–12,331	David McAllester	1958	22 hrs.
Navajo	14,058A	KTAR-Phoenix	1937	5 min.
Navajo	14,073*	Robert A. Black	1959	15 min.
Navajo	14,078	Geoffrey O'Hara	ca. 1914	1 hr.
Navajo	14,619A*	Willard Rhodes	1951	6 min.
Navajo	14,624–14,625*	Willard Rhodes	1952	1.1 hrs.
Navajo	14,742*	Washington Matthews	ca. 1900	15 min.
Navajo	16,152–16,236*	Laura Boulton	1933	8.7 hrs.
Navajo	16,699–16,844*	Laura Boulton	1941	?
Navajo	19,182*, 19,184	Monroe Benton	ca. 1969	35 min.
Navajo	20,210–20,218*	Washington Matthews	ca. 1900	8 hrs.
Navajo	21,294–21,317	George Herzog	1929–31	48 hrs.
Navajo	21,324–21,237	George Herzog	1932	28 hrs.

TRIBE	AFS NUMBERS	COLLECTOR	DATE	APPROXIMATE DURATION
Navajo	21,338–21,340	Fr. Berard Haile	1929–34	6 hrs.
Navajo	21,344–21,346	Harry Hoijer	ca. 1930	5 hrs.
Navajo	21,347–21,350*	Fr. Berard Haile	1929–34	7 hrs.
Navajo	22,177	Hubbell Trading Post (G. O'Hara?)	ca. 1914?	1 hr.
Navajo/Pueblo	14,773–14,778*	Wheelwright Museum	1920s	11.2 hrs.
Navajo/Taos/Cochiti	21,317–21,323*	Arnold Barrington	1927	11.3 hrs.
Nez Perce	9548–9553*	Willard Rhodes	1947	50 min.
Nez Perce	14,054	J.P. Harrington	1929	3 min.
Nez Perce	14,739*	Herbert Spinden	1907	2 hrs.
Nez Perce	16,905–16,906	Laura Boulton?	?	12 min.
Nez Perce	20,309*	Alice Fletcher	1897+	10 min.
Nez Perce	AFC 1990/030	Washington State University	1909–12	6 hrs.
Nitinat	10,092: A5, A12–A15	Willard Rhodes	1950	15 min.
Nitinat	10,694–10,697+	Frances Densmore	1926	1.5 hrs.
Nomlaki	11,028*	Helen Roberts	1926	5 min.
Nootka/Makah	14,368–14,372 [= 14,450A–14,451A]	Morris Swadesh	pre-1950	2 hrs.
Nootka	18,473*	Morris Swadesh	1933	8 min.
Nootka, etc.	23,252* [cf. 23,255, 24,980-24,981]	Edward Sapir	1934	4 min.
Omaha	11,728*	Melvin Gilmore	1905	10 min.
Omaha	13,574–13,576	Roger Welsch	1969	3 hrs.
Omaha	20,308–20,325*	Fletcher/La Flesche	1895–1905	7 hrs.
Omaha	20,330–20,332*	Frances Densmore	1941	2.5 hrs.
Omaha	21,255	Charles Cadman	1909	20 min.
Omaha	See ref. staff	Federal Cylinder Project	1983–85	62+ hrs.
Osage	20,200–20,209+	Francis La Flesche	1910–23	28 hrs.
Osage	20,314*+	Alice Fletcher	1897–98	1 hr.
Osage	26,144–26,153*	Indians for Indians Hour	1943–50	20 min.
Otoe	11,728*	Gilmore/Murie	1905	7 min.
Otoe	20,315–20,324*	Alice Fletcher	1895	45 min.
Otoe	26,068–26,165*	Indians for Indians Hour	1943–50	1.6 hrs.
Ottawa	8417	Charles Hofmann	1946	10 min.
Ottawa	14,316–14,328 [= 14,430–14,434A]	Jane Willets Ettawageshik	1947	8 hrs.
Paiute	9520–9522*	Willard Rhodes	1941	35 min.
Paiute	12,274–12,276	Willard Rhodes	1949	20 min.

TRIBE	AFS NUMBERS	COLLECTOR	DATE	APPROXIMATE DURATION
Paiute	14,038A	Charles & James Mooney	1894	2 min.
Paiute	15,090–15,096*	Omer C. Stewart	ca. 1938	15 min.
Panamint	19,890: 6–11	Not identified	?	15 min.
Papago	3314: A3–A4	M. Valiant (FSA)	1939	3 min.
Papago	10,606–10,622+	Frances Densmore	1920	6.5 hrs.
Papago	11,097: B3–B4	Charles Lummis	1904?	2 min.
Papago	17,621–17,623	Richard Spottswood	1975	1.5 hrs.
Papago	17,979	Richard Spottswood	1975	30 min.
Papago	19,736*–19,737	Richard Spottswood	1976	45 min.
Passamaquoddy	14,737–14,739*	Jesse Walter Fewkes	1890	1.6 hrs.
Passamaquoddy	23,259	David Francis re. Fewkes	1985	25 min.
Passamaquoddy	25,245–25,250	Am. Dialect Society	1934	45 min.?
Pawnee?	9414-9421	Martha Lincoln	1947	50 min.
Pawnee	9527A*	Willard Rhodes	1941	3 min.
Pawnee	10,053*	E.M. von Hornbostel	1906	2 min.
Pawnee	10,623–10,632+	Frances Densmore	1919–20	3 hrs.
Pawnee	11,728*	Addison Sheldon	1905	30 min.
Pawnee	14,618–14,622*	Willard Rhodes	1951	20 min.
Pawnee	20,316–20,320*	Alice Fletcher	1898–1901	2.1 hrs.
Pawnee	22,197–22,201	James Murie	1911–21	10 hrs.
Pawnee	26,144–26,161*	Indians for Indians Hour	1943–50	4.2 hrs.
Picuris	20,333–20,334*	J.P. Harrington	1918	1.5 hrs.
Pima	3315: A1, 3334: A1–A2	M. Valiant (FSA)	1939	5 min.
Pima	9519: A3	Willard Rhodes	1941	2 min.
Pima	11,097*	Charles Lummis	1904	12 min.
Pima	16,788–16,793	Laura Boulton	1940	35 min.
Pima	19,182*	Monroe Benton	1969	3 min.
Pomo	9563–9565*	Samuel Barrett	1902–7	45 min.
Pomo	9564–9565*	Henriette Kroeber	1908	20 min.
Pomo	9566*	A. Warburton	1909	3 min.
Pomo	9566–9568*	Edward W. Gifford	1919	50 min.
Pomo	9568–9572*	Derrick N. Lehmer	1926–27	1.2 hrs.
Pomo	11,029*	Helen Roberts	1926	5 min.
Pomo	11,102*+	Charles Lummis	1904	10 min.
Pomo	19,886: 24 to 19,888: 5	Quinn/Riddell/Peri/ Dawson-Norick	1949–63	1.6 hrs.

TRIBE	AFS NUMBERS	COLLECTOR	DATE	APPROXIMATE DURATION
Ponca	20,308–20,323*	Alice Fletcher	1896–1900	2 hrs.
Ponca	20,614	AFC/Chicago Ethnic Arts Project	1977	25 min.
Ponca	26,068–26,153*	Indians for Indians Hour	1943–50	2.7 hrs.
Ponca	AFC 1988/025	Buffalohead/Fenner/Orens	1980s	30 hrs.
Potowatomi	12,186	Willard Rhodes	1943	4 min.
Pueblo/Navajo	14,773–14,778*	Wheelwright Museum	1920s	11.2 hrs.
Pueblo?	20,334*	J.P. Harrington	pre-1940	30 min.
Quileute	10,093: A8-B8	Willard Rhodes	1950	40 min.
Quileute	10,672–10,673	Frances Densmore	1926	30 min.
Quileute	20,868–20,873	Leo Frachtenberg	1916–17	6.2 hrs.
Quinault	10,092: B5, B14–B15	Willard Rhodes	1950	8 min.
Sac and Fox	26,049–26,166*	Indians for Indians Hour	1943–50	2.7 hrs.
Sac and Fox	20,513*	Truman Michelson	1910s	15 min.
Salinan	20,349* 21,293*	J.P. Harrington	1930	10 min.
San Ildefonso	9527–9542*	Willard Rhodes	1941	10 min.
San Ildefonso	19,183*	Monroe Benton	1969	5 min.
San Ildefonso	19,502–19,508*	Helen H. Roberts	1929–30	3.8 hrs.
San Juan	9519B*	Willard Rhodes	1941	2 min.
San Juan	19,183*	Monroe Benton	1969	1 min.
Santa Ana	19,182*	Monroe Benton	1969	3 min.
Santa Clara	12,203: B3–B4	Willard Rhodes	1943	2 min.
Santa Clara	19,502–19,508*	Helen H. Roberts	1929–30	2 hrs.
Santo Domingo	10,743–10,744+, 21,259–21,260*	Frances Densmore	1936	2.8 hrs.
Seminole	3892–3895A	Corse/Cornwall/WPA	1940	30 min.
Seminole/Calusa	10,729–10,734+	Frances Densmore	1931–33	7 hrs.
Seminole	11,427	Harry & Josiah Jumper	1954	30 min.
Seminole	26,054–26,154*	Indians for Indians Hour	1943–50	45 min.
Serrano	11,099–11,100*+	Charles Lummis	1904	8 min.
Shasta	10,502: B21–B23	Jaime de Angulo	1949	4 min.
Shasta	18,471*	Leo Frachtenberg	1915	8 min.
Shawnee	14,624: A8–A9	Willard Rhodes	1952	5 min.
Shawnee	20,513–20,519	Truman Michelson	1911	6.5 hrs.
Shawnee	26,136	Indians for Indians Hour	1943–50	30 min.
Shinnecock	13,052	Dennis Starin	1966	< 15 min.
Shoshone/Bannock	10,094A	Willard Rhodes	1950	45 min.
Shoshone	14,618–14,619*	Willard Rhodes	1951	1 hr.

TRIBE	AFS NUMBERS	COLLECTOR	DATE	APPROXIMATE DURATION
Shoshone	14,625A*	Willard Rhodes	1952	15 min.
Sioux	6895–6896*	Frances Densmore	1933	12 min.
Sioux	8371–8372	Charles Hofmann	1946	15 min.
Sioux	9165–9167	Library of Congress	1941	1 hr.
Sioux (Pine Ridge)	9534B–9537B, 9542A–9543A	Willard Rhodes	1941	1.2 hrs.
Sioux (Pine Ridge, Stand.Rock)	9543B–9562*	Willard Rhodes	1947	3 hrs.
Sioux (Dakota)	10,453–10,485	Willard Rhodes	1940	4 hrs.
Sioux (Teton, Santee)	10,556–10,578	Frances Densmore	1911–14	10 hrs.
Sioux (Rosebud)	10,762	Toshi & Pete Seeger	1951	?
Sioux	10,902	Hartle/Howard	1951	?
Sioux (Oglala, Santee)	11,106	Charles Lummis	1905–7	10 min.
Sioux	11,403	Bates Littlehales	1955	1 hr.
Sioux (Pine Ridge)	12,139–12,173	Willard Rhodes	1942	4 hrs.
Sioux	13,561	Russell Mosby	1949	8 min.
Sioux (Dakota)	16,270–16,271	Laura Boulton	ca. 1933	12 min.
Sioux (Santee, Oglala)	16,908–16,909, 16,948	Laura Boulton	ca. 1931	12 min.
Sioux	17,995*	Thurlow Lieurance	1911–12?	2 min.
Sioux (Lakota)	19,038–19,040 (=19,187–19,219)	Evelyn Yellow Robe	1947	5.5 hrs.
Sioux?	19,514	"Hindus collection"	?	8 min.
Sioux	20,263–20,264*	Carter Inaugural	1977	25 min.
Sioux (Dakota, Oglala, Teton, Santee, Yankton)	20,309–20,325*	Alice Fletcher	1896–1904	50 min.
Sioux	21,957–21,958*	Maurice Smith	1930	8 min.
Skokomish/Twana	10,090B*, 10,093B*	Willard Rhodes	1950	20 min.
Snuqualmie (includes Nisqualli, Puyallup, Skagit, Snohomish)	10,090–10,094*	Willard Rhodes	1950	2.3 hrs.
Squamish	10,725–10,726*	Frances Densmore	1926	25 min.
Taos	9519A, 9533B–9534B	Willard Rhodes	1941	45 min.
Taos	9617–9625 (=10,393–10,401 and 15,462–15,463*)	J.D. Robb	1946	50 min.
Taos	13,565–13,572*	Russell Mosby	1949	40 min.
Taos	17,995*	Thurlow Lieurance	pre-1915	6 min.
Taos	19,183*	Monroe Benton	1969	2 min.
Taos	19,502–19,508*	Helen Roberts	1929–30	30 min.
Taos/Navajo/Cochiti	21,317–21,323*	Arnold Barrington	1927	11.3 hrs.
Tesuque?	8383A	Charles Hofmann	1946	4 min.
Tesuque	19,502–19,508*	Helen Roberts	1929–30	2.2 hrs.

TRIBE	AFS NUMBERS	COLLECTOR	DATE	APPROXIMATE DURATION
Tewa	14,067B–14,068B	Robert Black	1957–66	2 hrs.
Thompson/Okanagon	10,053*	Franz Boas	1897?	3 min.
Thompson	10,727–10,728+	Frances Densmore	1926	40 min.
Tlingit	10,499 = 14,373 [=14,451*]	De Laguna/McClellan	1950	45 min.
Tlingit	11,934–11,937	De Laguna	1954	8 hrs.
Tlingit	11,998–12,000*	De Laguna	1954	4.5 hrs.
Tlingit	12,057	De Laguna	1954	2 hrs.
Tlingit	14,052, 14,055	J.P. Harrington	1929	6 min.
Tlingit	14,619:A7	Willard Rhodes	1951?	3 min.
Tlingit	17,029, 21,251–21,254*	John Swanton	1904	4 hrs.
Tlingit	19,379–19,380	Carol B. Davis	ca. 1920	1 hr.
Tlingit	AFC 1986/017	Agnes Bellinger	ca. 1985	2.2 hrs.
Tlingit/Athabaskan	10,498	Catherine McClellan	1950–51	1 hr.
Tolowa	19,886: 1–7	Frank Quinn	1956	15 min.
Tonkawa?	9401–9413	Martha Lincoln	1948	1.5 hrs.
Tonkawa	13,571B	Russell Mosby	1949	4 min.
Tsimshian	10,499 = 14,373 [=14,451*]	De Laguna/McClellan	1950	10 min.
Tsimshian	10,693*	Frances Densmore	1926	1.5 hrs.
Tsimshian	16,579–16,586	Laura Boulton	1942	> 15 min.
Tsimshian	16,910–16,913	Laura Boulton?	1934	35 min.
Tsimshian	17,184–17,187	Laura Boulton	1942	40 min.
Tututni	18,471*	Leo Frachtenberg	1915	1.1 hrs.
Umpqua	18,471*	Leo Frachtenberg	1915	5 min.
Unidentified	10,879	William Fenton	1950	< 1 hr.
Unidentified (Plains)	11,728*	Gilmore/Sheldon/Murie	ca. 1905	12 min.
Unidentified	13,053	White House concert	1965	30 min.
Unidentified (Oregon)	17,125–17,134	Laura Boulton	1946–47	1.2 hrs.
Unidentified	20,263*	Carter Inaugural	1977	10 min.
Unidentified (California)	20,341*+	J.P. Harrington	?	2.2 hrs.
Unspecified (Flagstaff Powwow)	19,186	Monroe Benton	1969	30 min.
Unspecified ("Tucson, Meet Yourself")	19,731	R. Spottswood	1976	30 min.
Ute (N)	10,583–10,596+	Frances Densmore	1914–16	5.5 hrs.
Ute (S)	12,174–12,176A	Willard Rhodes	1942	20 min.
Ute (N)	14,619–14,620*	Willard Rhodes	1951	1.1 hrs.
Ute	15,092–15,096*	Omer C. Stewart	ca. 1938	8 min.

TRIBE	AFS NUMBERS	COLLECTOR	DATE	APPROXIMATE DURATION
Ute (S?)	19,182*	Monroe Benton	1969	3 min.
Wailaki	11,029*	Helen Roberts	1926	5 min.
Walapai	12,277–12,278	Willard Rhodes	1949	18 min.
Warm Springs	9548–9550*	Willard Rhodes	1947	40 min.
Warm Springs	14,625*	Willard Rhodes	1952	3 min.
Warm Springs	19,871	National Folk Festival	1972	?
Washo	12,263–12,264	Willard Rhodes	1949	20 min.
Washo	15,090B–15,095*	Omer C. Stewart	ca. 1938	30 min.
Wichita	14,621B–14,622*	Willard Rhodes	1951	7 min.
Wichita	20,323*	Alice Fletcher	1898	3 min.
Wichita	21,957–21,958*	Maurice Smith	1930	30 min.
Wichita	26,150	Indians for Indians Hour	1943–50	30 min.
Winnebago	3244: A1 3256: A1–B1	Sidney Robertson	1937	15 min.
Winnebago	8365–8413*	Charles Hofmann	1946	1.5 hrs.
Winnebago	8903	Huron H. Smith	1928	8 min.
Winnebago	8977–8978	Horace Beck	pre-1948	15 min.
Winnebago	9551: B3–B9	Willard Rhodes	1947	12 min.
Winnebago	10,698–10,707+	Frances Densmore	1927–32	8.2 hrs.
Winnebago?	16,236: B1-B5; 16,257–16,269	Laura Boulton	1933	1.4 hrs.
Winnebago	20,323–20,325*	Alice Fletcher	1897–1900	20 min.
Winnebago	21,356–21,360	Paul Radin	1908–12	4 hrs.
Winnebago	23,256–23,258	N.O. Lurie	1980	1 hr.
Wintu (Nomlaki, Patwin)	19,888: 6–16	Quinn/Dawson-Norick	n.d./1963	20 min.
Yakima	9545–9548*	Willard Rhodes	1947	1.3 hrs.
Yakima?	18,052	Leroy Selam	1975	30 min.
Yakima	21,266*	Frances Densmore	1926	3 min.
Yaqui	8187–8202	Henrietta Yurchenco	1946	2.2 hrs.
Yaqui	10,646–10,648*	Frances Densmore	1922	30 min.
Yaqui	14,374 (=14,451B–14,452A)	John Alden Mason	1954	1 hr.
Yaqui	14,381B (=14,453*)	Robert H. Barlow	ca. 1949	2 min.
Yaqui	16,794–16,795+	Laura Boulton	1940	15+ min.
Yaqui	19,735*, 19,745–19,746	Richard Spottswood	1976	1.1 hrs.
Yokuts (Tachi)	19,888–19,889*	Hatch/Marvin	1957/1961	35 min.
Yokuts	20,336–20,340*+	J.P. Harrington	1916–17	4+ hrs.
Yuki	11,132–11,133*	Samuel Barrett	1907	10 min.
Yuma (Quechan)	3334: A3–A4	M. Valiant (FSA)	1939	2 min.

TRIBE	AFS NUMBERS	COLLECTOR	DATE	APPROXIMATE DURATION
Yuma (Quechan)	10,633–10,641*+	Frances Densmore	1922	3.3 hrs.
Yurok	11,131*	Alfred Kroeber	1906	5 min.
Yurok	19,886: 8–13	Frank Quinn	1956	10 min.
Zia	9520A	Willard Rhodes	1941	2 min.
Zuni	8369-8376*	Charles Hofmann	1946	15 min.
Zuni	9519–9532*	Willard Rhodes	1941	1.2 hrs.
Zuni	12,292–12,294	Willard Rhodes	1949	10 min.
Zuni	14,068–14,069*	Robert Black	1957	1 hr.
Zuni	14,737–14,738*	Jesse W. Fewkes	1890–91	30 min.
Zuni	16,711, 16,827–16,830	Laura Boulton	1941–42	30 min.
Zuni	19,182–19,183*	Monroe Benton	1969	12 min.
Zuni	20,220	Frances Densmore	1940	35 min.
Zuni	AFC 1991/007	Zuni Story-Telling Project	1980s	53 hrs.

Additional relevant recordings:

Chinook jargon	10,093B	Willard Rhodes	1950	7 min.
Shaker Church (Puget Sound)	10,091B–10,092B	Willard Rhodes	1950	1.2 hrs.
Rhode Island Indians	14,004	Nat. Fed. of Music Clubs/ Mrs. Kaiser	1961	30 min.
Radio program "Am. Ind. music is alive and well"	16,979	David McAllester	1970s	30 min.
"Fuss and Feathers" (radio?)	16,982–16,983	John S. Candelairo	1950s–60s	1 hr.
Interview with Helen Roberts	19,894–19,899	LaVigna/McAllester	1979	3 hrs.

Arlee Powwow, Flathead Reservation, Arlee, Montana, July 1987. Photograph by Edwin Schupman, Jr. (Federal Cylinder Project: FCP-DS-87-ES-16A-8). American Folklife Center.

Women in buckskin dresses dance in place while fancy dancers move by. Many elements of dance regalia move as the people move—and some of the articles worn also make sounds (the sleigh bells often sewn on fancy dancers' belts and leggings; the shells on the one woman's shoulders and arms). This clothing with all the fringed, dangling, swiveling, and feathery elements emphasizes movement. The long fringes on the women's dresses and dance shawls, for example, can best be appreciated when they are swaying elegantly in response to dignified dance steps.

LEFT: *Drum group at powwow, Lafayette, Rhode Island, 1979*. Photograph by Carl Fleischhauer. (Rhode Island Project: RI79-CF8-1). American Folklife Center.

The drum is both the symbolic and often the literal center of such events, as dancers circle the cleared area. Both the instrument and the group of men seated around it, beating on the drumhead and singing, are called "the drum." Much information regarding songs and dances native to East Coast tribes has been lost, so many intertribal events use the Plains-style big drum and song repertory.

BELOW: Grand Entry at the 1983 Omaha powwow, Macy, Nebraska. Photograph by Carl Fleischhauer. (Federal Cylinder Project: FCP/0-CF9-6). American Folklife Center.

The Grand Entry begins each dance session at this annual event. The dancer carrying the American flag leads the procession that circles the arena, followed in this case by the powwow princess wearing a sash and a beaded crown. Other dancers follow, grouped by age, gender, and the type of dance regalia they are wearing. The male "fancy dancers" with brightly-colored feather bustles attached to their necks and waists are in the foreground.

LEFT: Cover of brochure for *Omaha Indian Music*. AFC L71 album. American Folklife Center.

This Library of Congress-published recording—a sampler of the cylinder recordings made by Alice Fletcher and Francis LaFlesche between 1895 and 1897—was produced in collaboration with the Omaha Tribal Council in 1985. The cover illustration is drawn after a photo of a Hethu'shka dancer at the Omaha Pow-wow, August 1925 (Nebraska State Historical Society photo); underneath is part of a photo of an Omaha gathering near Macy, Nebraska, ca. 1890, courtesy of the Presbyterian Historical Society.

BELOW: *Parents dressing their children for the Omaha powwow, 1983.* Photograph by Carl Fleischhauer. (Federal Cylinder Project: FCP-214061-11-frame 12A). American Folklife Center.

Traditions live by being passed along. In this photo, Omaha parents dress the next generation of dancers. Over time, children and youth learn how to put on—as well as to make—dance regalia themselves and to perfect their dance steps. But even the very young ones participate in cultural activities, wearing items of regalia that are made for them and appropriate to their size, and learn by doing.

Partial transcription of a Karuk song. (Federal Cylinder Project). American Folklife Center.

Helen Heffron Roberts made a partial transcription of a Karuk song she recorded from Fritz Hansen on wax cylinder in Orleans, California, on March 8, 1926. Transcriptions such as these are part of the documentation researchers may find for collections accessed in the Folklife Reading Room.

Federal Cylinder Project dissemination process, Sitka, Alaska, August 1986. Photograph by D. Toby James. (Federal Cylinder Project: FCP/DS-86-CC-257650-2, frame 1). American Folklife Center.

Federal Cylinder Project staff member, Carey Caldwell, meets with the Sitka Community Association Tribal Council, as part of the process of returning to the Sitka community a set of cassettes containing the Tlingit cylinder recordings made in 1904 by John Reed Swanton.

ABOVE: *Panoramic view of Crow Fair, Crow Agency, Montana, 1979.* Photograph by Michael Crummett. (Montana Project: MT9-MC20-7). American Folklife Center.

The Crow Fair is among the largest annual powwows. People from many places in Indian Country camp here for the duration of the event. Those who have tipis (nowadays most often made of heavy canvas) proudly erect them in family encampments that also include tents, arbors, sun shades, cooking areas, and the vehicles that people need in order to get food, water, ice, and other supplies.

RIGHT: *Dancer at the Crow Fair, Crow Agency, Montana, August 1979.* Photograph by Michael S. Crummett. (Montana Project: MT9-MC27-1). American Folklife Center.

Dance regalia consist of many components, some specific to certain dance styles. The dancer with his back to the camera is wearing, among other items, a dance bustle made of the skin and head of a raptor together with several kinds of feathers; sleigh bells hanging from his waist; beaded leather armbands, gauntlets, and belt; fringed cloth yoke over his shoulders; a porcupine-hair "roach" on his head to which feathers on swivels are attached; and hair ties that appear to be quilled "wheels." The colors and ornamentation patterns on his regalia and that of his neighbor may reflect personal tastes or, in some cases, tribal affiliation (some tribes historically have favored particular patterns and colors).

LEFT: *Interviewing teacher at a Flathead summer school, near Valley Creek, Montana, 1979.* Photograph by Carl Fleischhauer. (Montana Project: MT9-CF8-6). American Folklife Center.

American Folklife Center fieldworker Kay Young interviewing Agnes Vanderburg at the summer school where aspects of traditional Flathead culture were taught. Topics discussed included deerskin-processing methods, medicinal and food plants, childbirth customs, ways of learning traditional skills, and perceptions of powwows.

RIGHT: *Teaching Hupa legends at the Hupa Day Care Center, Hoopa Valley, California, 1982.* Photograph by Lee Davis. (Ethnic Heritage Schools Project: ES82-198934-4-11A). American Folklife Center.

Ruth Bennett used Red-Headed Woodpecker and Skunk puppets to help Hupa elder Alice Pratt teach young children about Hupa legends. In northern California as well as in many Indian communities elsewhere, parents are concerned about native language transmission, especially since many grew up at a time when use of native languages was discouraged, and therefore they themselves are not able to speak those languages in the home for the benefit of the next generations.

Poster on classroom door in Mesquakie Settlement School, Tama, Iowa, 1986. Photograph by Judith Gray. (Federal Cylinder Project: FCP/DS-86-JG-1-13). American Folklife Center.

Included on this poster are the names and emblems of the Mesquakie clans. The photograph was taken on the occasion of a visit to the community to return cassette copies of Mesquakie wax cylinder recordings made there between 1912 and 1916. Dissemination visits such as this usually included opportunities to see cultural retention programs and projects.

INDEX

Page numbers in **boldface type** refer to illustrations

ISBN 0-8444-0904-9